THE NATIVE AMERICAN ALMANAC

A PORTRAIT OF NATIVE AMERICA TODAY

Arlene Hirschfelder

Martha Kreipe de Montaño

MACMILLAN • USA

Macmillan General Reference
A Simon & Schuster Macmillan Company
1633 Broadway
New York, NY 10019-6785

MACMILLAN is a registered trademark of MacMillan, Inc.

Library of Congress Cataloging-in-Publication Data

Hirschfelder, Arlene B.
     The Native American almanac / Arlene Hirschfelder and Martha
Kreipe de Montaño.
         p.   cm.
     Includes bibliographical references and index.
     ISBN 0-671-85012-1
       1. Indians of North America—History—Handbooks, manuals, etc.
     2. Indians of North America—Social life and customs—Handbooks,
     manuals, etc.   I. De Montaño, Martha Kreipe.   II. Title.
     E77.H59   1993
     973'.0497'00202—dc20   93-1057
                                                                      CIP

Designed by Irving Perkins Associates
Manufactured in the United States of America

10   9   8   7   6   5   4   3

First Edition

Acknowledgments

Arlene B. Hirschfelder would like to give special thanks to the following people:

To Bill Byler and Bert Hirsch, two generous men who never were too busy to answer my questions or fine tune my prose about legal issues.

My gratitude to Robert Lyttle for saying "yes" to doing the Tribal Governments chapter and my admiration for his impeccable scholarship.

My gratitude to Karen Warth who weathered high winds, rain, fog, and desert heat to take all the photographs I asked her to. Her generous spirit is appreciated.

To Edna Paisano at the Bureau of the Census, Department of Commerce who patiently answered a zillion questions.

To my special neighbors Julie and Elaine Lugovoy who have always been there for me, especially when I am having a computer or printer crisis.

My appreciation to Leslie F. McKeon, a special neighbor, for her fine line drawings that she executes so effortlessly.

To Adam Hirschfelder for his magnificent research abilities.

To Ariane Baczynski who did flawless research and mastered the New York Public Library to boot!

To Colleen Hall who has always provided many kinds of support.

Martha Kreipe de Montaño would like to gratefully acknowledge the help of the following people:

To Ellen Jamieson, for her competent and cheerful assistance that goes beyond typing.

To Suzanna Prophet, Nanette Roubideaux, and Mara Hennessey for their research assistance.

To Gary Galante for photo research.

To Mary Davis of the Huntington Free Library for her suggestions and assistance with reference material.

To Clinton Elliott for his constructive criticism.

Robert Lyttle would like to thank the following:

Special thanks to Carey Vicente, attorney and Chief Judge of the Jicarilla Apache Tribal Court for his assistance with the historical introduction in the Tribal Governments chapter.

A substantial portion of the royalties from this publication will be given to the American Indian Higher Education Consortium.

Contents

Introduction

One can make a case that the Native people of the United States are perhaps the most studied and least understood of all those who make up the tapestry of American life. Stereotypes of Native Americans, as noble or savages, stolid or eloquent, fanciful, pagan, new age, or any number of images, saturate American popular culture. Daily we are bombarded with time-frozen American Indian images. School textbooks dwell on bloody conflicts between Indians and Europeans and the U.S. army paving the way for advocates of Manifest Destiny. Children all over the world play "cowboys and Indians," sports mascots "ugh-ugh" and wardance around stadiums. Greeting cards picture feathered Indians mouthing mangled grammar and broken English. Toy drums, head-dresses, and "peace" pipes trivialize spiritual values and beliefs of Native people. Newspapers report so much doom and gloom that even some Indians believe reservations belong in the past.

While current motion pictures treat viewers to authentic sights and sounds of mid-seventeenth century Huron villages in Northern Quebec (*Black Robe*), colonial-era Mohegan and Huron people in New York (*Last of the Mohicans*), and nineteenth-century Lakota band life in the Dakotas (*Dances with Wolves*), the films fixate on the past and portray the Hurons, Mohegans, and Lakotas as relics of history. Even museums, a potentially rich source of information about Indian cultures, often reinforce stereotypes by using the material culture of Native Americans to focus on values and ideals from white culture. True, many historians and anthropologists, including Native people themselves, have written volumes that try to accurately convey the richness

and diversity, the tragedy, struggles, dreams, and hopes of Native people, but still the public remains ignorant. It is hoped that *Native American Almanac: Portrait of Native Americans Today* will help to correct these misconceptions. It offers a glimpse into the history and contemporary reality of American Indian and Alaska Natives in the United States. A story that is tragic and triumphant, complex and dynamic.

This book uses "Native Americans" in its title, but "American Indians" also serves as shorthand for the hundreds of different peoples who have populated the present-day United States since before Europeans arrived. The term, "American Indian" is acceptable because of long usage, but many people prefer the term "Native American" because it is an acknowledgement of the fact that the people called American Indians are the true natives of the Americas.

Over hundreds of years, the spellings of the names of Native American nations have varied and still do to this day. The authors have used spellings preferred by native groups. The Navajos prefer this spelling over Navaho. The Blackfeet in the United States prefer this spelling to Blackfoot.

Tribal names vary as well as tribal spellings. Some of the people popularly called Eskimo prefer *Inuit*, the name meaning "people" in their language and *Yupik*—the self-designation of the Eskimos of southwestern Alaska or Inupiat, people from northwest Alaska. The people formerly called the Papago (a Spanish distortion of a Native word meaning "bean eaters") have officially declared a preference for *Tohono O'Odham*, the name by which they have always known themselves. Sioux is the popular name for the Siouan-speaking Dakota (eastern groups) and Lakota (western groups) peoples. Sometimes Lakota is used to refer to the entire tribal group. Some of the people popularly known as Fox prefer Mesquakie (Red Earth People), their traditional name.

The book is not designed to be an encyclopedic compendium of Native America, but rather a portrait that emphasizes Native American experiences, achievement, and point of view.

The book begins with "Historical Overview of Relations Between Native Americans and Whites in the United States," since the present is incomprehensible without reference to the past. The second chapter, "Native Americans Today" offers a demographic snapshot of the people, land, and tribal nations that make up Native America. "Supreme Court Decisions," describes ten key court rulings in the areas of tribal powers, the federal-tribal relationship, state-tribal relationships, resource rights, and religious rights. "Treaties" tells about Indian treaty fishing rights in the Pacific Northwest and Great Lakes, two regions that have endured conflict over the rights of Native people "to fish at usual and accustomed places." The fifth chapter "The Bureau of Indian Affairs and Indian Health Service," concerns the mission and organization of two of the federal agencies that influence the daily lives of Indians. In chapter six, "Tribal Governments" by Robert Lyttle provides an inside view of the operation of tribal governments today. "Education" is an overview of the double-edged sword of formal education and the

struggle of Native people to influence the process. "Religion" deals with sacred sites, repatriation and reburial, and the use of peyote—all contemporary issues of great concern. The ninth chapter, "Games and Sports" introduces traditional games and sports and explores Native American participation in non-native sports. The next chapter, "The Arts," provides a depiction of traditional and introduced arts—both visual and performing—including Native American depictions in film and video and the growing presence of Native Americans in the creation of film and video about Native Americans. The eleventh chapter, "Voices of Communication," focuses on contemporary Native press, radio broadcasting, autobiography, poetry, and fiction writers—voices that tell about Native American life in the contemporary United States. "Employment, Income and Economic Development" is concerned with Native American employment, the development of minerals, oil, gas, coal, and other resources found on reservations: agricultural resources; water rights; outdoor recreation opportunities on Indian lands; and the development of business and gaming on Indian reservations. The final chapter, "American Indians and Military Service" focuses on twentieth-century participation of Native American men and women in all branches of the armed services.

The *Native American Almanac* aims to give the reader not only information, but a Native American perception of Indian Country and the people who inhabit it today.

Historical Overview of Relations Between Native Americans and Whites in the United States

FIRST ENCOUNTERS

When Europeans arrived in the western hemisphere, native peoples were sovereign, strong militarily and numerically, and economically self-reliant. Trading partnerships and alliances developed between the two peoples. By the early 1600s, a period of Indian–European equality, Europeans maintained friendly relations and treated Native Americans with respect. Survival depended on it. Europeans recognized the prior right of Indians to the soil, and trading, negotiations, treaties, and land acquisitions were made between equals.

Holland, Spain, France, and England penetrated North America almost at the same time. Spain, England, and France sent out numerous exploratory expeditions but permanent settlements, with the exception of St. Augustine, Florida, a permanent settlement founded in 1565, were not established until the first decade of the seventeenth century. Jamestown was settled by the British in 1607, Quebec in Canada by the French in 1608, Santa Fe by the Spanish in 1610, and New Amsterdam by the Dutch in 1626. Russia established claims to land along the North Pacific Coast in the 1740s. The various colonial powers dealt with Indians in different ways. Alden T. Vaugh (1979) states however that in every area settled by Europeans, "Indians were victims . . . they suffered discrimination, exploitation, and wholesale destruction—by disease and demoralization if not by sword and bullet."

The French in Canada were primarily interested in the fur trade, which required minuscule amounts of land. They developed no permanent settlements in the interior and farmed little of mainland Canada. The French depended on the friendship of Indian trappers and go-betweens, both sides benefiting from the reciprocal economic relationship.

The Spanish wanted precious metals, and since Indians were forced to labor in their mines, ranches, farms, and public works, they were not driven from their territories. While the Spanish crown exploited their labor, missionaries carried on large-scale efforts to convert their souls.

Since Holland hungered at first for furs as well, the Dutch negotiated with the native peoples for small pieces of land for trading posts and villages. After furs were depleted in coastal areas by the 1630s, the Dutch turned to agriculture and used force and cajolery to acquire larger chunks of Indian lands.

The English wanted Indian lands for farming, although some were involved with fur trading. English agricultural practices destroyed native subsistence economies and forced tribes to move away or convert to English lifestyle. Since the British crown was unable to enforce uniform policy and regulations, treatment of Indians varied widely in the British colonies, which eventually fought with each other as well as with the crown over Indian land acquisition and trade policies and defense. In an effort to gain control over all Indian–white relations

EPIDEMICS

Early European explorers who came to North America searching for new passages to the "Orient," gold, spices, riches, and fame brought with them diseases to which Indian peoples had little or no resistance. Many more Indians died from these catastrophic diseases than from all their protracted warfare with colonists, regulars, militia, and U.S. troops. Epidemics of smallpox, cholera, and measles decimated whole peoples or annihilated them altogether. Some tribes lost most of their populations within a matter of weeks when illness infected the group. In 1614, English slave trader Captain Thomas Hunt kidnapped some Wampanoag and Nauset Indians on the Massachusetts coast. Some of his men, infected with smallpox, spread the disease to the Wampanoags, nearly wiping out their population by the 1620s, just about the time the Pilgrims came to America. William Bradford, governor of Plymouth Plantation recorded the horror of the disease in his journal: "A sorer disease [smallpox] cannot befall them, they fear it more than the plague . . . for want of bedding and linen and other helps they fall into a lamentable condition as they lie on their hard mats, the pox breaking and mattering and running out into another, their skin cleaving by reason therof to the mats they lie on. When they turn them, a whole side will flay off at once . . . And then being very sore, what with cold and other distempers, they die like rotten sheep."

In the nineteenth century, smallpox, measles, cholera, and tuberculosis decimated Indians in the West who had no exposure and therefore no immunity to these diseases. In 1837, a smallpox epidemic among the Mandans, Hidatsas, Arikaras, Blackfeet, Lakota, and Pawnees killed about 14,000 people. So few were the survivors that the Mandans (reduced from 1,600 individuals living in fifteen villages to thirty-one survivors), Hidatsas, and Arikaras reorganized after the epidemic into a single village.

Tribal historians noted these devastating illnesses. Numerous winter counts, pictographic historical calendars kept by the Lakotas, Kiowas, and Blackfeet, show drawings of figures filled with spots documenting the epidemic sieges that exterminated thousands of people with no resistance to the new diseases. The

throughout the colonies in the mid-eighteenth century, the British crown put Indian affairs under the control of Indian superintendents in the newly created Northern and Southern Departments. Lawless traders, settlers who moved into restricted Indian territories, and other problems interfered with the effectiveness of the system.

In the 1740s, Russia claimed lands along the north Pacific Coast. Throughout its tenure in North America, Russians forced native men to produce furs, children to prepare the hides, and women to become concubines. Russia established a permanent settlement in 1783 on Kodiak Island to administer the native people, whom they bullied and tortured. From 1812 to 1841, Russians maintained a fort in Bodega Bay, California. Finally, in 1867 when Russia ceded Alaska to the United States, its rule in North America ended.

In almost every instance, the first arrivals to North America were received with hospitality. Massasoit, the Wampanoags' principal chief in southern New England, and Wahunsonacock, known to the English as Powhatan, the principal chief of a large confederacy of eastern Virginia Algonquian tribes, offered food and shelter and showed the English how to survive in the North American environment. Both men maintained peace with the white colonists until they died.

From the beginning, however, English colonists pressured Indians to adopt the so-called civilized

Hardin winter count, believed to have been kept by a Brulé Lakota, shows that smallpox plagued his Lakota band at least eight times between 1776 and 1878. Eight figures covered with black spots represent the event for the winters of 1779, 1780, 1801, 1818, 1845, 1850, 1860, and 1873. The Lone Dog winter count reveals that the epidemic struck the Yanktonai Dakota the winter of 1801. Red Horse Owner, an Oglala Lakota historian, recorded smallpox and measle epidemics for 1799, 1850, and 1901. Bad Head, a Blackfeet chief of the Bloods, documented smallpox, brought to the Upper Missouri on the steamboat *St. Peters* of the American Fur Company, striking his band in 1837 and 1838. About two-thirds of the Blackfeet Nation, some 6,000 people, died during the epidemic.

In his novel, *Fools Crow* (1986), Blackfeet writer James Welch describes how the feared "white scabs plague" (smallpox) tortured Yellow Kidney, a member of the small, Lone Eater band of Pikuni (Blackfeet) in northwestern Montana around 1870:

I awoke in a sweat with a fearful pounding in my head. Then I began to get cold and my teeth chattered so I thought they would shatter. I tossed all night in such agony. When the medicine woman came to see me in the morning I had calmed down a little. But she looked at my face and her mouth fell open for I had begun to develop the little red sores. I saw them on my arms and I felt them around my mouth, and again I was besieged by the fever and chills. My body began to buck with such fury I was powerless to stop it. The old woman hurried out and returned with two older men. They had strips of rawhide in their hands. After they tied me down, the woman signed that all of them had lived through the last plague of white scabs. They would not get it again. But by now I was tortured by red sores which were bursting all over my body and I was terrified of dying such a horrible death. This went on for how long I don't know because I was out of my head.*

* From: Fools Crow by James Welch. Penguin: 1986. Reprinted with permission of Viking Penguin, a division of Penguin Books, U.S.A., Inc.

European lifestyle and Christianity and often employed repressive measures to overpower Indians who did not comply. They often used deceit to extinguish title to Indian lands when rightful owners refused to sell. When English settlements became stronger, permanent, and armed, they forced Indian peoples to obey their laws and to submit to their demands. Many Indians in New England tried to resist English seizure of their lands. Two major wars fought between the English and southern New England Indians in the seventeenth century—the Pequot War in 1637 and King Philip's War in 1675–6, involving Wampanoags and their allies—led to bitter defeat for the Indians and the end of organized resistance. In Virginia, two fiercely fought wars, in 1622 and 1644, also led to the defeat of the Indians and the decline of Indian political power in that region.

In New York, the Dutch and bands of Algonquian Indians engaged in border warfare until the Indians were defeated. By the end of the seventeenth century, tribes along the Atlantic seaboard had been weakened by disease, destroyed, dispersed, or subjected to the control of European colonists.

Before the French and Indian War began in 1754, almost every colony witnessed Indian–white conflicts. The Tuscarora War of 1711–1712, a revolt against white encroachments, resulted in the partial decimation of North Carolina Indians and the northward retreat of survivors. In the Yamassee War of

WINTER COUNTS

History-conscious Dakotas, Kiowas, and other native peoples of the Plains kept winter counts, calendars with pictographs or pictures that showed the outstanding event of each "winter," or year, the time extending from spring to spring. The tribal historian met with elders to determine the event to be recorded. They talked about new births and the deaths of important leaders, discussed severe weather and food shortages, and considered illnesses and encounters with Euro-americans. A text accompanied each event pictured, memorized by the tribal historian and transmitted orally from one generation to the next. The historian, who learned the story of each event from his father and grandfather, who most likely were historians before him, interpreted and explained the drawings for anyone who asked. The line drawings that reminded tribal members of critical events also marked the passage of time. Whatever the pattern, winter counts were easy to follow, and years could be counted forward and backward with accuracy. Originally drawn with dyes on buffalo or deer hides, later on pieces of white canvas or cotton or unbleached muslin, the pictographs may progress from left to right, right to left, follow a serpentine path, or spiral outward from the center. As skins deteriorated, figures were copied onto new hides.

One of the best known winter counts was kept by Lone Dog, a Yanktonai Dakota. It covered seventy years beginning with the winter of 1800–1801 to 1870–1871. Lone Dog, the artist, counseled by elders, selected the outstanding event of each year and painted it in colors on buffalo skin. Later, copies of the winter count were made on cotton cloth. Interpretations for the pictures, which follow a counterclockwise spiral outward from the center, were compiled through conversations with Indians in Dakota Territory in the late 1870s.

LONE DOG'S WINTER COUNT

1800–1801	Thirty Dakotas were killed by Crow Indians.
1801–1802	Many died of smallpox.
1802–1803	A Dakota stole some horses with shoes on, i.e., stole them either directly from whites or from some other Indians who obtained them from whites. Indians did not shoe their horses.
1803–1804	They stole some "surly horses" from the Crows.
1804–1805	The Dakota had a calumet (ceremonial pipe) dance and then went to war
1805–1806	The Crows killed eight Dakotas.
1806–1807	A Dakota killed an Arikara who was about to shoot an eagle.
1807–1808	Red Coat, a chief, was killed.
1808–1809	The Dakota who killed the Arikara, 1806–1807, was himself killed by the Arikaras in revenge.
1809–1810	Little Beaver, a chief, set fire to a trading store and was killed.
1810–1811	Black Stone made medicine. An albino buffalo head held over the man figure indicates the ceremony of making medicine.
1811–1812	The Dakota fought a battle with the Gros Ventres and killed many of them.
1812–1813	The Dakotas caught wild horses with lassos.
1813–1814	Whooping cough was fatal to many. (Sign suggests a blast of air coughed out by man-figure.)

1814–1815 A Dakota using a tomahawk killed an Arapaho in his lodge.

1815–1816 The San Arcs made the first attempt at a dirt lodge.

1816–1817 Drawing of the side of a buffalo indicates "buffalo belly was plenty."

1817–1818 Canadian La Framboise built a trading store with dry timber.

1818–1819 Measles broke out and many died.

1819–1820 Another trading store built, this time by Louis LaConte at Fort Pierre, Dakota. His timber was rotten.

1820–1821 The trader LaConte gave Two Arrow a war dress for his bravery.

1821–1822 A brilliant meteor was seen falling to earth.

1822–1823 Another trading house was built by a white man called Big Leggings at the mouth of the little Missouri.

1823–1824 U.S. soldiers and allied Dakotas attacked Arikara villages.

1824–1825 Swan, chief of the Two Kettle tribe, had all of his horses killed.

1825–1826 A number of Indians died in a remarkable flood of the Missouri river.

1826–1827 An Indian died of tympanites, resembling dropsy, probably from eating the rotting carcass of an old buffalo on which wolves had been feeding.

1827–1828 Dead Arm, an Indian with a withered arm, was stabbed with a knife or dirk by a Mandan.

1828–1829 A white man named Shadran built a dirt lodge.

1829–1830 A Yanktonai Dakota was killed by Bad Arrow Indians.

1830–1831 Bloody battle with the Crows, of whom it is said twenty-three were killed.

1831–1832 Le Beau, a white man, killed another named Kermel.

1832–1833 Lone-Horn had his leg "killed," probably fractured.

1833–1834 "The stars fell," the great meteoric shower observed all over the United States on night of November 12, 1834.

1834–1835 Medicine Hide, a chief, was killed.

1835–1836 Lame Deer shot a Crow Indian with an arrow, withdrew it, and shot him again with the same arrow.

1836–1837 Buffalo Breast (personal name), chief of the Two Kettles, died.

1837–1838 A successful hunt was held in which 100 elk were killed.

1838–1839 A dirt lodge was built for Iron Horn.

1839–1840 The Dakotas killed an entire village of Snake or Shoshone Indians.

1840–1841 The Dakotas made peace with the Cheyennes.

1841–1842 Feather-in-the-Ear stole thirty spotted ponies.

1842–1843 One Feather raised a large war party against the Crows.

1843–1844 The San Arcs made medicine to bring the buffalo.

1844–1845 The Minneconjous built their tipis in pine woods for protection from heavy snow.

1845–1846 There was plenty of buffalo meat.

(continued)

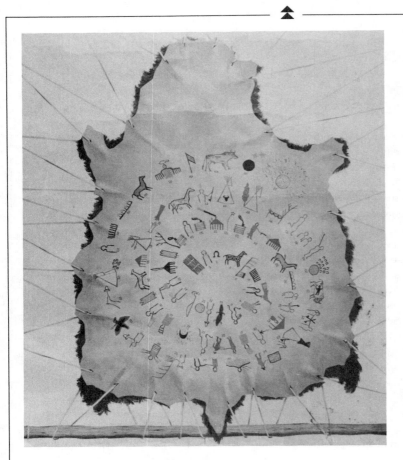

Lone Dog's winter count reckoned time by recording one outstanding event for each year. This count, known by a portion of the Dakota (Sioux) people, extended over seventy-one years, beginning in the winter of 1800–1801. From Picture Writing of the American Indians *by Garrick Mallery, 1893.*

1715, a rebellion of southern Indians prompted by general resentment against English economic exploitation and a fear of English agricultural expansion, settlers in South Carolina nearly exterminated the Yamasees.

THE FUR TRADE

Throughout the colonial period and well into the nineteenth century, the fur trade was one of the principal business enterprises in North America. European fashions demanded furs for making hats, coats, dress trimmings, and other items. Trading with Indian peoples for furs began immediately in colonies along the Atlantic Coast. Gradually, as fur-bearing animals were exterminated from Indian lands, traders moved inland looking for new sources. For a time, trading pelts for European goods benefited Indians. Guns made hunting bountiful, metal kettles were more practical to cook in, steel tools were more efficient than stone and bone. Cloth, needles, and scissors replaced clothing made from furs that required hours of preparation. Soon traders'

WINTER COUNTS (*cont.*)

1846–1847	Broken Leg, a Brulé, died.
1847–1848	Two Man was killed.
1848–1849	Humpback, a distinguished Minneconjou chief, was killed.
1849–1850	The Crows stole a large drove of horses from the Brulés.
1850–1851	A buffalo cow was killed and an old woman was found in her belly.
1851–1852	The Dakotas and the Crows made peace by exchanging pipes for a peace smoke.
1852–1853	The Nez Percés came to Lone Horn's lodge at midnight.
1853–1854	Spanish blankets were first brought to the Dakota by a white trader.
1854–1855	Brave Bear was killed.
1855–1856	General Harney made peace with a number of Dakota bands.
1856–1857	Four Horn, a subchief of the Uncpapas, was made a medicine man or calumet.
1857–1858	The Dakotas killed a Crow woman.
1858–1859	Lone Horn made buffalo medicine.
1859–1860	Big Crow, a Dakota chief, was killed by the Crows.
1860–1861	The-Elk-that-Holloes-Walking, Minneconjou chief, made buffalo medicine.
1861–1862	Buffalo were so plentiful their tracks came close to the tipis.
1862–1863	Red Feather, a Minneconjou, was killed.
1863–1864	Eight Dakotas were killed.
1864–1865	The Dakotas killed four Crows.
1865–1866	Many horses starved to death for lack of grass.
1866–1867	Swan, father of Swan, chief of the Minneconjous, died.
1867–1868	Many flags were given to the tribe by the Peace Commission, resulting in the Dakota Treaty of 1868.
1868–1869	Texas cattle were brought into the country.
1869–1870	The August 7, 1869, eclipse of the sun.
1870–1871	The Uncpapas had a battle with the Crows whose fort is shown as nearly surrounded, with bullets flying.

Source: Mallery, 1893.

goods became necessities as Indians discarded their own equivalent tools and technologies. With their basic economic systems disrupted, their wildlife resources depleted, and their subsistence areas diminished, the Native Americans became even more dependent on Europeans for commodities in order to survive.

By the mid-1700s, European traders wanted Indian lands as well as pelts. Unscrupulous English and French traders along the northeastern colonial frontier swindled Indians out of furs and large acres of land. Some traders forced tribes to trade entire catches of furs to them under threats of punishment. Deeply in debt to certain traders, tribes gave up immense areas of valuable land to cancel their obligations. Spanish, English, and French traders who competed for furs manipulated tribal peoples into supporting the country that supplied them with goods they wanted. The increasing demand for furs by rival European traders led to tribal competition for limited supplies of pelts. Incessant wars between European powers exacerbated intertribal conflicts as European nations encouraged tribes allied with them to attack tribes allied with other European powers.

Anglo-French rivalry in the fur trade, which contributed to the struggle for control of North America, culminated in the French and Indian War (1754–1763). The French and British also competed in giving presents to The Six Nations Iroquois and their allies, as well as Algonquian tribes, to secure their allegiance during the war. The British successfully recruited thousands of Indians as allies through tremendous outlays of gifts. Mutually exchanged presents cemented political relationships between an Indian nation and a European nation. European powers gave peace medals to heads of various Indian nations, a practice continued by American leaders. While medal giving secured diplomatic alliances, it cost colonial governments great sums of money.

Defeated in the war, the French lost control of Canada to England in the 1763 Treaty of Paris. The British substantially reduced the giving of presents to Indians, angering tribes who needed goods, especially ammunition for hunting, to alleviate their suffering after the war. Further, an extremely high schedule of prices for goods was instituted, which outraged Indians who could not go to English trading posts and obtain supplies on credit or as gifts, as had been the custom with the French. British forts, which reduced Indian hunting territories, and the British failure to supply western Indians enabled certain chiefs to mobilize Indian discontent. By 1763, tribal peoples along the whole northwestern frontier were ready to retaliate against Euroamericans. Pontiac, an Ottawa chief, and other chiefs led an angry Indian alliance of Ottawas, Hurons, Chippewas, Shawnees, Eries, Potawatomis, and Wyandots, against British aggressors in the area north of Ohio, capturing nine English forts and killing some 1,000 settlers. Unable to sustain the uprising, Pontiac agreed to peace on October 3, 1763.

Four days later, in an effort to protect Indian land rights and to avert further trouble with Indians, the British crown forbad white settlement in the region west of the Appalachian Mountains. However, the Proclamation of 1763, treaties setting boundary lines, and regulations concerning land purchases and trade with Indians were ineffectual.

Colonial governments purchased Indian lands in treaties or grabbed them by force. Agreements allowed some Indian people to remain on part of their original domain and opened the remaining land to public sale and speculators. Some of the colonies claimed territories west of their western boundaries, which were occupied by Indians. Settlers and land speculators alike simply ignored the British regulations and invaded the Indians' domain. John Stuart, superintendent of the Southern Indian Department, tried to maintain the Indian boundaries against American encroachment and settlement before the Revolution. The British government stationed a standing army in the colonies to enforce the Proclamation of 1763 and then taxed the colonists to help pay for the venture. The colonists protested and revolted against the British government, resenting the closing of the frontier, the British military force, and the taxes levied for its support. These and other grievances led to the American Revolution.

THE REVOLUTIONARY ERA

The majority of Indians allied themselves with the British, who posed as defenders of Indian lands against land-avaricious American settlers and who provided trade goods that Indians depended on. The new American Congress, which initially tried to secure Indian neutrality, later tried to engage Indians in the service of the United Colonies. When some factions of the Oneidas and Tuscaroras took the American side and most of the Six Nations [Iroquois] Confederacy took the British side, the confederacy, its allegiance split, weakened. Their homelands destroyed during the war, some went to Canada, others moved to reservations in New York. Southern tribes, especially the Creeks and Cherokees, supported the British, but the Catawbas aided the Americans. The Americans failed to win the allegiance of most Indians because their goods were no match for British goods, and Americans in the Ohio Valley were committing atrocities against Indians.

In the Treaty of Paris that ended the conflict, the British granted Americans title to the entire "Northwest Territory," disregarding the tribal peoples who lived there, and made no provisions for the Indian allies who supported the British cause. The British, however, held on to frontier posts around the Great Lakes from which they continued to trade English goods for Indian furs.

After the Revolution, settlers poured onto Indian lands north of the Ohio River ignoring Indian rights. In 1788 alone, 18,000 settlers moved into Ohio country. Chiefs such as Little Turtle, a Miami, reacted to the hordes of land-hungry settlers. Between 1783 and 1790, he and his allies killed some 1,500 settlers and routed Josiah Harmar's force in 1790 and Arthur St. Clair's in 1791, dealing the highest ranking officer in the U.S. Army the worst military disaster in its history. After U.S. troops defeated Little Turtle and Blue Jacket of the Shawnees, they were forced in the 1795 Treaty of Greenville to sign away huge tracts of lands northwest of the Ohio River, which became part of the public domain, but retained some land for themselves as promises of annuities and military protection against squatters.

The extent of the land cessions dissatisfied Shawnee Indian leaders such as Tecumseh (called Tekamthi, "Shooting Star," by his people), and his brother, a religious leader named Tenskwatawa, or the Prophet. Tecumseh believed only a united front could withstand American military power. While Tecumseh was away gathering support among southern tribes, William Henry Harrison marched on Tippecanoe (a town where Indian people of all tribes attempted to live a traditional lifestyle) and burned it to the ground. The British listened to Tecumseh's complaints against American intruders and led him to believe they would support him in driving Americans back from the Ohio country. A war between some of Tecumseh's followers and American troops began in 1811, which persisted through the War of 1812 between Americans and the British, the last war in which some Indians allied themselves with a foreign power. Again, some Indians were pro-American, although the sympathies of most tribes, in the Northeast and Southeast, were with the British. When the war broke out, most tribes in the Old Northwest, already hostile to Americans, became auxiliaries, scouts, and raiders for the British forces. Tecumseh, who had become a brigadier general in the British army at the beginning of the War of 1812, was shot in October 1813 at the Battle of the Thames, in what is now Ontario, where Harrison defeated the combined British and Indian forces.

In the South, a portion of the Creeks called the Red Sticks were armed against the Americans from 1813 to 1814. Andrew Jackson headed military operations in the upper Creek area and waged a campaign to level Creek towns. The tribe, with its forces split, suffered defeat by the American troops, resulting in the cession of 23 million acres, nearly all the Creek lands in Alabama. After the end of the War of 1812, tribes in the Northeast and Southeast, deprived of British allies, were coerced into signing a series of treaties extinguishing their title to large areas of land. Nearly all the tribes continued to occupy greatly reduced portions of their ancestral lands until Andrew Jackson became president, when eventually the government forcibly removed the tribes to west of the Mississippi River.

The early laws of the U.S. government that recognized the largely independent character of Native American tribes were built around policy confirming Indian land ownership on areas they occupied, which could not be taken without their consent. At the same time, the government actively encouraged Indians to adopt white technology and culture. The Indian Intercourse Acts of 1790, 1793, 1796, and 1802 governed Indian relations and attempted to control the trade relationship between Indians and Euro-american traders. They specified geographic boundaries separating "Indian country" from white settlements and sought to restrain lawless frontier whites who circumvented federal laws. Other laws governing the fur trade sought to prevent the use of liquor by traders among Indians.

The federal government attempted early on to compete with the British and private fur companies by creating a system of government-operated trading houses by act of Congress in 1795. Designed to help Indians secure goods at fair prices and to reduce warfare with tribes, the system established seventeen trade factories between 1795 and 1821. The system, which suffered heavy losses during the War of 1812, was criticized by Indians, agents, and private trading interests and by 1822, Congress closed down the factories.

EARLY FEDERAL INDIAN POLICY

Official U.S. Indian policy began in 1775, when the Second Continental Congress created three Indian departments, Northern, Middle, and Southern. Each was headed by commissioners who reported directly to Congress. (Patrick Henry and Benjamin Franklin served as commissioners.) The commissioners were responsible for winning the support of Indian nations during the American Revolution.

In 1781, the Articles of Confederation stipulated that Indian affairs were to be handled by the national government. By 1786, the three departments were organized into two regions. The heads of the departments, called superintendents, were responsible to the secretary of war who was charged with "such duties as shall from time to time be enjoined on, or entrusted to him by the President of the United States, agreeably to the Constitution, relative to . . . Indian affairs." With this arrangement, the basic structure of what was to become the Bureau of Indian Affairs (BIA) began to emerge. Indian agents, who were located in the field, reported to superintendents. Superintendents reported to the secretary of war, who reported to the president. During this time, Indian affairs consisted mainly of negotiating treaties, acquiring land, regulating Indian trade, and arranging payments to Indians as specified in treaties.

In the period after the Revolution, the American government increasingly turned its attention to the acquisition of land. Recognizing that the United States was not strong enough militarily to take Indian land by force and that peace with Indian nations was a matter of national security, Congress expressed an enduring, if often violated, commitment to treat Indians fairly and to respect their property rights. In the Northwest Ordinance of 1787, Congress set forth elements of an official U.S. policy toward Indians that is part of the basis for the trust responsibilities of the United States for Indian rights and property. The ordinance specifies that:

> The utmost faith shall always be observed toward Indians; their lands and property shall never be taken from them without their consent; and in their property, rights, and liberty, they shall never be invaded or disturbed, unless in just and lawful wars authorized by Congress; but laws founded in justice and humanity shall from time to time be made, for preventing wrongs done to them, and for preserving peace and friendship with them.

The superintendents were responsible for carrying out the commitments expressed in the Northwest Ordinance. Since the official policy was against taking Indian land by force, one of the main duties of the superintendents was to arrange for treaty negotiations in which the United States could acquire land within a legal framework, and the Indian people would get something in return. The superintendents were also responsible for the distribution of goods, money, and services to Indians as specified in treaties.

Beginning in 1789, as territories were created, the territorial governors were often appointed ex-officio superintendents of Indian affairs. They usually served until the territory was admitted as a state. In their capacity as governors of territories, they reported to the secretary of state; as superintendents of Indian affairs, they reported to the secretary of war. Their allegiance, however, was to the white citizens of their territories, not to the Indians.

As more and more treaties were signed, the work of the departments expanded. At the same time, the governmental process became increasingly bureaucratic. Treaties stipulated that Indian title to land was exchanged for a variety of things, most often money, goods, and/or services. It was often stipulated that a specified amount of money was to be distributed for a specified number of years, sometimes forever. The money payment was called an annuity. The accounting procedure for appropriating money from Congress and for acquiring the goods was, then as now, time consuming and complicated. The secretary of war was responsible for dealing with each purchase order; each appropriation for money, goods, or services, and all correspondence, no matter how routine. New treaties were signed every year, each one stipulating a different mix of money, goods, and services in payment for land. In addition, non-Indians were pushing back the frontier and encroaching on Indian land, causing hostilities. The whites began to demand reparation for damages from attacks by Indians. The secretary was authorized to make payments to whites whose property was damaged by Indian attack. The money was to come from money owed to Indians as a result of land transfers. This meant that in addition to seeing that each tribe received its annuities, goods, and services, the secretary of war had to assess the validity of claims and make arrangements for payments from treaty money. The secretary could not keep up with the work. By 1816, the War Department was eighteen years behind in settling the accounts of the Indian departments.

In 1824, the secretary of war, John C. Calhoun, without authorization from Congress, upgraded the Indian Department to bureau status and appointed Thomas L. McKenny, the former superintendent of Indian trade, to handle the day-to-day business. Calhoun's reasoning was to establish an independent bureau so that it could be responsible for its own complex accounting and record keeping. He used the term "the Bureau of Indian Affairs" for the first time in his letter of appointment to McKenny on March 11, 1824. However, since Secretary Calhoun did not have authorization from Congress, he did not actually have the power to transfer some of his authority to someone else or to create a separate branch in the War Department. Nevertheless, the Indian Office grew, and the question of its legality was overlooked for a time.

In 1832, Congress passed an act that legalized McKenny's position to that of commissioner of Indian affairs. A House committee investigation then reported that it could find no basis in law for making the Indian Office an independent branch of the War Department and recommended that Congress enact a statute to make the office legal. Congress did so on June 30, 1834. The Act of 1834 is therefore considered the "organic act" of the Indian Office (the law by which an organization exists). This meant that the commissioner of Indian affairs could handle the daily business of the Indian Office under the supervision of the secretary of war. The Indian Office, as it was called at the time, remained part of the War Department until 1849, when Congress created the Department of the Interior and transferred the Indian Office to its jurisdiction.

The mission of the Indian Office reflected the government's policy toward Indians. Initially, the government was concerned with peace and land acquisition. Activities were aimed at achieving peaceful co-existence with Indian nations, securing equitable trade relations, and acquiring land. Treaties contained clauses that defined boundaries that separated Indian land from white land. But whites often encroached on Indian land, taking it for themselves, destroying the environment, and treating Indians with aggressive hostility. Often the government did not even try to keep the intruders off of Indian land. By 1803, however, the policy switched from peaceful co-existence to aggressive destruction of the Indian way of life. This was to be accomplished either by the physical removal of Indians or by making Indians indistinguishable from white Americans. Both the first option, "removal," and the second, "assimilation," became government policy for many years.

REMOVAL AND ASSIMILATION

During the 1820s, government officials and religious and reform organizations who argued for the assimilation of Native Americans into white society merged this philosophy with that of moving eastern natives west of the Mississippi River, where they thought the "civilizing" program could be pursued

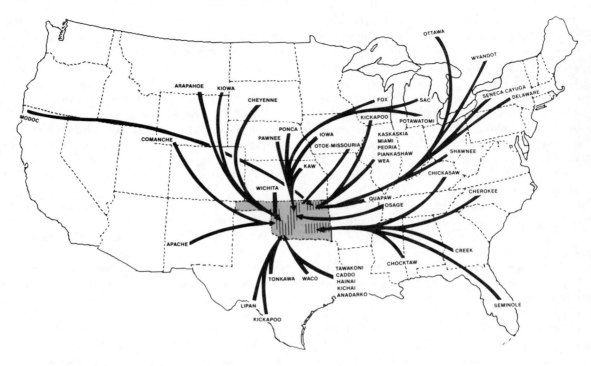

Removal of Indian Nations to Oklahoma. During the 1800s, many Indian nations were forced to move to Indian Territory, which later became Oklahoma. Courtesy of Division of Indian Health, U.S. Public Health Service.

more successfully. President Thomas Jefferson first suggested the removal policy in 1803. The Jeffersonian generation initially believed in a program of civilizing Indians through secular and religious education which would transform them into individual farmers who eventually would be incorporated into white society. That generation witnessed, however, the disintegration of Indian tribal and personal life, as a result of the "civilization" program, renewed warfare with whites, exposure to European diseases, and the influence of liquor. Some Jeffersonians argued that Indians in the east should be removed west of the Mississippi River where the "civilizing" program that failed in the east could be carried on. During the Jefferson era, there were three unsuccessful attempts to remove voluntarily southeastern tribal groups to unsettled portions of the Louisiana Territory acquired by the United States from France.

Subsequent presidents James Monroe and John Adams were unwilling to use military force to remove tribes, but in 1830, President Andrew Jackson sponsored the Indian Removal Act, which called for the forcible removal of Indian people from their homelands in the eastern United States to tracts of land west of the Mississippi. In the southeast, great numbers of settlers demanded that prospering tribes with extensive land holdings be cleared out of their way.

The role of the Indian Office was to negotiate removal treaties and to convince Indian leaders to leave voluntarily. In order to deal more effectively with Indians, the Indian agents learned to adopt the rich descriptive language of Indian oratory to conduct treaty negotiations. In 1866, an Indian agent tried to convince a chief of the Mille Lac Chippewa to sign a treaty exchanging their wild rice fields, hunting grounds, and fisheries for land unsuitable for hunting, horticulture, or fishing. The agent opened the negotiations with these words:

> My red brothers, the winds of fifty-five winters have blown over my head and have silvered it with gray. In all that time I have not done wrong to a single human being. As the representative of the Great Father and as your friend, I advise you to sign this treaty at once.

The Mille Lac chief replied:

> My father, look at me! The winds of fifty-five winters have blown over my head and have silvered it with gray. But—they haven't blown my brains away.

From 1828 to 1830, Georgia passed laws imposing state jurisdiction over Cherokee Territory. The Supreme Court decided two landmark cases, Cherokee Nation v. Georgia (1831) and Worcester v. Georgia (1832), recognizing an "expansive [federal] protection of the tribe's status as a self-governing entity." State interference with the Cherokee Nation continued despite the court mandate. Bribery, threats, intimidation, force, and coercing a particular group to represent the entire tribe secured some kind of assent to removal treaties. A series of treaties with the Cherokees, Creeks, Choctaws, Chickasaws, and Seminoles, whose lands were coveted by plantation owners, forced them to move west under military escort. In what is referred to as the "Trail of Tears," 18,000 Cherokees were forced from their homes in the southeast. Because of inadequate government preparations, the emigrants suffered hunger, extreme cold, cholera, and many perished along the forced marches to Indian Territory, now Oklahoma. Of the 18,000 who were removed, 4,000 died, either in stockades where they were imprisoned before the removal, or along the way.

After forcing the Cherokees to move to Oklahoma, the state of Georgia distributed their lands through a lottery to become slave plantations. Usually ceded lands were offered for public sale, bought by speculators, and subdivided for sale to settlers at much higher prices.

Some tribes resisted removal, particularly the Florida Seminoles. The resistance, led by Osceola, raided farms and settlements, destroyed bridges essential to transporting troops and artillery, and ambushed Florida militia. Lured into captivity through treachery, Osceola died at Fort Moultrie, South Carolina, in 1838. By 1842, the U.S. government gave up trying to evict the remaining Seminoles hiding in the Everglades.

In the Great Lakes area, settlers thirsty for valuable resources overran tribal lands. To control the competition among settlers and traders and to prevent war with Indians, the government removed the Indians to solve the "problem." Over fifty tribes, including Delawares, Ottawas, Wyandots, Potawatomis, Miamis, Illinois, Kickapoos, Sac, and Foxes, also known as Mesquakies, who lived in Ohio, Michigan, Indiana, and Illinois, were forced west of the Mississippi. Indians in this region fought fiercely against removal and the strongest Indian nations remained. The Sac and Foxes led by Black Hawk resisted removal from Illinois, but General Henry Atkinson and Colonel Henry Dodge, with a 1,300-man command, massacred the Indians in 1832, captured Black Hawk, and forced the Sac and Foxes to cede some six million acres of Iowa's Mississippi River frontage. Later, in 1857, the Foxes (Mesquakies) purchased eighty acres of land near Tama, Iowa, so determined were they to move back there. Serious problems arose for the Chippewas who managed to remain in their homeland. After treaty negotiations left them with a reduced homeland, and not enough funds and annuities, their economies fell apart.

The removal process that began in 1830 was completed around 1840, with the establishment of a large, unorganized "permanent" Indian country west of Arkansas, Missouri, and Iowa. About 100,000 Native Americans were removed forcibly or voluntarily from their ancestral homes in the northeast and southeast and isolated in enclaves west of the Mississippi River, where missionaries and government officials pursued their goals of "educating" Indians. White greed for land motivated Indian removals, but publicly the policy was masked with arguments

During negotiations with the U.S. government in 1834 for the removal of his people from present-day Florida, Seminole leader Osceola plunged a knife into the treaty he refused to sign. Courtesy of Florida State Archives.

for removal as the only way to save Indians from extinction. President Andrew Jackson argued that removing Indians from the corrupting influence of white culture would slow the Indians' decline and cause them to gradually lose their "savage" habits and become "civilized," Christianized people.

Assimilation, the replacement of one culture by another, was considered the humane solution to the problem of peaceful coexistence of peoples from such different cultures as Indians and whites. It was always assumed by non-Indians that Indian cultures would give way to white culture—that Indians should and would disappear into the mainstream of American culture. Education was the primary tool for the assimilation of American Indians, and many treaties with Indian nations stipulated that the United States would provide for education.

In 1819, the Civilization Fund Act provided for an annual appropriation for the education of Indians. In the beginning, the funds were given to mission-

aries to allow them to continue and expand their network of schools for Indians. Later, with legislation that made it illegal for the government to support religious organizations, the federal government took on the responsibility of eventually establishing and operating hundreds of schools (see the chapter, "Education").

INTERTRIBAL CONFLICTS

By 1840, most of the Indians from east of the Mississippi River were settled in the area which is now Nebraska, Kansas, and Oklahoma. Clashes occurred between the removed tribes and the indigenous tribes who surrendered some of their lands to make room for the displaced people. These Indians resented the displaced tribes with whom they now had to compete in hunting buffalo, their chief source of food. Because the government failed to protect the displaced Indians in their new locations, they resorted to fighting in order to survive. Cherokees, Choctaws, Creeks, and Chickasaws, and Seminoles had difficulty establishing amicable relations with the Osages, Pawnees, Kiowas, Comanches, and other indigenous nations. The so-called "Five Civilized Tribes," demoralized and impoverished by forced removal from the southeast, nevertheless reconstructed their lives in Indian Territory. The Sac and Foxes, moved to a Kansas reservation from Illinois, also battled Plains tribes in order to survive.

Lands west of the Mississippi River were forever guaranteed to the tribes who were removed there. But white settlers did not stop at the Mississippi River, and the government formulated new policies. In the 1840s, the Kansas, Otoes, and Missourias, who were moved to small reservations in Kansas and Nebraska, were again forced to cede lands to make room for settlers moving in on their lands. Almost all the groups went to Indian Territory. Territorial governments were organized to protect settlers, and in 1854, the Kansas-Nebraska bill completely dispossessed Indians of lands in those regions.

In 1845, Texas, with its many Indian peoples, entered the Union, as well as Oregon and Washington Territory, acquired from Great Britain in 1846. In 1848, the United States acquired portions of the Southwest and California from Mexico. European emigrants and American settlers created additional pressures on newly acquired lands and lands permanently set aside for native peoples removed from east of the Mississippi. Friction developed along travel routes crossing Indian-owned land. Western trade routes and railroads increased the number of settlers who drove buffalo herds from Indian hunting grounds and whose wasteful hunting practices wiped out the buffalo, so necessary to the Plains Indian way of life. Government agents concerned with securing the safe passage of travelers along the Oregon and Santa Fe trails convinced thousands of Plains Indians from numerous tribes to sign the Fort Laramie Treaty in 1851. The treaty set boundaries between tribes, authorized roads and military posts within their territories, where troops were stationed to protect emigrants and punish Indians, and guaranteed safety to white travelers along the travel routes. In return Indians were promised annuities.

THE CIVIL WAR

The Civil War, which slowed down the westward movement of settlers, was disastrous for many Indians. When the war broke out in 1861, the question of allegiance divided the Cherokees, Creeks, Chickasaws, Choctaws, and Seminoles. The federal government's failure to protect the "Five Civilized Tribes" in their new environment led some to support the Confederacy. The Choctaws and Chickasaws were overwhelmingly pro-South, and the Creek and Cherokees were evenly divided in their allegiance. Indian Territory figured prominently in Confederate designs for the West because of its geographic position and economic importance. Confederate diplomacy secured alliance treaties and assurances of military assistance from the five tribes. The instability of the Indian–Confederate alliance, Confederate mismanagement of Indian affairs, and the pitting of Indians from each side against each other led to the growth of unionist sentiment among southern Indians. Reconstruction treaties in 1866 readjusted tribal relations with the federal government after the war.

Violent Indian–white clashes bloodied Civil War history. In 1862, the Santee Dakotas attacked whites in Minnesota, their resentments fired, in part, by the failure of the government to deliver needed goods. In the Southwest, Union Colonel James Henry Carlton turned his attention to total warfare against raiding Mescalero and Jicarilla Apaches and Navajos provoked by citizens intent on capturing and selling Navajos as slaves. Carlton called on Christopher "Kit" Carson to round up Apaches and Navajos and ship them to Bosque Redondo, a forty-square-mile reservation on the Pecos River in New Mexico. Many Mescaleros fled to Mexico, while others marched to Bosque Redondo. Carson had to starve the Navajos out, steal their horses and sheep, burn their crops and peach orchards, and destroy hogans before he succeeded in forcing 8,000 Navajos to walk some 350 miles to the reservation, where they remained in captivity for five years. In Colorado, Black Kettle's band of peaceful Cheyennes, confident they were safe from attack by militia, camped at Sand Creek, near Fort Lyon on Territorial Governor John Evan's authorization. On November 29, 1864, they were wantonly massacred by Colonel John M. Chivington, who had ordered his troops to "kill and scalp all, big and little," and his 100-day enlistees.

RESERVATION POLICY

After the Civil War, the government turned its attention to the area west of the Mississippi. New territories were added to the growing country: The states of Texas and California joined the Union in 1845 and 1850 respectively, portions of present-day Arizona and New Mexico were purchased in 1847 from Mexico, railroads were pushing through west of the Mississippi, and in 1848 gold was discovered in California. All this combined to lure white entrepreneurs, adventurers, and homesteaders. The rush to the West was accompanied by white encroachment on Indian land and a destructive exploitation of natural resources. The degradation of the environment impoverished Indian people who depended on its resources. Indians retaliated by attacking the trespassers. The government replied by all-out military campaigns.

When the Indians west of the Mississippi were defeated militarily, they were forced to relinquish much of their homeland. Small portions were reserved for the use of the defeated tribes, and they were required to relocate to these smaller portions, called reservations. Initially, federal policy was to keep native populations racially segregated until "civilized." This was carried out by confining all Indians to a general area, such as the Indian Territory. This barrier philosophy ended because of the pressures of westward expansion, which virtually eliminated the line. In the 1850s, the federal government created reservations in California and after

Washington Territory was established in 1853, created reservations there, separating Indians from whites. By the 1860s, the government had confined tribes in the West to separate parcels with specific boundaries.

The Indian Office was responsible for overseeing the organization and running of the reservations. Agencies were established on each reservation. Schools, farm buildings, storerooms, offices, and housing were built for agency employees. The Indian Office funded reservation schools, and the agents oversaw the training of Indian men in agricultural methods. The Indian Office's field personnel grew by 1,000 percent between 1852 and 1872.

A major duty of the Indian Office was to provide subsistence for the people who were confined to the reservations. By 1871, with the end of treaty making, the federal government began treating Indians as wards and the government as their guardian. Indian agents were responsible for distributing annuity goods, food rations, and supplies on a regular basis. For example, the 1876 agreement with the Sioux, which reduced the size of their reservation, stipulated that until the Sioux were able to support themselves, the government would supply to each Indian "a pound and a half of beef, one-half pound of flour, and one-half pound of corn; and for every one hundred rations, four pounds of coffee, eight pounds of sugar, and three pounds of beans."

During this time, the Indian Office was growing more and more corrupt. The Indian Peace Commission, appointed to examine the problem, of 1867 reported:

> The records are abundant to show that agents have pocketed the funds appropriated by the government and driven the Indians to starvation. It cannot be doubted that Indian wars have originated from this cause. The Sioux war, in Minnesota, is supposed to have been produced in this way. For a long time these officers have been selected from partisan ranks, not so much on account of honesty and qualification as for devotion to party interests and their willingness to apply the money of the Indian to promote the selfish schemes of local politicians.

It was said that an agent could retire a wealthy man after working four years on an agent's salary of only $1,500 per year. Presidents often appointed agents to return political favors, not because the prospective agent was qualified for the job. The agents often defrauded Indians by skimming money off the top and providing the Indians with spoiled food and poor quality goods. The commission also reported that Indians were decreasing in number, that a large majority of Indian wars could be traced to the aggressions of lawless white men, that Indians were being impoverished by the loss of their hunting grounds and the destruction of game. They concluded that the problems could not be remedied until the Indians were all "civilized" or extinct.

During President Ulysses S. Grant's administration (1869–1877), the Indian Office was reorganized in the hope of eliminating inefficiencies and corrupt agents. A major reform was in the way field personnel were chosen. Agents were no longer selected from the political ranks, but were chosen from nominees submitted by missionaries in the field. In addition, the president organized the Board of Indian Commissioners to "exercise joint control with the Secretary of the Interior over the disbursement of the appropriations made by this act." The board began to oversee the purchasing of rations, annuity goods, and supplies. Grant's crusade against corruption eventually resulted in an important reform, the 1883 Civil Service Act, which, for the first time, required competency as a basis for eligibility for federal jobs. However, the Indian Office was not initially subject to the provisions of the act.

WESTERN INDIAN–WHITE CONFLICTS

During the late sixteenth century, the Spanish moved into southwestern lands for wealth, converts, and slaves and ruled there until 1821. Hostility eventually developed between the Spanish and the Apaches and Pueblo peoples. The harsh rule of some Spanish governors plus religious and economic oppression led to an allied Pueblo-Apache revolt against the Spanish empire in northern New Spain.

The 1680 Pueblo Revolt was ended by Spanish counter-offenses in 1692.

In the 1820s and 1830s, American and British fur trappers and traders moved into Indian lands of the interior and the Rocky Mountains, and fur trappers, traders, Mormon missionaries, miners, and settlers moved into the Nevada, Utah, Idaho, California, and Oregon lands of the Northern and Southern Paiutes, Washos, and Western Shoshones. From the trappers and traders, some tribes learned of Christianity and requested religious instruction for their people. In the 1840s, Catholic and Protestant missionaries traveled to the interior to open missions among the Cayuses, Nez Percés, Confederated Salish–Kootenai, and others. Competition among missionaries for converts ultimately undermined tribal institutions and created bitter factions that weakened tribes.

Between 1850 and 1890, incessant conflicts took place on the Plains and in Texas, the Southwest, the Pacific Northwest, California, and the Basin-Plateau areas.

Missionary writings encouraged more American settlements in Oregon country. Miners poured into Spokane country when gold was discovered. Mining towns soon crowded out Indian villages in the Wallowa Valley in the 1860s. Clashes and wars eventually occurred in the 1850s between Oregon and Washington settlers, miners, and troops and Indian tribes. During the 1850s, Rogue River Indians unsuccessfully tried to resist white settlers and miners who had moved onto their lands. Eventually, troops defeated tribes in Idaho, Oregon, and Washington, with the Indians relocated on reservations, and their "excess" lands opened to settlers.

During the gold rush in California, whites poured over Indian villages and hunting and fishing grounds. By the early 1850s, the American government extinguished Indian titles to California land and established reservations for Indians, by agreement, not treaties, between 1853 and 1860. Indian populations declined due to armed conflicts with Americans, disease, depletion of the food supply, and starvation.

In Texas, laws denying Indians all rights resulted

BUFFALO

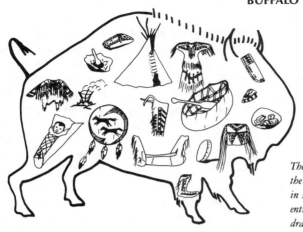

The buffalo, or American bison, was put to ingenious use by the Native peoples living in the plains areas who honored it in sacred ceremonies and depended on it for survival. The entire buffalo was used and never wasted. Contemporary drawing by Leslie Frank McKeon.

NORTH AMERICAN BUFFALO POPULATIONS

1800	40,000,000	1880	395,000
1850	20,000,000	1885	20,000
1865	15,000,000	1895	less than 1,000
1875	1,000,000	1983	50,000

HOW INDIANS USED THE BUFFALO

Meat	Food and ceremonial use	Hide	Tipis, robes, dresses, gloves, breech cloth, shirts, leggings, moccasins, bedding, dolls, regalia, cradleboards, implements, drums, tipi furnishings
Fat and Marrow	Food, paint, and cosmetics		
Bones	Tools, weapons, knives, pipes, soup, sleds		
Brain	Food, used to tan hides		
Intestine	Cord		
Hoofs	Implements, utensils, glue, jewelry, food, ceremonial use		
		Skull	Ceremonial use
Bladder	Storage pouches	Horns	Implements, ornaments, ceremonial use, games
Rawhide	Moccasin soles, shields, containers, ornaments, rattles, snow shoes, mortars, lariats, bridles, boats, luggage, food boiling, medicine bundle, saddles, thongs, stirrups	Hair	Rope, stuffing, ornaments, ceremonial use
		Dung	Fuel
		Sinew and Muscle	Thread, cord, bow strings
		Tail	Fly brush
		Stomach	Cooking vessel, container for carrying/storing water

in guerrilla warfare between the Texas Rangers and Comanches, Kiowas, and bands of Apaches for several decades until the Indians were defeated. The Spanish, Mexicans, and Texans in turn almost completely exterminated Texas Indians.

From 1860 to 1890, white settlements continued to expand over Indian lands, wiping out the two great buffalo herds, and usurping and depleting other resources—game, wood, and water—with government encouragement. The southern buffalo herd was destroyed by 1880, and the northern herd was almost gone from the Plains by 1885.

Between 1860 and 1886, Apache bands in Arizona and New Mexico waged "hit and run" warfare against large numbers of U.S. troops and citizens, who were encouraged to kill Apaches. One by one, Apache leaders surrendered, were killed, became prisoners of war, such as Geronimo, or were forced onto reservations.

Although some warfare had occurred earlier, the years 1860 to 1877 witnessed the major assault by the U.S. government on the lands of the Plains Indians and the general defensive warfare waged by the Lakotas [Sioux], Cheyennes, Arapahos, Kiowas, Kiowa Apaches, and Comanches from the Dakotas to Texas. White settlers encroached on Sioux lands between 1861 and 1870, especially in South Dakota's Black Hills during the 1870s. In 1868, Indian peace commissioners were appointed to make peace with so-called belligerent tribes throughout the West.

FEDERAL ASSIMILATION POLICIES

By 1877, powerful white armies and technology militarily defeated the Plains Indians and destroyed their economies. They were confined to reservations and subjected to Indian Office programs of cultural assimilation designed to train them to become farmers. At the end of the 1870s, the federal government removed large numbers of Indian children from their families and communities and placed them in distant federal boarding schools such as the precedent-setting Carlisle School in Pennsylvania,

founded in 1879. Children were stripped of their native clothing and hair, forced to speak English, prohibited from speaking their native language, and subjected to a routine of discipline and moral Christian training.

By 1878, the Indian Office established tribal police forces and courts under the administrative control of its agents. The Office frequently appointed "chiefs" through whom it governed the tribes. The agency also outlawed Indian religious practices such as the Plains Indian Sun Dance.

In the late 1880s, the prophecies of the Paiute Wovoka, who lived in what is now Nevada, spread to other tribes beyond the Rocky Mountains to the Dakotas. The Ghost Dance, which promised the return of the Indian dead and the buffalo, the end of misery, and among some adherents, the disappearance of white people from the country, expressed itself through worship in the form of ghost dancing. In December 1890, hundreds of Lakota ghost dancers were slaughtered at Wounded Knee, South Dakota, ending overt resistance to white authority.

After the Civil War and through the turn of the century, movements to reform Indian affairs developed because of the desperate situation of Indian peoples. President Grant's Peace Policy was created with two components, the Board of Indian Commissioners and the appointment of different evangelizing missionary societies to Indian reservations. Antimilitaristic reformers fought off the army, which wanted to resume control over Indian policy and transfer the Indian Bureau to the War Department. Organizations such as the Board of Indian Commissioners, the Indian Rights Association, and the Lake Mohonk Conference of Friends of the Indians tried to persuade the government to allot reservations in severalty (distribute parcels of reservation lands to individuals), assimilate Indians through formal schooling, and dissolve Indian nations of Indian territory, lands that were coveted by farmers. The reformers believed that by breaking up reservations, dissolving tribes, and making individual Indians into property owners the problem of assimilating Indians into the American mainstream would be solved. The policy of allotting lands in severalty to Indians was not a new idea. Wresting land from Indians through allotments first appeared in Indian treaties in 1817 and became a regular feature of treaties with tribes in the Kansas and Nebraska territories and other areas after 1854 until 1887, when the General Allotment Act enshrined the allotment philosophy into federal law.

THE GENERAL ALLOTMENT ACT

The General Allotment Act, also called the Dawes Act after Congressman Henry L. Dawes, who sponsored it, ignored Indian land use patterns that were thousands of years old. It enshrined in law the idea that American Indians should be assimilated into

WARS

Native Americans fought valiantly against the Europeans and Euro-americans who invaded their homelands. The following chronology lists major wars and campaigns fought by Native peoples in the present-day United States from the seventeenth through the nineteenth centuries.

1636–1638	Pequot War, Connecticut Valley
1675–1676	King Philip's War, Wampanoags and Narragansetts in southern New England
1675–1676	War with Susquehannocks in Maryland, Bacon's Rebellion
1711–1713	Tuscarora War, North Carolina
1715–1716	Yamassee War, South Carolina
1754–1763	French and Indian War, Iroquois and Algonquian
1774	War with Shawnees in Ohio Valley, also called Lord Dunmore's War
1774–1784	American Revolutionary War period
1779	War with Six Nations (Iroquois) in Wyoming Valley, Pennsylvania
1790–1795	War with Mingo, Miami, Wyandot, Delaware, Potawatomi, Shawnee, Chippewa, and Ottawa Indians of "Old Northwest," also known as Little Turtle's War

1811–1813	War with Shawnee, Potawatomi, Winnebago, Chippewa, and Wyandot Indians in Indiana
1813	Peoria Indian War in Illinois
1813–1814	Creek Indian War in Alabama, Georgia, Mississippi, and Tennessee
1817–1818	First Seminole Indian War in Georgia and Florida
1823	Campaign against Arikara Indians, upper Missouri River
1827	War with Winnebagos in Wisconsin, also called La Fevre Indian War
1832	Black Hawk's War (Sac and Fox Indians) in Illinois and Wisconsin
1834	Expedition against Pawnees in Indian Territory (Oklahoma)
1835–1842	Second Seminole War in Florida, Georgia, and Alabama
1837	War with Osage Indians in Missouri
1847–1850	War with Cayuse Indians in Oregon
1850–1851	Mariposa War with Miwoks and Yokuts in California
1851–1852	Yuma and Mohave uprisings in California and Arizona
1854	Campaign against Jicarilla Apaches in New Mexico
1855–1856	War with Takelma and Tututni Indians in Oregon, also called Rogue River War

white civilization, embrace agrarian values, and become individual land owners. Nearly all tribal members received allotments of land. Indian heads of family received 160-acre allotments of reservation land, single persons over eighteen years and orphans regardless of age received eighty acres. Single Indians under eighteen years received forty acres. Any remaining land the government put up for public

sale or would buy from the Indians and open to homesteaders under the 1862 Homestead Act. The federal government retained trusteeship over the individual's allotment for twenty-five years, protecting land from taxation during that time, while Indians established their "competency." After the trust period ended, the land became taxable and the allottee became a citizen. If an Indian died during the

1855–1856	War with Yakima, Walla Walla, Umatilla, and Cayuse Indians in Washington Territory
1855–1858	Third Seminole War in Florida
1858	War with Spokane, Coeur d'Alene, Palouse, Yakima, and Northern Paiute Indians in Washington Territory
1860	War with Paiute Indians in Nevada, also known as Pyramid Lake War
1861–1886	Campaign against Apaches in New Mexico and Arizona
1862–1863	War with Dakotas in Minnesota and Dakota territory
1863	War with Shoshone Indians in Utah and Idaho
1863–1866	War against Navajos in Arizona and New Mexico
1864–1865	War with Cheyenne and Arapaho Indians in Colorado and Kansas
1865	War with Northern Plains Indians, known as the Powder River Expedition
1866–1868	War with Northern Paiutes in Oregon, Idaho, and California, also known as Snake War
1866–1868	War with Lakota, Cheyenne, and Arapaho Indians in Wyoming and Montana, also known as Red Cloud's War for Bozeman Trail
1868–1869	War with Cheyenne, Arapaho,

	Lakota, Kiowa, and Comanche Indians on southern and northern Plains
1872–1873	War with Modocs in Oregon and California
1874–1875	Campaign against Kiowa, Southern Cheyenne, and Comanche Indians in Indian Territory, also known as the Red River War
1876–1877	War with Lakota, Cheyenne, and Arapaho Indians in South Dakota, Montana, and Wyoming, also known as the Black Hills War
1876–1879	War with Northern Cheyenne Indians in Indian Territory, Kansas, Nebraska, Wyoming, Montana and Dakota Territory
1877	War with Nez Percé Indians in Idaho
1878	War with Bannock, Northern Paiute, and Cayuse Indians in Idaho and Washington Territory
1879	War with Shoshone and Bannock Indians in Idaho, also known as Sheepeater War
1879	Campaign against Ute Indians in Colorado and Utah

twenty-five–year trust period, the act required division of land according to state or territory inheritance laws where the allotment was located. Indians of future generations were landless except for property acquired through heirs.

The Indian Office became the manager of all the details involved in the allotment process. They reviewed tribal rolls and decided who was and who was not eligible to be a member of a specific tribe. The agents were responsible for surveying land, dividing it up, and allotting portions to individuals. The office hired farmers to teach Indian men how to farm and raise cattle on their land. The agencies bought equipment, seeds, tools, and livestock to help transform hunters into farmers and ranchers. But there was never enough money to accomplish the goal. During the first twelve years of the allotment program, the government spent approximately $1.62 per allottee for supplies, seeds, equipment, and livestock, hardly enough money to plant a flower garden and not nearly enough to buy farm machinery or livestock.

The Bureau of Indian Affairs (BIA) was authorized in 1891 to lease the land (mostly to non-Indians) of those unable because of age or infirmity to work their land. Agents gradually became the real estate agents for all reservation land, leasing and collecting rents and handling the income, which was placed in trust for the allottees. An act in 1902 authorized the sale of land belonging to heirs of allottees, and in 1907, a congressional act provided that the BIA could sell land belonging to original allottees. Much of the allotted land was unsuitable for farming, and many Indians could not farm their land because they lacked equipment. In addition, there was a cultural bias for some tribal people, who did not consider farming men's work. In 1906, the Burke Act authorized Indians who were judged competent to sell their land, although the twenty-five–year trust period had not expired, and many Indians, unable to make a living from the land, sold it. By the end of allotment in 1934, 100,000 Indians were landless, deprived of over 90 million acres of original reservation land.

A massive loss of Indian property resulted from the clause in the Dawes Act requiring estates to be partitioned in accord with state or territorial inheritance law which maximized the number of heirs to an allotment and minimized the acreage each heir received. In 1910, a reform law permitted allottees to limit the number of heirs so as to pass on inheritances large enough to be useful. By the late 1920s, federal officials were faced with a growing Indian population living on a fixed and severely limited amount of land. Tribes attempted to reopen tribal rolls to provide land to children born since the first allotments. Many of these children were born to second-generation Indians who sold heirship lands under the 1902 law and had no hope of ever obtaining land unless new allotments were made.

In response to large mining and timber companies, various presidents used executive orders to alienate reservation lands and allocate them to the public domain, enabling companies to circumvent Indian land-leasing procedures. Congress also enacted laws that allowed speculators to acquire large tracts of public lands to lease to timber and mining companies. The 1920 Mineral Leasing Act also eased access to Indian lands.

THE INDIAN REORGANIZATION ACT

With tribal institutions seriously undermined by military defeat and the land base broken up through allotment, the BIA began to intrude on the daily lives and personal habits of the people in their care. In 1901, the Commissioner of Indian Affairs issued a circular to agents in the field detailing BIA actions toward Indian customs that "should be modified or discontinued." Forbidden were the wearing of long hair by males, face painting of both sexes, and wearing Indian dress. Dances and feasts were forbidden on the grounds that they were "simply subterfuges to cover degrading acts and to disguise immoral purposes." Offenders could be punished by having rations—which were owed to Indians in exchange for land—withheld or by imprisonment at hard labor.

The reservation system became the arena for a forced experiment in social change. Reservations were occupied by a legion of paternalistic bureau brainwashers who took over and effectively became the government of the tribe. BIA employees became the teachers and the health care workers. They provided police protection, built and ran schools and hospitals, and maintained roads. They employed farmers, stockmen, teachers, and administrators to run every aspect of the lives of reservation Indians.

Managing the details of a peoples' life requires staff to do the work. The BIA continued to grow and with growth, corruption once again became an issue. In response to criticism, inspectors were assigned to help keep agents honest by overseeing the purchase of goods. Eventually agents were placed under civil service regulations and were no longer appointed as a reward for political favors. Growth also brought about the creation of different divisions within the BIA. Within the BIA there were five divisions: Accounts, Records and Files, Land and Law, and Superintendent of Indian Schools. In order to administer the affairs on reservations which were spread out across the country, the BIA divided the United States into geographical regions called districts. Each district encompassed numerous reservations and had an office located in a large city within the district. The local-level employees were supervised by administrators at the division offices.

The BIA continued to operate on the premise that the "Indian problem" would be solved when there were no more identifiable Indians. It was assumed that it was necessary to force Indian people into giving up their heritage. It did not occur to the reformers of that time that there was anything about Indian culture that should be encouraged. By the early twentieth century, it was obvious that allotment, education, and coercion failed to turn Native Americans into prosperous Christian farmers; rather, the results were enclaves of poverty stricken, landless people surrounded by growing numbers of whites.

In the 1920s there was a growing concern that Indian affairs were being mishandled. A reform movement was led by John Collier, one of the founders of the American Indian Defense Association. He championed the rights of Native Americans to freedom of religion and defended the land rights of the Pueblo people of the Southwest. Several Indian defense societies called for investigations into the conditions of Indian people, and in 1926, the secretary of the interior authorized the Institute for Government Research (now the Brookings Institution) to conduct a study of the BIA. The resulting report, *The Problem of Indian Administration*, commonly called the *Meriam Report* after Lewis Meriam who headed the study, was severely critical of the BIA and its programs. The publication in 1928 of the *Meriam Report* was the beginning of a shift in policy in the BIA.

The *Meriam Report* recommended an end to allotment, better pay for bureau employees, the hiring of Indians in the BIA, and more funds for health and education. In 1933 President Franklin D. Roosevelt appointed John Collier as Indian Affairs Commissioner. Collier instituted an "Indian New Deal," and many of the recommendations of the *Meriam Report* were enacted in the 1934 Indian Reorganization Act (IRA), or the Wheeler-Howard Act. The IRA was important in that its passage marks a change in government policy. The act repealed the forty-seven–year old allotment system and forbade further allotments of Indian land in severalty and the sale to whites of unallotted or heirship lands. Its fundamental aims were development of Indian economic resources and restoration of Indian self-determination through revival of tribal governments. Tribes, at their own option, could incorporate under provisions of the act and elect tribal governments invested with certain legal powers. A revolving loan fund was created for economic development and provisions were included for scholarships for Indians attending vocational and trade schools, Indian employment preference for federal government jobs, and adding land to reservations. The act invested the interior secretary with a great deal of power in approving tribal constitutions, vetoing certain tribal council actions, and making rules for managing forests and grazing lands. Also in 1934, Congress enacted the Johnson-O'Malley Act to promote, with federal monies, federal–state cooperation in providing services to Indians, especially in education.

The Indian New Deal was not entirely successful. Hostility in Congress and a misunderstanding of Indian needs by the white community hampered the reform program. Tribal reorganization failed because Collier and his coworkers had basic misconceptions about Indian peoples and how they functioned. New tribal governments aroused little support among the people they were supposed to represent. There was intratribal factionalism and rivalry, and the political structures that were established were foreign to Indian societies. (See TRIBAL GOVERNMENTS for more information about the IRA.)

In 1946, Congress created the Indian Claims Commission (ICC) to adjudicate claims against the U.S. government by tribes for compensation for land stolen during the treaty period. Before the commission was created, claims of tribes, bands, and other groups against the United States could only be brought to court if Congress authorized the action. Lasting until 1978, when unheard claims were transferred back to the Court of Claims, the ICC granted awards, not land, to cases brought before it.

TERMINATION

After the reforms of the 1930s, the policies of the next two decades reflected a backlash. In 1943, a congressional study again found serious problems in

INDIAN CLAIMS COMMISSION (ICC)

By the 1890s, the United States, through formal treaty or agreement with Indian tribes, had purchased 90 percent of its public domain for some $800 million. But though the U.S. government was contented with its record in these dealings, Indians were not. One historian noted, "It would be difficult, indeed, to find a land cession made by the Indians entirely of their own volition." The Americans' right to buy always superseded the Indians' right not to sell.

Indians were not allowed to submit claims arising from treaty issues until 1881, when by a special act of Congress, the Choctaws were granted access to the Court of Claims for resolution of their fifty-year-old grievances. With the last of the hostilities and resistance fading, the legal forum replaced the military arena. Indians, however, required special jurisdictional acts of Congress to open the court to the petitioning tribes—an arduous process that forced tribes to go to Washington. By 1946, almost 200 claims were filed with the Court of Claims, but only 29 received awards, while the bulk of the rest were dismissed on technicalities.

The Court of Claims, narrowly circumscribed by the acts granting it jurisdiction, tried for sixty-five years to deal conclusively with Indian claims and failed. Although the Court of Claims had jurisdiction in some cases, often the court's authority did not extend to all aspects of tribal claims. To rectify the situation, Congress passed the Indian Claims Commission Act in 1946. The act created a judicial body expressly to resolve the large numbers of Indian claims that had accumulated before 1946. The act also enlarged the scope of claims that Indians could bring against the government and established a cut-off date for filing claims.

The ICC was established to give Indians wider scope to make claims against the government, Tribes had to hire their own attorneys subject to approval of the secretary of the interior. The attorney general represented the U.S. government. Initially composed of three commissioners, the ICC was expanded to five members in 1967. Of the eleven commissioners who served on the ICC, Brantley Blue, a Lumbee Indian, appointed in 1969 by President Richard Nixon, was the first and only Indian on the commission.

If the ICC determined that the United States was

the administration of Indian affairs. This time the "Indian problem" was to be solved by ending the special relationship between Indians and the federal government. Many Indian leaders felt that the trust status of Indian land was a protection of their land base. They felt threatened by laws that ended that relationship and subjected the land to taxation and alienation. In 1947, the BIA began to identify Indian groups that they believed were able to manage without the benefit of the federal trust relationship and services to Indian tribes. More than 100 tribal groups were singled out as ready for "termination." One factor determining "readiness" was a tribe's commercially valuable resources. In 1953, House Concurrent Resolution 108 was adopted, which

called for termination of the federal relationship with tribes as soon as possible.

Although Indian opposition to termination was substantial, congressional opposition was meager, and the consent of affected Indian groups was not considered necessary to the implementation of the termination policy. Within a year after the adoption of HCR 108, Congress began passing individual acts designed to carry forward the termination policy. Between 1954 and 1964, Congress terminated California rancherias, the Poncas of Nebraska, Peoria, Ottawa, and Wyandot Tribes in Oklahoma, the Klamath Tribe of Oregon, sixty-one other tribes and bands in western Oregon, the Catawbas of South Carolina, the Alabama-Couchattas of Texas, the

liable, it authorized monetary awards to the Indian claimants in whatever amounts it found they were entitled to, at the market value of the land at the date of its acquisition by the United States. The ICC did not restore land. Indians paid the expenses of the litigation, including attorneys' fees, 10 percent of the total judgment award. Some tribes borrowed money from the BIA Revolving Loan Fund and paid back the loan from judgment money. Final awards were deposited in the U.S. Treasury until Congress directed how it should be distributed among various tribal members. The interior secretary had the right to approve or reject any decision by any tribe as to the distribution of their own funds.

Many legislators felt that once the federal government settled all its outstanding claims and paid its debts to tribes, the government could mark the end of any special relationship with the Indian tribes. Indians, then, would have less incentive to retain tribal membership and residence on reservations. Thus, the way would be cleared for termination of federal trust over tribes and eventual assimilation into non-Indian society.

The ICC took years to resolve claims. Because of the government's deduction of its expenditures and tribal expenses, a tribe might receive only 8 to 10 percent of its original claim. Appeals to the Court of Claims or the Supreme Court tacked on more time. Because investigation and adjudicating claims was a slow and tedious process, the ICC's tenure was repeatedly extended, expiring in 1978. The time span of thirty-two years was not an exorbitant one to resolve the immense and complex backlog of work involved in over 600 claims covering 150 years.

The ICC completed 342 dockets and awarded some $818 million to Indian tribes for land taken unjustly, government fraud, and government mismanagement of affairs. The ICC transferred over sixty unresolved cases to the Court of Claims.

Southern Paiutes, Utes of the Uintahs and Ourays of Utah, and the Menominees of Wisconsin. The tide turned, and the decade of the 1970s opened with repeal or modification of other termination bills.

Certain provisions were common to most termination bills. Periods ranging from two to five years were authorized for completion of the termination process. During that time, final tribal rolls were to be prepared. After completing the rolls, each tribal member was to be given a personal property right in the undivided tribal assets. Various methods for distribution were authorized. Termination legislation ended most aspects of the historic relationship between the federal government and the terminated tribes, transferring responsibility for these tribes to the states. Federal programs of education, health, welfare, and housing assistance, as well as other social programs, were no longer available. State legislative jurisdiction was imposed, giving state and local legislative bodies broad authority over terminated Indians in matters basic to Indian cultural integrity, such as education, adoption, and land use.

Moreover, affected Indians became subject to state taxation from which they previously had enjoyed immunity. Since state judicial jurisdiction was imposed, criminal and civil cases were handled by state courts, and federal and tribal law were no longer applicable. In addition, termination ended federal trusteeship over tribal and individual landholdings of terminated groups. Some reservations remained real property held by the Indian government as a corporation. Others were allotted to individual members with the "surplus" sold to the government and retained as public land. Lands of many smaller tribes were sold, and proceeds distributed among tribal members. Members of other affected tribes were permitted to choose between receiving payment and participation in private trusts or having their lands placed with Indian-controlled state corporations. Most, though not all, terminated tribes ultimately relinquished their lands and once again large amounts of Indian lands passed into non-Indian hands.

Finally, another practical effect of termination was

HISTORICAL NOVELS BY NATIVE AMERICAN AUTHORS

Contemporary Native American writers use the genre of historical fiction to portray the human warmth, daily life, and traditions of Indian cultures as well as the systematic failure of Indian–white relations during the nineteenth and twentieth centuries. The reform-minded government agent to the Little Elk Indians in D'Arcy McNickle's novel *Wind From An Enemy Sky* expresses this relationship this way: "The problem is communciation . . . we [Indians and non-Indians] do not speak to each other—and language is only part of the problem."

Bruchac, Joseph, Abenaki. *Dawn Land* (1993). Pre-contact native people in New England.

Robert J. Conley, Cherokee. *Mountain Wind Song* (1992). About the 1838 Trail of Tears; the forced removal of Cherokees from their southeastern homeland to what is now Oklahoma.

Ella Cara Deloria, Dakota. *Waterlily* (1988). Mid-nineteenth century Dakota [Sioux] life in the northern Plains.

Linda Hogan, Chickasaw. *Mean Spirit* (1990). Osage Indians during the 1920s Oklahoma oil boom period.

Anna Lee Walters, Pawnee-Otoe. *Ghost Singer* (1988). About nineteenth century federal policy and twentieth century museum collection policies.

James Welch, Blackfeet-Gros Ventre. *Fools Crow* (1986). About a small band of Blackfeet in 1870s Montana.

TERMINATION LEGISLATION

	Date of Termination	Tribal Membership	Tribal Land (Acres)
Alabama–Couchatta Tribes, Texas	1955	450	3,200
California Rancherias and Reservations	1969	1,107	4,315.5
Catawba of South Carolina	1962	631	3,388
Klamath Tribe of Oregon	1961	2,133	862,662
Menominee Tribe of Wisconsin	1961	3,270	233,881
Ottawa Tribe of Oklahoma	1959	630	0
Paiute Indians of Utah	1957	232	42,839
Peoria Tribe of Oklahoma	1959	640	0
Ponca Tribe of Nebraska	1966	442	834
Uintah & Ouray Utes of Utah	1961	490	211,430
60 bands of western Oregon Indians	1956	2,081	3,158
Wyandot Tribe of Oklahoma	1959	1,157	94.36
Totals		13,263	1,365,801.86

Source: Taylor, 1972.

to remove the sovereignty of terminated tribes. Although the termination acts did not expressly extinguish the governmental authority of such tribes, most were not able to exercise their governmental powers after the loss of their land base.

A major step toward termination of federal responsibility over Indian affairs was the passage in 1953 of Public Law 280. This law transferred criminal and civil jurisdiction over Indian lands from the federal to state governments in five states and allowed for future assumptions of jurisdiction by all other states—without Indian consent. PL 280 provided for the mandatory transfer of criminal and civil jurisdiction to California, Minnesota [except for Red Lake Reservation], Nebraska, Oregon [except for the Warm Springs Reservation], and Wisconsin [except for the Menominee Reservation]. In 1958, Alaska was granted jurisdiction over Indian lands within its boundaries. PL 280 also extended to all other states the option of assuming jurisdiction on their own initiative at some future time. Indians criticized PL

280 in part because it did not include a provision requiring Indian consent to subsequent transfers of jurisdiction. By 1968, when Congress passed a statute requiring Indian consent, nine more states had extended partial or full jurisdiction over Indian lands within their boundaries.

URBAN LIFE

In the early 1950s, the federal government launched a massive program to relocate reservation Indians to urban centers. World War II prompted some Indians to head for cities, where they worked in defense-related factories. But after the war, when Indians returned home, they faced hard times on reservations where jobs were few. Capitalizing on the lack of opportunities, the BIA offered employment assistance to Indians who would leave their reservations and relocate in urban communities. The tactic became another way for the government to get out of

NATIVE AMERICANS IN CITIES

TOTAL NATIVE POPULATION IN URBAN AND METROPOLITAN AREAS

Over the decades, census-takers used different procedures to identify Indians, therefore, it is difficult to estimate precisely how much, in percentage terms, the urban/metropolitan Indian population has grown over the decades. Nevertheless, the figures show the percentage of Indians moving to cities and metropolitan areas has grown steadily over fifty years.

1940	5% (urban)
1950	nearly 20% (urban)
1960	nearly 30% (urban)
1970	44.5% (urban)
1980	49% (metropolitan area)
1990	51% (metropolitan area)

URBAN AREAS WITH THE GREATEST AMERICAN INDIAN POPULATION

The figures below represent approximate, 1990 figures for the metropolitan areas of the cities represented.

Los Angeles, California	87,500
Tulsa, Oklahoma	48,000
New York, New York	46,000
Oklahoma City, Oklahoma	45,700
San Francisco, California	40,800
Phoenix, Arizona	38,000
Seattle–Tacoma, Washington	32,000
Minneapolis–St. Paul, Minnesota	24,000
Tucson, Arizona	20,000
San Diego, California	20,000

CITIES IN LITERARY WORKS BY INDIANS

Now that substantial numbers of Native Americans live in cities, Native authors have written contemporary novels and short fiction set in places where they offer glimpses into daily lives of urban-dwelling Indians. The city that figures in each work is noted.

Paula Gunn Allen, Laguna Pueblo/Sioux. *The Woman Who Owned the Shadows* (1983). San Francisco, California.

Janet Campbell Hale, Coeur d'Alene. *The Jailing of Cecelia Capture* (1985). San Francisco, California.

N. Scott Momaday, Kiowa. *House Made of Dawn* (1968). Los Angeles, California.

Simon Ortiz, Acoma Pueblo. "The San Francisco Indians" in *The Man To Send Rain Clouds* (1974).

the Indian business; the chief of the BIA Relocation Division stated at the outset, "The sooner we can get out, the better it will be." The Voluntary Relocation Program, renamed the Employment Assistance Program in 1954, provided one-way bus tickets, temporary low-cost housing, and new clothing. The program expanded over the decade. Relocation field offices grew from the first two, in Chicago and Los Angeles, to twelve by 1958, by adding Denver, San Francisco, San Jose, St. Louis, Joliet, Waukegan, Oakland, Cincinnati, Cleveland, and Dallas. By 1960, only eight field offices remained, as numbers of jobs in cities decreased.

By 1953, the BIA established that one-third of Indians, discouraged by urban life, returned to reservations. Yet, many others stayed and more came. Home reservations devoid of economic opportunities propelled thousands of Indians to find work and money in cities. Soon Indian populations in cities outdistanced some reservations.

In cities, Indians were separated from kinship ties, tribal languages, tribal communities, and cere-

Gerald Vizenor, Chippewa. *Wordarrows: Indians and Whites in the New Fur Trade* (1978). Minneapolis, Minnesota.

James Welch, Blackfeet. *The Indian Lawyer* (1990). Helena, Montana.

URBAN INDIAN CENTERS

Native Americans have created Indian centers in urban areas to provide social, economic, educational, and cultural services in cities where there are substantial Native American populations. Some of these centers have powwows, gift shops, art galleries, and other outreach programs for the public. Besides the centers listed here, which run programs for the public, there are many located in other cities around the United States. Look for their names and addresses in Barry Klein's *Reference Encyclopedia of the American Indian*, 6th edition. West Nyack, New York: Todd Publications, 1992, a work available in most library reference sections.

Arizona: Flagstaff Indian Center, 2717 N. Steves Boulevard, Suite 11, Flagstaff, Arizona 86004

California: Intertribal Friendship House, 523 E. 14th Street, Oakland, California 94606

Colorado: Denver Indian Center, 4407 Morrison Road, Denver, Colorado 80219

Illinois: American Indian Center, 1630 W. Wilson, Chicago, Illinois 60640

Maryland: Baltimore American Indian Center, 113 S. Broadway, Baltimore, Maryland 21231

Massachusetts: North American Indian Center of Boston, 105 S. Huntington, Boston, Massachusetts 02130

Michigan: North American Indian Association of Detroit, 22720 Plymouth Road, Detroit 48239

Minnesota: Minneapolis American Indian Center, 1530 E. Franklin, Minneapolis, Minnesota 55407

New York: American Indian Community House, 404 Lafayette Street, 2nd Floor, New York, New York 10003

Oklahoma: Native American Coalition of Tulsa, 1740 W. 41st Street, Tulsa, Oklahoma 74107

Pennsylvania: United American Indians of the Delaware Valley, 225 Chestnut Street, Philadelphia, Pennsylvania 19106

Texas: Dallas Inter-Tribal Center, 209 E. Jefferson, Dallas, Texas 75203

monies and were thrust into a strange environment. Indian centers were created to provide "a touch of traditional life." Centers sponsored powwows and social dance events that provided opportunities to perpetuate traditional Indian music and dance and other social, cultural, and spiritual activities for their multitribal populations. Centers found jobs for people, and ran health clinics, day care, and soup kitchens.

However, left alone in urban ghettos, far away from kin, relocated individuals became an undif-

ferentiated part of the inner-city poor. Some families and individuals prospered and some did not. Many tribal leaders preferred programs of economic development on reservations, so that people would not have to leave in order to find work, but the BIA was not ready to involve the people in decisions about their destiny. Over 30,000 people were relocated before the program ended in 1980.

In 1952, Congress authorized the interior secretary to transfer Indian health facilities to states or other governmental or private, nonprofit entities. The final step toward terminating BIA responsibility for Indian health care was taken in 1954 with the passage of Public Law 568, which provided for the transfer of the entire Indian health program to the U.S. Public Health Service in the Department of Health, Education and Welfare. The transfer constituted the largest reduction of program responsibilities in the history of the BIA. This congressional action fit with termination goals to eliminate "laws which set Indians apart from other citizens" and to abolish "duplicating and overlapping functions provided by the Indian Bureau." At the same time, the government also aimed to transfer the basic responsibility for educating Indian children from the federal government to state public schools.

By the end of the 1950s, Indian resistance and national public protest caused the federal government to abandon its termination policies. By the mid-1960s, it was clear that termination usually resulted in further impoverishment, land loss, and unsupportable costs to state and local units of government. Congressional members began to speak out against termination and even some formerly staunch supporters of assimilationist policies recanted as the inadequacies of the individual termination programs became increasingly apparent. Recognizing the disastrous effects of termination, Congress restored federal recognition to a number of tribes terminated in the 1950s and early 1960s. And it has granted federal recognition to several other tribes that had never been recognized. Indians witnessed a historic shift from assimilationist goals and policies toward a policy in which the federal government recognized and respected cultural differences, encouraged self-determination, and financially aided tribes in achieving this goal.

SELF-DETERMINATION

In the 1960s, Indians began uniting to take control of their own future. A nationwide Indian conference was held at the University of Chicago in June 1961. Approximately 700 Indians from over sixty tribes participated and created a "Declaration of Indian Purpose," which attacked termination and supported the right of a tribal community to maintain itself and develop with government assistance.

The move toward self-determination gained momentum during the administration of Lyndon Johnson. Indians were included in much of the president's "Great Society" legislation, continuing a trend begun during the previous administration. Agencies created to administer new poverty and community development programs were responsible for a major breakthrough in Indian policy. Under grant programs administered by these agencies, Indian communities were treated as viable units of local government capable of delivering services to their constituencies and eligible for national programs in addition to those special services they received from Bureau of Indian Affairs and the Indian Health Service. By 1968, sixty-three community action agencies served 129 reservations. In 1966, President Johnson appointed Robert Bennett, an Oneida, commissioner of Indian Affairs, the first Indian in almost a century to hold that office. Bennett supported greater Indian involvement in development and administration of bureau programs. BIA officials were directed to make use of the bureau's authority to contract with Indian communities to operate Indian service programs.

On March 6, 1968, President Johnson delivered a "Special Message to the Congress on the Problems of the American Indian: 'The Forgotten American.' " The president proposed a "new goal for our Indian programs: A goal that ends the old debate about 'termination' of Indian programs and stresses self-determination; a goal that erases old attitudes of paternalism and promotes partnership and self-help." The president established by executive order the National Council on Indian Opportunity, a committee chaired by Vice President Hubert H. Humphrey, to coordinate the many agencies dealing with Indians and to promote Indian participation in planning Indian programs.

The widely accepted goals of Indian control over planning and implementation of Indian programs were the foundation of President Richard Nixon's Indian policy.

LEGAL ORGANIZATIONS PROTECTING NATIVE RIGHTS

The late 1960s and 1970s saw an increase in the number of Indian law cases being litigated. Legal service programs were established to provide national legal representation to protect the rights of Indians. The organizations also made available relevant Indian law decisions published in hard-to-obtain court reporters and trained practitioners of Indian law.

American Indian Law Center
Post Office Box 4456, Station A
1117 Stanford, N.E.
Albuquerque, New Mexico 87196

Founded in 1967, this staff of lawyers located at the University of New Mexico researches and trains tribal judges and prosecutors, assists tribes in making legal decisions, and administers a scholarship program for Indians studying law. Publishes manuals and a newsletter.

American Indian Lawyer Training Program (AILTP)
319 MacArthur Boulevard
Oakland, California 94610

Founded in 1973, AILTP provides access to complex legal developments affecting Indian tribes and members, publishes resource materials focused on vital areas of law, especially water and natural resources, and promotes tribal sovereignty through training programs. In 1985, it established the American Indian Resources Institute.

Native American Rites Fund (NARF)
1506 Broadway
Boulder, Colorado 80302

Founded in 1970, NARF works in five priority areas: preservation of tribal existence, protection of tribal natural resources, promotion of human rights, accountability of governments to Native Americans, and development of Indian law. In 1972, NARF founded a National Indian Law Library (NILL), a central clearinghouse on Indian legal materials which has developed a rich collection of materials relating to federal Indian law and Native Americans.

In 1969, President Nixon appointed Louis Bruce, a Sioux-Mohawk, to head the BIA, only the third Indian to do so. Commissioner Bruce reorganized the BIA and appointed Native Americans to fill most of the positions in his administrative staff.

Nixon also articulated a new policy in his 1970 message to Congress. He stressed three points: (1) no tribe would be terminated without its consent, (2) tribal governments would be encouraged to take over federally funded programs for their benefit, and (3) tribes would be helped to become economically self-sufficient. This policy, called self-determination, is the official policy today. In 1975, Congress passed the Indian Self-Determination and Education Assis-

tance Act, which strengthened the abilities of tribal governments to manage federally funded programs themselves. The next year, when contracting began, tribes contracted for 800 programs. By 1988, 345 tribes entered into nearly 1,500 contracts for a total of $300 million, approximately one-third of the total BIA budget.

During the Nixon administration, the sacred Blue Lake was restored to the Taos Pueblo, and 21,000 acres were returned to the Yakimas, both significant restorations of land rather than financial awards and important results of the Nixon self-determination policy. Also during the Nixon era, in 1973 Congress reinstated the Menominees as a federally recognized

SELECTED NATIVE ORGANIZATIONS

Native Americans decided one of the best ways to promote their interests and protect their resources from government, industry, and others who want what they have was to band together and create organizations that try to influence policy makers at all levels of government. During the twentieth century, Native Americans created dozens of these organizations of all sizes. Some are national organizations, some regional or state; some include non-Indians as members and some do not. As they became stronger and more practiced, these organizations used the communications media to demand and receive the attention of non-Indians. The following list shows the variety of Indian organizations headquartered around the United States. These and dozens of others and their addresses are listed in Barry Kein's *Reference Encyclopedia of the American Indian*, 6th edition. West Nyack, New York: Todd Publications, 1992, a work available in most library reference sections.

Alaska Federation of Natives—Anchorage, Alaska

All Indian Pueblo Council—Albuquerque, New Mexico

American Indian Adoption Resource Exchange—Pittsburgh, Pennsylvania

American Indian Health Care Association—St. Paul, Minnesota

American Indian Higher Education Consortium—Washington, D.C.

American Indian Law Center—Albuquerque, New Mexico

American Indian Lawyer Training Program—Oakland, California

American Indian Library Association—Chicago, Illinois

American Indian Movement—San Francisco, California

American Indian Registry for the Performing Arts—Hollywood, California

American Indian Resources Institute—Oakland, California

American Indian Science and Engineering Society—Boulder, Colorado

American Native Press Archives—Little Rock, Arkansas

Americans for Indian Opportunity—Washington, D.C.

Association of American Indian and Alaska Native Social Workers—Portland, Oregon

Association of American Indian Physicians—Oklahoma City, Oklahoma

Association of Community Tribal Schools—Vermillion, South Dakota

Atlatl (Arts service organization)—Phoenix, Arizona

California Indian Legal Services—Oakland, California

Columbia River Inter-Tribal Fish Commission—Portland, Oregon

Council of Energy Resource Tribes—Denver, Colorado

First Nations Financial Project—Falmouth, Virginia

Great Lakes Indian Fish and Wildlife Commission—Odanah, Wisconsin

Honor Our Neighbors Origins and Rights—Milwaukee, Wisconsin

Indian Law Resource Center—Washington, D.C.

Indian Youth of America—Sioux City, Iowa

Indians Into Medicine—Grand Forks, North Dakota

Indigenous People's Network—Highland, Maryland

Institute of Alaska Native Arts—Fairbanks, Alaska

International Native American Language Issues Institute—Choctaw, Oklahoma

Intertribal Agriculture Council—Billings, Montana

Intertribal Timber Council—Portland, Oregon

Inuit Circumpolar Conference—Anchorage, Alaska

Keepers of the Treasures: Cultural Council of American Indians, Alaska Natives, and Native Hawaiians—Hominy, Oklahoma

Migizi Communications—Minneapolis, Minnesota

National American Indian Cattleman's Association—Toppenish, Washington

National American Indian Court Judges Association—Washington, D.C.

National Indian Business Council—Englewood, Colorado

National Indian Council on Aging—Albuquerque, New Mexico

National Indian Education Association—Washington, D.C.

National Indian Gaming Association—Washington, D.C.

National Indian Justice Center—Petaluma, California

National Indian Social Workers Association—Oklahoma City, Oklahoma

National Indian Training and Research Center—Tempe, Arizona

National Indian Youth Council—Albuquerque, New Mexico

National Native American Co-op—San Carlos, Arizona

National Urban Indian Council—Denver, Colorado

Native American Fish and Wildlife Society—Broomfield, Colorado

Native American Journalists Association—Minneapolis, Minnesota

Native American Public Broadcasting Consortium—Lincoln, Nebraska

Native American Rights Fund—Boulder, Colorado

Northwest Indian Fisheries Commission—Olympia, Washington

Seventh Generation Fund for Indian Development—Forestville, California

Survival of American Indian Associations—Olympia, Washington

United Indian Development Association—Los Angeles, California

United Indians of All Tribes Foundation—Seattle, Washington

United National Indian Tribal Youth (UNITY)—Oklahoma City, Oklahoma

United South and Eastern Tribes—Nashville, Tennessee

Vietnam Era Veterans Inter-Tribal Association—Oklahoma City, Oklahoma

Women of All Red Nations—Rapid City, South Dakota

tribe, and Alaska natives' land claims were settled as well with the passage in 1971 of the Alaska Native Land Claims Settlement Act. The law granted natives legal title to some 44 million acres; in return, all native claims in Alaska were extinguished. The law provided a $962.5 million cash award, and division of Alaska into twelve geographic regions each of which had a native regional corporation. Alaska natives became shareholders in one of the twelve or a thirteenth corporation set up for nonresident Alaska natives. Native village corporations, also created by the law, held surface rights to lands, while the regional corporations held subsurface mineral rights.

During the Ford administration, the Havasupais succeeded in their peaceful struggle to get trust title to a portion of their ancient homeland along the Grand Canyon's south rim. The 1975 Grand Canyon National Park Enlargement Act authorized the United States to hold in trust for the Havasupai 185,000 acres of the land they have used and occupied for centuries. Also in 1975, during the Ford administration, the Indian Self-Determination and Education Assistance Act was passed. One of the most significant pieces of legislation since 1934, the law contained language repudiating termination policy, committing the federal government to a relationship with Indians and obliging it to foster Indian involvement and participation in directing education and service programs. The act also provided for tribes to contract to administer certain programs such as education.

During the Carter administration, Congress enacted the American Indian Religious Freedom Act in 1978 and the Archaeological Resources Protection Act in 1979, which assured Native Americans that their religious beliefs and practices and cultural values were secure from interference. Two U.S. Supreme Court rulings, however, limited considerably those Native religious practices that the U.S. government promised to protect. In the 1988 *Lyng, Secretary of Agriculture, et al. v. Northwest Indian Cemetery Protective Association, et al.* decision, the Court ruled in favor of permitting the U.S. Forest Service to pave a stretch of road in the high country of the Six Rivers National Forest sacred to the Karok, Yurok, and

Tolowa Indians of northern California. Further, the Forest Service ignored its expert witness who concluded that the road would destroy the religion of the three tribes. In the 1990 *Employment Division of Oregon v. Smith*, the Court denied Alfred Smith unemployment benefits because he had been discharged from his position as a drug rehabilitation counselor for "misconduct." He attended a prayer meeting of the Native American Church and used peyote, a sacred, hallucinogenic cactus "button" as a sacrament in much the same way that wine is used in holy communion in the Catholic church, but the court failed to recognize the practice. The ruling alarmed the Indian community and the Christian-Judaic community as well, which organized a coalition to restore religious freedom through legislative means.

During the Nixon administration, a generation of Indian activists fired up with the need to take responsibility for their own communities forced the public and the federal government to look at massive policy failures. In 1968, they developed new pan-Indian organizations, such as the American Indian Movement (AIM), committed to direct action. They occupied Alcatraz Island in 1969, took over the Bureau of Indian Affairs building in Washington in 1972, and occupied the town of Wounded Knee, South Dakota, in 1973.

Beginning in the 1960s, American Indian tribes, seeking to reverse 150 years of repressive and vacillating federal policies, sought to re-establish Indian reservations as substantially independent, economically viable communities. The task has not been easy. Tribes have faced seemingly insurmountable obstacles, including the dogged resistance of powerful economic and political interests and deep poverty and a sense of alienation among Indian people, resulting from generations of economic deprivation and attacks on tribal cultures and traditions.

During the 1970s, Indians went to federal and state courts to claim land and protect their treaty rights. In the eastern United States, Indian groups claimed lands taken illegally by eastern states during the late 1790s. Based on a section of the Indian Trade and Intercourse Act of 1790 that stated "no sale of lands made by any Indians . . . shall be valid to any person or persons, or to any state . . . unless the same shall be made and duly executed at some public treaty, held under the authority of the United States," Indians in Maine, Rhode Island, and Connecticut succeeded in reclaiming some state lands illegally taken in violation of the 1790 law.

In the 1970s, Indian activists demanded that water rights be protected. As trustee of Indian resources, the federal government litigated scores of Indian water rights cases against states and private interests, especially in the Southwest where water is scarce. Increasingly, Congress, the courts, and the administration have recognized a trust obligation to protect the land and its resources and to ensure that the people occupying the land have the services and financial resources to prosper in the future. These resources include fish, and the 1970s witnessed court actions taken by Indians in the Great Lakes and northern Pacific coast region to protect their treaty rights to fish at "accustomed" places ceded to the federal government in nineteenth-century treaties.

During the 1980s, the Supreme Court reaffirmed three sources of sovereignty within the constitutional system—the federal and state governments and American Indian tribal governments. This affirmation of tribal sovereignty gave Indian people the right to control land, natural resources, economic development, law and order, education, and health within reservation boundaries. By the end of the decade, however, the Supreme Court took a sharp turn away from the recognition of tribal rights. Decisions in 1989 threatened tribal sovereignty and signaled that the Court would no longer be the ultimate protector of essential tribal interests in difficult cases.

In addition to congressional and court challenges to their sovereignty, tribal people faced organized opposition from small, regional anti-Indian organizations scattered throughout the country. Most vocal during the 1970s and 1980s, when Indian fishing rights were confirmed in the Pacific Northwest and Great Lakes, these groups wanted "nation unto nation" treatment of Native Americans abrogated, reservations terminated, and the BIA abolished. Successful in terms of staging demonstrations and attracting press attention, anti-Indian groups have used discontent, racism, and economic troubles to drive home their message that the "special treatment" of Indians deprive citizens of their hopes and dreams. In response, organizations of people appalled by the performance of peers and neighbors vocalized support of treaties and tribal rights.

Despite the opposition, tribal efforts to build serious, working sovereignty in Indian country progress. Native Americans have been negotiating with state governments and talking with the private business sector to generate economic projects in Indian country. Tribal people intent on maintaining cultural identities now run their own elementary schools and community colleges, manage health services, and operate hotels, motels, factories, and other businesses. Indians have organized professional groups that advocate for legal, social, educational, economic, health, and veterans' rights. These activities, while they do not garner the media spotlight, contribute substantially to the determination by Native Americans of their own future.

Native Americans Today

POPULATION

Native Americans are a small minority in their ancestral homelands. According to the 1990 census, there are 1,959,234 Native Americans in the United States, which represents less than 1 percent of the total population. Census figures for any minority group are always subject to error and there is no proven way to test their accuracy. In addition, the Census Bureau has changed its definition of who is an American Indian numerous times, and each changed definition affects the reported numbers of American Indians. The definition of who is considered a Native American is important because American Indians have been mixing with Eastern Hemisphere people for 500 years, and the resulting progeny present a problem for the Census Bureau. At various times, people of obvious mixed heritage were classed as either Indian, white, or black, at the discretion of the enumerator. At other times, enumerators were instructed to classify mixed bloods as the race of the father and at other times as the race of the mother. In 1910 and 1930, mixed bloods were classed as Indian, while in 1950, they were classed as "other." Sometimes an Indian was defined as one who was recognized as an Indian in the community or as someone who was on the tribal rolls.

Before the 1960 census, the observations of enumerators were used to decided who was an Indian. Beginning with the 1960 census, respondents were allowed for the first time to self-identify for race, and the population figure for Native Americans increased by nearly 50 percent over the figure for 1950, a growth rate that is not a result of an excess of births over deaths alone. It seems likely that many people who were identified as some other race in 1950 claimed Indian identity in 1960. Perhaps more people felt pride in their Indian ancestry in 1960, and they identified themselves as Native American. On the other hand, some Native Americans are suspicious of government representatives of any kind and may withhold information. Some reservation communities did not allow census enumerators to complete their survey. And, contributing to the confusion, several independent researchers have concluded that Indians were undercounted in 1960 and in 1970. Census figures should always be used with caution.

If contemporary population numbers are subject to inaccuracies, estimates of the past are even more problematic. For the first half of the twentieth century, scholars estimated the pre-Columbian population of North America at from 900,000 to 2 million. In 1966, anthropologist Henry Dobyns challenged demographers to consider the question of pre-Columbian population using different methods. Dobyns estimated that there were between 9.8 and 12 million Native North Americans before 1492. Russell Thornton, a historical demographer at the University of California at Berkeley, estimated in 1978 that the aboriginal population of the conterminous United States area was more than 5 million before contact.

Whatever the figure, it seems likely that early estimates are too low. What is clear is that contact with people from the Eastern Hemisphere caused a Native-American holocaust. By 1890, the population of American Indians in the conterminous United States was reduced to 250,000, a decline of at least 95 percent based on Thornton's estimate. The American Indian population remained fairly static in the decade between 1890 and 1900. After

NATIVE AMERICAN POPULATION

NATIVE AMERICAN POPULATION, 1890–1990

Date	Size	Change from Previous Decade
1890	248,000	
1900	237,196	−4.5%
1910	276,927	16.8%
1920	244,437	−11.7%
1930	343,352	40.5%
1940	345,252	0.6%
1950	357,499	3.5%
1960	523,591	46.5%
1970	792,730	51.4%
1980	1,366,676	72.4%
1990	1,959,234	37.9%

Source: Thornton, 1987: 160, and United States Bureau of the Census, 1990

Ten States with the Largest American Indian, Eskimo or Aleut Population, 1990 (In Thousands, Rank in 1980 in parentheses)

Oklahoma (2)	252
California (1)	242
Arizona (3)	204
New Mexico (4)	134
Alaska (6)	86
Washington (7)	81
North Carolina (5)	80
Texas (9)	66
New York (11)	63
Michigan (10)	56

Source: United States Bureau of the Census, 1990.

Ten States with the Highest Percentage American Indian, Eskimo, or Aleut (Rank in 1980 in parentheses)

Alaska (1)	15.6
New Mexico (2)	8.9
Oklahoma (5)	8.0
South Dakota (3)	7.3
Montana (6)	6.0
Arizona (4)	5.6
North Dakota (7)	4.1
Wyoming (9)	2.1
Washington (10)	1.7
Nevada (8)	1.6

Source: United States Bureau of the Census, 1990.

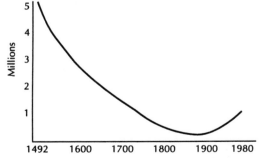

American Indian Population Decline and Recovery in the United States Area, 1492–1980.

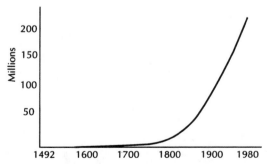

Non-Indian Population Growth in the United States Area, 1492–1980.

Charts from: American Indian Holocaust and Survival: A Population History Since 1492 by Russell Thornton. Copyright © 1987 by the University of Oklahoma Press.

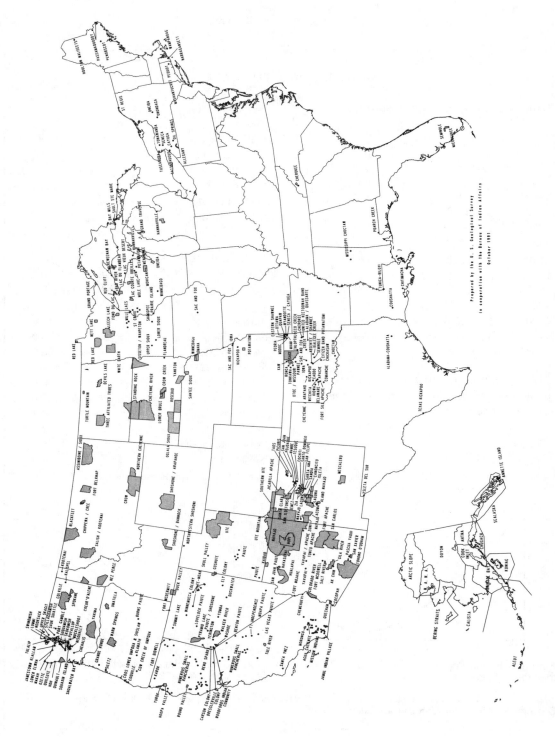

Location of Federally Recognized Indian Tribes. Courtesy of the Bureau of Indian Affairs.

1900, the population began a recovery, and fluctuations are largely a result of changing definitions of who is an Indian.

The reasons for the decimation are, in order of importance, diseases brought by Europeans, warfare (intertribal and genocidal wars with Europeans), forced relocation and removals, and destruction of traditional lifestyles. Among the diseases that Europeans brought with them are smallpox, influenza, measles, bubonic plague, colds, scarlet fever, mumps, and typhoid. These diseases and others were not present in the Western Hemisphere before the arrival of Europeans, and native people had no immunity to them. The diseases spread in cyclic epidemics and pandemics that killed Native Americans by the millions. Eastern Hemisphere diseases are the most significant cause of the rapid decline of the Native American population; warfare was a significant cause of depopulation and forced relocation and destruction of traditional lifestyles also contributed to the decline. At the same time, the non-Indian population began to increase, both in the Americas and in Europe.

TRIBES

The many different terms used to describe Native American groups reflects the diversity of Native American organizational structures as well as the application of European-derived terms to Native American realities. The most commonly used descriptive word, *tribe*, comes from the Latin, *tribus*, which refers to a division of the Roman people. Although tribe does not fit all the groups of aboriginal Americans, it has long been used as a convenient way to classify the many diverse social and political organizations in the Americas, where people joined together in groups ranging from simple egalitarian family units to complex confederacies composed of several nations. The word *tribe* is often used to refer to them all. *Tribe* is often used interchangeably with *nation*, and today, Native Americans use a wide range of terms to describe their political organizations,

including *confederacy, nation, tribe, band, community, village* and *corporation*.

Partly as a result of the disastrous effects of contact with Europeans, some tribes have politically merged with others, like the Cheyenne–Arapahoe of Oklahoma, and the Sac and Fox of Iowa, Kansas, and Oklahoma. Others have splintered into several autonomous tribal nations. The Kickapoo, for example, are now divided into three tribes, one in Kansas, one in Oklahoma, and one in Texas. Each one has its own governing body, usually a tribal council, recognized by the U.S. government.

American Indian tribes were legally defined by the Supreme Court in 1831 (*Cherokee Nation v. Georgia*) as "domestic dependent nations." Federal recognition of a tribe means that the U.S. government acknowledges that the tribal nation exists as a unique political entity with a government-to-government relationship to the United States. As far as the federal government is concerned, recognition entails certain rights reserved for, or granted to, Indian nations by treaties, executive orders, or special acts of Congress, or rights determined by the courts to be available to the tribe and its members. Tribes are often acknowledged by the fact that they have signed a treaty with the United States. Others have been acknowledged through an executive order, a presidential proclamation, or by legislation that mentioned the group. Some tribes are recognized by their state government, but not by the federal government.

Some tribes, like the Mashpee Wampanoag and the Lumbee, are not recognized by the federal government because they were never at war with the United States and did not sign any treaties. Some groups, especially in the East, managed to evade the army during forced removal, hiding out in isolated areas, keeping to themselves in order to stay in their homelands. These groups avoided the government but retained their identity. Some tribes had their relationship with the government ended by termination, the withdrawal of federal responsibility and services to tribes.

Until the enactment of the Federal Acknowledgement Project in 1978, there was no formal procedure

by which a tribe could seek recognition. When the
staff of the project was organized, there were forty
petitioners on hand. The longest-standing petition
was that of the Tunica-Biloxi of Louisiana, who petitioned for recognition in 1826. They were recognized in 1981. As of March 1992, there were 132
groups seeking recognition. Twenty-seven cases have
been resolved: eight were acknowledged; twelve
were denied acknowledgement. The Texas Kickapoo
were judged to be part of a recognized tribe, the
Oklahoma Kickapoo. The Lac Vieux Chippewa had
their status clarified and four groups that were terminated have had their recognized status restored or
have been recognized by Congress; and one merged
with another petitioner. The rest are awaiting legislative action, being litigated, or are pending. (A
complete list of tribes appears at the end of this
volume.)

RESERVATIONS, TRUSTS, AND OTHER INDIAN LANDS

At present, the Native American land base in the
United States is approximately 54 million acres.
Indian lands take many forms, including reservations, rancherias, colonies, native villages, historic
Indian areas, Indian trust land, and joint use areas of
reservations. In California and Nevada, Indian reservations are often referred to as "rancherias" and "colonies."

In 1990, about 685,000 Indians or 35 percent of
Native Americans in the United States lived on In-
dian land (reservations, rancherias, trust land, native
Alaskan villages, etc.). In 1980, 37 percent lived on
Indian land.

Horses on the Crow reservation near Lodge Grass, Montana. Photograph by Gary Galante.

A family reunion at the Catholic church hall on the Prairie Band Potawatomi Reservation in Kansas. Photograph by M.K. de Montaño.

Ten Reservations with the Largest Population of American Indians, in Thousands, 1990

Navajo, AZ, NM, UT*	143.4
Pine Ridge, NE, SD*	11.2
Fort Apache, AZ	9.8
Gila River, AZ	9.1
Papago, AZ	8.5
Rosebud, SD*	8.0
San Carlos, AZ	7.1
Zuni Pueblo, AZ, NM	7.1
Hopi, AZ*	7.1
Blackfeet, MT	7.0

*Includes trust lands.
Source: United States Bureau of Census, 1990.

Most reservations are lands that were not relinquished to the United States but were reserved for Indians. Federal Indian reservations are areas that are recognized by the federal government as territory in which American Indian tribes have jurisdiction. Indians on reservations are not subject to state laws unless and until Congress permits state laws to apply, or the tribe adopts the state law as its law. Indian property on a reservation is not subject to state or local taxation without the consent of Congress, however non-Indians on a reservation are not covered by this immunity.

Reservations were created in a number of ways including by treaty, executive order, act of Congress, and agreement. The first reservation was established by the Puritans in 1638 for the Quinnipiacs in Connecticut. The Quinnipiacs, like many other tribal groups in Connecticut, were forced out of the state and eventually merged with other tribes. Their land then became open for white occupancy. Some were converted from other government uses. The Fort Bidwell and Fort Mohave reservations in California, for example, were created from abandoned military posts that were turned over to the Indian Bureau for schools and are now considered Indian reservations.

TWENTIETH CENTURY RESERVATION AND PUEBLO LIFE IN NOVELS BY NATIVE AMERICANS

Native American writers use their art to draw portraits of twentieth-century Indian reservation and pueblo life beset with cultural conflicts and the impact of U.S. government policies, as well as to paint the revival of identity, traditions, and rituals in these homelands.

Elizabeth Cook-Lynn, Crow Creek Sioux. *From the River's Edge* (1991). Crow Creek Reservation in South Dakota.

Michael Dorris, Modoc. *A Yellow Raft in Blue Water* (1987). Montana Indian reservation life.

Louise Erdrich, Turtle Mountain Chippewa. *Love Medicine* (1984). North Dakota reservation life.

D'Arcy McNickle, Salish-Kootenai. *Surrounded* (1936). Montana's Flathead Reservation and *Wind from an Enemy Sky* (1978). Northwest reservation life.

John Joseph Mathews, Osage. *Sundown* (1934). Oklahoma's Osage reservation life.

N. Scott Momoday, Kiowa. *House Made of Dawn* (1968). Jemez Pueblo, New Mexico life.

Louis Owens, Choctaw/Cherokee. *Wolfsong* (1991). Washington State reservation life.

Leslie Silko, Laguna Pueblo. *Ceremony* (1977). Laguna Pueblo, New Mexico life.

James Welch, Blackfeet, *Winter in the Blood* (1974). Blackfeet Reservation in Montana.

A few Indian tribes have purchased the land for their reservations; the Reno Indian Colony in Nevada was purchased with funds appropriated by Congress, as were a few others. Some reservations cross state and other jurisdictional boundaries.

At one time, Indians held their land in common. Since the 1887 allotment act, many, but not all, reservations have been allotted to individuals rather than to tribes. Since allotment meant individual ownership of land, it came with the right to sell, which resulted in non-Indian ownership of much reservation land. Many reservations are "checkerboarded" with non-Indian ownership, but they are still reservations.

In Oklahoma, all the reservations except the Osage were dissolved just prior to Oklahoma statehood in 1907. The former reservations in Oklahoma are called "historic Indian areas," or "tribal jurisdiction statistical areas" by the Census Bureau. Trust lands are property associated with a particular tribe or reservation, held in trust either for a tribe or for an Indian individual member of a tribe.

In Alaska, all the reservations, except the Annette Island Reserve, have been dissolved, and the native people have organized pursuant to the Alaska Native Claims Settlement Act of 1971. Under the terms of this act, Alaska was divided into twelve geographical regions. Each region was organized as a for-profit corporation, and villages were organized into profit or nonprofit corporations. Aboriginal title to the land was extinguished, and in return, the native corporations received patents to over 40 million acres of land, with the native residents as shareholders. There are twelve regional corporations and over 200 native village corporations in Alaska.

The date that a reservation was established sometimes refers to the date at which the United States officially recognized its existence. The Pueblos in the Southwest, for example, have existed for many centuries in their present locations. The Spanish Crown recognized the Rio Grande Pueblos' rights to their land before the United States was formed, and the United States confirmed the right in 1864. In other cases, the people were moved, some times more than once, from their homelands and assigned new, smaller parcels of land in the form of reservations.

The size of reservations is by no means static. Reservations, of course, represent a small portion of the aboriginal holdings. Many reservations were originally large enough to allow the people to continue to live off the land for a time. Then the reservations were made progressively smaller and smaller as the land was opened to white settlement, or in some cases, reservation land was declared "surplus" in order to legitimize illegal white settlement on Indian land. Some reservations, however, have grown as tribes successfully sue for the return of illegally taken land.

No description fits all reservations. The Shinnecock Reservation in New York is located in an expensive, densely populated area of Long Island, while many reservations are located in remote, economically depressed and sparsely populated areas.

The Navajo reservation is about the size of the state of West Virginia and extends into three states, while the Golden Hill Reservation in Connecticut has only one-third of an acre.

Reservations were originally conceived as places where Indians could be segregated from whites and separated from their land. In the nineteenth century, they served as concentration camps, where Indians were disarmed and forbidden to leave. Today, they are tangible proof of Indian sovereignty, where the tribal council has jurisdiction. They are what is left of homelands, and although only about one-third of American Indians live on reservations, many native people are tied to the reservations, returning to the "res" for special occasions and to renew family ties.

Supreme Court Decisions Affecting Native Americans

Since 1810, when the first Indian case was decided by the U.S. Supreme Court, several hundred cases dealing with Indian rights have been decided by the Court. Opinions rendered in these cases reflect shifts in judicial interpretations. In *Cherokee Nation v. Georgia* (1831) and *Worcester v. Georgia* (1832), the court handed down decisions in which tribes were viewed as largely autonomous governments retaining inherent powers not expressly ceded away by the tribes or extinguished by Congress and essentially independent of state control. In *United States v. Kagama* (1886), the court recognized a seemingly unlimited federal power to alter tribal property without tribal approval and infringe on internal tribal resolution of disputes. Over a half century later in 1959, the court ushered in a new era of Indian law. In *Williams v. Lee*, the court recognized Indian tribes as permanent governments within the federal constitutional system.

The Supreme Court has developed a set of judicial rules that treaties, agreements, and statutes be construed as the Indians would have understood them, that ambiguities be read in their favor, and that Indian laws be read liberally in favor of the Indians. Despite these doctrines of construction favoring Indian rights, the court has set limits and stated "a canon of construction is not a license to disregard clear expressions of . . . congressional intent."

In his renowned treatise, *Handbook of Federal Indian Law* published in 1942 by the Department of the Interior, Felix S. Cohen stated:

> The whole course of judicial decision on the nature of Indian tribal powers is marked by adherence to three fundamental principles: (1) An Indian tribe possesses, in the first instance, all the powers of any sovereign state. (2) Conquest renders the tribe subject to the legislative power of the United States and, in substance, terminates the external powers of sovereignty of the tribe, e.g., its power to enter into treaties with foreign nations, but does not by itself affect the internal sovereignty of the tribe, i.e., its powers of local self-government. (3) These powers are subject to qualification by treaties and by express legislation of Congress, but, save as thus expressly qualified, full powers of internal sovereignty are vested in the Indian tribes and in their duly elected organs of government.

The following brief discussions of ten key Supreme Court cases introduce broad philosophical directions of the Court as well as some specific principles in the areas of tribal powers, the federal–tribal relationship, tribal–state relationships, resource rights, and religious rights.

CHEROKEE NATION v. GEORGIA (1831)

In 1828 and 1829, Wilson Lumpkin, the governor of Georgia signed acts to parcel out Cherokee territory to four counties in Georgia, "to extend the laws of this State over the same" and "to annul all laws and ordinances made by the Cherokee Nations of Indians." Other Georgia laws authorized the survey and distribution by lottery of Cherokee lands to people in Georgia and prevented white persons from residing within Cherokee territory without a license from the governor. The Georgia governor was also authorized to take over gold, silver, and other mines in Cherokee country, to state citizen armed forces at the gold mines, and to punish anyone "found trespassing upon the mines."

The Cherokee National declared these laws "null and void" owing to its status as "a foreign state, not owing allegiance to the United States, nor to any State of this Union, nor to any prince, potentate or States, other than their own." The Cherokees, who believed themselves to be sovereign, independent, and self-governing, stated that Georgia, in its efforts to force the Cherokees from their homeland, violated at least a dozen treaties the Cherokees made with the U.S. government; "all of which treaties and conventions were duly ratified and confirmed by the Senate of the United States, and . . . a part of the supreme law of the land" and violated various acts of Congress that consecrated the Indian boundaries and recognized the exclusive Cherokee "right to give and to execute the law within that boundary."

The Cherokees, determined to resist Georgia efforts to force them from their homeland, filed suit in the Supreme Court for an injunction to prevent the enforcement of Georgia state statutes. The Cherokees believed the Supreme Court had original jurisdiction for their case because the third article of the Constitution gave the Supreme Court jurisdiction in controversies "between the State or the citizens thereof, and foreign states, citizens, or subjects."

In a brief opinion by Chief Justice John Marshall, the majority of the Court held that the Cherokee Nation lacked original jurisdiction because an Indian tribe or nation within the United States was not a "foreign state" in the sense of the Constitution because their lands "compose a part of the United States;" it was, rather, a "domestic, dependent nation" that "cannot maintain an action in the courts of the United States." The Chief Justice described the federal–Indian relationship as "perhaps unlike that of any other two people in existence" and "marked by peculiar and cardinal distinctions which exist nowhere else." Marshall agreed with the Cherokees that they were a state, "a distinct political society . . . capable of managing its own affairs and governing itself" but that owing to the treaties they made, the Cherokees were considered by foreign nations and by the U.S. government "as being . . . completely un-der the sovereignty and dominion of the United States" Regarding the actions of the Georgia legislature, however, the Court stated "the point respecting parties makes it unnecessary to decide the question."

WORCESTER v. GEORGIA (1832)

In 1829 and 1830, the Georgia legislature passed acts trying to seize Cherokee country, parcel it out among neighboring counties of the state, extend its code over the Cherokees, abolish its institutions and laws, and annihilate its political existence. One act stated that "all white persons residing within the limits of the Cherokee Nation . . . without a license or permit from his excellency the governor . . . shall be guilty of a high misdemeanor."

In July 1831, Samuel Worcester, a missionary to the Cherokee Nation, was indicted in a county court for residing in the Cherokee Nation without a license or permit from the governor and for not taking the oath to support and defend the constitution and laws of Georgia. Despite Worcester's contention that he, a Vermont citizen and a missionary authorized by the President of the United States and the Cherokees to preach the gospel, was in the sovereign Cherokee Nation completely separated from the other states by U.S. treaties and laws and therefore outside the jurisdiction of the county court, the state prosecuted him. Convicted, Worcester was sentenced to "hard labor in the penitentiary for four years" for violating some of the same statutes challenged in *Cherokee Nation* the year before.

Worcester took his case to the Supreme Court which first decided that it had jurisdiction, under the 1789 Judicial Act, to decide the controversy because the missionary's indictment and plea in this case drew into question the validity of U.S. treaties and Georgia statutes which tried to regulate and control the "intercourse with the Cherokee Nation which belongs exclusively to Congress."

Speaking for the court in one of its most lasting statements (since 1970, Worcester has been cited by state and federal courts more than virtually any other case handed down by the Court between 1789 and

TWENTY SUPREME COURT CASES

The following important cases have shaped federal Indian law by establishing tribes as sovereign governments or limiting tribal powers as indicated.

1823 *Johnson v. McIntosh.* Indian title; aboriginal possessory right.

1870 *Cherokee Tobacco Case.* Law of Congress supersedes provisions of treaty.

1881 *United States v. McBratney.* State law in Indian country.

1896 *Talton v. Mayes.* Tribal self-government.

1903 *Lone Wolf v. Hitchcock.* Federal power over Indian affairs; treaty abrogation.

1905 *United States v. Winans.* Treaty rights; reserved access to fishing sites.

1955 *Tee-Hit-Ton Indians v. United States.* Federal power over Indian affairs; land seized without compensation.

1968 *Menominee Tribe of Indians v. United States.* Treaty hunting and fishing rights preserved.

1974 *Morton v. Mancari.* Indian hiring preference.

1979 *Washington v. Washington State Commercial Passenger Fishing Vessel Association.* Off-reservation treaty fishing rights.

1980 *Washington v. Confederated Tribes of the Colville Indian Reservation.* State jurisdiction; state sales tax.

1982 *Merrion v. Jicarilla Apache Tribe.* Tribal sovereignty; tribal severance taxes.

1983 *New Mexico v. Mescalero Apache Tribe.* Tribal regulatory jurisdiction; hunting and fishing.

1985 *County of Oneida, New York v. Oneida Indian Nation of New York State.* Tribal right to sue to enforce aboriginal land rights.

1985 *Kerr-McGee Corp. v. Navajo Tribe of Indians.* Tribal sovereignty; non-IRA tribal taxation power.

1985 *United States v. Dann.* Aboriginal title extinguished.

1986 *United States v. Dion.* Treaty rights to hunt eagles abrogated.

1987 *California v. Cabazon Band of Mission Indians.* Gaming; state regulation not permitted.

1988 *Lyng, Secretary of Agriculture, et al. v. Northwest Indian Cemetery Protective Association, et al.* First Amendment, free exercise claim denied; sacred site on public land.

1989 *Mississippi Band of Choctaw Indians v. Holyfield.* Tribal jurisdiction in adoptions; Indian Child Welfare Act.

1865), Justice John Marshall held that Georgia's statutes were unlawful because they were "repugnant to the Constitution, treaties, and laws of the United States." In reaching this decision, the Court announced virtually every basic doctrine in Indian law: federal plenary power: "The whole intercourse between the United States and this nation is, by our Constitution and laws, vested in the government of the United States;" trust relationship: "From the commencement of our government Congress has passed acts to regulate trade and intercourse with the Indians; which treat them as nations, respect their rights, and manifest a firm purpose to afford that protection which treaties stipulate;" reserved rights: "the Indian nations possessed a full right to the lands they occupied, until that right should be extinguished by the United States, with their consent;" and the general exclusion of state law from Indian country: "The Cherokee nation . . . is a distinct community, occupying its own territory, with boundaries accurately described, in which the laws of Georgia can have no force."

UNITED STATES v. KAGAMA (1886)

Kagama (alias Pactah Billy), a Hoopa Indian, murdered Iyouse, (alias Ike), another Indian on the Hoopa Reservation in Humboldt County, California. Kagama, prosecuted under the Major Crimes Act of 1885, challenged its constitutionality. Before 1885, federal criminal law had not extended to Indians committing crimes against other Indians on Indian reservations. In 1885, however, the Major Crimes Act, which gave federal courts jurisdiction in cases of major offenses committed on all Indian reservations, made the murder of an Indian by another Indian on an Indian reservation within a state a federal crime and "subject to the same laws, tried in the same courts . . . and subject to the same penalties as are all other persons committing any of the . . . crimes within the exclusive jurisdiction of the United States.

The Court upheld the constitutionality of the Major Crimes Act and stated that the U.S. circuit court for the district of California indeed had jurisdiction of the offense. The court also denied the existence of tribal sovereignty: "Indians are within the geographical limits of the United States. The soil and the people within these limits are under the political control of the Government of the United States, or of the States of the Union. There exist within the broad domain of sovereignty but these two."

The Court found that protecting Indians was a national problem and referred to the practical necessity of protecting Indians and withholding such a power from the states. This case, therefore, was one

among others that established the principle that a state has no criminal jurisdiction over offenses involving Indians committed on an Indian reservation, unless such a jurisdiction has been granted by Congress. A famous statement explaining the limitations on state power within the territory of an Indian tribe also enunciated a doctrine of plenary federal power:

These Indian tribes are the wards of the nation. They are communities dependent on the United States. Dependent largely for their daily food. Dependent for their political rights. They owe no allegiance to the States, and receive from them no protection. Because of the local ill feeling, the people of the States where they are found are often their deadliest enemies. From their very weakness and helplessness, so largely due to the course of dealing with the Federal Government with them and the treaties in which it has been promised, there arises the duty of protection, and with it the power. This has always been recognized by the Executive and by Congress, and by this court, whenever the question has arisen.

The power of the General Government over these remnants of a race once powerful, now weak and diminished in numbers, is necessary to their protection, as well as to the safety of those among whom they dwell. It must exist in the government, because it never has existed anywhere else, because the theater of its exercise is within the geographical limits of the United States . . . and because it alone can enforce its laws on all the tribes.

WINTERS v. UNITED STATES (1908)

On May 1, 1888, an act of Congress created the Fort Belknap Indian Reservation out of a much larger tract of land for the Gros Ventre and Assiniboine bands of Indians in the then territory of Montana, designating the Milk River as the northern boundary of the reservation. Beginning in 1889, the United States and the Indians diverted and used the waters of the Milk, the government for its reservation agency and the Indians for irrigating arid portions of their land.

In 1900, Henry Winters and other settlers, whose land also bordered the Milk River, appropriated upstream water for agricultural purposes to the detriment of downstream United States and Indian irrigators. Arguing that under U.S. homestead and desert land laws and Montana laws, they were entitled to use the waters, the settlers claimed "their lands will be ruined, it will be necessary to abandon their homes." They also argued that the 1888 act of Congress did not contain any reservation of waters because with their cession of land, the Indians also ceded their waters. On behalf of the Fort Belknap Indians, the federal government argued that all waters of the Milk River were essential to fulfilling the purposes of the reservation, although it was alleged that the reservation contained springs and streams which could be used for stock watering.

The Court argued that ambiguities in Indian treaties and agreements be resolved in favor of the Indians: "We realize that there is a conflict of implications, but that which makes for the retention of the waters is of greater force than that which makes for the cession." It held that the Agreement of May 1, 1888 implicitly reserved from appropriation under state law an amount of water sufficient for irrigation purposes. The Court also held that sufficient water impliedly was reserved to fulfill the purposes of the reservation at the time the reservation was established—1888. Tribal rights date, therefore, from the date of the reservation rather than the date when a tribe puts the water to actual use. The Court also rejected the notion that Congress' admission of Montana to the union in 1889 repealed the reservation of waters made the year before. The Court stated "the power of the government to reserve the waters and exempt them from appropriation cannot be denied . . . That the government did reserve them we have decided, and for a use which would necessarily continue through the years . . . and it would be extreme to believe that within a year Congress destroyed the reservation and took from the Indians the consideration of their grant, leaving them a barren waste."

The Winters doctrine did not address the quantity of water reserved by Indian tribes. Indeed, Indian water rights were not perfected for more than fifty years after the famous Winters doctrine was enunciated. In 1963, the Court tackled the question of defining the quantity of water reserved for Indian reservations in *Arizona v. California*. Quantifying water is of considerable important today in the water-hungry western states because of the effects of waters so "reserved" being exempt from appropriation by non-Indian farmers, ranchers, municipalities and mines.

WILLIAMS v. LEE (1959)

Hugh Lee, a non-Indian, operated a general store on the Navajo Reservation in Arizona under a license required by a federal statute. He brought action in the Apache County, Arizona Supreme Court against Paul and Lorena Williams, a Navajo husband and wife who lived on the reservation, to collect for goods sold them there on credit. The Williams argued for dismissal on the ground that jurisdiction lay in the tribal court rather than in the state court, but judgement, affirmed by the Supreme Court of Arizona, favored Lee. The Supreme Court heard the case because of the important question of state power over Indian affairs.

Justice Hugo Black, who delivered the majority opinion of the Court, discussed *Worcester v. Georgia* at some length, calling it "one of (Chief Justice Marshall's) most courageous and eloquent opinions." Arguing that the basic policy of *Worcester* had remained—a protective stance toward tribal self-government—the Court ruled that exclusive jurisdiction over this case involving a non-Indian doing business on the reservation and an Indian lay with the Navajo court thus reversing the Arizona Supreme Court. The opinion pointed to the fact that "the Tribe itself has in recent years greatly improved its legal system through increased expenditures and better-trained personnel. Today the Navajo Courts of Indian Offenses exercise broad criminal and civil jurisdiction which cover suits by outsiders against Indian defendants" and further stated that "to date, Arizona has not accepted jurisdiction" over such controversies. Finally, Justice Black concluded: "There can be no doubt that to allow the exercise of state jurisdiction here would undermine the authority of the tribal courts over Reservation affairs and hence would infringe on the right of the Indians to govern themselves. It is immaterial that respondent is not an Indian. He was on the Reservation and the transaction with an Indian took place there."

Therefore, the Court held Indian tribes retain inherent sovereignty to exercise some forms of civil jurisdiction over actions involving contracts entered into on an Indian reservation between a non-Indian plaintiff and Indian defendant. A tribe may regulate, through taxation, licensing, or other means, the activities of nonmembers who enter consensual relationships with the tribe or its members through commercial dealings, contracts, leases, or other arrangements.

This case has been widely cited because it was a leading example of rules recognized by the Supreme Court to protect tribal governments in Indian country in contemporary America and its findings gave incentive to tribes to exercise long-dormant powers of self-government.

OLIPHANT v. SUQUAMISH INDIAN TRIBE (1978)

In 1973, The Suquamish Indian Tribe in Washington state adopted a Law and Order Code which extended the Tribe's criminal jurisdiction over both Indians and non-Indians. The Tribe posted notices in prominent places at the entrances to the Port Madison Reservation informing the public that entry onto the Reservation would be deemed implied consent to the criminal jurisdiction of the Suquamish tribal court.

Subsequently, during the annual Chief Seattle Day celebration, tribal authorities arrested and charged two non-Indian residents of the reservation with criminal behavior—Mark David Oliphant for assaulting a tribal officer and resisting arrest and Daniel B. Belgarde for a high-speed race along reservation highways that ended in his collision with a tribal police vehicle. After they were arraigned before the tribal court, both petitioners applied for a writ of *habeas corpus* to the U.S. District Court for the Western Division of Washington arguing that the Suquamish Court did not have criminal jurisdiction over non-Indians. After the District Court denied the petitions, affirmed by the Court of Appeals for the Ninth Circuit, the Supreme Court took Oliphant's case (Belgarde's case was still pending before the Court of Appeals) and decided that Indian tribal courts did not have criminal jurisdiction over non-Indians because it was inconsistent with its "dependent status."

Chief Justice William Rehnquist, who delivered the opinion, cited congressional policy about law enforcement on reservations and judicial precedents that satisfied the Court that Indians did not have inherent criminal jurisdiction to try and punish non-Indians unless Congress delegated such power to the tribe. The opinion went on to cite other inherent limitations on Indian tribal authority including limitations on the tribes' power to transfer lands or exercise external political sovereignty. Although the Court acknowledged that the prevalence of non-Indian crime on today's reservations requires the ability of tribes to try non-Indians, it stated "these are considerations for Congress to weigh in deciding whether Indian tribes should finally be authorized to try non-Indians."

SANTA CLARA PUEBLO ET AL. v. MARTINEZ ET AL. (1978)

Julia Martinez, a member of the Santa Clara Pueblo in New Mexico, and her daughter Audrey brought suit in federal court against the Pueblo and its

Governor because of a 1939 tribal ordinance denying tribal membership to children of female members who marry outside the tribe, while extending membership to children of male members who married outside the tribe. The Pueblo barred admission of the Martinez children to the tribe because their father was not a Santa Claran. The Martinez women claimed that tracing membership patrilineally was sexist and violated Title 1 of the Indian Civil Rights Act of 1968 (ICRA) which provides that "no Indian tribe in exercising powers of self-government shall . . . deny to any person within its jurisdiction the equal protection of its laws."

The ICRA's only express remedial provision to protect individual interests at stake was federal judicial review of the validity of an Indian tribe's ordinance. The tribe moved to dismiss the complaint on the ground that the District Court lacked jurisdiction to decide intratribal controversies affecting matters of tribal self-government and sovereignty. The U.S. District Court for the District of New Mexico, which denied the motion to dismiss the case, favored the tribe while the Court of Appeals reversed the judgement. The Supreme Court heard the case and held that suits against the tribe under the Indian Civil Rights Act were barred by its sovereign immunity from suit.

In delivering the court opinion, Justice Thurgood Marshall reviewed court decisions that stated Indian tribes are "distinct, independent political communities, retaining their original natural rights" in matters of local self-government but also subject to congressional plenary authority to limit, modify, or eliminate the powers of local self-government. He further explained that federal enforcement of Title 1 would be at odds with the congressional goal of protecting tribal self-government. "Tribal courts," he stated "have repeatedly been recognized as appropriate forums for the exclusive adjudication of disputes affecting important personal and property interests of both Indians and non-Indians." Indeed, the Court declined to interfere with the Santa Clara definition of membership.

MONTANA v. UNITED STATES (1981)

By a tribal regulation, the Crow Tribe of Montana sought to prohibit hunting and fishing within its reservation by anyone not a member of the tribe. Relying on its purported ownership of the bed of the Big Horn River, on treaties which created its reservation, and on its inherent power as a sovereign, the Tribe claimed authority to prohibit hunting and fishing by nonmembers of the tribe even on non-Indian property lands within reservation boundaries. Montana, however, continued to assert its authority to regulate hunting and fishing by non-Indians within the reservation. The Supreme Court decided to hear the case to review the decision of the United States Court of Appeals for the Ninth Circuit that substantially upheld the Crow claim.

Justice Potter Stewart delivered the opinion of the Court that concluded title to the bed of the Big Horn River passed to the state of Montana on its admission to the Union and that the Court of Appeals erred in holding otherwise. The Court held that the treaties of 1851 and 1868 did not create tribal power to restrict or prohibit non-Indian hunting and fishing on lands held in fee by non-Indians. Tribal authority extends to land on which the tribe exercises "absolute and undisturbed use and occupation" (1868 treaty language) and cannot apply to subsequently alienated lands held in fee by non-Indians. Further, the Court held that regulating hunting and fishing by nonmembers of the tribe on lands no longer owned by the tribe bore no clear relationship to tribal self-government. Non-Indian hunters and fishermen on non-Indian fee land did not enter into any agreements or dealings with the Crow Tribe so as to subject themselves to tribal civil jurisdiction. Therefore, the general principles of inherent sovereignty, which previous Court decisions held do not extend to the activities of nonmembers of the tribe, did not authorize the Crow Tribe to adopt the tribal resolution barring non-Indian hunting and fishing on lands no longer owned by the tribe. Applying previous judicial thought that a tribe may exercise civil authority over non-Indians when their conduct directly affects the tribe's political integrity or economic security, the opinion concluded "nothing in this case suggests that such non-Indian hunting and fishing so threaten the Tribe's political or economic security as to justify tribal regulations."

BRENDALE v. CONFEDERATED TRIBES AND BANDS OF YAKIMA INDIAN NATION; WILKINSON v. CONFEDERATED TRIBES AND BANDS OF YAKIMA INDIAN NATION; COUNTY OF YAKIMA v. CONFEDERATED TRIBES AND BANDS OF YAKIMA INDIAN NATION (1989)

The treaty between the United States and the Yakima Indian Nation of Washington State provided that the tribe would retain its reservation for its "exclusive use and benefit" and that "no white man [shall] be permitted to reside upon the said reservation without [the Tribe's] permission." Roughly 20 percent of the reservation is owned in fee simple by Indian or non-Indian owners. The reservation is divided in two parts: a "closed" area of predominantly forest land (closed to the general public since 1972) which contains a small portion of fee land and an "open" area heavily populated by non-Indians due to the late nineteenth-century federal policy of alloting Indian tribal lands to individuals.

Over time, through sale and inheritance, nonmembers of the tribe came to own a substantial portion of the alloted land. Almost half of the open area was fee land, the rest range and agricultural land and land used for residential and commercial development. The tribe's zoning ordinance applied to all lands within the reservation, including fee lands owned by Indians or non-Indians. Yakima County's zoning ordinance applied to all lands within its boundaries, except for Indian trust lands which fall within its borders.

Petitioners Brendale and Wilkinson, nonmembers of the tribe who owned land in the closed and open areas respectively, filed applications with the Yakima County Planning Department to develop their lands in ways prohibited by the tribe's ordinance but permitted by county ordinance. After the Department authorized the developments, the tribe challenged them because it believed it had exclusive authority to zone the properties in question. The District Court held the Yakima Nation had exclusive zoning authority over the Brendale property but lacked authority over the Wilkinson property and determined Yakima County had no zoning authority over lands in the closed area. On appeal, the Ninth Circuit consolidated the cases and affirmed as to the Brendale property but reversed as to the Wilkinson property. Brendale, Wilkinson, and Yakima County petitioned the Supreme Court for a review. The justices who heard the case split widely, issuing three separate opinions.

In one judgement, Justice John Paul Stevens announced the tribe had zoning authority over the Brendale property in the reservation closed to the general public where the amount of non-Indian land was insignificant and the tribe "preserved the power to define the area's essential character" as well as to protect the tribe's welfare. Nonmember Brendale's planned development of recreation housing within the area would have endangered economically important timber production and threaten the cultural and spiritual values of the unique and undeveloped character of the closed area.

In the second judgement, Justice Byron White struck down the tribe's right to zone the Wilkinson property in the "open" area of the reservation where almost half of the land was owned by nonmembers of the tribe and the tribe "no longer possesse[d] the power to determine the basic character of the area." Indeed the Court said that as a practical matter the open area had become an integrated portion of the Yakima County whose exercise of zoning power over the Wilkinson property would have had no effect on the tribe's political integrity, economic security, or health and welfare.

In a third dissenting judgement, Justice Harry Blackmun concluded that the Court was wrong to judge that the tribe did not have zoning authority over non-Indian fee land in the reservation's "open" area. He judged that the Indian tribe had exclusive zoning authority over all the lands within its reservations and the county lacked authority to zone the Yakima Nation's reservation fee lands in both the "open" and "closed" areas.

EMPLOYMENT DIVISION, DEPARTMENT OF HUMAN RESOURCES OF OREGON ET AL. v. SMITH, ET AL. (1990)

In a case that originated in Oregon, Alfred Smith and Galen Black were fired from their jobs with a private drug rehabilitation organization because they ingested peyote for sacramental purposes at a ceremony of the Native American Church, of which both were members. When they applied to the Employment Division for unemployment compensation, they were determined to be ineligible for benefits because they had been discharged under a state law disqualifying employees for work-related "misconduct."

The Oregon Court of Appeals reversed that determination, holding that the denial of benefits violated Smith and Black's free exercise rights under the First Amendment. The Oregon Supreme Court affirmed, but the Supreme Court vacated the judgement, refusing to decide whether such use was protected by the Constitution, and remanding it for a determination whether sacramental peyote use was proscribed by the state's controlled substance law, which made it a felony to knowingly possess the drug. The Oregon Supreme Court confirmed that Oregon law prohibited the sacramental use of peyote and concluded that the prohibition was invalid under the Free Exercise Clause and the state could not deny unemployment benefits to Smith and Black for ingesting peyote.

The Supreme Court reviewed the case a second time and found that the Free Exercise Clause permitted the state to prohibit sacramental peyote use and thus to deny unemployment benefits to persons discharged for such use. Justice Antonin Scalia delivered the majority opinion of the Court that a state prohibition of peyote use in a Native American Church ceremony is constitutionally permissible under the Free Exercise Clause because Oregon's drug law does not represent an attempt to regulate religious beliefs. Justice Scalia noted that the Free Exercise Clause of the Constitution "does not relieve an individual of the obligation to comply with a law that incidentally forbids (or requires) the performance of an act that his religious belief requires (or forbids) if the law is not specifically directed to religious practice and is otherwise constitutional as applied to those who engage in the specified act for nonreligious reasons." Scalia, in rejecting the Sherbert test, that governmental actions that substantially burden a religious practice must be justified by a compelling governmental interest, the majority concluded prohibitions of socially harmful conduct "cannot depend on measuring the effects of a governmental action on a religious objector's spiritual development." In sum, this case determined that the legality of peyote is a matter decided by each state legislature. For many Native people, the ruling represented a devastating blow to Native American religious freedom.

Treaties

The Constitution of the United States gave Congress plenary power over Indian affairs and reserved to the United States the power to make treaties to acquire land for a growing population and westward expansion.* Beginning in 1778 and for almost a hundred years, the treaty was the principal instrument of federal Indian policy.

The United States made treaties with over 100 Indian nations, ranging from a couple with the Navajos to over forty with Potawatomi bands between 1789 and 1867. The first treaty was written in September 1778 and the last in August 1868. Indian nations in the Northeast, Southeast, Midwest, Upper Great Lakes, Great Plains, Southwest, Great Basin, and Pacific Northwest participated in treaty councils at forts, beside rivers, and in cities.

Between 1778 and 1871, the U.S. Senate ratified approximately 372 treaties with Indian tribes. Some treaties were negotiated with the Indians on a basis of equality, some were dictated to defeated tribes. Some treaties were negotiated by only a portion of the tribe presuming to represent the entire nation. Sometimes, certain members of the tribe rejected a treaty, while others were unaware that it was being negotiated. The peak period for treaties was between 1853 and 1856, during which time more Indian acreage was alienated than in any other period. Congress opened the Kansas and Nebraska territories in 1854 and thousands of land-hungry settlers rushed in, many squatting on Indian lands. Sometimes treaties transferred large tracts of land to railroads that subdivided the land and sold small pieces to settlers. Congress ended treaty making in 1871 by

* See Appendix III for a more detailed list of significant treaties.

means of a rider attached to an appropriations bill. With the abandonment of the treaty process as the legal link between tribes and the federal government, acts of Congress took on the role of treaties. The government subsequently made "agreements" with tribes, which were submitted to both houses of Congress for ratification instead of to the Senate, which alone ratified treaties.

No law prescribed the form of treaties. They could be written or oral. In practice, American Indian treaties have been written, and they contained a beginning (a preamble), a middle (terms) and an end (signatures).

Most treaties began with a preamble which named the parties—the United States and the particular Indian nations negotiating the agreement—and usually included the date and place where the document was arranged. A typical preamble might read:

> Articles of a treaty concluded at Fort M'Intosh, the twenty-first day of January, one thousand seven hundred and eighty-five, between the Commissioners of Plenipotentiary of the United States of America, on the one part, and the Sachems and Warriors of the Wiandot, Delaware, Chippewa, and Ottawa Nations of the other.

The middle portion of treaties contained terms that spelled out what the United States and Indian nations agreed to give one another, and they explained how the parties planned to compensate each other. The number or terms, each written separately in an article, varied from treaty to treaty. A handful of treaties contained one article, while others included over two dozen articles.

Indian nations reluctantly agreed under pressure

to terms that diminished their homelands and their right to govern themselves. In over 230 treaties, about two-thirds of the total negotiated, Indian nations agreed to cede portions of their homelands. These land cessions were valuable properties. In the Treaty of 1795, at Greenville in the Ohio Valley, which ended years of conflict between Indians and Americans, twelve Indian nations ceded to the United States "one piece of land six miles square at the mouth of Chikago river, emptying into the south-west end of Lake Michigan, where a fort for-

mally stood." The American government wanted this property. It had a strategic location near waterways and at the edge of the western frontier of the young country. By the early 1800s, Chicago was the busiest port in America, and by 1860, it was a great railroad center. Today, of course, this six-mile square piece of land is part of one of the biggest cities in the country and its value is incalculable.

In many cases, the government simply wanted to clear away title to Indian lands so settlers could homestead them. In a treaty with the Sac and Fox in

TREATY MAKING

Between 1778 and 1871, over 370 treaties between Indian nations and the U.S. government were signed. By the end of the 1860s, numerous federal, military, and church people called for the end of treaty making. An Appropriations Act of March 3, 1871, stated: "No Indian nation or tribe . . . shall be acknowledged or recognized as an independent nation, tribe, or power with whom the United States may contract by treaty." The law did not in any way repeal or change treaties signed and ratified prior to that date. The following list states other important information about treaties.

1. A treaty is a contract between two or more sovereign nations that is as binding today on the governments that signed it as when agreed to more than 100 years ago.
2. The U.S. Constitution in Article 6, Section 2, states that treaties are the supreme law of the land.
3. Indian treaties have as much force as treaties made with any other nation. U.S. courts repeatedly uphold the validity of Indian treaties and the continued sovereignty of Indian nations.
4. Treaties are not simply old historical documents nor are they outdated. Their age does not invalidate them any more than age invalidates the U.S. Constitution.

5. Treaties as "supreme law of the land" are superior to the law of any states. As the U.S. Constitution points out, "the judges in every state shall be bound thereby, anything in the Constitution or laws of any state to the contrary notwithstanding."
6. At different points in history, states and individual citizens have challenged the legal force of Indian treaties, but the Supreme Court has upheld their validity.
7. Violations of treaties do not nullify them any more than committing a crime nullifies the law that forbids the crime.
8. The fact that the United States has broken treaties reflects on the integrity of the United States, not on the integrity of treaties.
9. Some treaties contain the right to use off-reservation land for Indians' traditional subsistence activities of hunting, fishing, and gathering, which do not necessarily require that the tribes have title to the land.
10. Although a statute ended Indian treaty making in 1871, all treaties are still in full force to this day and "no obligation or any treaty lawfully made and ratified with any such Indian nation or tribe prior to March 3, 1871, shall be thereby invalidated or impaired."

The first treaty between an Indian nation and the U.S. government, negotiated on September 17, 1778, with the Delaware (Lenape) Indians. Courtesy National Archives.

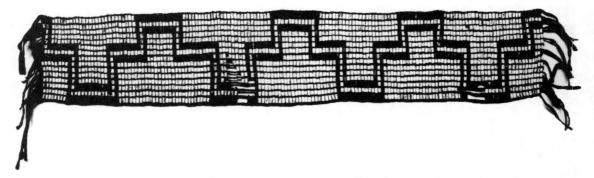

The designs woven into wampum belts, which are made of shell beads, represent the terms of agreements, treaties, or important occasions. This belt is one of three that commemorates a seventeenth-century sale of Delaware land to a colonial representative. Although the land was sold, the Delaware retained the freedom to travel and use the land, and the dark meander represents the freedom paths over the land. Courtesy of the National Museum of the American Indian/Smithsonian Institution.

September 1832 at Rock Island, Illinois, the Indians ceded a part of eastern Iowa to the U.S. government. This treaty, unlike several dozen others, forbade the Sac and Fox from planting, fishing, or hunting on any of the ceded land after June 1, 1833, the date the territory became part of the public domain. The government had already permitted large numbers of settlers to move into Iowa territory and establish log cabin homes, contrary to federal laws. The Sac and Fox had barely left their homeland, when Dubuque, Iowa, was founded at the end of 1833. Davenport, Iowa, was founded in 1836, also on former Sac and Fox homelands.

In nearly eighty treaties, Indians agreed to terms that permitted roads or railroads to be built across their lands. As early as 1791 in a treaty with the Cherokees, the U.S. government insisted on the "unmolested use of a road" from Washington District to Mero district (Tennessee). In November 1808, five Indian nations agreed to give the United States "a tract of land for a road, of one hundred and twenty feet in width . . . and all the land within one mile of the said road, on each side thereof, for the purpose of establishing settlements along the same." As late as 1868, in a treaty with the Navajos, the United States required the people to "make no opposition to the construction of railroads now being built or hereafter to be built across the continent."

Indian nations made other kinds of concessions besides giving up homelands. In nearly ninety treaties, Indian nations agreed to keep "perpetual peace" with the United States and in another two dozen agreements, Indian nations allowed the government to regulate their trade.

In exchange for Indian land cessions, rights of way for roads and railroads, and exclusive trade agreements, the U.S. government agreed in several dozen treaties to permit Indians to hunt and fish, gather foods or plant crops within territories they ceded to the government as long as the Indians acted "peaceably" and as long as the ceded land continued to be U.S. property. In at least two dozen treaties, the government agreed to give Indians land in other locations in exchange for homelands that were ceded.

In most of the treaties, the U.S. government agreed to provide payments of "consideration." "Consideration" was something valuable the government offered Indian nations to persuade them to accept treaty terms.

The United States usually promised "annuities," payments of money or goods or both, for certain periods of time. In at least thirty treaties, the U.S. government promised to pay annuities forever. In the 1829 treaty with the Chippewa, Ottawa, and Potawatomis, for example, the government agreed to "pay to the . . . Indians the sum of sixteen thousand

HISTORICAL OVERVIEW OF TREATIES

Treaty making, involving Native Americans and Europeans and then the United States government, spanned the period of the early 1600s to 1868. The list that follows gives a historical overview of five periods of treaty making.

COLONIAL TREATIES (1600–1776)

- Period of independence and equality for most Indians.
- Indians held positions of power in Western hemisphere.
- European settlers still small in number.
- England and France sought military assistance from the Indians.
- Colonists treated Indians with respect.
- Boundaries delineated.
- Trade relations.

TREATIES OF ALLIANCE AND PEACE (1776–1816)

- Indians still strong militarily, numerically, and economically.
- Indians could choose which European powers with which to align.
- Increasing need to clarify boundaries between Indian governments and United States arose.
- U.S. government recognized that Indians owned their land and to seize it would mean constant warfare, which the U.S. government wanted to avoid.
- Prevent powerful Indian nations from joining forces against the United States.

THE BEGINNING OF LAND CESSIONS (1784–1817)

- Land cessions began in New England and Middle Atlantic states in exchange for annuities and specific services delivered to tribes.

- Treaties in this period began to be used to legally extinguish Indian title to land.
- Methods used to wipe out title were (1) the drawing of boundaries between Indian country and U.S. territory and (2) the securing of "rights of way" and land for military forts and trading posts.
- The effect of drawing boundaries was that Indians permanently lost lands.
- By securing "rights of way," the United States gained important footholds in Indian country.
- With the establishing of boundaries and land cessions, the concept of "reservation" came into American policy.

TREATIES OF REMOVAL (1817–1846)

- The departure of France, England, and Spain diminished Indians regaining power.
- As settlers wanted more land, the primary goal of the United States in making treaties became the removal of Indians from that land.
- The removal policy meant that the Indian nations of the Southeast and Great Lakes exchanged their homelands for lands west of the Mississippi River (now Arkansas, Kansas, and Oklahoma).
- The primary goal was removal of eastern tribes to the west.
- The Indians of the Great Lakes fought fiercely against removal.

WESTERN TREATIES (1846–1868)

- Now clear that the policy of removing Indians farther west would not work because U.S. citizens kept demanding more lands.
- A new policy was to force Indians to smaller, well-defined reservations.

dollars, annually, forever, in specie." In a handful of treaties, mostly written in 1818 and 1819, the United States promised a perpetual annuity in silver. In 1819, the government agreed to pay the Chippewa in Michigan, in consideration of its land cession, "annually, for ever, the sum of one thousand dollars in silver."

In most treaties, however, the U.S. government promised to pay annuities for a certain period of time, for example, thirty years. Payments for land cessions could be complicated. In the treaty with the Omahas in 1854, the United States agreed to pay the Omahas $40,000 per year for three years, then $30,000 for the next ten years, then $20,000 for the next fifteen years, and then $10,000 for the next twelve years.

In many treaties, the government promised goods to Indian nations as payment of consideration for ceded lands or rights of way. In the 1847 treaty with the Pillager Band of Chippewas, the United States agreed to furnish the following annually for five years:

Fifty-three point Mackinaw blankets, three hundred two and a half point Mackinaw blankets, . . . three hundred and forty yards of white list scarlet cloth, eighteen hundred yards of strong dark prints, assorted colors, one hundred and fifty pounds three thread gray gilling-twine, seventy-five pounds turtle-twine, fifty bunches sturgeon-twine, twenty-five pounds of linen thread, two hundred combs, five thousand assorted needles, one hundred and fifty medal looking glasses, ten pounds of vermilion, thirty nests (fourteen each) heavy tin kettles, five hundred pounds of tobacco, and five barrels of salt.

In a 1853 treaty with the Cow Creek Band of the Umpqua Tribe in Oregon, the United States agreed to pay to the band, in consideration of its land cession, $1,000 spent immediately on "twenty blankets, eighteen pairs pants, eighteen pairs shoes, eighteen hickory shirts, . . . forty cotton flags, . . . one gross buttons, two lbs. thread, ten papers needles" plus another $11,000 to be paid in twenty

equal annual installments on more "blankets, clothing, provisions, stock, farming implements."

Occasionally, annuity goods were promised forever. In the 1829 treaty, the United States agreed to deliver to the Chippewas, Ottawas, and Potawatomis at Chicago "fifty barrels of salt annually, forever." In the 1818 treaty with the Quapaws, the government promised the value of $1,000 dollars of merchandise to be delivered to them "yearly, and every year."

In more than 80 treaties, the United States promised to deliver domestic animals and "implements of husbandry;" in another thirty treaties, it agreed to supply vaccines and other medicines, as well as hospitals; and in at least sixty treaties, it vowed to build saw or grist mills.

The U.S. government also promised services as consideration for ceded lands. In the treaty of 1794 with the Oneida, Tuscarora, and Stockbridge nations, the government promised for the first time a person who would "instruct some young men of the three nations in the arts of the miller and sawyer, and to provide teams and utensils for carrying on the work of the mills." This was the first education provision, and at least another eighty to ninety treaties promised teachers, school houses, and books. In about 100 treaties, the United States guaranteed the services of blacksmiths; in another seventy-two, it promised the services of farmers; in forty-two, it provided millers; and in eighteen it listed carpenters.

The treaties ended with the signatures, seals, or marks of authorized representatives of the United States and Indian nations. In some treaties, only a handful of people signed their names or made their marks; in others, dozens signed. In the treaty with the Sioux bands in 1868, nearly 200 Indian people made their marks.

In a treaty with the Cherokees in 1828, four Cherokees signed the agreement using Cherokee language symbols invented in 1821 by Sequoyah, or George Guess. Sequoyah was one of the four who signed this treaty. He was able to reduce all the sounds in the Cherokee language to a set of eighty-six symbols that he either made up or copied and modified from English spelling books.

INDIAN TREATY FISHING RIGHTS IN THE PACIFIC NORTHWEST

For over a century, a controversy raged over the question of the off-reservation fishing rights of Indian people in the Pacific Northwest. Before white people arrived, Native Americans of the Pacific Northwest had thriving fisheries in Puget Sound and on the Columbia River and its tributaries. The great salmon runs were at the core of tribal economic, cultural, and ceremonial life. In legislation creating the Oregon Territory, which opened the area to non-Indian settlement, Congress promised fair dealings with the tribes and to preserve "rights to person or property now pertaining to the Indians." In the series of treaties negotiated between the U.S. government and Indian tribes in the 1850s, tribes gave up much of their land in return for promises of cash payments, other aid, and retention of their fishing rights "at all usual and accustomed grounds and stations." Tribes conceded, however, to share these off-reservation fishing grounds with white settlers. Tribes assured by 1855 treaty negotiators that "this paper [treaty] secures your fish" continued to fish at their usual places on Puget Sound and along the Columbia River and its tributaries.

By the late 1880s, however, white trap users, gillnetters, seiners, and trollers encroached upon and even blocked Indian access to their usual and accustomed fishing grounds. By the 1920s, sportsmen were competing with commercial fishermen for the salmon-like steelhead trout, declared "a game fish" in 1925. The 1930s and 1940s brought a new threat to Indian fishing rights. Some 300 dams, big and small, built by 1948 by the Army Corps of Engineers and private utility companies in the Columbia River Basin—which pose environmental threats to salmon by cutting off their spawning migrations—inundated ancient fishing grounds. Logging, farming, and industrial development have also taken tolls on salmon runs and depleted their numbers.

Despite opposition from state agencies and non-Indian fishermen and the demands of more people, more industry, and more recreation, Indians initi-

Northwest Indian Fisheries Commission

Members of Northwest Indian Fisheries Commission
2625 Parkmont Lane, S.W.
Olympia, Washington 98502

TREATY OF MEDICINE CREEK (December 26, 1854)
Nisqually
Puyallup
Squaxin Island

TREATY OF POINT ELLIOTT (January 22, 1855)

Lummi	Suquamish
Muckleshoot	Swinomish
Nooksack	Tulalip
Sauk-Suiattle	Upper Skagit
Stillaguamish	

TREATY OF NEAH BAY (January 31, 1855)
Makah

TREATY OF POINT NO POINT (January 26, 1855)
Lower Elwha Klallam
Port Gamble Klallam
Skokomish

TREATY OF QUINAULT (January 25, 1856)
Hoh
Quileute
Quinault

Logo of the Northwest Indian Fisheries Commission. Courtesy of the Northwest Indian Fisheries Commission.

Members of Columbia River
Inter-Tribal Fish Commission
729 N.E. Oregon, Suite 200
Portland, Oregon 97232

Confederated Tribes of the Umatilla Indian Reservation
Confederated Tribes of the Warm Springs Reservation
Confederated Tribes and Bands of the Yakima Indian
   Reservation
Nez Percé Tribe

Logo of the Columbia River Inter-Tribal Fish Commission.
Courtesy of the Columbia River Inter-Tribal Fish Commission.

ated court cases and "fish-ins"—fishing in defiance
of state law but in accord with Indian treaty rights—
to assert their rights. Several court decisions in the
late 1960s and 1970s firmly established in law the
tribes' right to take fish at usual fishing grounds. The
Boldt decision of 1974, as *U.S. v. Washington* came to
be called, set off a shock wave of controversy. En-
raged non-Indian commercial fishers mounted a
campaign against the decision that permitted treaty
tribes to catch 50 percent of the harvestable fish
destined to pass through their usual and accustomed
fishing grounds and stations. For years after the decision, non-Indian commercial fisherman protested in
courts, in public areas, on rivers where they fished
illegally in defiance of state fishing regulations, and
against Judge Boldt, who was the object of bumper
stickers, protests, and petitions.

Since the Boldt ruling, procedures have been put
into place that should contribute to the long-term
well-being of salmon. The struggle to preserve Indian fishing rights in the Northwest still continues.
During the 1980s, a vocal anti-Indian movement
that refused to recognize Indian treaty fishing rights
organized Steelhead-Salmon Protective Association
and Wildlife Network (S/SPAWN). New alliances
formed in response among sports organizations, environmental groups, religious and civic groups,
treaty tribes, state governments, and natural resource management agencies. Their cooperation has
squelched uprisings of anti-Indian sentiments when
they appear.

INDIAN TREATY FISHING RIGHTS IN THE GREAT LAKES

In the Great Lakes area of Michigan, Minnesota, and
Wisconsin, treaty rights have become a controversial
issue today. Prior to the nineteenth century "treaty
era," the lives of Chippewa people revolved around
the seasonal harvests of the area's abundant resources.
Wild rice, fish, and venison were mainstays of their
diet. Even after the white culture rooted itself, hunting and fishing remained critical for trade as well as
subsistence.

Members of Great Lakes Indian
Fish and Wildlife Commission
P.O. Box 9
Odanah, Wisconsin 54861

WISCONSIN
Bad River Chippewa Tribe
Lac Du Flambeau Chippewa Tribe
Lac Courte Oreilles Chippewa Tribe
Mole Lake Chippewa Tribe
Red Cliff Chippewa Tribe
St. Croix Chippewa Tribe

MINNESOTA
Bois Forte (Nett Lake)
Fond du Lac Chippewa Tribe
Mille Lacs Chippewa Tribe
Grand Portage Chippewa Tribe

MICHIGAN
Bay Mills Indian Community Lac Veiux Desert Band of
   Lake Superior Chippewa Indians
Keeweenaw Bay Indian Community

*Logo of the Great Lakes Indian Fish and Wildlife
Commission. Courtesy of the Great Lakes Fish and Wildlife
Commission.*

During the first half of the nineteenth century, in
the treaties of 1836, 1837, and 1842, the Chippewas
of the Lake Superior area ceded or sold land in what is
now northern Wisconsin and parts of Michigan and
Minnesota in exchange for cash, goods, schools, and
other benefits. They also reserved the right to hunt,
fish, and gather foods on their former homelands. In
1854, the Lake Superior Chippewas ceded their remaining homeland in Minnesota in exchange for permanent sites in Wisconsin (Red Cliff, Bad River, St.
Croix, Lac Court Oreilles, Lac du Flambeau, Mole
Lake); Michigan (Bay Mills, Keeweenaw Bay); and
Minnesota (Fond du Lac, Grand Portage). As a conse-
quence of land cessions that divided the Lake Superior
Chippewas onto small, separate reservations, the Indians faired poorly amidst a sea of development by
non-Indian neighbors. Further, federal policies of termination and assimilation attempted to abolish
Chippewa and other Indian cultures, religions, and
tribal identities.

In the mid-twentieth century, the separate reservations recovered and began to reassert their treaty
rights. The 1972 Gurnoe and 1981 Fox decisions
reaffirmed the treaty rights to commercially fish in
the Great Lakes. The 1983 Voight decision upheld
the treaty rights of the Lake Superior Chippewas to
hunt, fish, and gather on ceded territories in northern Wisconsin.

Once the Chippewas began hunting and fishing
according to ancient custom and treaty-protected
rights, antitreaty sentiment reached a fever pitch in
northern Wisconsin. During the 1980s, antitreaty
protestors, members of Stop Treaty Abuse (STA) and
other groups, disrupted Chippewa spear fishing, especially on small northern Wisconsin lakes. Because
of the violence and outright racist activities, Honor
Our Neighbors Origins and Rights (HONOR) and
several other organizations supporting treaty rights
formed. Members have provided peaceful witness at
Wisconsin spear fishing landings and focuses on
public education regarding tribal sovereignty and
tribal rights.

The Bureau of Indian Affairs and the Indian Health Service

The Bureau of Indian Affairs (BIA) is a division of the Department of the Interior and is the principal government agency that carries out the government-to-government relationship between the United States and federally recognized Indian tribes. This relationship is affirmed by the treaties the two groups have approved, and the treaty-making process itself. The BIA also carries out the responsibilities that the United States has as trustee for the 54 million acres of land it holds in trust for federally recognized tribes and individual Indians. According to the Department of the Interior's *Departmental Manual* for the Bureau of Indian Affairs:

> The principal objectives of the Bureau are to actively encourage and train Indian and Alaska Native people to manage their own affairs under a trust relationship with the Federal Government; to facilitate, with maximum involvement of Indian and Alaska Native people, full development of their human and natural resource potentials; to mobilize all public and private aids to the advancement of Indian and Alaska Native people for use by them; and to utilize the skill and capabilities of Indian and Alaska Native people in the direction and management of programs for their benefit.

The BIA has not always sought to include Indians in the management of their own affairs. Indian relations were initially handled by the War Department. The goal was to keep the peace, while separating Indian people from their land and resources. Indians were impoverished and their rights violated as the United States grew in size. Indians were not consulted about the direction of Indian policy; until the mid 1960s, Indian people had no input into policies and practices that directly affected their future. (See HISTORICAL OVERVIEW for the early history of the BIA.)

Today, the official mission of the BIA is to protect Native Americans and their land and resources and to turn federal programs that benefit Indians over to the administration of the tribes. Since 1972, hiring, training, and promotions in the BIA have been governed by Indian preference. Each president since Richard Nixon has reaffirmed the government-to-government relationship. Yet the BIA is often accused of paternalism and, recently, of efforts to defeat Indian preference by moving high-level positions out of the BIA and into the Department of Interior.

Native American leaders often point out that the position of the BIA within the Department of the Interior creates a conflict of interest. That conflict of interest was evident when the government flooded Indian homesites in 1956 on the Fort Berthold Reservation in North Dakota in order to build the Garrison dam. When the tribe turned to the BIA lawyers for protection of their homes and businesses, they could not get help from lawyers, who worked for the same government that flooded the reservation. Throughout its history, the bureau has been accused of corruption, inefficiency, wastefulness, and bureaucratic excesses. Many people including Indians, politicians, and special interest groups, have called for the abolishment of the BIA. It has been investigated, castigated, reformed, and reorganized dozens of times. However, some feel that the abolishment of the BIA is the first step in getting rid of tribal governments and ending the trust relationship. Other Indian leaders would like to see the BIA abolished, and some feel that the BIA should be reorganized by Indian people so that it truly represents Indian interests. Yet, it remains the official U.S. government authority in dealing with the sovereign Indian nations.

Section 12 of the 1934 Indian Reorganization Act provided that the BIA must use Indian preference in hiring. In 1972, Commissioner Louis Bruce extended Indian preference to include training, reinstatements, and promotions in the bureau. The law was quickly challenged in court by non-Indian federal employees. The Supreme Court upheld Indian preference in the BIA and said it was not based on race, but on the special legal status of Indians. By

1983, an estimated 80 percent of the 14,000 employees of the BIA were Indian.

Indian leaders have articulated a number of suggestions and criticisms of the BIA. Many of the suggestions have been repeated in every task force study since 1960 that has involved Indian participants. The following are consistent suggestions:

- Involve Indian people in any plan to reorganize the BIA.
- Take the BIA out of the Department of the Interior and make an independent cabinet-level agency.
- Make the BIA an advocate for Indian needs.
- Establish legal counsel that is accountable to the BIA, but is outside of the Department of the Interior.
- Abolish the area offices, perhaps change them into technical assistance centers.
- Move decision making out of the Central Office

George Gillette (second from left), a member of the Fort Berthold Tribal Business Council, is overcome with emotion as Secretary of the Interior Julius Krug signs a contract on May 20, 1948, ceding 155,000 acres of the Fort Berthold reservation for construction of the Garrison Reservoir. The reservoir, which was opposed by the tribal council, forced tribal members from their ancient homeland in North Dakota. Courtesy of Associated Press/Wide World Photos.

in Washington, D.C., and out of the area offices and place it within agencies, which are closer to the tribes and know their needs.

- Change the present budget system to respond to needs at the tribal level, instead of a top down system that begins with an appropriation that is not based on need.
- Involve tribal leaders in the formulation of budgets.
- Appoint a commissioner of Indian affairs from a list of candidates prepared by tribes.
- Change the BIA from a management to a service organization.

Today, the BIA has four main functions: (1) education, (2) reservation services (these are the same types of services that non-Indians receive from local governments), (3) trust responsibility/economic development, and (4) BIA operations. Since 1849, the BIA has been a division of the Department of the Interior. Until 1977, the BIA had a three-tiered organizational structure consisting of a central headquarters located in Washington, D.C.; area offices in each of twelve geographic regions, and local organizational units located on or near reservations. Until recently, the commissioner of the BIA reported to the assistant secretary of the interior for Public Land Management, who was also responsible for the Bureau of Land Management, the National Park Service, and other federal agencies. In 1977, a new position, the assistant secretary for Indian affairs (ASIA), was created in the Department of the Interior to head the BIA. The position of commissioner of Indian affairs, which was created by Congressional statute, still exists, but is vacant. The addition of the ASIA created another level to the organization and is an apparent upgrading of the head of the BIA, something Indian leaders have wanted for a long time. However, some Indian leaders are suspicious of the intentions of the Department of the Interior. Indian preference does not apply to the Department of Interior, and some see the creation of a hierarchy of senior staff outside of the BIA as circumventing Indian preference and accountability to Indian people.

STRUCTURAL ORGANIZATION OF THE BIA

Some of the offices organized within the BIA are described below:

Headquarters, Washington, D.C. (unless otherwise noted)

Office of the Assistant Secretary—Indian Affairs. Responsible for planning, organizing, coordinating, controlling, and directing all activities, programs, and functions assigned to the BIA.

Alcohol and Substance Abuse Staff. Functions within the Office of the ASIA, and under the day-to-day supervision of the director, Office of Tribal Services, is responsible for the implementation of the provisions of the Anti-Drug Abuse Act of 1986.

Commissioner of Indian Affairs. Responsible for the direction of the noneducation portions of the BIA. This position has been vacant since 1977.

Public Information Staff. Under the supervision of the office of the Commissioner of Indian Affairs and with guidance from the Office of the ASIA, maintains liaison with the media, the public, and other federal and state agencies.

Office of Trust Funds Management. Located in Albuquerque, New Mexico, and is responsible for professional, technical, and management leadership of the bureau's activities, programs, and functions related to and affecting funds held in trust for individual Indians and Indian tribes.

Office of Tribal Services. Under the supervision of a director, manages those headquarters organizations, activities, and functions that promote the attainment of goals and objectives designed to assist tribes in delivering local governmental services, such as social services, housing, training, job placement, law enforcement, judicial services, and developing self-governing capabilities. Includes five divisions.

Division of Housing Services. Provides staff assistance for Bureau programs designed to provide and improve housing for Indians who cannot be served under other federal-assisted housing programs. The division serves as liaison to the Department of Housing and Urban Development and the Indian Health Service, coordinating the sanitation facilities construction program with housing construction and improvement programs.

Division of Job Placement and Training.
Provides staff assistance to the director regarding programs leading to the development of job opportunities, on-the-job training, and other services needed to enable Indian individuals seeking work to secure and retain suitable employment.

Division of Law Enforcement Services.
With staff located in Albuquerque, New Mexico, and Marana, Arizona, develops standards and criteria for the selection, training, and duties of law enforcement officers, including programs related to enforcement of trading, hunting, and fishing regulations, and the co-ordination of such programs with other agencies. The division is responsible for the direction and operation of special investigations of alleged or suspected violations of major federal criminal statutes relating to Indian country.

Division of Self-Determination Services.
Provides staff assistance to the director in carrying out the responsibilities for the Indian Self-Determination and Education Assistance Act and other legislation as it pertains to Indian self-determination.

Division of Social Services. Provides staff assistance to the director in bureau programs designed to provide social services to Indians and Indian communities. The programs include financial assistance for needy Indians living on reservations; arranging foster care for dependent, neglected and handicapped Indian children; referral of Indians to local and state agencies for assistance when appropriate; preventive services in both adult and juvenile crime; individual and family counseling services; community organizational services to improve the lives of Indian people; and assistance to tribes in the development of tribal social services programs and tribal work experience programs for employable recipients of assistance.

Division of Tribal Government Services.
With staff located in Albuquerque, New Mexico, is responsible for training and technical assistance ac-

tivities of the judicial services program, provides staff assistance to the director in bureau programs relating to tribal special services, tribal management services, and tribal enrollment services.

Office of Trust and Economic Development. Under the supervision of a director, manages those headquarters organizations, activities, and functions associated with economic development and the development, enhancement, and protection of trust property, natural resources, and treaty and statutory rights of Indian tribes and individual Indians in or affecting property held in trust by the federal government. Includes seven divisions.

Environmental Services Staff. Provides assistance and advice to the director regarding all matters involving environmental statutes which have application to, or implications for, Indian trust land, including statutes dealing with the environment and the preservation of cultural and archaeological resources.

Division of Energy and Minerals Resources.
Located in Lakewood, Colorado, with liaison staff in Washington, D.C., provides staff assistance and advice to the director in analyzing, evaluating, developing, and coordinating bureauwide policies pertaining to the conservation, development, and leasing of mineral resources on Indian lands. The division is responsible for economic analyses and other activities related to coal, oil, gas, uranium, copper, molybdenum, tungsten, and other energy and mineral resources.

Division of Financial Assistance. Provides staff assistance to the director regarding specific programs designed to aid Indians in obtaining adequate capital for development of Indian resources and to provide credit and financing services to tribal organizations and individual Indians. This includes services to obtain funds from conventional and government sources to finance Indian economic self-development, including loans for housing, education, and Indian governmental purposes, and in the investment and use of their own monies for the same purposes.

Division of Forestry. With staff located in Portland, Oregon, and at the Interagency Fire

Control Center in Boise, Idaho, provides staff advice and assistance to the director and technical assistance to bureau and tribal organizations in forestry matters, including multiple-use management plans for the forest land, forest improvement projects, and forest protection.

Division of Real Estate Services.   Provides staff assistance and advice to the director in activities related to land resources and property management.

Division of Transportation.   With staff located in Albuquerque, New Mexico, provides staff

assistance to the director regarding bureau programs for analysis, design, construction, and maintenance of roads, bridges, airfields, and other transportation facilities with the ultimate objective of enhancing reservation economies and services to Indian and Alaska Native people.

Division of Water and Land Resources.   The division provides staff advice for all activities related to the planning, management, conservation, development, and utilization of the Indians' soil, water, range land, fish, and wildlife resources; it directs the

ADMINISTRATORS OF INDIAN AFFAIRS

From 1789 to 1824, the Secretaries of War were the administrators of American Indian affairs. From 1824 to 1832, the Secretaries of War were still officially in charge of Indian affairs, even though during this time there was an unofficial head of the Indian Office. In 1832, the position of Commissioner of Indian Affairs was officially created by Congress. In 1849, the Indian Bureau was transferred out of the Department of War and into the Department of the Interior. In 1977 a new position, the Assistant Secretary for Indian Affairs, was created to head the Bureau of Indian Affairs within the Department of the Interior. Since 1977, the position of Commissioner of Indian Affairs has been vacant, with an "acting" commissioner in place up to 1979. Since 1979, the head of Indian Affairs is the Assistant Secretary for Indian Affairs.

Samuel Dexter	1800
Henry Dearborn	1801
William Eustis	1809
John Armstrong	1813
James Monroe	1814
William H. Crawford	1815
John C. Calhoun	1817
James Barbour	1825
Peter B. Porter	1828
John H. Eaton	1829
Lewis Cass	1831

Heads of Indian Affairs, War Department

Thomas L. McKenney	1824
Samuel S. Hamilton	1830
Elbert Herring	1831

Secretaries of War, War Department	*Year Appointed*
Henry Knox	1789
Thomas Pickering	1795
James McHenry	1796

Commissioners of Indian Affairs, War Department

Elbert Herring	1832
Carey A. Harris	1836
T. Hartley Crawford	1838
William Medill	1845

bureau's flood plains management program. It provides technical advice and assistance, as required, for the authorization, planning, design, construction, management, and operation of Indian irrigation and power projects, water development projects, accounting for irrigation water utilization, and protection of water rights.

Office of Indian Education Programs. Under the supervision of a director, who reports to the assistant secretary—Indian affairs, is responsible for all BIA education functions, programs, activities,

field operations and offices. The director executes education programs at area offices, agencies, schools, and postsecondary institutions operated by the bureau.

FIELD ORGANIZATION

The BIA has divided the United States into twelve areas for the purpose of administering its field activities (except for Indian Education Programs). Each area is designated by the name of the city in which

Commissioners of Indian Affairs, Department of the Interior

Orlando Brown	1849	Charles J. Rhoads	1929
Luke Lea	1850	John Collier	1933
George Manypenny	1853	William A. Brophy	1945
James W. Denver	1857, 1858	John R. Nichols	1949
Charles E. Mix	1858	Dillon S. Myer	1950
Alfred B. Greenwood	1859	Glenn L. Emmons	1953
William P. Dole	1859	Philleo Nash	1961
Dennis Cooley	1865	Robert L. Bennett (Oneida)	1966
Lewis V. Bogy	1866	Louis Rook Bruce (Sioux-Mohawk)	1969
Nathaniel G. Taylor	1867	Morris Thompson (Tanana)	1973
Ely S. Parker (Seneca)	1869	Benjamin Reifel (Sioux)	1976
Francis A. Walker	1871	Raymond Butler (Blackfeet) acting	
Edward P. Smith	1873	commissioner	1977
John Q. Smith	1875	Martin Seneca, Jr. (Seneca) acting	
Ezra A. Hayt	1877	commissioner	1978
Roland E. Trowbridge	1880	William Hallett (Chippewa)	1979
Hiram Price	1881		
John D. C. Atkins	1885		
John H. Overly	1888	*Assistant Secretaries for Indian Affairs, Department*	
Thomas J. Morgan	1889	*of the Interior*	
Daniel M. Browning	1893	Forrest Gerard (Blackfeet)	1977
William A. Jones	1897	Tom Fredericks (Mandan-Hidatsa) temporary	1981
Francis E. Leupp	1905	Kenneth Smith (Wasco)	1981
Robert G. Valentine	1909	Ross Swimmer (Cherokee)	1985
Cato Sells	1913	Ed Brown (Pascua Yaqui)	1985
Charles H. Burke	1921	Ada Deer (Menominee)	1993

the area office is located, except the Navajo Area Office which is located in Window Rock, Arizona, and Gallup, New Mexico, and the Eastern Area Office, which is located in Washington, D.C. Subordinate to the area offices are agency offices, subagencies, field stations, and irrigation project offices, which provide program service delivery to Indian tribes and Indian people. Following is a list of addresses for the central and area offices:

Central Office

Bureau of Indian Affairs
1951 Constitution Ave., NW
Washington, DC 20245
Carl Shaw, Director of Public Affairs
(202) 343-2315

Area Offices

Aberdeen Area Office
115 4th Avenue, SE
Aberdeen, South Dakota
57401

Albuquerque Area Office
P.O. Box 26567
615 N. 1st Street
Albuquerque, New Mexico
87125-6587

Anadarko Area Office
P.O. Box 368
Anadarko, Oklahoma
73005

Billings Area Office
316 N. 26th Street
Billings, Montana 59101

Eastern Area Office
1951 Constitution Avenue, NW
Washington, DC 20245

Juneau Area Office
Box 3-8000
Juneau, Alaska 99802

Minneapolis Area Office
15 S. 5th Street
Minneapolis, Minnesota
55402

Muskogee Area Office
Old Federal Building
Muskogee, Oklahoma
74401

Navajo Area Office
P.O. Box M
Window Rock, Arizona
86515

Navajo Area Office
(Administrative)
P.O. Box 1060
Gallup, New Mexico 87301

Phoenix Area Office
P.O. Box 7007
3030 N. Central
Phoenix, Arizona 85001

Portland Area Office
P.O. Box 3785
1425 NE Irving Street
Portland, Oregon 97208

Sacramento Area Office
2800 Cottage Way
Sacramento, California
95825

INDIAN HEALTH SERVICE

The Indian Health Service (IHS), an agency of the Public Health Service, administers the principal federal health programs for American Indians and Alaska Natives. It provides comprehensive health services to people living on or near federal Indian reservations or in traditional Indian territory, such as Oklahoma and Alaska. The organization and deliv-

INDIAN MORBIDITY

"Civilized medicine has for generations been considerably preoccupied by contagious diseases and, as a result of vast experience with bacterial disease, has developed a technique of prevention and cure. What the whites most scorned in the Indians' practice of medicine was the inability to cope with the recently introduced contagious diseases. The Indian had no racial immunity, and when yellow fever, smallpox, measles, or scarlet fever were introduced by a passing white, the Indian community was decimated by the disease. Instances are recorded in which a party of apparently healthy whites merely camped without so much as seeing an Indian, and the next year other travelers arrived and found the whole neighboring community wiped out, and so rapidly that the woods and deserted village were littered with unburied bodies. In truth, the Indian might more justly scorn a civilization that lived under such circumstances that plagues were sufficiently frequent to allow its physicians to become adept in treating infectious diseases."

From: *Medicine Among the American Indians* by Eric Stone (1932).

ery of health care by IHS is based on treaties, laws enacted by Congress, and judicial rulings first set forth in the 1830s by the U.S. Supreme Court under Chief Justice John Marshall. Principal among the laws is the Snyder Act of 1921 that provided the basic authority for most Indian health services provided by the federal government to native people.

As of October 1991, IHS provided health care in 42 hospitals, 65 health centers, 4 school health centers, and 52 smaller health stations. Through contracts with IHS, tribes and tribal groups operated 8 hospitals and 331 outpatient facilities which include 93 health centers, 3 school health centers, 63 smaller health stations and satellite clinics, and 172 Alaska village clinics. IHS funds 34 Indian health organizations operating at 41 sites located in cities throughout the United States to provide culturally acceptable, accessible, affordable, accountable, and available health services to the underserved urban Indian population.

The IHS program is community-oriented offering medical and dental care and services including maternal and child health, eye care, diabetes, otitis media, family planning, mental health, social services, alcoholism treatment, nutrition counseling, public health nursing, health education, and environmental health and sanitation.

During the twentieth century, health conditions of native people markedly changed. For hundreds of years, natives were victimized by repeated and severe epidemics of communicable and infectious diseases such as influenza, measles, whooping cough, diphtheria, and tuberculosis, one of the worst killers. By the 1960s, Indians displayed disease patterns characteristic of their economic status—alcohol and drug abuse, spouse abuse, homicides, suicides, child neglect, and violent crimes.

Since the mid-1950s, when the Public Health Service became responsible for Indian health care, the health of Native Americans has improved, but Indians continue to be sicker and die younger than other Americans. Owing to their geographic isolation, many Native Americans have less access to health care than does the general U.S. population. There are proportionately fewer primary care provider visits among Indians and Alaska Natives and proportionately fewer health providers in facilities serving them. Indians on reservations rarely see Indian doctors, and the doctors that do come usually do not stay for more than two or three years, and they do not communicate effectively with their Indian patients. Rarely is there long-term continuity in health care provided the Indian community.

Limited access is compounded by the greater morbidity experienced by Native Americans. Many diseases occur at much higher rates, and Native Americans are three times more likely to die young than are other Americans. During the period from 1980 to 1982, 37 percent of deaths among Indian and Alaska Natives occurred before age forty-five, compared to 12 percent of all U.S. deaths in the same age group. In 1992, the ten leading causes of death among Indians were heart disease, accidents, malignancies, cerebrovascular diseases, cirrhosis, diabetes, influenza and pneumonia, suicide, homicide, and chronic pulmonary diseases.

Some elderly American Indians delay or avoid seeking IHS medical help because of significant language and cultural barriers. Few health care professionals speak native languages. Often Indian elders cannot explain in English what is wrong with their bodies nor can they understand what doctors tell them or the treatments, injections, X-rays, and other tests they receive. "Medicine" embraces much more than treating disease and healing injuries to traditional native people who believe that the body, mind, and spirit are interrelated and function together. Western medicine with its tendency to focus on bodily sickness alienates traditional Indians who prefer Indian medicine men and women who treat the entire person.

The life expectancy of American Indians and Alaska Natives continues to increase at a rate faster than other races in the United States. In 1980, the life expectancy at birth for Native Americans had increased to 71.1 years (67.1 years for males and 75.1 for females), an increase of 19 percent since 1950, during which period the increase for the U.S.

white population was 8 percent. From 1986 to 1988, the infant mortality rate among Native Americans fell to 9.7 infant deaths per 1,000 live births. The death rate for native infants was 62.7 per 1,000 live births in 1955 when IHS became part of the Public Health Service.

IHS consists of headquarters and twelve area office operations.

Headquarters

Indian Health Service
Parklawn Building
5600 Fishers Lane
Rockville, Maryland 20857

Area Offices

- Aberdeen, South Dakota, servicing North and South Dakota and Iowa
- Alaska servicing Alaska
- Albuquerque, New Mexico, servicing New Mexico and Colorado
- Bemidji, Minnesota, servicing Minnesota, Michigan, and Wisconsin
- Billings, Montana, servicing Montana, Wyoming, and Utah
- Nashville, Tennessee, servicing the eastern United States
- Navajo, Arizona, servicing the northeast section of Arizona, the northwest section of New Mexico, the southern section of San Juan County, Utah
- Oklahoma City, Oklahoma, servicing Kansas and Oklahoma
- Phoenix, Arizona, servicing Arizona, Nevada, and Utah
- Portland, Oregon, servicing Idaho, Oregon, and Washington
- Sacramento, California, servicing California
- Tucson, Arizona, servicing Arizona (Sells only)

Tribal Governments*

HISTORICAL TRIBAL GOVERNMENTS

Indian tribes have experienced much change in the past five centuries. Indian tribal governments existed for thousands of years before European contact. Tribal governments exercised full sovereign powers as independent nations. It is difficult to describe accurately the exact structure of any single traditional or historical tribal government. Each of the hundreds of Indian tribes in North America developed unique forms of government that varied greatly from tribe to tribe.

Much of what was known about tribal governments before European contact has been lost. Tribal histories were often contained in stories handed down from one generation to the next. With European contact and the disruptions that followed, much of the evidence of the past is gone. But there are clues as to those times. For every tribe, there is some remnant of those past times.

The creation story of a tribe is an important starting point for understanding tribal governments. It can often lend understanding to a tribe's philosophy of power and politics. Sometimes the stories help define the roles of man and woman in the greater

design. For example, in some tribes where religious figures take on female attributes, the woman is more likely to have a central place in politics and governance of the tribe.

The selection of tribal leadership varied for each tribe. Some tribes selected leaders through election. Leaders in other tribes came to power through individual initiative. Sometimes leadership was vested in a group or groups of individuals who made decisions for the tribe. With some tribes, family clan systems developed. Each clan would select its own leader. Agreements and decisions between clans required still different mechanisms. Religion could play an important role in tribal government. Some tribes received spiritual guidance from a single spiritual leader. Sometimes a council provided spiritual leadership.

Internal decision making tended to focus on the well-being of the group. Daily concerns of the tribe included child rearing, care for the elderly, food supply, and safety. Internal disputes and controversies were less often philosophical ones, and more often ones of personal pride or greed. Tribal governments developed mechanisms to deal with internal tribal disputes. Laws and religious rules were known and followed by most. New controversies were referred to established internal mechanisms, such as the political and religious leadership.

The dividing line between religious infractions and crimes was not clear. Among the Cherokee and the Cheyenne, a murder, for instance, became a taint on the entire tribe, which, therefore, had to undergo a ritual cleansing. In many tribes, lying was considered one of the most terrible religious crimes; telling

* The following chapter is by Robert J. Lyttle, an attorney and member of the Cheyenne and Arapaho Tribes of Oklahoma. Mr. Lyttle has assisted several tribes with successful constitutional revision projects. He has organized and conducted numerous conferences and workshops on tribal government and he regularly makes presentations to tribal councils, tribal communities, high schools, and colleges. Mr. Lyttle currently serves as the Attorney General for the Yavapai-Apache Tribe of Arizona. He also serves as an adjunct professor at Arizona State University College of Law.

the truth was considered a virtue. When crimes did take place, often the transgressor would freely confess his or her guilt. The tribe's primary problem was not determining guilt, but fashioning a punishment or remedy.

Tribes were also concerned with external conflict. Some tribes developed sophisticated systems of commerce and trade. Internal mechanisms were needed to prepare for and engage in trade or common social activities. Trading and commerce brought tribes in contact with other tribes, which allowed tribes to witness how power was distributed in another group. Adaptations in tribal governments occurred. Some practices spread across whole regions of the country. Intertribal contact sometimes resulted in serious conflict and war. Decisions regarding relationships between groups were often treated seriously and involved all leaders and leadership groups.

Since European contact, tribal governments have been in flux. Each tribe and its government had to make decisions regarding its own unique circumstances. The arrival of European settlers, the migration of eastern Indians into the west, the encroachment on Indian lands, and war with other tribes and the United States all caused severe disruptions in tribal governments.

The federal Indian policy of the U.S. government has had a profound impact on tribal governments and has shifted dramatically over the past 200 years.

In the late 1700s, the newly formed U.S. government treated Indian tribes as independent sovereign nations often seeking their allegiance and support and negotiating with them as equals. During the mid-1800s, traditional tribal governments came under increasing attack by the federal government. The federal policy of forced relocation to Indian reservations caused severe disruptions in traditional governing bodies. From the late 1800s to the early 1930s, the federal government implemented a policy of breaking apart Indian reservations and assimilating Indian people into mainstream non-Indian society. The allotment of Indian lands and the forced assimilation of Indian people further eroded tribal governments.

Federal Indian Policy: Historical Perspective

Discovery, Conquest and Treaty Making	(up to 1871)
Removal and Relocation	(1828–1887)
Allotment and Assimilation	(1887–1934)
Reorganization and Self-government	**(1934–1945)**
Termination	(1945–1961)
Self-determination	(1961–present)

THE INDIAN REORGANIZATION ACT OF 1934

As noted earlier in this volume, the U.S. government passed the Indian Reorganization Act (IRA) in 1934. The IRA represented a dramatic shift in federal Indian policy. It ended the further allotment of Indian lands and proposed that Indian tribes organize their governments under written tribal constitutions.

Congress designed the IRA to stop the further loss of Indian lands; support and recognize the legitimacy of tribal governments; and encourage economic development and self-determination.

Summary of IRA Provisions

Section 1.   Indian lands shall not be allotted.

Section 2.   Trust status of Indian lands shall be extended indefinitely.

Section 3.   Surplus Indian land opened for settlement may be restored to Indian ownership.

Section 4.   Indian lands cannot be sold or transferred without the approval of the U.S. Secretary of the Interior.

Section 5.   The U.S. Secretary of the Interior may purchase or obtain additional lands for Indian tribes.

Section 6. Rules and regulations for managing Indian forests and livestock grazing are required.

Section 7. The U.S. Secretary of the Interior can create new Indian reservations on newly acquired lands or can add land to existing reservations.

Section 8. Individual Indian allotments or homesteads outside existing reservations shall not be affected by the IRA.

Section 9. UP to $250,000 per fiscal year may be appropriated to defray expenses of organizing under the IRA.

Section 10. Up to $10,000,000 may be appropriated to establish a revolving fund for the Secretary of the Interior to make loans to Indian-chartered corporations to promote economic development.

Section 11. Up to $250,000 may be appropriated to make loans to Indians for tuition and expenses at recognized vocational and trade schools, and that up to $50,000 of this amount shall be available to Indian students in high schools and colleges.

Section 12. Indian preference standards for employment in the Indian Office (BIA), without regard to existing civil service laws, must be established.

Section 13. Key sections of the IRA are not applied to Alaska or to Oklahoma tribes.

Section 14. Certain acts covering Indian allotments may still be applied to qualified Sioux Indians.

Section 15. The IRA shall not impair or prejudice any suit by a tribe against the United States.

Section 16. Indian tribes may adopt a constitution. ("Any Indian tribe or tribes, residing on the same reservation, shall have the right to organize for its common welfare, and may adopt an appropriate constitution and bylaws." "Amendments to the constitution and bylaws may be ratified and approved by the Secretary in the same manner as the original constitution and bylaws.")

Section 17. Tribes may request the U.S. Secretary of the Interior to issue a charter of incorporation to the tribe.

Section 18. The IRA shall not apply to tribes which have voted against the IRA.

Section 19. This section defines the terms: "Indian," "tribe," and "adult Indian."

The original IRA gave tribes one year to vote on whether to accept or reject the IRA. In June 1935, Congress extended the IRA for an additional one-year period. In a controversial move, the U.S. government decided that tribes that did not vote to exclude itself from the IRA were automatically included under the IRA. In some cases, opposition to the IRA was strong and participation in the voting was discouraged; however, under BIA interpretation, a "no-show" vote was considered a "yes" vote.

The Alaska Act, passed by Congress in May 1936, applied certain sections of the IRA to Alaska tribes and villages. Many native Alaska groups organized under written tribal constitutions similar to tribes in the lower 48 states.

The Oklahoma Indian Welfare Act of 1936, also called the Thomas Rogers Act, applied certain sections of the IRA to Oklahoma Indian tribes. Many Oklahoma tribes organized their governments under written tribal constitutions.

During the two-year period, officials from the Department of the Interior/BIA traveled throughout Indian country to encourage tribes to accept the provisions of the IRA. From 1934 to 1936, BIA records indicate that 181 tribes voted to accept the IRA and 77 tribes voted to reject the IRA. Today, tribes may still organize under the IRA.

The BIA drafted IRA constitutions for tribes with little or no tribal input. IRA constitutions ignored traditional tribal governments that had existed for thousands of years. Despite differences that existed from one tribal government to another, the BIA used a "boiler-plate" constitution for most tribes. Although some adjustments were made for each tribe, most IRA tribes received nearly identical BIA-drafted constitutions.

Once a tribe voted to accept the IRA, the BIA held a second election for a tribe to vote on a specific tribal constitution. Typically, the second election on a specific document took years to schedule and conduct. Some tribes that voted to accept the IRA never held a second election to vote on a specific tribal constitution; thus, some IRA tribes do not have a tribal constitution.

Both IRA and non-IRA tribes enjoy the same government-to-government relationship with the federal government. The Navajo Tribe, the largest tribe in the United States, rejected the IRA and is not organized under a written tribal constitution.

The form of government for tribes not organized under the IRA can vary widely from tribe to tribe. Some traditional tribal governments remain intact and functioning. For example, some Pueblo groups retain much of their traditional tribal governments. However, many tribes that voted to reject the IRA later adopted a governmental structure similar to an IRA government. Today, an IRA tribe may schedule an election to revoke its IRA structure and become a non-IRA tribe.

Varied Governments from Tribe to Tribe

Names	*Examples*
Nation	Navajo Nation
Tribe	Minnesota Chippewa Tribe
Tribes	Cheyenne and Arapaho Tribes of Oklahoma
Confederated Tribes	Confederated Tribes of the Warm Springs Reservation
Indian Community	Fort Belknap Indian Community
Indian Colony	Burns Paiute Indian Colony
Pueblo	Pueblo of Sandia
Village	Akhiok Native Village
Rancheria	Elk Valley Rancheria
Band	Coyote Valley Band of Pomo Indians

Governing Body	*Examples*
Tribal Council	Kickapoo Tribal Council
General Council	Sherwood Valley General Council
Business Committee	Cheyenne and Arapaho Business Committee
Legislature	Menominee Tribal Legislature
Board of Directors	The Tulalip Board of Directors
Business Council	Fort Hall Business Council
Board of Trustees	Umatilla Board of Trustees
Executive Committee	Nez Percé Tribal Executive Committee
Council	Mashantucket Pequot Council

Tribal Committee	Viejas Tribal Committee	Territory & Jurisdiction	Establishes the territory or land base of the tribe often citing various treaties, executive orders, legislation, or other official documents; may also address the extent of tribal jurisdiction over persons, property, and activities.
Leadership	*Examples*		
President	Navajo Nation		
Governor	Isleta Pueblo		
Chairman	Yankton Sioux Tribe		
Vice Chairman	Quapaw Tribe		
Legislator	Menominee Indian Tribe	Membership	Establishes the criteria for membership in the tribe; blood quantum and residency are typical requirements for tribal membership; BIA initially set most membership requirements at $1/2$ degree blood quantum, but many tribes today have made changes to membership criteria including lowering the requirement to $1/4$ degree blood quantum.
Business Committee Member	Miccosukee Tribe		
Tribal Council Member	Crow Tribe		
Spokesman	Enterprise Rancheria		
Representative	Jackson Rancheria		
Chief	Miami Tribe		
Principal Chief	Cherokee Nation		

TRIBAL CONSTITUTIONS

Just as the U.S. Constitution is the foundation for the U.S. government, a tribal constitution is the foundation for a tribal government. Each tribe is free to determine its own form of government. A tribe may choose to accept the standard IRA form of government. Tribes may accept all, some, or none of the standard provisions.

Typical Provisions Found in IRA Constitutions

Constitution		Governing Body	Establishes the leadership of the tribe, usually a tribal council or business committee comprised of 5–11 members; tribal council includes the chairman and vice chairman.
Title	Name of the tribe or other Indian group.		
Preamble	Sets out the goals of the tribe; often begins with the words, "We the people of the _____ Tribe. . . ."	Powers	Lists the powers of the governing body including a general statement "to act in all matters that concern the welfare of the tribe"; sometimes includes the power to establish a tribal court system.
		Elections	Determines the timing and procedures for conducting tribal elections to vote for tribal leadership positions.

Vacancies	Establishes the procedures for filing vacancies on the governing body which usually includes appointing a person to fill the vacancy or scheduling a special election to fill the vacancy.
Popular Participation	Establishes a referendum and initiative process for tribal members to revoke enactments of the governing body or to propose decisions or actions; procedure is generally not used but the popularity of the referendum/initiative is increasing.
Civil Rights	Sets out basic rights of tribal members but usually does not include a full listing of the Bill of Rights from the U.S. Constitution; however, the Indian Civil Rights Act of 1968 applies many of the provisions of the U.S. Bill of Rights to tribes.
Amendment	Sets the criteria for amending the tribal constitution which typically includes three requirements: a majority vote of registered tribal members, voting at a secreterial (BIA) election, and at least 30% of the registered members must actually vote.

Bylaws

Duties of the Officers	Lists the duties of the Chairman, Vice Chairman,

Secretary and the Treasurer; sometimes includes a provision requiring the secretary of the tribe to send minutes from all tribal meetings to the BIA.

Meetings	Sets the dates for regular tribal council meetings usually held once per month, and for general meetings of the entire tribe.
Order of Business	Sets the order of business for tribal council meetings.
Adoption or Ratification Clause	Refers to the requirements for adopting or ratifying the constitution.
Certification of Election Results	BIA form which certifies the election results.
Certificate of Approval or Ratification	BIA approval of the constitution or amendments.

THE BUREAU OF INDIAN AFFAIRS

In the 1930s, the BIA often dictated the form of government for each tribe. The BIA usually established the form of tribal leadership and the requirements for membership in the tribe. Today, changes to the system still require BIA approval.

The BIA exercises a considerable amount of supervision over internal tribal matters. A typical IRA constitution allows the BIA to supervise a tribe by requiring secretarial (BIA) approval for many tribal council actions.

The phrase, "with the approval of the Secretary of the Interior" can be found in most IRA tribal constitutions. A tribe must seek BIA approval to act in certain matters.

"WE'RE HERE FOR YOUR BEST INTERESTS."

Artist Marvin Cook suggests the nature of Bureau of Indian Affairs supervision over tribal matters. Courtesy of Marvin Cook.

BIA Supervision of Tribal Governments

According to many IRA constitutions, the BIA must review and approve numerous tribal council actions. The BIA intrudes itself into internal tribal matters in the following ways:

1. BIA approval needed to make changes to tribal membership criteria
2. BIA approval needed for contracts and agreements
3. BIA approval needed to employ legal counsel
4. BIA approval needed for tribal budgets
5. BIA approval needed to borrow money
6. BIA approval needed to lease tribal lands
7. BIA approval needed to pass tax ordinances
8. BIA approval needed to set rules for adoption of minor children
9. BIA approval needed to establish a tribal court
10. BIA approval needed to establish a law enforcement department
11. BIA approval needed to regulate domestic relations
12. BIA approval needed to regulate inheritance
13. BIA approval needed to exclude non-members of the tribe
14. BIA approval needed to exercise further powers not listed in the constitution
15. BIA establishes the procedures for review and approval of tribal council actions
16. BIA can hold a tribal election if a dispute arises
17. BIA approval needed to pass a land ordinance
18. BIA approval needed to pass amendments to the constitution
19. BIA must receive a copy of the minutes of all tribal meetings
20. BIA must receive a copy of the tribe's audit once a year
21. BIA must approve a surety bond for the tribal treasurer
22. BIA can call a special meeting of the tribal council
23. BIA can call for a tribal election (first elections).
24. BIA approval needed to impose license fees on non-members
25. BIA approval needed to pass a law and order code.

The BIA supervises tribes at four levels: the local agency, the area office, the central office, and by the secretary of the interior in Washington, D.C. Tribal decisions that require BIA approval must go through the various levels (see chart on following page).

To change or amend an IRA tribal constitution, the tribe must request a BIA election, called a secretarial election, for tribal members to vote on the amendments. A normal tribal election follows tribal rules. However, a secretarial election follows complicated federal BIA rules and regulations. Some tribes have experienced problems with amending their constitutions. BIA delays in reviewing the proposed changes and scheduling elections often caused many amendments to fail. One California tribe waited four years for the BIA to review its proposed constitutional amendments. Eventually, the tribe successfully sued the BIA.

BIA Process for Changing IRA Constitutions

STEP 1   Tribe formulates and drafts amendments; tribe sends amendments to BIA for review and requests a secretarial (BIA) election.

STEP 2   BIA completes a review and sends the proposed amendments back to tribe with comments and recommendations.

STEP 3   Tribe accepts or rejects the BIA comments and recommendations and sends its answer back to the BIA.

STEP 4   BIA authorizes the election on the proposed amendments.

STEP 5   If tribal voters pass the amendments, tribe sends amendments back to BIA for final approval.

The BIA agreed to hold elections in a timely manner but continued to enjoy the discretion to approve or deny voter-passed amendments based upon its interpretation of federal law and federal Indian policy. Thus, BIA officials could determine federal Indian policy and could decide whether certain constitutional amendments were in the best interests of the tribe. Congress changed this situation in 1988 with the passage of the Indian Reorganization Act Amendments.

Indian Reorganization Act Amendments of 1988

Congress amended the IRA in 1988 because of persistent BIA delays. The important changes are summarized below:

• The Secretary (BIA) shall call and hold an election . . . within ninety days after receipt of a

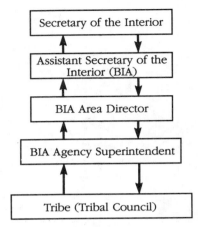

Tribal Council actions that require Bureau of Indian Affairs approval must work their way up four levels to the Secretary of the Interior in Washington, D.C., and back down the levels for implementation by the Tribal Council.

tribal request to ratify an amendment to a tribal constitution.

• The Secretary (BIA) shall approve the . . . amendments . . . unless . . . amendments are contrary to applicable laws.

• If the Secretary (BIA) does not approve or disapprove the . . . amendments within forty-five days, the Secretary's approval shall be considered as given.

• Actions to enforce the provisions of (this law) may be brought in the appropriate federal district court.

Two major changes contained in the 1988 law include:

1. BIA must hold an election on proposed constitutional amendments in a timely manner, and

2. BIA must approve the voter-passed amendments unless the amendments are contrary to applicable law.

TRIBAL GOVERNMENT OPERATION

A typical tribal government is governed by a legislative body called a tribal council. The chairman of the tribal council serves as the executive officer in charge of the tribal administration. The tribal court, which is usually established through enactment of the tribal council and is thus subject to political influences, serves as a second semi-independent branch of government.

The U.S. Congress operates through formal actions, such as committee hearings, debate, and legislative drafting, and informal means, such as discussions with constituents and other interested persons. Similarly, tribal councils operate through formal and informal methods. Many tribes schedule regular tribal council meetings to discuss current issues facing the tribe. These meetings are usually open to the public. Tribal councils will often call special meetings to address specific issues.

Most formal tribal council actions are taken through the adoption of tribal council resolutions. Tribal councils also take action through the adoption of formal ordinances or laws. Sometimes, a tribal council acts through voice vote or by way of consensus, which is then noted in the minutes to the meeting.

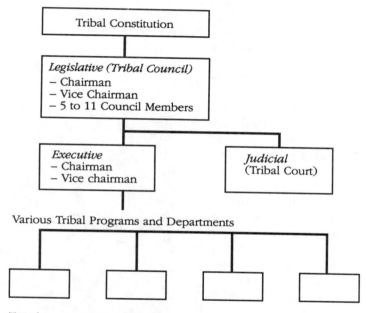

Typical organization of a Tribal Government.

A typical IRA tribal constitution includes:

- A legislative body usually called a tribal council
- A chairman and vice chairman of the tribal council
- A chairman and vice chairman who serve as the executive branch of government in charge of tribal administration, including all departments and programs
- A tribal judiciary or tribal court system which is usually established through enactments of the tribal council.

In 1883, the U.S. government established the Courts of Indian Offenses governed by federal rules and regulations. U.S. Indian agents appointed the judges. Despite the passage of the IRA in 1934, the BIA was reluctant to encourage tribes to establish their own tribal courts. Today, however, most tribes have established their own tribal courts which follow tribal laws and customs.

Most tribal governments operate a tribal court system which can vary from highly formalized courts modeled after Anglo-American courts to less formal bodies designed for informal dispute resolution. Some tribal courts use a mix of both Western and traditional dispute resolution techniques.

A typical tribal court is established through a tribal ordinance or code. The code will determine the jurisdiction of the courts, the number of courts, the number of judges, their term of office, and the procedures for removing judges. Many tribal courts include a tribal prosecutor and defense advocates for criminal matters. Most tribal court judges are not lawyers but do undergo some judicial training.

Most tribal courts consist of a trial-level court, called the tribal court, and a court of appeals, which is seldom used. Some tribes have an appellate court called a supreme court.

A wide variation of tribal court systems exists. For example, in some New Mexico Pueblos, the governing body serves as the tribal court. In other tribes, the tribal council will serve as the tribal court of appeals. Some tribes establish specialty courts to hear juvenile matters or probate matters.

The predominate type of case in a typical tribal court is a criminal misdemeanor action. Tribal courts also handle other serious criminal actions, although the most serious criminal actions are handled in federal court pursuant to the Major Crimes Act (18 U.S.C. 1153) which includes murder, manslaughter, kidnapping, maiming, sexual abuse, incest, assault with intent to commit murder, assault with a dangerous weapon, assault resulting in serious bodily injury, arson, burglary, robbery, and felony theft.

The Major Crimes Act stands as an intrusion into tribal sovereignty in that federal courts have jurisdiction over major crimes committed by Indians in Indian country. Some tribes continue to prosecute major crimes because of lax federal enforcement of major crimes on Indian reservations. The tribes will prosecute these actions under tribal law. However,

Chief Peggy Big Eagle sworn in by Judge Connie Hart in the Cheyenne–Arapaho tribal court. Photograph by Clifford Whiteman.

Graffiti supporting removal of Bureau of Indian Affairs supervision over internal tribal matters of the Havasupai Tribe, Arizona in 1991. Photograph by Cate Gilles.

tribes do not have criminal jurisdiction over non-Indians.

Tribal courts also handle a wide range of civil matters, and the use of the tribal court to settle civil disputes is increasing. Civil matters include marriages, divorces, child custody disputes, actions between tribal members, and actions between tribal members and non-tribal members.

TRIBAL GOVERNMENT REFORM

Many tribal governments operate under an array of complicated systems. These systems often include informal personal procedures and formal impersonal procedures for dealing with problems.

IRA constitutions have imposed a foreign system on many tribes and most tribes have experienced difficulties operating under their old IRA constitutions. Some tribes have ignored these IRA-imposed systems for a more effective and practical means of dealing with problems or have revised their tribal constitutions to implement governmental reform.

Limited Tribal Sovereignty

Tribal governments today exercise limited sovereignty. Below are examples of areas where tribal sovereignty has been limited.

Power to carry on relations with other nations	Prohibited by federal law.
Disposition and use of tribal lands	Federal sale, transfer, use and zoning restrictions apply to tribal lands.
Major Crimes Act	Federal Courts have jurisdiction over major crimes committed in Indian country.
Tribal Criminal Jurisdiction over Non-Indians	U.S. Supreme Court decision eliminates tribal criminal jurisdiction over non-Indians.

Taxes	Case law and state pressure force some tribes to collect taxes on sales of products to non-tribal members.
Gaming	Federal law requires tribes to enter into a tribal–state compact before conducting certain gaming operations.
Indian Civil Rights Act	Federal act applies certain civil rights to Indian tribes.
Sales of Alcohol	Limited by federal law.
Hunting and Fishing rights	Federal law limits these rights under certain circumstances.
Power to freely change the form of the Tribal government	Federal BIA approval needed for all IRA tribes.

In December 1991, the Havasupai Tribe of Arizona adopted ten amendments to their tribal constitution. The first seven amendments removed the federal government (BIA) from the internal affairs of the tribe. The next two amendments expanded tribal jurisdiction to the fullest extent allowed under law. The last amendment banned uranium mining on the reservation.

In early 1992, the Yavapai-Apache Tribe of Arizona completely reformed its tribal government with the adoption of a new tribal constitution. The new form of government marked an historic turning point for the tribe by guaranteeing greater independence and more freedom from BIA control. The old constitution had unclear election laws, no mention of the tribe's sovereign rights, and required BIA approval for many tribal actions. The new constitution revised the election laws, set up a new tribal court system, removed BIA control over internal tribal matters, and clearly established the tribe's inherent sovereign rights and powers. The new constitution was adopted by a 94 percent approval rate of those who voted.

Many tribes today are seeking to reform their governments to gain greater freedom and automony. A strong tribal government provides a more effective means to address critical issues which may face the tribe in the future.

Languages

Although English is the common language spoken by Indians in the United States—some native people in the Southwest speak Spanish and some in the Northeast speak French—Indian languages survive. In 1492, an estimated 500 or more native languages were spoken; today, some 200 languages are spoken in the United States and Canada. These languages have complex systems of grammar and pronunciation and vocabularies with thousands of words. It is reported, for example, that in the Ahtna Athabascan language, the verb theme "to go" has been calculated to have over 500,000 forms. Besides the Athabascan language, other Indian language families north of Mexico, none of which derive from Indo-European languages, are called Eskimo-Aleut, Algonquian, Muskogean, Siouan, Iroquoian, Caddoan, Yuman, Penutian, Tanoan, Keresan, Salishan, Uto-Aztecan, and Zuni. Some of the languages are related and belong to language families, but this does not guarantee that speakers within language families understand one another. Dialects spoken for thousands of years by Natives Americans diverged and evolved into languages of their own. Navajos of Arizona and Tlingits of Alaska, who both speak an Athabascan language, do not automatically understand one another.

Traditionally, these languages passed orally from generation to generation. Later, missionaries among others captured on paper the sounds they heard native people speak. Jesuit missionary Jean de Brebeuf who lived among Huron people in Canada until his death in 1649, compiled a dictionary and grammar of their language. Christian Le Clerq, Recollet missionary to the Micmacs from 1675 to 1686 developed a system of ideographs, or figurative letters, for their language that is still used today. In 1821, Sequoyah, a Cherokee from the Cherokee town of Tuskegee, Tennessee, known to Americans as George Guess, was inspired by the "talking leaves" of the English and devised a written language for his people. His eighty-six–character (actually eighty-five characters as one is not currently used) syllabary or alphabet permitted him to capture all the sounds of the Cherokee language on paper. In a little over a year, thousands of Cherokee were reading and writing their own language. In 1828, the Cherokees published a newspaper, *Cherokee Phoenix*, in their own language and in English. (The syllabary, still used by thousands of Cherokee speakers, shows up today in comic books, on voting ballots, and on computer screens. Charles West, a Cherokee who taught the language in Indianapolis, and Morgan Fraley, a computer programmer, developed a computer program that prints the Cherokee syllabary.)

When Europeans arrived in what is now the United States, the Indians had names, in their own languages, for their tribes and for rivers and mountains, trees, the animals and plants, and their towns and villages. Many of the settlers who moved from Europe found these names too difficult to pronounce or misunderstood the Indian pronunciation. In time, the original Indian personal, tribal, and place names were replaced by names chosen by Spanish, German, Dutch, French, English, and other newcomers.

The names by which most Indian tribes are commonly known today are not usually those applied by the tribes to themselves. During the twentieth century, some tribes, in order to restore tribal identity, have cast off names given to them by the French, Spanish, and Americans or thrown out nicknames

CHEROKEE SYLLABARY

For twelve years, Sequoyah worked to create a writing system for his people. Eventually he captured on paper all the sounds of the Cherokee language in a set of 86 symbols that he either made up or copied and modified from English spelling books. At first his mysterious marks on pieces of bark caused people to think he was crazy or engaged in witchcraft. After he and his daughter demonstrated the value of the system in 1821 before the tribal council and onlookers, it took less than a year for the Cherokees to become literate. Today, Sequoyah's name and brilliant invention are honored throughout the world. A county seat in Oklahoma, a presidential yacht with the alternative spelling, Sequoia, businesses, a nuclear power plant near Chattanooga, Tennessee, and the giant redwood trees in California carry his name.

The *Cherokee Advocate* has this to say about Sequoyah's system:

"Cherokee letters painted or cut on the trees by the roadside, or fences, houses, and often on pieces of bark or board lying about the houses. The alphabet of George Guess has never been taught in schools. The people have learned it from one another; and that without books, or paper, or any of the common facilities for writing or teaching. They cut the letters, or drew them with a piece of coal, or with paint. Bark, trees, fences, the walls of houses, etc. answered the purpose of slates."

THE CHEROKEE ALPHABET

Cherokee syllabary created by Sequoyah, a Cherokee, in the early 1820s. Courtesy Bureau of American Ethnology.

given them by other tribes. In 1984, the tribe formerly called Papago changed its name to Tohono O'odham, or Desert People, in its traditional language. In 1992, the Navajo Nation President Peterson Zah sponsored a resolution to change the official name of the Navajo people from Navajo to "Dineh."

The resolution states: "The People are proud of the name they have for themselves, and the official adoption of the names 'Dineh' and 'Dineh Nation' would signify the pride of the Dineh in their culture, language, and traditions." Many Dakota or Lakota people prefer these traditional names to Sioux, a French corruption of a name given them by traditional Ojibwa tribal enemies. Some Wampanoags on Martha's Vineyard now call the island Noepe in their original Algonquian dialect, and some people, commonly called Chippewa or Ojibwa, prefer to be called Anishinabe, their own native name in Algonquian.

Ancient Indian names are still attached to some states, cities, towns, villages, counties, mountains, hills, rivers, lakes, bays, and other geographic features in this country, although the pronunciation has changed over the years. In 1990, the United States Board of Geographic Names declared these American Indian names "an important and integral part" of American cultural heritage. For Native Americans, ancient place names are not just labels on a map.

NATIVE-AMERICAN WORDS USED IN ENGLISH

Bayou—From the Choctaw (Muskogean) language; a sluggish stream forming the inlet or outlet of a lake or bay, or connecting two bodies of water or a branch of a river flowing through a delta.

Caribou—From the Micmac tongue; the common name of the American reindeer.

Catalpa—From the Creek (Muskogean) language meaning "winged head," any tree of the genus *Catalpa* belonging to the family Bignoniaceae.

Caucus—From several Algonquian languages; a public meeting of the voters of a ward of a city, town, or a representative district held for the nomination of a candidate for election, for the election of a political committee, or for delegates to a political convention.

Chipmunk—From an Algonquian language; the common name of the striped ground squirrel.

Hominy—From an Algonquian language; a dish prepared from Indian corn pounded or cracked and boiled.

Iglu or Igloo—From the Eskimo language; a snow house of the Inuit (Eskimo) people in Canada.

Kaiak (Kayak)—From the Eskimo language; a boat of the Inuit (Eskimo) of northeastern North America.

Klondike—From an Athabascan language; a corruption of the name of an Alaskan river meaning a rich strike, a fortune.

Maize—From the Arawak language; the word for Indian corn.

Moccasin—From an Algonquian language; the soft-skin shoe of the North American Indians.

Moose—From an Algonquian language; the common name of a species of large deer.

Pecan—From Algonquian language; a term for a hard-shelled nut.

Podunk—From an Algonquian language, meaning a neck or corner of land; a term applied to an imaginary place in burlesque writing or speaking.

Quahog—From Algonquian language; the name used in New England for the round or hard clam.

Succotash—From an Algonquian language, meaning "the grains are whole."

Squash—From an Algonquian language, meaning "vegetables eaten green."

Tipi—From the Siouan language; *ti* meaning "to dwell" and *pi* meaning "used for."

Toboggan—From an Algonquian language; a term meaning "what is used for dragging."

Wigwam—From an Algonquian language; a term meaning "a dwelling."

STATES WITH INDIAN NAMES

Hundreds of Indian place names persist today in the United States, including the names for these states:

Alabama—The word is from an Indian tribe of the Creek Confederacy originally called the Alabamas or Alibamons, who in turn gave the name to a river from which the state name was derived.

Alaska—The word is either from Eskimo word *al-akshak* meaning "peninsula" or Aleut word *Alaxsxaq* designating "their land"; also said to mean "great lands."

Arizona—Many authorites attribute the meaning to a word meaning arid zone or desert. Others claim the name is Aztec, from *arizuma* meaning "silver bearing." Still another version attributes the origin to the Tohono O'odham (Papago) Tribe of Arizona who named it from the locality in which they lived called Arizonac, meaning "site of the small springs" (lack of water). This place was near the present town of Nogales, and in the early 1700s, silver was discovered near here, which gives some credence to the Aztec word *arizuma*.

Arkansas—Origin is uncertain. Various spellings for the state name include Alkansia, Alkansas, and Akamsea. According to some, the word is of Algonquian origin. Other say that Arkansas is a French version of *Kansas*, a Sioux Indian name for "south wind people."

Connecticut—The word appears to be derived from the Indian word *Quonoktacut* (also *Quonecktacut*) interpreted by some to mean "river whose water is driven in waves by tides or winds." Other interpretations include "long river," "the long (without end) river," and "long river place."

Idaho—The origin of the word is uncertain, although some claim it to derive from an Indian word of unknown meaning while others claim the meaning "gem of the mountains." Some claim the word to be a Shoshone translation of *edah hoe*, meaning "light on the mountain." Also *ida* means "salmon" and *ho* means "tribe" or literally "eaters," hence, "salmon eaters."

Illinois—The word from the Illini Indian word means "men" or "warriors," supplemented by the French adjective ending *ois*.

Indiana—The word presumably comes from the fact that the land lying along the Ohio River was purchased from the Indians. Others claim it was named for the Indian tribes who settled in western Pennsylvania.

Iowa—The word comes from an Indian tribe called Ah-hee-oo-ba, meaning "sleepy ones" or "drowsy ones." They lived in the valley of the state's principal river, which they named for the tribe, and in turn, the name was applied to the state.

Kansas—The state was named for the Kansas or Kanza tribe of the Siouan language family whose name translates as "south wind people" or "wind people."

Kentucky—The origin and meaning are controversial. Pioneer George Rogers Clark claimed the name was derived from the Indian word *Kentake*, meaning "meadow land." The claim is also made that it stems from the Shawnee word meaning "at the head of a river," inasmuch as they used the Kentucky River in traveling throughout the area. It is also claimed that the word stems from the Wyandot word *Ken-tah-ten* meaning "land of tomorrow."

Massachusetts—The word comes from the Algonquian language and means "great-hill-small-place," possibly for the hills around Boston as seen from the bay.

Michigan—The word comes from the Algonquian word *Mishagamaw* meaning "bit lake" or "great water"; derived its name from the lake of the same name. It is also said to be from *Michi* meaning "great" and *gama* meaning "water."

Minnesota—The word comes from the Sioux word meaning "cloudy water" or "sky-tinted water"; derived its name from the river of the same name.

Mississippi—The word means "great river" or "gathering in of all the water," sometimes referred to as the "father of waters," indicating the Indians were aware of the immensity of the river.

Missouri—The word is from a tribal name denoting "muddy water" and named for the large river.

Nebraska—The Sioux word describes the river from which the state gets its name, meaning "shallow water" or "broad water." Also said to be an Otoe Indian word meaning "flat river," referring to the Platte River.

New Mexico—The word was used by the Mexicans to refer to the territory north and west of the Rio Grande in the sixteenth century. It may have been derived from the name of the Aztec war god Mixitli. Still another interpretation is that it means "habitation of the god of war."

North Dakota—The word comes from the Sioux name meaning "allies." *Allies* was used to signify the common name of the confederated Sioux tribes.

Ohio—The Iroquois Indian word means "beautiful river"; taken from the river of the same name.

Oklahoma—Believed to have been coined about 1866 by a Choctaw-speaking missionary; the Choctaw Indian word means "red people."

South Dakota—The word comes from the Sioux Indian name meaning "allies." *Allies* was used to signify the common name of the confederated Sioux tribes.

Tennessee—The word is of Cherokee origin from a tribe located at a village site called Tanasee (also spelled *Tennese*). The state is named for its principal river, which has been interpreted by some as meaning "bend in the river."

Texas—The word is generally accepted as an Indian word meaning "tejas" or "friends" or "allies."

Utah—The name is taken from the Ute Indians who inhabited the region, but origin of the word is unknown. Also, it is believed it is an Apache word meaning "one that is higher up" referring to the Ute Indians who lived higher in mountain country than the Navajo or Apache of the area.

Wisconsin—This word is believed to be an Indian name whose meaning is uncertain. The state was named after its principal river, which is said to mean "wild rushing channel" or "holes in the banks of the stream in which birds nest." It was spelled *Ouiconsin* and *Misconsing* by early chroniclers.

Wyoming—Authorities interpret this name as either "extensive plains" (from the Delaware or Lenni Lenape word *maugh-wau-wama*) or "mountains, with valleys alternating."

Navajos keep their Athabascan language alive on stores and schools on the reservation. Tse bit'a'i *Shopping Center and Middle School in Shiprock, Navajo Nation, New Mexico.* Tse bit'a'i *is the Navajo name for Shiprock Pinnacle near the town of Shiprock and translates into English as "rock with wings." Navajo tradition tells that this volcanic rock formation was once a giant bird. Anglo settlers thought the peak looked like a ship in sail hence its Anglo name "Shiprock." Photographs by Karen Warth.*

Dotting Indian lands from Alaska to Florida, place names are matters of cultural and tribal survival for Indian societies whose identities are rooted in land. The names symbolize the long-term relationship native people have had with the land. Some names describe places, serving as visual aids, to native travelers who rarely used maps. Other places are named for animals or tell what kind of activity went on at a place. In some instances, names have spiritual meanings, which Indians refuse to divulge.

Indian place names and over 2,000 common and scientific words derived from Indian languages of North and South America have made their way into the English language. People around the United States use native words when they speak about food (squash), the weather (hurricane), transportation (canoe), animals (coyote), and shoes (moccasin).

Virtually every Native American nation had its own language names for the divisions of the year called "moons" (equivalent to a month). The names of each moon, derived from the climate, budding, blooming, leafing, and fruiting of vegetation and the growth and activities of animals, birds, and fish,

varied from region to region according to environment and latitude. Today, various native groups use bilingual calendars—ancient moon names along side the names from the Gregorian calendar.

Many Indian languages were lost in the 1880s and early 1900s, when Indian children were forced to go to boarding schools run by the U.S. government. From December 14, 1886, when federal policy forbidding the use of any Indian language was announced, through the 1950s, federal policy destroyed or discouraged Indian languages in schools and public settings. In some federal boarding schools, children were beaten for using their own languages. The ban on Indian languages wiped out over 150 languages.

Ancient native languages continue to be spoken in many Indian, Inuit, and Aleut communities today despite destructive federal policies. While large tribes such as the Navajos of Arizona, New Mexico, and Utah and the Lakotas of South and North Dakota have retained their languages partly because of their size, small groups such as the Hualapai and Tohono O'odham of Arizona also have successfully retained their languages. On the Coushatta reservation in Louisiana and the Choctaw reservation in Mississippi, children enter school speaking their native languages exclusively. The Cherokee, Creek, Choctaw, Mohawk, Muckleshoot, Lummi, Sioux, Navajo, and other Indian nations produce dictionaries and school curricula in their native tongues. Dozens of counties and political districts print voting ballots in tribal languages. Radio stations broadcast programs in Navajo, Zuni, Lakota, and other native languages. In 1991, KYUK-AM (Yuk means "you" in Yupik), a public radio station serving fifty-two Yupik villages in southwest Alaska, received the Wassaja Award, the Native American Journalists Association's highest honor for journalistic excellence. The station provides up-to-date news in Yupik and English and other bilingual programs to 20,000 residents in Alaska's tundra region. Many of the tribal community colleges and some urban Indian schools give classes in native languages.

On some reservations during the 1980s, native people raced against the clock to videotape and tape record the few remaining elders speaking their unwritten languages. Linguists say dozens of languages are on the verge of extinction; languages such as Yuchi, spoken by fewer than fifty people; Mandan, spoken by six people in 1991; Osage, spoken by five in 1991; and Eyak spoken by three out of a population of twenty in 1991. On other reservations, quiet revivals of languages, once forbidden in schools, reflect the growing interest in native languages among native communities throughout the country. Chil-

NATIVE LANGUAGES: FORBIDDEN AND PROTECTED

The attitude toward the preservation of Native American languages has changed over time. Below are some provisions from instructions to Indian agents in 1886 and from the Native American Languages Act, passed in 1990.

December 14, 1886. Orders to Indian Agents from Commissioner of Indian Affairs. In all schools conducted by missionary organizations it is required that all instructions shall be given in the English language.

February 2, 1887. . . . The rule applies to all schools on Indian reservations, whether they be Government or mission schools. The instruction of the Indians in the vernacular is not only of no use to them, but is detrimental to the cause of their education and civilization, and no school will be permitted on the reservation in which the English language is not exclusively taught.

July 16, 1887. Your attention is called to the regulation of this office which forbids instruction in schools in any Indian language. . . . You are instructed to see that this rule is rigidly enforced in all schools upon the reservation under your charge.

THE NATIVE AMERICAN LANGUAGES ACT

October 30, 1990. (3) the traditional languages of Native Americans are an integral part of their cultures and identities and form the basic medium for the transmission, and thus survival, of Native American cultures, literatures, histories, religions, political institutions, and values.

(8) acts of suppression and extermination directed against Native American languages are in conflict with United States policy of self-determination for Native Americans.

(9) languages are the means of communication for the full range of human experiences and are critical to the survival of cultural and political integrity of any people.

TRADITIONAL NATIVE CALENDAR NAMES

In the past, virtually all native peoples measured their year in "moons," some of which came at almost the same time as the months in the Euro-american calendar used today. While some tribes reckoned twelve months, Algonquian tribes in New England counted thirteen. Among the Zuni, half the months were "nameless," the other half "named." The Creeks counted twelve-and-a-half moons to the year, adding a moon at the end of every second year, half counted in the preceding and half in the following year.

Every Indian group named each moon in tribal tongue with words that usually reflected seasonal changes, the major subsistence activity taking place that month, and the close relationship native people had to the land. Calendar names differed from region to region and even within geographic regions, depending on the native group's activities during each "moon."

About 1650, John Pynchon, who lived in what is now western Massachusetts, copied down the calendar used by the Algonquian Indians in that area. Pynchon noted that the Indians divided the year into thirteen *kesos*, or moons, and (unlike the English calendar which began in March) started the year with *Squanni kesos*, "the month when they set their corn," which corresponded to the English months of late April and early May. He wrote, "Papsapquoho and Lowatanassick, they say are both one. And then if they be reckoned both for one, they reckon but 12 months to the year as we do. And they make the year to begin with *Squanni kesos*." Pynchon reported the following as the Algonquian calendar:

1. *Suquanni Kesos*, part of April and part of May, when they set Indian corn.
2. *Moonesquanimock Kesos*, part of May and part of June, when the women weed their corn.
3. *Twowa Kesos*, part of June and part of July, when they hill Indian corn.
4. *Matterllawaw Kesos*, when squashes are ripe and Indian beans begin to be eatable.
5. *Micheenee Kesos*, when Indian corn is eatable.
6. *Pohquitaqunk Kesos*, the middle between harvest and eating Indian corn.
7. *Pepewarr*, because of white frost on the grass and ground.
8. *Quinne Kesos*, same as *Pepewarr*.
9. *Papsapquoho*, or about January 6.—*Lowatanassick*, so called because they account for it the middle of winter.
10. *Squochee Kesos*, because the sun has (not) strength to thaw.

NATIVE AMERICAN LANGUAGES IN U.S. MILITARY HISTORY

The U.S. government used Native American languages as codes during World War I and World War II. The Choctaw language played important roles in both wars, and the Comanche language was used in World War II. The Navajo language played a legendary role during World War II. Some 400 Navajo who served in the Marine's code talker program used a coded Navajo language to call in air strikes, direct troop movements, report enemy locations and transmit sensitive military information. (See NATIVE AMERICANS IN THE MILITARY for more information about the code talkers.)

11. *Wapicummilcum*, part of February and part of March, because the ice in the river is all gone.
12. *Namossack Kesos*, part of March and part of April, because of catching fish.

Today, many native peoples in the United States whose languages were banned in U.S. boarding schools have rejected English-only instruction for their children and insist on teaching native youngsters ancestral tribal languages to ensure continuation of cultural heritage, unity, and identification. Besides native language workbooks and computerized language instruction, traditional native calendar names posted in classrooms daily remind native children and young adults that their people had their own distinctive language names for months. "Navajo Calendar Flashcards" decorate Navajo classrooms at Rough Rock Demonstration School in Rough Rock, Arizona. The cards show June is *Ta'iishjaashcili* in Navajo or "early planting time"; October is *Ghaaji* or "dividing of the seasons." In 1981, the Minnesota Chippewa Tribe of Cass Lake, Minnesota, produced "Ojibwe Calendar Unit" to teach Ojibwe language names for the months of the year. September may be called *Manoominikegiizis* or "ricing moon," *Waatebagaa-giizi* or "leaves changing color moon," or *Moozo-giizis* or "Moose

month." At the Mohawk School in Hogansburg, New York, Mohawk teachers teach "January in Mohawk is *Tsiothokrko:wa*. It is hunting time and the coldest time of the year" or "May is *Onerahtohko:wa*. Buds on the trees turn into leaves and the blessing of seeds takes place before planting." The calendar of the Bacavi School in Hotevilla, Arizona, tells students that January is *Paamiyaw* or "Play Moon," the month for social dances, and July is *Nimanmuya* or "Going Home Moon," the end of Kachina dances for the year.

Other calendars produced by native groups provide daily doses of native language. The May 1992–April 1993 New England Native American Calendar authored by Narragansett Harold Champlin and published by the Algonquin Indian Arts and Culture Association in Providence, Rhode Island, faithfully reaffirms Algonquian New England native tradition by starting the year with "*Sequanankeeswuch*—Indian New Year, Late April to May, Corn Planting" and ending with "*Namassack Keeswush*—Time of Catching Fish." In the early 1980s, the masthead of the *Lac Courte Oreilles Journal*, now *News from Indian Country*, spelled out Lake Superior Ojibwe names for the months. *Min Gisiss* or "Blueberry Moon" corresponds to August, while *Gashkadino Gizis* or "Freezing Moon" corresponds to November.

dren at Isleta and Zuni Pueblo schools in New Mexico use computers to learn their languages. Children plug in disks that graphically teach them body parts, names of animals, numbers, and hundreds of other words.

In the late 1980s, a grassroots movement among Native Americans and Anglo educators and linguists

led to the passage of the Native American Language Act signed by President George Bush in October 1990. The act, officially recognizing the right of native languages to exist, states that it is U.S. policy to "preserve, protect, and promote the rights and freedom of Native Americans to use, practice, and develop Native American languages."

Education

Indian education is thousands of years old. Before Europeans established formal schools in the Americas, Indian education was an integral part of life that involved everyone in schooling the young children. Native Americans possess an incredible body of knowledge based on thousands of years of living in a spiritual relationship with the natural world. In the past, each new generation had to learn to make and use everything it needed to survive. The community had to know how to process and store food crops, anticipate the habits of prey animals, process meat and fish, make clothing, and defend itself. Each group was guided by spiritual beliefs that included an extension of moral considerations to animals and to elements of the landscape. Survival was based on a religious respect for the natural world and an understanding that humans are part of nature, not above it. This accumulated knowledge was not kept in books, but in the hearts and minds of the people.

Everyone had a stake in the education of the young, especially in the transmittal of the particular ethos of the group. Hopi children, for example, learned the "Hopi Way." Lakota children learned to see the world the way the Lakota saw it. Before the coming of Europeans, Indian education meant that Native Americans were assured of their continued existence as distinct peoples.

The first formal school for North American Indians was founded by Jesuit missionaries in 1568. From the beginning, Europeans saw education as a way to induce Indians to adopt their lifeways so they would disappear as distinct peoples. It was almost 400 years before there was serious official questioning of educational policies designed to force Indians to give up their culture. Euro-americans consistently

assumed that European-based culture was superior to the cultures of Native Americans. They saw little of value in Native American lifeways and tried to substitute Christianity and Euro-american culture for Native American cultures and religious expressions. The main tool for forced assimilation was education.

The colonies of Virginia, Plymouth, Massachusetts, Pennsylvania, and Connecticut justified their existence in large part on the basis of a professed desire to convert Indians. Dartmouth, Harvard and The College of William and Mary are among those schools that were founded for the education of Indian and English youths.

Although some Indians voluntarily sent their children to missionary schools, and a few converts were made, the efforts of missionaries in the colonial period were mostly ineffective. Early missionaries did not convert Indians in significant numbers, and they often earned the disdain of Indian leaders. In 1744, Benjamin Franklin reported that when the government of Virginia offered to educate six young Iroquois men at the Anglican College of William and Mary, the Iroquois replied:

> Several of our young people were formerly brought up at the Colleges of Northern Provinces; they were instructed in all your Sciences; but when they came back to us, they were bad Runners, ignorant of every means of living in the Woods; unable to bear either Cold or Hunger, knew neither how to build a Cabin, take a Deer, or kill an Enemy, spoke our Language imperfectly, were therefore neither fit for Hunters, Warriors, or Counselors; they were totally good for nothing. We are however not the less oblig'd by your kind Offer, tho' we decline accepting it; and, to

show our grateful Sense of it, if the Gentlemen of Virginia will send us a Dozen of their Sons, we will take great Care of their Education, instruct them in all we know, and make *Men* of them.

After the Revolutionary War, the newly established government began a continuing involvement in Indian education. In 1776, the Continental Congress appropriated funds for education of the Indians of New York and for the education of Indian students at Dartmouth. Some Indian leaders believed that it would be important for their children to learn the new ways, and in 1792, Chief Cornplanter of the Seneca asked George Washington to "send smiths among us, and, above all, that you will teach our children to read and write, and our women to spin and weave."

The dilemma faced by Seneca chiefs 200 years ago is still with us today. How can Native Americans survive and prosper in the non-Indian world without giving up their culture? It is important to note that the Seneca chiefs just quoted did not want to send

their children away to school. Chief Cornplanter desired education, but he asked the government to send teachers to the Seneca, where they would presumably have some oversight in the process and a continuing influence on their children. Native Americans want to take advantage of the opportunities that education brings, but not at the expense of losing their identity. This has been very difficult for non-Indians to understand. For a variety of reasons, the U.S. government has felt an obligation to educate the original owners of the land, but until recently, education was designed to be a form of cultural genocide.

The history of Indian education in the United States parallels the history of U.S. Indian policy as a whole. When the U.S. government was new, and as long as tribal nations had the balance of power, the fledgling U.S. government was eager to make treaties with the powerful Indian nations, and education of native children was often promised in return. This responsibility to educate Indians created an alliance of religious evangelists and the federal

RELIGIOUS SANCTION FOR TAKING LAND IN EXCHANGE FOR "SALVATION"

Not only did Europeans feel superior to Indians, they felt morally obliged by the precepts of their faith to convert all non-Christians and were given religious sanction to take their land. Land acquisition was tied to education by a European theological principle that originated to give religious blessings to conquest of the Holy Land, but was later extended to include the Americas. In 1455, Pope Nicholas V decreed that Catholic kings and princes were morally obliged to:

Invade, search out, capture, vanquish, and subdue all Saracens and pagans whatsoever, and other enemies of Christ wheresoever placed, and the kingdoms, dukedoms, principalities, dominions, possessions, and all movable and immovable goods whatsoever held and possessed by

them and to reduce their persons to perpetual slavery, and to apply and appropriate to himself and his successors the kingdoms, dukedoms, counties, principalities, dominions, possessions, and goods, and to convert them to his and their use and profit.

In the minds of many Europeans, conquering and enslaving non-Christians and expropriating their land was justified "for the defense and increase of the faith." This meant that Indians must be converted in order to legitimize the takeover. Explorers were closely followed by or accompanied by missionaries: Jesuits and Franciscans at first, followed by various Protestant denominations.

government. Both shared a goal—to "civilize and Christianize" Indians.

The first U.S.–Indian treaty to contain a provision for education was the 1794 treaty with the Oneida, Tuscarora, and Stockbridge. Eventually, Congress approved 118 treaties between Indian tribes and the United States in which Indians ceded over one billion acres of land. Ninety-five of the treaties specifically mentioned that Indian ownership of land would be exchanged for a variety of things, including education. Education still meant forced assimilation, and at the time, it was considered the humanitarian solution to the so-called Indian problem. In many ways, the Indian problem was that Indians still had much of the land and the whites wanted it. How to get it was debated in Congress. There seemed to be two choices, as the House Committee on Appropriations put it in 1818, "In the present state of our country one of two things seems to be necessary. Either that those sons of the forest should be moralized or exterminated."

At first, missionaries were funded by the federal government to do the moralizing. In 1819, Congress passed the Civilization Fund Act which appropriated $10,000 annually to various missionary groups to teach the "habits and arts of civilization" to Indians. The president was authorized to "employ capable persons of good moral character, to instruct them in the mode of agriculture suited to their situation; and for teaching their children in reading, writing, and arithmetic and performing such other duties as may be enjoined." The partnership of the federal government and missionaries was ended in 1917 by an act that mandated the separation of church and state.

In 1832, the Indian Office, part of the Department of War, became responsible for the government's relationship with Indians, including general supervision of the 32 schools for Indians operated by various religious denominations. Fifteen years later, there were 103 government schools of various types, including day schools and boarding schools on and off reservations. Most were manual labor schools, some were academies. In the Southeast, several tribes established their own schools.

By the 1840s, the Choctaw and Cherokee operated a common school system, which was better than that provided by many states for their non-Indian citizens. These tribes were forced westward in the 1830s and 1840s into Indian Territory, where they re-established their schools. In 1898, the Curtis Act, which abolished tribal governments in Indian Territory, closed these schools. With their closing, Indian control of education for their children was lost. It has taken over sixty years to once again regain some measure of control over education.

Since Indian land was often exchanged for services that included education, the U.S. government began to fulfill treaty obligations by establishing schools and appropriating money to build, staff, and run them. Indian tribes also contributed directly (with money) and indirectly (with land) to the education of their children. Indian land was often exchanged for a combination of money and services. Some of the money from land sales was applied to education, which eventually became compulsory, and over which Indian people had no say. In 1855, Commissioner of Indian Affairs George Manypenny reported the following accounting of money spent for Indian education in a ten-year period from 1845 to 1855:

U.S. government	$102,107.14
Indian treaty funds	$824,160.61
Indian tribes	over $400,000.00
Private donations	$830,000.00

In the post-Civil War era, there was a renewed demand for land and for an end to the "Indian problem." The government stepped up its involvement in Indian education and began military campaigns in the Plains to subdue the last independent tribes and force them onto reservations, opening up the land for white prospectors, entrepreneurs, and farmers. In 1870, $100,000 was appropriated for schools, and by 1877, the Indian commissioner proposed that education be compulsory. During this time there was considerable animosity toward Indians as a result of the struggle to force the Plains tribes off of their land. The Custer defeat was fresh in people's minds, and appropriations for Indians who were forced into dependency on reservations were frequently cut, resulting in malnourishment and sickness on the reservations and equally poor conditions in government reservation schools.

In the last decades of the nineteenth century, the policy of the government was to dispose of the Indian problem by destroying tribal organizations and dispersing what was left of Indian land through allotments to individuals of tribally held communal property. During this time, while the Indian population was at its lowest point, and the U.S. government was now stronger than tribal nations, Congress passed a law forbidding the making of further treaties with Indian nations. Indian children were held virtual hostages in boarding schools against the good behavior of their parents. At the schools, they were taught that traditional ways were wrong, that they must forget their Indian heritage and become copies of white Americans.

As Commissioner of Indian Affairs J. D. C. Atkins put it in 1887, "The first step to be taken toward civilization, toward teaching the Indians the mischief and folly of continuing in their barbarous practices, is to teach them the English language." In the annual report for 1889, Indian Affairs Commissioner Thomas Morgan explained that the government's Indian education policy was that

Education should seek the disintegration of the tribes, and not their segregation. They should be educated, not as Indians, but as Americans. In short, the public school should do for them what it is so successfully doing for all the other races in this county, assimilate them. . . . In all proper ways, teachers in the Indian schools should endeavor to appeal to the highest elements of manhood and womanhood in their pupils, exciting in them an ambition after excellence in character and dignity of surroundings, and they should carefully avoid any unnecessary reference to the fact that they are Indians.

In 1878, the Carlisle Indian Industrial School was established in a closed army installation in Carlisle, Pennsylvania. It was an experiment to test the feasibility of educating Indians in boarding schools located far from tribal and parental influence. The idea was not new; boarding schools for Indian students had been proposed a century earlier by Reverend Eleazer Wheelock, a missionary who thought that if children were removed from their parents and homes and sent to schools far away, it would be easier to force them to abandon their culture.

Lieutenant Richard Henry Pratt, a former Indian fighter and founder of Carlisle, took this idea a step further. He began a practice called "outing," in which students were not allowed to return home for vacations, but were placed as servants with white families. He hoped that the students would adopt the language, religion, and values of the families in which they were placed. The Indian problem would be solved by making Indians disappear, and Carlisle became the model for future federal boarding schools for Indians.

In 1882, the government authorized using abandoned military forts and stockades for schools and the use of military officers as teachers. By 1885, there were 177 government schools spread across the country from Carlisle, Pennsylvania, to Parker, Arizona. Many of the school buildings were overcrowded and unsuitable for education, the teachers were often poorly trained (some were military men, fresh from the Indian wars), and there was a lack of instructional material.

At the schools, the students typically wore military uniforms, marched to class, were forbidden to speak their native languages, and attended mandatory Christian services. The schools were often underfunded and were supported in part by the work of the children. The boys worked cleaning, constructing buildings, planting and harvesting food crops, caring for farm animals, digging wells, quarrying stones, and making shoes, boots, and wagons. The girls were responsible for sewing, repairing, washing, and ironing clothing; cooking; and cleaning for the whole school. These chores were in addition to their school work. In fact, students spent more hours working every day than they spent learning in the classroom.

By the last decade of the nineteenth century, the remaining tribes of the Plains were confined to reser-

Young boys learning the "white man's way" at Riverside Indian Boarding School in Oklahoma. Although the students were supposed to learn to read and write, they spent more hours working around the school than they did learning in the classroom. Courtesy of the Western History Collections, University of Oklahoma Library.

vations, disarmed, forbidden to hunt, and issued government rations for food. In 1893, an act was passed authorizing the withholding of food rations from parents who kept their children from school. Indian children were captured by Indian agents and put into schools. Little wonder that Indian parents hid their children to keep them from the schools. Some children repeatedly ran away, some died from diseases while at school and were buried in the schools' graveyards, and some committed suicide.

In spite of the hardships and demoralizing aspects of Indian education, there were Indian graduates of the boarding schools who prospered from the experience at school, and some spent their lives working for Indian people. Other graduates joined white society, never quite belonging there and no longer able to fit in with their own people. "We leave confused and bewildered," said the Sioux medicine man John Lame Deer of school experience, "When we enter the schools we at least know we are Indian. We come out half red and half white."

By 1913, the government was operating 233 Indian day schools on reservations, 76 boarding schools on reservations, and 35 boarding schools off reservations. Of an estimated 65,000 school age Indian children, government schools cared for 25,000; mission and public schools were serving 22,500, and 17,500 children received no schooling.

In 1916, a uniform course of study for all federal Indian schools was implemented that was based on courses offered for non-Indians by the various states, as well as from suggestions "from every source from which it was thought practical suggestions could be gotten," except of course, from Indians.

On the whole, the various types of schools were unsuccessful in their goal of making Indians disappear into the mainstream. Official reports of the Indian Bureau record a litany of failure. In 1897, the superintendent of Indian schools reported that students "return to their respective reservations merely to relapse into so-called Indian savagism, in most cases, even an aggravated form." In 1916, the com-

DR. HENRY ROE CLOUD AND ELIZABETH BENDER ROE CLOUD

Henry Roe Cloud, a Winnebago who attended the Indian school in Genoa, Nebraska, graduated from Yale in 1910 and spent the rest of his life working for Indian people. He founded a college prep school for Indians in 1915, when the government schools were offering vocational training. Dr. Roe Cloud was the only Indian member of the staff of the Institute for Government Research (now the Brookings Institu-

tion), and in 1933 he became the first Indian president of Haskell Institute, a government school for Indians in Lawrence, Kansas. His wife, Elizabeth Bender Roe Cloud graduated from Hampton Institute, the University of Wichita, and the University of Kansas. She assisted her husband and was an active member of the National Congress of American Indians and the Society of American Indians.

missioner of Indian affairs described a "chasm, often impassable, between the completion of a course in school and the selection of a vocation in life."

In 1928, the Institute for Government Research released a report, *The Problem of Indian Administration*, which was highly critical of the Indian educational system. The *Meriam Report*, as it was popularly known, was the basis for much needed reform in Indian education. The report revealed shocking conditions in the boarding schools, including severe overcrowding and grossly inadequate student care.

The *Meriam Report* uncovered the fact that the schools were partly supported by the labor of the children and that the teachers were often poorly trained. Although the *Meriam Report* suggested that teachers try to fit curriculum and instruction to the needs of the children, the report affirmed that the ultimate goal was to assimilate the students.

During the term of John Collier as Indian Affairs commissioner (1933–1945), there were reforms in government Indian policy, and Collier planted the seeds of progressive reform in Indian education. He

Students outside a school near the Potawatomi reservation in Kansas. Around 1899, when this picture was taken, the children were rounded up by Indian agents and sent to school, where they were forbidden to acknowledge their heritage. Note the expressions on the children's faces. Courtesy M. K. de Montaño.

instituted bilingual education and teacher training in Indian culture. He began to replace boarding schools with day schools, until the Second World War intervened. Some of the politicians and bureaucrats of the day disagreed with Collier's ideas, and in 1945, he resigned over differences in the direction of Indian policy.

With Collier gone, there was a backlash in the 1950s. Termination ended federal responsibility and jurisdiction over several tribal nations. Relocation encouraged Indian families to move away from reservations and relocate in cities. The small gains Collier made in officially recognizing that Indian cultures had value in their own right were for a time halted by the renewed assimilationist climate in government. During this time, Indians came to be the most poorly educated people in the nation.

Beginning in the 1960s, educators began to explore the "cultural-difference hypothesis" that suggested that poor academic achievement of minority students was related to differences between the students' culture and the culture of the classroom. In 1969, the Senate report, *Indian Education: A National Tragedy—A National Challenge*, concluded that "our national policies for educating American

Indians are a failure of major proportions." The committee found, among other things, that

> the average educational level for all Indians under Federal supervision is 5 school years . . . dropout rates for Indians are twice the national average. . . . Only 18 percent of the students in Federal Indian schools go on to college. . . . Only 3 percent of Indian students who enroll in college graduate; the national average is 32 percent.

While the committee made many recommendations, one concept was reiterated throughout: "Increased Indian participation and control of their own education programs" was now an officially recognized goal. "For far too long," the committee noted, "the Nation has paid only token heed to the notion that Indians should have a strong voice in their own destiny."

In the next decade, several laws were passed that began to lay the groundwork for parental and community involvement in Indian education. It did not happen rapidly or completely, nor did it happen without a struggle, but the Bilingual Education Act of 1968, the Indian Education Act of 1972, the Indian Self-Determination and Education Assistance

1972 INDIAN EDUCATION ACT

The most significant legislation affecting Indian education is the Indian Education Act of June 23, 1972, which recognized that Indian students have special educational needs and provided financial assistance to meet those needs. The act also mandated parental and community involvement in educational programs funded by the act. It created the Office of Indian Education and the National Advisory Council on Indian Education (NACIE).

NACIE is composed of fifteen American Indian and Alaska Natives appointed by the president from nominees submitted by Indian tribes and organizations.

NACIE was set up to review applications for grants under the new act and

> to advise the Secretary of Education with respect to the administration of any program in which Indian children and adults participate or from which they can benefit, and the duty to submit to the Congress each year an annual report, including any recommendations necessary for the improvement of federal education programs in which Indian children and adults participate or from which they can benefit.

Act of 1975, and the Education Amendments Act of 1978 began to give Indian parents control over money spent for the education of their children and an opportunity for Indian communities to be involved in the development of their own educational programs.

Since the 1960s, Indian communities have had a growing voice in and control over the education of their people. The BIA began to establish Indian advisory boards for its schools and to contract with tribal entities for tribal schools. In 1966, the Navajo Nation created Rough Rock Demonstration School, a highly successful Indian-controlled elementary school located on the Navajo reservation. It has an all-Indian school board, classes in Navajo and English, and curriculum that was developed by the community. The Navajo also established the first tribally controlled college, Navajo Community College, in Tsaile, Arizona. Other schools followed, and today, there are seventy-five elementary and secondary schools controlled by tribes or tribal organizations, and twenty-four tribally controlled colleges funded through the BIA. The BIA operates ninety-one elementary and secondary schools and two postsecondary schools.

In 1990, the Office of Indian Education funded 1,153 programs in forty-two states, serving the special educational and culturally related academic needs of over 354,000 elementary and secondary Indian students. The programs offer tutoring, Indian history and culture, counseling, and home-school liaison. The BIA educational programs serve approximately 10 percent of the total K–12 Indian student population attending U.S. schools. The remaining 90 percent of Indian students are served by either public or private schools.

Despite the gains in Indian control since the 1960s, it is not enough to offset four centuries of domination and paternalism. The Indian Nations At Risk Task Force, which was chartered on March 8, 1990, to study the status of native education, reported that

> the existing educational systems, whether they be public or federal, have not effectively met the educational, cultural, economic, and social needs of Native communities. . . . If Native cultures remain important today, as many Native political and educational leaders believe they do, they must again become a part of the educational process. Tribal groups must develop educational structures built on their cultural priorities and foster continued development and growth. Schools must do their part in supporting this movement.

Today, many Indian students are in public schools, which for the most part have remained unresponsive and unable to address their needs. In most public schools Indian educational programs are chronically underfunded; there are few Indian teachers and little parent involvement; the curriculum lacks a native viewpoint; and non-Indian teachers do not have an orientation toward Indian students.

Indian children are at a disadvantage when teachers do not understand cultural differences. Learning styles are affected by a person's culture. Indian children have traditionally been taught first by watching and then doing. Children are expected to be attentive and to have good observational skills. It is not surprising that studies suggest that Indian children have a strong visual approach to learning. The visual approach is at odds with a schoolroom environment that stresses learning through listening, reading, and writing.

Indian children often do not attempt an activity until they feel they can accomplish it, while non-Indian children often learn by repeated attempts, until they get it right. "If at first you don't succeed, try, try again" is contrary to an Indian philosophy of learning. This may explain why many Indian children are uncomfortable when asked to perform publicly before a skill is mastered.

Indian values affect the learning environment as well. The traditional Native American stress on a strong sense of community and on co-operative effort is at odds with the stress in non-Indian culture on individualism and competition. Indian children are often unwilling to show competence in the classroom when they feel that to do so would put them in competition with their fellow students. Indian

ROUGH ROCK DEMONSTRATION SCHOOL

In 1964, Navajo leaders presented a proposal to the Office of Economic Opportunity to fund a demonstration project on the Navajo reservation. The leaders were concerned about the unique needs of Navajo students that were unmet by the present schools. The community leaders organized an all-Navajo nonprofit organization, DINE (Demonstration in Navajo Education) to receive funds for the school project. The BIA turned over to DINE a new $3 million school, the Navajos hired their own teachers, and Rough Rock Demonstration School was born the first school to operate under a contract from the BIA. It has become a well-known example of the wisdom of local control and involvement. The school received more than 12,000 visitors during its first year and a half and has become a model of effective teaching and community involvement for countless schools.

The people of Rough Rock, a remote and very traditional community on the reservation, control the school. DINE receives the funds and the all-Navajo school board and the board of directors establish the policies and create programs. Parents from the community work in the dormitories as foster parents on a rotating basis. Navajo culture is an integral and significant part of the school program. Children are taught in Navajo and English.

"A lot of us are uneducated and couldn't work here if this were a BIA school," explained Ada Singer, a member of the original school board. "I am glad our children are learning to read and write English, but I'm also very glad they're learning about the Navajo culture and the Navajo way. We want our children to be proud they are Navajos and this is what our school is doing." Robert A. Roessel, Jr. explains the significance of the school in the foreword of his book, *Navajo Education in Action: Rough Rock Demonstration School.*

The heart (of the Rough Rock Demonstration School) lies in the involvement of Indian parents and the leadership of the all-Navajo school board. That is the most significant area in which the demonstration school is pioneering. Certainly, extra funds have had a considerable impact on pupil achievement, student attitudes and community participation, but the kind of leadership which the school board has displayed . . . is the type which can be acquired only through a change in attitude and not merely through increased funds.

A kindergarten song and dance group from the Rough Rock Demonstration School on the Navajo reservation, Arizona in the 1970s. The school is controlled by an all Navajo school board and students are taught about their own culture as well as the "three Rs." Note how happy the children seem in contrast to turn of the century photos of Indian children in boarding schools. Courtesy of the Rough Rock Demonstration School Board.

CORNEL PEWEWARDY AND THE INDIAN MAGNET SCHOOL IN MINNEAPOLIS

Dr. Cornel Pewewardy, a thirty-nine-year-old Comanche-Kiowa from Oklahoma was named National Indian Educator of the Year by the National Indian Education Association in October 1991. Dr. Pewewardy earned a D.Ed. (Doctor of Education) degree in Educational Administration from Pennsylvania State University. He is the principal of the new American Indian Magnet School, a public elementary school in St. Paul, Minnesota.

The school houses two programs, the World Cultures and Language Magnet and the American Indian Magnet School, which complement each other with an emphasis on multicultural education. The school, from the architecture to the curriculum, is based on Native American philosophy. This school is unique in that while most of the students are Native American, it is a public school open to all.

The teachers have to be familiar with Indian culture and have the "knowledge base that will trigger a culturally relevant curriculum," explains Dr. Pewewardy. Students receive a solid foundation of basic skills "coupled with an environment surrounded by Native American culture." The expectation is that this will enhance the self-esteem of the students.

Teachers use a holistic approach, but at the same time, high technology is seen as an important tool for cultural preservation. Elders and other resource per-

Dr. Cornell Pewewardy, principal of the Minneapolis American Indian Magnet School. Dr. Pewewardy, a Comanche-Kiowa from Oklahoma, was named Teacher of the Year in 1991 by the National Indian Education Association. Photograph by Dale Kakkak.

sons are brought into the classroom either in person or, eventually, through satellite link-up with distant reservations.

students often feel more at ease in co-operative, rather than in competitive, situations. The Native American cultural bias toward co-operation places some students at a disadvantage in competitive classroom situations.

There is a growing cadre of professional Native American educators dedicated to improving the education of Indian children. The National Indian Education Association (NIEA) was founded in 1969 to help American Indian and Alaska Native students

keep traditional tribal values while learning to be productive citizens. Dedicated to excellence through the promotion of quality education for all American Indian/Alaska Native people, the NIEA protects and maintains traditional cultures and values while advocating for quality Indian education. The NIEA has an annual national conference and a national newsletter. NIEA lobbyists work closely with Congress and the executive branch. They also function as a clearinghouse for information and provide technical assistance and professional development for Indian educators.

Since colonial times, a few Native Americans have been educated in colleges and universities, but there has been little emphasis on higher education until recently. During the period from 1870 to 1920, when federal support for educating Indian children was growing, there were no provisions for support of postsecondary education. In 1932, it is estimated that only fifty-two Indians graduated from college, and only five colleges offered scholarships for Indian students.

In the aftermath of the *Meriam Report*, some attention was directed at the problem, and in 1934, the Indian Reorganization Act authorized a $250,000 loan fund for higher education. After World War II, the GI Bill allowed Indian veterans the opportunity to attend colleges and universities, and in 1969, the BIA allocated $3 million for scholarships. During the 1960s, the BIA began to emphasize academic education instead of vocational training in its schools. In 1970, two postsecondary BIA schools were established: Haskell Institute became Haskell Indian Junior College and the Institute of American Indian Art became a two-year college.

The social activism and consciousness raising of the 1960s had a profound effect on Indian education. The American Indian Movement was founded, and mainstream universities added Native American Studies to their offerings. Native American leaders were no longer willing to accept an education that meant giving up Indian identity or to be satisfied with white-conceived and operated Native American programs. The passage of Title III of the Education Act of 1965 and the Indian Self-Determination and Assistance Act of 1975 (PL 93-638) provided funds to help in the development of postsecondary educational institutions for, not just about, Native Americans. The Indian Education Act of 1972 helped train Native Americans by providing scholarships for Indian students in the fields of medicine, law, education, engineering, forestry, and business.

In 1968, the first college controlled by Native Americans was established on the Navajo reserva-

tion. In the next ten years, Navajo Community College was followed by fifteen tribally controlled colleges on or near reservations. Today there are twenty-four Indian controlled colleges. The Bureau of Indian Affairs operates two postsecondary educational institutions: Haskell Indian Junior College and Southwestern Indian Polytechnic. Today there are almost 100,000 Native American/Alaska Native students in higher education.

Indian education has meant different things to different people. Once, it meant the ways Native American communities passed their cumulative knowledge to the coming generations. For many years since the arrival of Europeans, Indian education has meant forced change. Today, for Native American educators, according to the 1976 report by the National Advisory Council on Indian Education (NACIE), Indian education means

> A method of teaching that recognizes the educational needs of Indian people as unique and offers a challenge to the educators and policy makers to redress the present inadequacy in meeting those needs. . . . A method of teaching that revives an appreciation for Indian heritage and generates a positive self-image . . . educational policies should respect the wishes and the desires of the Indian people to design and manage their own educational programs . . . (they should have) full involvement of Indian parents and community members . . . (and) include the method and content of teachings which are designed and developed by Indian educators and Indian people reflecting Indian concepts and cultural values . . . (Indian education) is necessary because conventional education puts the Indian child at a disadvantage so far as learning is concerned . . . Indian concepts about humanity adds to the more conventional emphasis on technical learning skills by putting equal emphasis on universal harmony and creates a basis for deeper appreciation for life and the universe in a spiritual context. . . . Creates in a child a positive outlook for learning new skills and knowledge . . . to develop the intrinsic values of an individual so that one's ability is balanced with one's appreciation and understanding.

It has taken a long time to educate the Euro-Americans.

INDIAN-CONTROLLED POSTSECONDARY SCHOOLS

Arizona

Navajo Community College
Tsaile Rural Post Office
Tsaile, Arizona 86556
(602) 724-3311

California

D-Q University
Post Office Box 409
Davis, California 95617
(916) 758-0470

Michigan

Bay Mills Community College
Route 1, Box 315 A
Bromley, Michigan 49715
(906) 248-3354

Minnesota

Fond du Lac Community College
302 14th Street
Cloquet, Minnesota 55720
(218) 879-0880

Montana

Blackfeet Community College
Post Office Box 819
Browning, Montana 56417
(406) 338-5441

Dull Knife Memorial College
Post Office Box 98
Lame Deer, Montana 59043
(406) 477-6215

Fort Belknap Community College
Post Office Box 159
Harlem, Montana 59526
(406) 353-2607

Fort Peck Community College
Post Office Box 398
Popular, Montana 59255-0398
(406) 768-5552

Little Big Horn College
Post Office Box 370
Crow Agency, Montana 59022
(406) 638-2228

Salish Kootenai College
Post Office Box 117
Pablo, Montana 59855
(406) 675-4800

Stone Child Community College
Rocky Boy Route 1082
Box Elder, Montana 59521
(406) 395-4313

Nebraska

Nebraska Indian Community College
Post Office Box 752
Winnebago, Nebraska 68071
(402) 878-2414

New Mexico

Crownpoint Institute of Technology
Post Office Box 849
Crownpoint, New Mexico 87313
(505) 786-5851

North Dakota

Fort Berthold Community College
Post Office Box 490
New Town, North Dakota 58763
(701) 627-3665

Little Hoop Community College
Post Office Box 269
Fort Totten, North Dakota 58335
(701) 766-4415

(continued)

INDIAN-CONTROLLED POSTSECONDARY SCHOOLS (*cont.*)

Standing Rock College
HC 1, Box 4
Fort Yates, North Dakota 58538
(701) 854-3861

Turtle Mountain Community College
Post Office Box 340
Belcourt, North Dakota 58316
(701) 477-5605

United Tribes Technical College
3315 University Drive
Bismarck, North Dakota 58501
(701) 255-3285

South Dakota
Cheyenne River Community College
Post Office Box 220
Eagle Butte, South Dakota 57625
(605) 964-8635

Oglala Lakota College
Post Office Box 490
Kyle, South Dakota 57752
(605) 455-2321

Sint'e Gleska University
Post Office Box 490
Rosebud, South Dakota 57570
(605) 747-2263

Sisseton Wahpeton Community College
Old Agency, Post Office Box 689
Sisseton, South Dakota 57262
(605) 689-3966

Washington
Northwest Indian College
2522 Kwina Road
Bellingham, Washington 98226
(206) 676-2772

Wisconsin
Lac Courte Oreilles Ojibwa Community College
Rural Route 2, Box 2357
Hayward, Wisconsin 54843
(715) 634-4790

Source: Tribal College Magazine

BUREAU OF INDIAN AFFAIRS POSTSECONDARY SCHOOLS

Southwestern Indian Polytechnic Institute
Post Office Box 10146
9169 Coors Road NW
Albuquerque, New Mexico 87184
(505) 897-5347

Haskell Indian Junior College
155 Indian Avenue, #1305
Lawrence, Kansas 66046-4800
(913) 749-8403

STATISTICS IN ELEMENTARY AND SECONDARY EDUCATION, 1990

Native American/Alaska Native
   students in public schools   333,494

Native American/Alaska Native students
   in National Catholic Educational
    Association schools   9,743
Native American/Alaska Native
   students in BIA schools   39,791

• Native American/Alaska Natives make up approximately one percent of the total public school enrollment in the nation.

• The BIA serves approximately 10 percent of the total enrolled students.

• Approximately 50 percent of Native American/ Alaska Native students live on reservations and attend public schools.

EDUCATION ORGANIZATIONS AND PROGRAMS

American Indian Graduate Center

4520 Montgomery Boulevard, NE, Suite 1B
Albuquerque, New Mexico 87109
(505) 881-4584

The American Indian Graduate Center assists American Indian/Alaskan Native students who are members of federally recognized tribes. Applicants must be attending an accredited graduate school on a full-time basis, working on a master's or doctorate degree. Scholarship awards are based upon the applicants' unmet needs as verified by the school financial aids office. Deadline for submitting an application is June 1 for the forthcoming academic year.

American Indian Higher Education Consortium

333 Pennsylvania, SE
Washington, DC 20003

The American Indian Higher Education Consortium represents twenty-eight Indian-controlled colleges in the United States and Canada.

American Indian Library Association

c/o Office for Library Outreach Services
50 East Huron Street
Chicago, Illinois 60611
(312) 944-6780
(800) 545-2433

The association is a membership action group that addresses the library-related needs of American Indians and Alaska Natives. AILA is interested in the development of programs to improve Indian library, cultural, and informational services in school, public, and research libraries on reservations and is dedicated to disseminating information about Indian cultures, languages, values, and information needs to the library community.

American Indian Research & Development, Inc.

Resource & Evaluation Center V
2424 Springer Drive, Suite 200
Norman, Oklahoma 73069
(405) 364-0656

AIRD is a nonprofit program that primarily develops and provides services to American Indian gifted and talented students and conducts research. In general, the program assists others in proposal development and fund raising. Established in 1982, it sponsors a summer institute for gifted and talented Indian secondary students.

American Indian Science and Engineering Society

1085 Fourteenth Street, Suite 1506
Boulder, Colorado 80302
(303) 492-8658

AISES provides American Indian youth with the opportunity to enter the world of science and engineering while preserving their rich cultural heritage. AISES membership comprises over 500 student members and 300 professional/corporate members. Two components of AISES are precollegiate, which assists in teacher training and curriculum development, and collegiate, which offers scholarships and oversees chapters at universities and colleges. Established in 1977, AISES sponsors a four-day annual conference, has an educational newsletter containing precollegiate information, has a quarterly newsletter on employment/scholarship opportunities, *On the Way Up*, and has a magazine, *Winds of Change*.

Americans for Indian Opportunity

3508 Garfield Street, NW
Washington, DC 20007
(202) 338-8809

AIO is founded upon the premise that the tribes that comprise Indian America must be free to exercise their legal and rightful powers of self-government and to pursue self-determination, including the right to cultural autonomy and the right to control their own economic and financial resources. AIO stands for equality of opportunity, including educational opportunity, for all Indian people wherever they may live—from the reservations to the cities of America.

Association of American Indian Physicians

10015 South Pennsylvania, Building D
Oklahoma City, Oklahoma 73159
(405) 692-1202

The AAIP assists and recruits American Indian students into health careers. It helps students identify health career opportunities and helps students take advantage of those opportunities by identifying sources of financial aid, prerequisities for admission, and special programs to enhance the students' chances for professional school admission. Established in 1971, AAIP sponsors an annual conference and has a quarterly newsletter.

Association of Community Tribal Schools

Pierre Indian Learning Center
449 N. Plum Street
Vermillion, South Dakota 57069
(605) 624-9755

ACTS provides advocacy, communication, training, and services to schools, communities, and tribes interested in operating their own elementary and/or secondary school systems.

Association of Navajo Community Controlled School Boards

Box 2568
Window Rock, Arizona 86515
(602) 729-2764

Association on American Indian Affairs

95 Madison Avenue
New York, New York 10016
(212) 689-8720

The AAIA is a private, not-for-profit national citizens' organization funded by its members and contributors, who are Indian and non-Indian. The staff works from offices in New York City and in the field with Native American tribes and organizations nationwide. AAIA works in areas of community and economic development, education and scholarship support, health, legal defense, and youth and child welfare.

Bureau of Indian Affairs Advisory Committee for Exceptional Children

18th & C Street, NW (MIB) 4659
Washington, DC 20245
(202) 208-3711

The committee operates in an advisory role to see that educational needs of handicapped and gifted Indian children are met. Membership on the committee is by appointment from the secretary of the interior upon recommendation of the assistant secretary for Indian affairs. Established in 1977, the committee sponsors quarterly meetings through the Bureau of Indian Affairs and produces an annual report.

Coalition for Indian Education

3620 Wyoming Boulevard, NE, Suite 206
Albuquerque, New Mexico 87109
(505) 275-9788

CIE is an organization of professional Indian educators who are advocates for quality education for Indian children and adults. It is a membership organization established in 1987. It holds an annual conference in the fall and publishes a quarterly newsletter.

Community Development Institute

3812 Central Avenue, SE, Room 205
Albuquerque, New Mexico 87108
(505) 265-8344

CDI is a nonprofit organization, which since 1979 has provided training, consultation, and technical assistance to Indian and non-Indian Head Start programs, public and private agencies serving preschool-aged children. CDI staff members' areas of expertise include (but are not limited to) management, early childhood education, child abuse, career development, parenting curricula, and CDA advisor training.

Council for Exceptional Children

1920 Association Drive
Reston, Virginia 22091
(703) 620-3660

CEC is a national professional association dedicated to advancing the education of handicapped and gifted and talented children. CEC has been especially active in seeking improved federal special education policy for American Indian/Alaska Native exceptional children. Council conventions, conferences, symposia, and publications frequently feature information on American Indian/Alaska Native exceptional children and youth. Within CEC, there is an American Indian Caucus. CEC has an ethnic and multicultural bulletin, and the CEC American Indian Caucus has a biannual newsletter.

ERIC Clearinghouse on Rural Education and Small Schools

1031 Quarrier Street, 8th Floor
Post Office Box 1348
Charleston, West Virginia 25325
(304) 347-0461
(800) 344-6646 (in West Virginia)
(800) 624-9120 (outside West Virginia)

ERIC/CRESS acquires, processes, and disseminates materials, including news releases, related to all aspects of American Indian education, Mexican-American education, migrant education, outdoor education, rural education, and small schools. The clearinghouse prepares bibliographies, guides, and state-of-the-art papers and ERIC digests; conducts computer searches; prepares quick-response items; responds to questions; refers to other sources when appropriate; and facilitates networking and encourages development of organizations at all levels. Established in 1966, ERIC/CRESS makes presentations to facilitate educators' use of the ERIC system.

Indian Resource Development

Box 30003, Department 31RD
New Mexico State University
Las Cruces, New Mexico 88003
(505) 646-1347

IRD encourages American Indian students to attend the university of their choice and major in natural resource-related fields, such as agriculture, physical science, computers, engineering, business, or related fields. Information is provided to participants on careers, financial aid, academic assistance, and work experience, such as cooperative education internships and summer jobs. Established in 1977, IRD sponsors precollege career seminars for high school students and has a semiannual newsletter, *Indian Country Student News*.

Indians Into Medicine

University of North Dakota School of Medicine
501 North Columbia Road
Grand Forks, North Dakota 58203
(701) 777-3037

INMED assists American Indian students in finding health education opportunities. Multifaceted programs serve Indian students preparing for health careers. Assistance includes academic, financial, and personal support for summer high school, college, and medical preparatory students. Established in 1973, INMED has a newsletter, *Serpent, Staff and Drum*.

National Advisory Council on Indian Education

330 C Street, SW, Room 4072
Switzer Building
Washington, DC 20202-7556
(202) 732-1353

The council's primary responsibility is with the education of American Indians as established in Title IV of the Indian Education Act of 1972 as amended. The council advises the Congress and the secretary of education in regard to programs benefitting Indian children and adults. Established in 1972, the council sponsors a Full Council Meeting, has a newsletter, and produces an annual report.

National Indian Education Association

1819 H Street, NW, Suite 800
Washington, DC 20006
(202) 835-3001

The membership of NIEA is composed of 2,000 individuals who are interested in the promotion and provision of quality education to American Indians and Alaska Natives. The organization's goals pertain to communication, advocacy, and technical assistance. Established in 1970, NIEA sponsors an annual conference and publishes a newsletter approximately six times per year.

National Indian Education Clearinghouse

Hayden Library, Arizona Collection
Arizona State University
Tempe, Arizona 85287-1006
(602) 965-6490

The overall mission of the NIEC is to strengthen the communication flow between American Indian tribes and the national education community. The NIEC acts as a central repository for American Indian cultural curriculum and related retrospective materials. Currently in its developmental phase, the NIEC plans to develop a resource-sharing network among the university, the national education community, and the national Indian community, focusing on quality American Indian/Alaska Native curriculum and research. The NIEC requests copies of existing American Indian/Alaska Native curriculum materials and program information.

National Indian School Board Association

c/o Wilson Contracting Services
1 Tandy Center Plaza, 4th Floor
Fort Worth, Texas 76102
(817) 626-6410

NISBA is a professional membership association which was established in 1982 as a nonprofit education and service organization. Its major purpose is to facilitate the implementation of the BIA policy of Indian control in all matters relating to Indian education. Membership is open to BIA-funded schools, public schools, Indian parent committees, and tribal education committees. Congressional oversight and advocacy, training, and information sharing are the primary activities. An annual conference and regional workshops are conducted.

National Indian Training and Research Center

2121 South Mill Avenue, Suite 218
Tempe, Arizona 85282
(602) 967-9484

The NITRC provides special services in program development, curriculum design, evaluation, training for administrators, teachers, boards of education, education committees, and technical assistance in the human and health services. It was established in 1969.

Native American Scholarship Fund

3620 Wyoming Boulevard, NE, Suite 208 C
Albuquerque, New Mexico 87111
(505) 275-9788

NASF is a national organization making grants to Indian students at the college level. Concentration is on undergraduate level, but grants are also made to graduate students. Priority areas are math, engineering, science, business, education, and computers (MESBEC). Within the education priority area, the fund operates the Native American Leadership in Education (NALE) program. This program helps native paraprofessionals to return to college full-time and become certified teachers. Priority is given to those who are majoring in the MESBEC areas. Students must have high grades, high test scores, excellent leadership ability, high motivation, and excellent communication skills. They should have decided on a major field of study and have planned their work in school for this major.

Navajo Area School Board Association

Post Office Box 578
Window Rock, Arizona 86515
(602) 871-5225

Navajo Nation Public School Boards Association

Post Office Box 337
Kayenta, Arizona 86033
(602) 697-3251

Office of Indian Education

U.S. Department of Education
400 Maryland Avenue, SE
Washington, DC 20202
(202) 401-1887

ORBIS Associates

1411 K Street, NW, Suite 200
Washington, DC 20005
(202) 628-4444

ORBIS is an Indian nonprofit corporation providing education training and management consulting. Major areas include whole language curriculum, cultural instruction methods, learning styles assessment and use, holistic consulting techniques, and strategies.

Research and Development for Indian Education

Northwest Regional Educational Laboratory
101 SW Main Street, Suite 500
Portland, Oregon 97204
(503) 275-9500

The Research and Development Program for Indian Education at NWREL assists educators in using effective practices in administration, teaching, and curriculum in Indian education. The program also conducts studies of issues and qualities of Indian education. NWREL assists teachers

and administrators at schools serving Indian students as they implement practices that have proven effective in Indian education. Inservice training is available in school improvement and substance abuse prevention. Products are *Effective Practices in Indian Education*, Teacher's Monograph, Administrator's Monograph, and Curriculum Monograph. NWREL was established in 1966 and has a newsletter, *Northwest Report*.

REGIONAL RESOURCE AND EVALUATION CENTERS

The purpose of the regional centers is to assist Indian Education Act Title V grantees and potential grantees in meeting the special educational and culturally related academic needs of Indian children and adults. The centers provide technical assistance and training at no cost and upon specific request to Indian tribes, organizations, institutions, local educational agencies, and parent committees in the planning, developing, and administering of Title V projects.

Resource and Evaluation Center I

ORBIS Associates
1411 K Street, NW, Suite 200
Washington, DC 20005
(202) 628-4444
(800) 621-2998 (For Title V grantees in states served)

Serving: District of Columbia and all states east of the Mississippi River.

Northern Plains Resource and Evaluation Center II

3315 University Drive
Bismarck, North Dakota 58504
(701) 258-0437
(800) 932-8997 (In North Dakota)
(800) 437-8054 (For Title V grantees in states served)

Serving: Iowa, Minnesota, Montana, Nebraska, North Dakota, South Dakota, and Wyoming

Indian Education Resource and Evaluation Center III

School of Education
Gonzaga University
502 East Sharp
Spokane, Washington 99258-0001
(509) 328-4220
(800) 533-2554 (For Title V grantees in states
    served)

   Serving: Alaska, Idaho, Oregon, and Washington

Southwest Resource and Evaluation Center IV

2121 South Mill Avenue, Suite 216
Tempe, Arizona 85282
(602) 967-9428
(800) 352-6498 (For Title V grantees in Arizona)
(800) 528-6425 (For Title V grantees in states
    served)

   Serving: Arizona, California, Colorado, Hawaii,
   Nevada, New Mexico, and Utah

South Plains Resource and Evaluation Center V

American Indian Research and Development, Inc.
2424 South Springer Drive, Suite 200
Norman, Oklahoma 73069
(405) 360-1163
(800) 422-0966 (For Title V grantees in Oklahoma)
(800) 451-2191 (For Title V grantees in states
    served)

   Serving: Arkansas, Kansas, Louisiana, Missouri,
   Oklahoma, and Texas

Religion

Indian country today is home to hundreds of religious traditions that have endured despite the long history of forced removals, sacred site destruction, the jailing of native religious practitioners, and pressures to assimilate by the U.S. federal government and missionaries. Many sacred beliefs, knowledge, ceremonies, and rituals live on as the heart of Native American cultural identity.

Ancient traditional religions survive and remain strong among some native peoples while others practice Christianity exclusively. Some Indian people pray in church and attend Indian healing ceremonies, finding that both traditions offer spiritual comfort. Some people mix Catholicism and ancient practices, and others follow the practices of the Native American Church, which attracts followers from many tribes.

Each tribe has its own "Genesis" to explain the universe and the unknown. Each tribe performs ceremonies according to instructions given in the sacred stories. Some of the most important ceremonies need to be conducted at certain sacred places at specific times of the year. These ceremonies mark important life-cycle events in a person's life and take place at important times, such as solstices and equinoxes. Ceremonies heal the sick, renew relationships with spiritual beings, initiate people into religious societies, ensure success in hunting and growing crops, bring rain, and give thanks for harvests of food. Some ceremonies must be performed in order that the earth and all forms of life might survive. Today, as in the past, native peoples worship by dancing. Many Indians continue to dance to keep ancient ways alive and to connect themselves to the past.

Traditional religious practices are inseparably bound to natural formations. Since time immemorial, Indian religious practitioners have gone into sacred high places, lakes, and isolated sanctuaries to pray, fast, make vision quests or pilgrimages, receive guidance, and train young people in the spiritual life of their community. In these sacred places, native people relate to ancestors, humans, plants, animals, and especially to spirits that most often reveal themselves there.

Physical conditions affect sacred sites, however. Spraying and logging trees, dams, fencing, building roads, mining, hydroelectric plants, urban housing, tourists, and vandals damage the sacred nature of land. Many of the Indians' most revered places are not under their control but are on public lands governed by federal agencies intent on uranium mining, clear cutting, and tourist development. Traditional religious leaders were sometimes able to work out informal arrangements with federal agencies to allow them access to these places for religious purposes. But since the 1970s, bureaucrats began restricting access to sacred sites by establishing increasingly narrow rules and regulations of managing public lands. If sacred sites are restricted or destroyed, so too are the religious rituals connected to those places. Since native people cannot substitute another site for one considered sacred, unlike Judeo-Christian religions which arbitrarily create sacred spaces and times through special rituals, religious practices once again are threatened. Without the religious rites that form the cornerstone of Indian cultures, the essence of Native American identities may cease to exist.

SACRED SITES

Every religion has its sacred sites where members gather to worship. Native Americans consider the whole earth sacred, but certain lakes, hot springs, and mountains are believed to be even more so. The Indian Chief Seattle expressed this concept in 1887:

> "Every part of this country is sacred to my people. Every hillside, every valley, every plain and grove has been hallowed by some fond memory or some sad experience of my tribe. Even the rocks, which seem to lie dumb as they swelter in the sun along the silent shore in solemn grandeur thrill with memories of past events connected with the fate of my people."

Today, because tribes lost much of their land through treaties with the U.S. Government, many traditional prayer sites of tribes are located on public domain lands controlled by the U.S. Forest Service, U.S. Park Service, and U.S. Bureau of Land Management.

In 1978, when Congress passed the American Indian Religious Freedom Act (AIRFA), a policy statement declaring Congress' intention to protect and preserve the inherent right of American Indians to believe, express, and practice their traditional religions, Indians hoped worship at sacred sites would be incorporated into American law and social policy. Almost unanimously, however, federal courts changed that. They have ruled that AIRFA contained nothing in it to protect or preserve the right of Indians to conduct ceremonies at sacred sites on public lands. Courts unwilling to find any protections under the First Amendment or any other statute have allowed federal land managing agencies to destroy irreplaceable native sacred sites.

The U.S. Commission on Civil Rights noted in 1983:

> In large part, the Federal Government's failure to protect Native American religion stems from its long history of antagonism and refusal to treat them as "significant" as western religions. Over the past three centuries, white colonists and Federal agents have actively suppressed the practice of 1,000-year-old rituals and sacraments that served a central and life-sustaining function for American Indians. The attitudes of the young American government toward Native American religions were influenced to some extent by the policy of previous governments in their dealings with the Indian peoples.

Bear Butte, a sacred site near Sturgis, South Dakota, is called Noaha-vose *by Cheyenne people and* Paha Wakan *or* Mato Paha *by Lakota (Sioux) people. Photograph by Paul Conklin.*

ENDANGERED SACRED LANDS

Traditional Native American spiritual practices are inseparably bound to land and natural formations. Ceremonies, vision quests, prayers, fasts, or pilgrimages must take place at sacred sites that have not been disturbed by mining, logging, dams, fencing, road building, hydroelectric plants, tourists and vandals. In a few cases, sacred lands have been protected or returned to Indian peoples; in others, sacred sites have been destroyed. The following sites have been classified as destroyed, saved, or threatened. Many more sites are threatened.

ENDANGERED SACRED LANDS

Badger-Two Medicine, Montana. Site bordering Blackfeet Reservation in Lewis and Clark National Forest sacred to Blackfeet and other tribes since pre-horse times. Threatened by oil and gas companies that want to drill the site for oil and gas.

Canyon Mine, Arizona. Site in Kaibab National Forest sacred to the Havasupai people. Threatened by uranium mining, permitted by the U.S. Forest Service.

Medicine Wheel, Wyoming. Site in Big Horn Mountains of Wyoming sacred to Arapaho, Blackfeet, Crow, Cheyenne, Lakota, and Shoshone Indians. In 1991, the U.S. Forest Service proposed measures to develop the Medicine Wheel area as a tourist attraction and promote future logging activities in the vicinity of the wheel.

Mount Graham, Arizona. San Carlos Apache ancient sacred site in Coronado National Forest managed by the U.S. Forest Service. Endangered by construction of seven-telescope observatory ("Columbus Project") on Mount Graham by the Vatican, University of Arizona, Germany's Max Planck Institute for Radio Astronomy, and Italy's Arcetri Astrophysical Observatory.

DESECRATED SACRED SITES

Celilo Falls, Oregon. Ancient place of worship and fishery on the Columbia River for the Umatilla, Nez Percé, Yakima, and Warm Springs Indians. Flooded by the Dalles Dam, which was completed in 1957.

Rainbow Natural Bridge, Utah. Huge sandstone arch sacred to Navajo, Paiute, and Pueblo peoples. Desecrated by the completion of Glen Canyon Dam on the Colorado River in 1963 and the rising of Lake Powell.

San Francisco Peaks, Arizona. Site in Coconino National Forest sacred to Apaches, Hopis, Navajos, and Zunis. Desecrated by the development of the Snow Bowl, a portion of the peaks used for downhill skiing.

PRESERVED SACRED SITES

Blue Lake, New Mexico. Sacred Taos Pueblo site located in the Sangre de Cristo Mountains. Seized by the federal government in 1960, made part of Carson National Forest, and restored to the Taos people in December 1970.

Kootenai Falls, Montana. Site on Kootenai River sacred to Kootanai Indians of Montana, Idaho, and British Columbia. Preserved by a Federal Energy Regulatory Commission ruling in June 1987, denying the license to seven Montana-Idaho electric co-operatives that tried to get a dam and hydroelectric power plant approved for Kootenai Falls.

Mount Adams, Washington. Mountain sacred to Yakima people. Taken around the turn of the century by the federal government, included in Gifford Pinchot National Forest, and restored to the Yakimas in May 1972.

The struggle culminated in 1988 when the Supreme Court ruling in *Lyng, Secretary of Agriculture, et al. v. Northwest Indian Cemetery Protective Association, et al.* permitted the U.S. Forest Service to pave a six-mile logging road in the Chimney Rock area of the Six Rivers National Forest in northern California, which would have disturbed the sacred sites of the Yurok, Karok, and Tolowa tribes and opened the high country to commercial logging. Although the California Wilderness Act protecting the Chimney Rock area made the point almost moot, the Supreme Court insisted on deciding religious issues and ruled that the Free Exercise clause did not prevent the government from using its property in any way it saw fit.

The *Lyng* decision created a crisis in Indian country. Since there are no legal safeguards to protect native worship at sacred sites under the U.S. Constitution and laws, including the AIRFA, which Indians now view as a policy statement "with no teeth," traditional Indian worship stands without any legal protections in American jurisprudence.

MISSIONARIES

The English, Spanish, and French missionaries tended to view Native American religions as heathenistic and contemptible. French priests in Canada who sought to convert Indians to Catholicism and French culture ridiculed traditional Indian rituals and ceremonies. English colonial charters frequently carried a clause urging grantees to convert and "civilize" the Indians. Puritans formed fourteen "praying towns" among southern New England Algonquians from the late 1640s to the 1670s. Potential converts were removed to and isolated in the towns away from English settlers encroaching on their lands and other unconverted Indians. The English stopped trying to convert the Indians when it became clear that the Indians were not abandoning traditional beliefs. Before this realization, however, the English, who were intolerant of "different" religions, denounced the Indian world view. The Spanish missionaries in the Southwest directed all their efforts toward concen-

CALIFORNIA MISSIONS

Missions South to North	Year Founded	Territory of Tribes	Missions South to North	Year Founded	Territory of Tribes
San Diego de Alcalá	1769	Diegueño	San Antonio de Padua	1771	Salinan
San Luis Ray de Francia	1798	Luiseño	Nuestra Señora de la Soledad	1791	Costanoan
San Juan Capistrano	1776	Juaneño	San Carlos Borromeo de Carmelo	1770	Costanoan
San Gabriel Arcángel	1771	Grabrieleño	San Juan Bautista	1797	Costanoan
San Fernando Rey de España	1797	Fernandeño	Santa Cruz	1791	Costanoan
San Buenaventura	1782	Chumash	Santa Clara de Asís	1776	Costanoan
Santa Bárbara	1786	Chumash	San Jose de Guadalupe	1797	Costanoan
Santa Inez	1804	Chumash	San Francisco de Asís	1776	Costanoan
La Purísima Concepción	1787	Chumash	San Rafael Arcángel	1817	Coast Miwok
San Luis Obispo de Tolosa	1772	Chumash	San Francisco Solano	1823	Coast Miwok
San Miguel Arcángel	1797	Salinan			

NATIVE AMERICAN MISSIONARIES

Since the end of the seventeenth century, Native American preachers had converted their people to Christianity and preached to congregations made up of Christian Indians. Today, many Native preachers help their people preserve their cultural traditions rather than proselytizing or converting them away from their beliefs. Native Catholic priests, Episcopal bishops, and Methodist reverends bridge traditional Indian beliefs and Christian theology. They explore ways to bring together both traditions without violating the sacredness of either. There are, of course, many Indians who worship in churches without any reference to their heritage.

Anawangmani, Simon, Dakota (c. 1808–1891) Congregational

Apes, William, Pequot (1798–?) Methodist

Arthur, Mark K., Nez Percé (1873–1947) Presbyterian

Aupaument, Hendrick, Mahican (1757–1830) Congregational

Belvin, B. Frank, Choctaw (b. 1914) Baptist

Bemo, John, Seminole (fl. 19th century) Presbyterian and Baptist

Billie, Josie, Seminole (c. 1887–?) Baptist

Black Fox, Cherokee (?–1895) Methodist

Bouchard, James Chrysostom, Delaware (1823–1889) Roman Catholic

Bushyhead, Jesse, Cherokee (?–1844) Baptist

Checote, Samuel, Creek (c. 1819–1884) Methodist

Cook, Charles Smith, Lakota (?–1892) Protestant

Coolidge, Sherman, Arapaho (1862–c. 1933) Episcopal

Copway, George, Ojibwa (1818–1869) Methodist

Crawford, Charles Renville, Dakota (1837–1920) Presbyterian

Cusick, Albert, Onondaga-Tuscarora (1846–?) Episcopal

Custalow, Otha Thomas, Mattaponi (fl. 20th century) Baptist

Davis, Gloria Ann, Navajo-Choctaw (b. 1933) Roman Catholic nun

Deloria, Philip Joseph, Dakota (1854–1931) Episcopal

Deloria, Vine Sr., Dakota (1901–1990) Episcopal

Dukes, Joseph, Choctaw (1811–1861) Presbyterian

Eastman, John, Dakota (b. 1848) Presbyterian

Ehnamani, Artemas, Dakota (1827–c. 1902) Congregational

Enmegahbowh, Ojibwa-Ottawa (c. 1810–1902) Methodist, later Episcopal

Foreman, Stephen, Cherokee (1807–1881) Presbyterian

Frazier, Francis Philip, Dakota (fl. 1880s–1890) Congregational

Goodbird, Edward, Hidatsa (1869–1938) Congregational

Green, Joe, Northern Paiute (fl. 1930s–1950s) Episcopal

Grey Cloud, David, Dakota (1840–1890) Congregational

Hascall, John, Ojibwa, (1941–) Roman Catholic

Hiacoomes, Pokanoket (c. 1610–1690) Congregational

Hill, Cornelius, Oneida (?–1907) Episcopal

Jacobs, Peter, Ojibwa (c. 1807–1890) Methodist

Jones, Peter, Ojibwa (1802–1856) Methodist

Journeycake, Charles, Delaware (1817–1894) Baptist

Jumper, John, Seminole (c. 1822–1896) Baptist

Kaneeda, Cherokee (fl. 1800s) Baptist

Kushuwe, Jack, Iowa (fl. late 19th–early 20th century) Presbyterian

Lawyer, Archie B., Nez Percé (?–1893) Presbyterian

Lee, George, Navajo (b. 1943) Mormon

Lonewolf, Delos Knowles, Kiowa (1870–1945) Methodist

Lowry, Henry H., Lumbee (?–1935) Lumbee Methodist

(continued)

NATIVE AMERICAN MISSIONARIES (*cont.*)

Marksman, Peter, Ojibwa (c. 1815–1892) Methodist

Moore, William Luther, Lumbee (?–1931) Lumbee Methodist

Morgan, Jacob, Navajo (1879–1950) Methodist

Napeshnee, Joseph, Dakota (c. 1800–1870) Presbyterian

Oakchiah, Choctaw (c. 1810–1849) Methodist

Oakerhater, David Pendleton, Cheyenne (1844–1931) Episcopal

Occum, Samson, Mohegan (1723–1792) Presbyterian

Onasakenrat, Joseph, Mohawk (1845–1881) Methodist

Osunkhirhine, Pierre Paul, Abenaki (fl. 1830–1849) Presbyterian

Owl, W. David, Cherokee (1893–c. 1981) Baptist

Pelotte, Donald E., Abenaki (b. 1945) Roman Catholic

Perryman, James, Creek (?–c. 1882) Baptist

Perryman, Joseph M., Creek (1883–?) Presbyterian and Baptist

Perryman, Thomas Ward, Creek (1839–1903) Presbyterian

Poor Man, Mercy, Lakota (c. 1922) Christian Life Fellowship Church

Renville, Isaac, Dakota (c. 1840–1919) Congregational

Renville, John B., Dakota (1831–1903) Presbyterian

Renville, Victor, Dakota (1849–1927) Episcopal

Smith, Stanley, Creek (fl. 1940s) Baptist

Steinhauer, Henry Bird, Ojibwa (1816–1884) Methodist

Sunday, John, Ojibwa (c. 1795–1875) Methodist

Suyeta, Cherokee (c. 1825–?) Baptist

Tanenolee, Cherokee (fl. mid-19th century) Baptist

Tunkanshaiciye, Dakota (1833–1910) Presbyterian

Waters, George, Klickitat (?–1923) Methodist

Winslett, David, Creek (c. 1830–1862) Presbyterian

Wright, Allen, Choctaw (1825–1885) Presbyterian

Wright, Frank Hall, Choctaw (1860–1922) Presbyterian

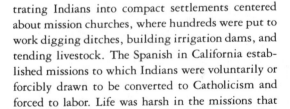

trating Indians into compact settlements centered about mission churches, where hundreds were put to work digging ditches, building irrigation dams, and tending livestock. The Spanish in California established missions to which Indians were voluntarily or forcibly drawn to be converted to Catholicism and forced to labor. Life was harsh in the missions that lined the California coast in the eighteenth century.

In the end, despite their efforts to eradicate native beliefs and practices labeled "heathen," "pagan," and "primitive," the Spanish, French, and English missionaries failed to convert and "civilize" the majority of Indians. Many tribal people simply preferred their own beliefs and practices to those of the invaders. Missionaries succeeded, however, in dividing tribal societies into converts and traditionalists pitted against each other in bitter ideological conflicts.

RELIGIOUS MOVEMENTS

Native Americans responded to the assaults on their way of life with new religious movements that offered hope that the land would be restored, the dead returned, as well as buffalo and other game, and the disappearance of the Euro-americans. These movements and prophets worked to reclaim Indian people from promiscuity, drinking alcohol, stealing, following customs adopted from the whites, and abandoning native traditions and goods. The movements included:

- Big Head Religion
- Bole-Maru Religion
- Cherokee Religious Revival of 1811 to 1813

- Delaware Prophet's Message in 1760s
- Dream Dance
- Earth Lodge Religion
- Feather Religion
- Ghost Dance of 1870
- Ghost Dance of 1890
- Handsome Lake Religion
- Indian Shaker Religion
- Kenekuk Prophet's Message in early nineteenth century
- Prophet Dance
- Redbird Smith's Movement of late 1800s, early 1900s
- Skolaskin Prophet's Message in 1870s
- Tenskwatawa Prophet's Message in early 1800s
- Wabokieshiek Prophet's Message in 1830s
- Washani Religion
- Washat Dance

REPATRIATION AND REBURIAL

Today, ancient Indian graves are endangered. Over the course of time, erosion and river flooding have exposed grave sites. Farmers plowing their field have unearthed skeletal remains and burial goods. Urban developers have bulldozed mounds to make way for buildings. Road builders have destroyed Indian cemeteries. Land-clearing techniques and seismic line construction and logging operations have taken their toll. And worst of all, pothunting vandals deliberately plunder Indian burial sites to steal objects valued by collectors in domestic and international markets. These grave looters scatter bones of the dead in their frenzy to find grave goods. By all accounts, grave desecration and looting reached epidemic proportions across the nation in the 1980s.

Native American tribes, outraged by the desecration, looting, and disregard of their dead, demanded the return of skeletal remains, burial goods, and other sacred objects taken from them. Despite opposition to native efforts to reclaim ancestral remains and sacred objects, native people persevered and eventually helped win passage of important legisla-

tion protecting native gravesites from looting and giving native people legal procedures for reclaiming artifacts of religious or ceremonial importance. The following chronology testifies to native perseverance in repatriating human remains, grave goods, and sacred objects.

May 1988—Indian people throughout the country trekked to Uniontown, Kentucky, site of the largest Indian burial desecration yet discovered, to rebury more than 1,000 remains of Indian men, women, and children scattered across fields, the result of mining equipment used to blow skeletal remains out of the ground.

June 1988—The North Dakota Historical Board approved rules to release boxes of Indian skeletal remains for reburial, but a four-year dispute about the proper disposal of state-owned remains prevented immediate action.

August 1988—In Bemidji, Minnesota, the bones of sixteen to twenty Indians were reburied after being disturbed during a construction project.

September 1988—A Blackfeet delegation brought home to the reservation fifteen skeletal remains of their ancestors, the first successful return of Indian remains to native people by the Smithsonian Institution in Washington, D.C.

September 1988—In a ceremony in Annapolis, Maryland, three ceremonial eagle feather headdresses were returned to the Blackfeet Indian tribe after an auctioneer discovered the tribe considered the feathers sacred.

April 1989—Under new Kansas laws, the remains of 146 Indians on public display at a roadside tourist attraction were properly reburied by three related Caddoan tribes at state expense.

April 1989—The American Museum of Natural History in New York City refused to give a 150-year-old sacred bundle back to a Canadian Cree man who ran 2,700 miles in his quest to retrieve the object for his people.

June 1989—Stanford University in California agreed to return all of the Native American skeletal remains in its collection to local Ohlone/Costonoan people for reburial.

SELECTED CONTEMPORARY RELIGIOUS CEREMONIES

Important tribal ceremonies take place all across the United States. Each tribe has its own ceremonies to perform according to instructions given in sacred stories. Contemporary ceremonies mark important changes in an individual's life—birth, coming-of-age, death. They mark important times of the year such as the winter and summer solstices. There are ceremonies for healing sickness, renewing relationships with spirit beings, initiating people into religious societies, assuring success in hunting, planting, and growing crops, bringing rain, and giving thanks for the harvest of food. The following list names some of the tribal ceremonies performed throughout North America.

Apache—Ceremonial Relay Race, Holiness Rite, Long Life Ceremony, Mountain Spirit (Gan) Dances, Naihes (Sunrise)

Athabascan—Stick Dance

Cocopah—Mourning Ceremony

Confederated Tribes of Warm Springs—Root Feast

Creek—Green Corn Ceremony, Stickball Game, Stomp Dance

Crow—Sun Dance

Havasupai—Peach Dance

Hopi—Flute Ceremony, New Fire Ceremony, Niman Kachina Ceremony, Pachavu Ceremony, Powamu Ceremony, Snake-Antelope Ceremony, Soyal, Wuwuchim Ceremony

Hupa—World Renewal Ceremonial

Inuit—Bladder Festival, Feast to the Dead, Masquerade Feast, Messenger Feast, Sedna Ceremony, Whale Feast

Kiowa—Gourd Dance

Kwakiutl—Hamatsa Dance, Memorial Potlatch, Winter Ceremonial

Lakota/Dakota—Sweat Lodge Ritual, Sun Dance, Vision Quest, Yuwipi

Maidu—Hesi Ceremony, Spring Rite

Navajo—Blessing Way Rite; Enemy Way, Evil Way, Holy Way, and Life Way Ceremonies; House Blessing Rite, Night Way

Ojibwa—Midewiwin Religion

Omaha—Anointing the Sacred Pole Ceremony

Osage—I'n-lon-schka Ceremonial Dance

Pueblo—Animal Dances, Basket Dance, Comanche Dance, Corn Dance, Eagle Dance, Feast Day

Salish—Spirit Dance Ceremonial

Seminole—Green Corn, Single Pole Ball Game

Six Nations (Iroquois)—Bean Ceremony, Bowl (Peach Stone) Game, Condolence Ceremony, Eagle Dance, Feast to the Dead, Feather Dance, False Face Ceremony, Green Corn, Harvest Festival, Lacrosse, Maple Festival, Midwinter Festival, Our Life Supporter Dances, Snow-Snake, Strawberry Festival, Stirring Ashes Rite, Thanksgiving Address, Thanksgiving Dance, Tobacco Invocation

Tohono O'odham—Saguaro Festival

Tolowa—World Renewal Ceremonial

Ute—Bear Dance

Wampanoag—Cranberry Day

Yakima—Washat Dance

Yaqui—Pahko, Pascola Dance, Waehma

Yurok—World Renewal Ceremonial

Zuni—New Fire Ceremony, Shalako Ceremony, Teshkwi

August 1989—The University of Nebraska at Lincoln agreed to give to the Omaha Tribe a collection of more than 100 tribal skeletal remains and burial goods housed at the university for decades.

October 1989—The State Museum in Albany, New York, returned twelve wampum belts to the Onondaga Nation of New York.

November 1989—President George Bush signed the National Museum of the American Indian Act that requires the Smithsonian Institution to repatriate some of its 18,000 skeletal remains and thousands of associated funerary objects to requesting tribes for reburial after evidence links the remains to the tribes.

February 1990—The Zuni Tribal Council in New Mexico contacted all museums in the United States known to have Ahayu:das (War Gods) to request their repatriation. Within two months, thirty-eight War Gods were repatriated from twenty-four institutions and private collections.

September 1990—The Omaha Tribe of Nebraska held a ceremony to bless about 270 artifacts returned by the Peabody Museum at Harvard University in Cambridge, Massachusetts.

November 1990—President George Bush signed the Native American Grave Protection and Repatriation Act, landmark human rights legislation that will help protect Indian gravesites from looting and requires repatriation to tribes of culturally identifiable remains, funerary objects, and sacred objects.

April 1991—The Natural History Museum of the Smithsonian Institution in Washington, D.C., agreed to return more than 700 human remains and associated burial goods to Larsen Bay Tribal Council of Kodiak Island, Alaska, the largest single collection to be returned under new federal laws.

COURT CASES AND PEYOTE

Opposition to peyote, a sacrament as integral to Native American Church ceremonies as wine is to Catholic ritual, stretches back to 1620 when Catholic missionaries banned it. Over 370 years later, opposition continues. Federal, state, and local governments suppress peyote through directives, legislation, and litigation, despite medical testimony attesting to its nonharmful effects and testimony about its power to heal and transform the lives of many Native Americans who were former alcoholics. Peyotists have been raided, arrested, and jailed. On April 17, 1990, the Supreme Court struck a major blow by ruling that the U.S. Constitution does not inherently protect the right to use peyote in religious ceremonies. The decision in *Employment Division, Department of Human Resources of Oregon v. Smith et al.* discarded the longstanding test for evaluating whether a governmental action unconstitutionally interferes with a religious practice. Since then, over forty lower court decisions have curtailed the free exercise of religion, citing *Smith* as justification.

There have been a number of other court cases involving peyote:

Employment Division, Department of Human Resources of Oregon et al v. Smith, et al., 1990

Indian Inmates of Nebraska Penitentiary v. Grammer, 1986

Peyote Way Church of God, Inc. v. Smith, 1983

Native American Church of New York v. United States, 1979

State of Washington v. Robin H. Gunshows, et al., 1978

Whitehorn v. State of Oklahoma, 1977

State v. Soto, 1975

Golden Eagle v. Deputy Sheriff Johnson, 1974

State of Arizona v. Janice and Fred Whittingham, 1973

State of New Mexico v. Robert Dan Pedro, 1971

People v. Foster Alphonse Red Elk, 1970

People v. Woody, 1964

State of Arizona v. Mary Attakai, 1960

Native American Church v. Navajo Tribal Council, 1959

Games and Sports

Traditional native games and sports, which were an integral part of each tribe's culture and religion, were often played in a spiritual manner to benefit the tribe. As potential beneficiaries of spiritually motivated games, tribal members were avid participants and spectators. Waging on the outcome of an engagement, which did not diminish the spiritual value of the game, was nearly universal and served to redistribute goods among tribal members and to reaffirm social ties. Games and sports were often featured in tribal mythologies, attesting to their antiquity among Native Americans.

There was limited exchange of games and sports between the natives and non-natives from the mid-seventeenth century to the early nineteenth century. French Canadians learned to play lacrosse from the Mohawks in 1750. In 1856, the first lacrosse club was formed in Montreal, and it was made the national sport of Canada in 1867. In the last decades of the nineteenth century, with the continued development of boarding schools and a federal policy to assimilate Indians, Native Americans began to formally learn and adopt non-native games and sports.

Since the 1960s, there have been efforts to rekindle Native American involvement in traditional sports and to recognize the achievements of Indians in nontraditional sports. The World Eskimo–Indian Olympics was established in 1961 to promote indigenous sports and culture of Alaska. The American Indian Athletic Hall of Fame, founded in 1972 at Haskell Indian Junior College in Lawrence, Kansas, recognizes the contributions of Indian athletes. The Iroquois Nationals, founded in 1983, has built a lacrosse team to ensure that Native Americans are represented in international lacrosse competition. The National Indian Activities Association was founded in 1974 to organize national basketball tournaments for Indian teams and has recently expanded to include softball, golf, and bowling tournaments. UNION (Unite Now Indian Olympic Nation), formed in 1991, seeks to establish an independent American Indian Olympic team to compete in the Olympics.

Albert Henry, Choctaw stickball player from Mississippi poses with a racket in 1908. Stickball is a Southeastern variation of lacrosse. Courtesy of the National Museum of the American Indian/Smithsonian Institution.

A group of Cherokee stickball (a variation of lacrosse) players in 1908. Courtesy of the National Museum of the American Indian/Smithsonian Institution.

TRADITIONAL PURPOSE OF GAMES AND SPORTS

Historically, there was an integral connection between athletic abilities and the cultural life of the tribe. Survival skills were often developed and honed by participation in sports activities. The hoop and pole game, for example, is widely played north of Mexico. It consists of a hoop, often with a network of webbing, that is pierced by a spear, by darts, or by arrows shot from a bow. The game is played by two boys or men. The hoop is rolled along the ground and

the players try to impale the hoop with the spears, darts, or arrows. Points are given for different locations of penetration of the spears, and spectators bet on the outcome of the game. The game sharpens the aim of men and boys who hunt for food.

The hoops are often painted in colors representing the four winds or the four directions and are sometimes sacred in nature. There are ceremonial versions of the game among many tribes, including the Zuni, Hopi, Sioux, and Cheyenne. The game figures among the oral tradition of many tribes. Among the Arapaho, a story is told of twin boys, one of whom is blown away by a strong wind. He is found by an old

Football players around 1900 on the Onondaga reservation in New York. Courtesy of the National Museum of the American Indian/Smithsonian Institution.

Southern Cheyenne youth playing the hoop and pole game near Colony, Oklahoma. Courtesy of National Museum of the American Indian/ Smithsonian Institution.

woman who makes for him a small netted wheel, a bow, and arrows. Grandmother rolls the wheel toward the boy saying, "A fat buffalo cow is running toward you," and a red cow runs toward him, which he shoots with his bow and arrows. The game is repeated and a supply of meat is secured. Miniature hoop and poles are made as offerings for ceremonial altars among the Zuni, and miniature hoops are worn by dancers in ceremonies among many tribes and are sometimes used in ceremonies to aid in healing of the sick.

Although many games began as religious rites and evolved into sports over time, they often retain their connection to customs and traditions. According to Black Elk, Oglala Lakota, the game of "throwing the ball" was originally a sacred rite. In Joseph Epes Brown's classic book, *The Sacred Pipe; Black Elk's Account of the Seven Rites of the Oglala Sioux* (1953), Black Elk related that there were "only a few of us

today who still understand why the game is sacred, or what the game originally was long ago, when it was not really a game, but one of our most important rites." Some games may have been played as a secular activity and evolved into a ritual expression to fill a need. The Pawnee Ghost Dance Handgame seems to be a case of a game, originally played for amusement, that acquired a sacred nature in response to the stress of forced acculturation in the nineteenth century.

Games and sports have a spiritual connection in Native American cultures. In the past, and to some extent today, games were played to honor the dead, comfort the bereaved, placate spirits, influence weather, heal the sick, and to end misfortune. There were games to ensure the fertility of people, prey animals, and food plants. Native Americans are often fervent players and spectators of games that benefit the tribe as a whole. The athletic abilities that are a part of sports provide a means of communication

THE ORIGIN OF THE PEACH BOWL GAME AMONG THE SIX NATIONS (IROQUOIS)

The Peach Bowl Game is often played as part of, or at the conclusion of, ceremonial gatherings. The game is played with six peach stones that are ground to about half their original size. One side of each stone is blackened by burning, the other side is white. The stones are placed in a carved wooden bowl and the bowl is struck on a blanket that is folded on the floor. When the stones stop rolling, the number of peach stones of one color facing up, either blackened or white, are noted. If there are five of one color facing up, the person who struck the bowl wins a point. If all six are of one color, that person wins the game. Scores are kept and people bet on the outcome, usually wagering articles of clothing.

According to *Traditional Teachings*, a publication of the North American Indian Travelling College, the Peach Bowl game originated as a sacred ceremony to express thanks and to please the Creator. Long ago,

they say, before the *Hotinonshonni* (Six Nations Iroquois) had spiritual beliefs and laws to guide them, a boy was sent to them to teach them how to be grateful to the Creator for all the things that they have. He taught them three great dances to pay respect to the earth, the sun, the moon, the plants and animals, and to all the forces of nature that sustain life. He left the *Hotinonshonni* for a time, and he returned to teach them one more ceremony, the Great Peach Bowl Game. He showed them how the game was played and told them it was to be played for the amusement of the Creator. He said the main purpose of the game was "to remind you that the things you have around you are not yours. They do not belong to you. They belong to the world." By playing the game and losing things when gambling, it sends a message to the Creator that you are grateful for your material belongings and are willing to share them with others.

with the supernatural. Sometimes misfortune can be attributed to an imbalance between invisible forces, which may be corrected by a struggle between opposite sides.

Running has been an important activity for Native Americans since ancient times. In the past, runners served as messengers, uniting large territories by carrying information to distant villages. The Six Nations (Iroquois) territory, from Albany to Buffalo, New York, was united by a trail. When the runners arrived at their destination, they repeated carefully memorized messages, or delivered messages indicated by strands of purple and white wampum. Messages, generally the number of days before a meeting, were sometimes recorded by knots on a woven strand carried by the runners. Some messengers were ceremonial runners whose lives revolved around their sacred duties. They observed food taboos, abstained from sexual contact, and were considered blessed.

COMMON TRADITIONAL GAMES WITH GENERAL DESCRIPTIONS

Dice Games—(Peach pit, bowl game, basket game) Dice, made from a variety of materials (bone, seed, wood, leather, cane, etc.) that are light on one side and dark on the other or are carved to represent different animals or marked with different designs, are tossed in a bowl or basket. The score is determined by the numbers of dice of one color or design that face upward. Often played by women, but played by both sexes in some areas. The game has ritual forms. Played widely over North America, with many variations, by many tribes.

Stick Games—Played with sticks similar to arrowshafts that are painted with colored bands or with a number of splints or straws, of which one or more are marked, or with unmarked sticks. The sticks, from ten to one hundred, are divided into two bundles and the object is to guess the location of the marked sticks. In some games, the object is to guess which hand holds the odd (or even) number of sticks. Sometimes played to the accompaniment of songs.

Hand Games—Played over most of North America in different forms. In general, it is played by two sides who sit opposite each other. Both men and women play; in the past men played separately from women, but today they play together. A player (sometimes two) from one side conceals two bone or wood cylinders in the hands. One is marked around the middle. While the players sing accompanied by drums, the players with the cylinders keep time to the music with their hands and their bodies. A person from the opposite side tries to guess which hand contains the marked cylinder. The guesser signifies his guess with hand signals. The score is kept with marked sticks. The games are accompanied by much excitement, merriment, and occasional exuberant whoops. The ceremonial hand game is sedate.

4-Stick Game—Played by several tribes in the Far West. Two players sit opposite each other, one places four sticks that are differently marked, or of different sizes, under a mat, bowl, or blanket. The guesser tries to determine the relative position of the four sticks: whether the large (or marked) sticks are placed on the outside, the inside, or alternating with the other sticks. Sometimes the game is accompanied by singing.

Hidden Ball or Moccasin Game—Played widely over North America. The object of the game is to guess the location of an object that is hidden under four moccasins or pieces of some kind of material (cloth or buckskin), or in cups or cylinders. In some areas, the choice of the guesser is indicated by pointing to it with a stick. The game is often accompanied by songs. This game, as with many others, has ritual aspects.

Races are part of the oral traditions of many tribal nations. The outcome of mythic races long ago determined much of the present world order. The Cheyenne relate how the arrogant buffalo and other animals with split hooves challenged the people and the birds to a race. The people defeated the split-hooves and won the race with the help of a hawk. The split-hooved animals forever after became the food of humans.

Running was, and to a certain extent still is, an important means of physical training and an activity grounded in ritual and mythology. Running was a way to prepare the body for hunting and warfare. The Pima are said to have run down deer and to smother them. The Apache put young boys on their way to becoming warriors through endurance training that included distance running. Apache women run during their coming of age ceremony in order to symbolically make them strong, beautiful, and long lived.

Snow Snake—A 5- or 6-foot missile is thrown along a trough made in the snow to see how far it will slide. Played widely in the northern United States and Canada where there is snow in winter. The snow snake is still a popular activity for the Six Nations (Iroquois) people of upstate New York and Canada.

Hoop and Pole—Men or boys throw or shoot a spear, dart, or arrows at a rolling hoop that often has a network or web in the center. The game has a ritual form.

Ring and Pin—A small ring is attached to a stick about eight inches long. The ring is tossed into the air and the player attempts to catch the ring by impaling it on the stick.

Lacrosse—The lacrosse racket is made of a sapling, bent at one end into a hook and laced with thongs to form a net in which the ball is caught and thrown. The ball was at one time made of wood; later it was made of stuffed hide, and today, the ball is often made of synthetic material. The object of the game is to catch the ball with the racket and throw it over, or into, the opponents' goal, which is placed at one end of a playing field. At one time, the goals were often miles apart, and the game was quite rough. Among the people of the Southeast, it was referred to as the "little brother of war." Lacrosse was played over much of North America, and today is played internationally. According to the Six Nations (Iroquois), lacrosse was a gift from the Creator. It is part of the cultural and spiritual heritage of North American Indians and was often played to heal the sick.

Shinny—A game similar to lacrosse. Played with a stick that is crooked on one end, but does not have a net with which to catch the ball.

Double Ball—Played mainly by women, using a stick with a crook on one end and two balls connected by a thong. The game was similar to the men's game of lacrosse, the object being to hook the thong with the crooked stick and toss the balls over the opponent's goal.

Swimming—Swimming was an important sport for many Indian people. It was a necessary skill for people who lived close to nature and who often used watercraft for transportation. In the 1830s, George Catlin described the Mandan swimming in a river in a manner unknown in Europe. The stroke he described is known as the American crawl today, and it is a powerful stroke that is widely used in competition and leisure swimming.

Canoeing and Kayaking—American Indians invented the canoe, and the Eskimos invented the kayak; both have been adopted by non-Indians.

Running is also a means of communication with the forces of nature. Ritual foot races are conducted to induce rain and bountiful harvests in the Southwest, to locate buffalo on the Plains, and to accompany the spirits of the dead in the Arctic. Races are run between two people or clans of a village, between different villages, or by nearly every one in a village. There are races for men and for women and betting on the outcome is common.

In the Southwest and in California, there is a variation called the kick-stick race, in which runners kick a small stick ahead of them as they run. Among the Pueblo people of the Southwest the kick-stick is associated with rain. They say that the rain comes down in uneven bursts and torrents because the kachinas play kick-stick. The kick-ball race is a variation on the kick-stick race.

Before the arrival of Europeans, the game of lacrosse was played over much of what became the United States. The game was part of the lives of the numerous Algonquian-speaking people and the Iroquois-speaking people of the Northeast Woodlands, the Dakota and Cheyenne of the Great Plains, the Muskhogean and Cherokee tribes of the Southeast, the Chinook and Salish of the Northwest, and of some tribes in California. Most tribes observed rituals and ceremonies before the game. For the Cherokee, preparation for the game involved elaborate observances. The players had to observe food and behavioral taboos, avoiding the eating of meat of animals such as the timid rabbit, the frog, whose bones are brittle, and a certain slow moving fish. Men had to abstain from physical contact with women before a game and participate in rituals designed to bring success. A night-long dance with men and women as participants was held the night before the game. Just before the game began, the spiritual leader performed a ceremonial bloodletting by scratching twenty-eight shallow cuts on the limbs of the players prior to the start of the game. Finally, the players rubbed their bodies with the juice from a root and washed themselves in the river. The webbing on lacrosse rackets were often intertwined with the whiskers of a bat, and the players adorned their bodies with paint and wore a feather in their hair from the powerful eagle or hawk.

The antiquity of traditional sports among Native Americans is evident from the presence of lacrosse in the oral literature of many tribes. The Menominee of the Great Lakes tell how the beings above challenged the beings below to a game of lacrosse. The beings below were represented by the fishes and the creatures of the fields, the beings above were represented by the birds of the air; all took human form for the game. The goals for this primordial game were placed far apart, one at present-day Chicago and the other at Detroit. The Cherokee tell how two new animals were created in the course of a lacrosse game. The ground animals once challenged the birds to a ball game. The birds assembled in trees overlooking the playing field, and the four-legged animals were preparing themselves below. Before the start of the game, two small creatures climbed up the birds' tree and asked if they could join the game. The birds asked them why they did not join the ground animals, and the small creatures said the ground animals did not want them because they were so small. So the birds took pity on them and made a tiny pair of wings from the edge of their drumhead, which was made of groundhog skin. They fastened the skin to the front and back legs of the first small creature and taught him to fly, creating the first bat. The skin on the drumhead was used up on the first creature, so they stretched the skin between the front and back legs of the other animal and created the flying squirrel.

In addition to the spiritual connection of traditional native games and sports, there was an important social aspect as well. Sports were open to all tribal members, involvement was not based on social or economic class, and most sports were team-oriented rather than individual efforts. Teams were often based on kinship ties or on membership in a moiety, which is a division of a tribe into two parts (for example, earth and sky, summer and winter, red and blue moieties). Sometimes, teams consisted of members of one village or town, which would play teams from another town. The games reinforced kinship, moiety, and village ties and stressed the value of co-operation. The more important the ceremony, the greater the number of participants and spectators. A lacrosse game could have a dozen or several hundred participants.

Women and men played prominent roles in sports, but with differences. In some tribes, women played a slightly different version of lacrosse, which was played with a stick, rather than a racket, and two balls connected by a thong. In both forms, touching the ball with the hands was forbidden. Gambling was an integral and universal component of all sports and was not associated with unsavory elements, as it often is in non-Indian culture, but was a component of the spiritual aspect of the games.

MODERN SPORTS INVOLVEMENT

Through the process of assimilation, attendance at boarding schools, reduced military conflict, and re-settlement, Native Americans began to play non-traditional modern sports. They attained national visibility through the emergence of team sports, especially football and baseball. The Indian schools were important factors in Indian participation in non-traditional sports. The two schools that became sports powerhouses were Carlisle Indian Industrial School and Haskell Institute. Although these gov-ernment schools did not offer college-level courses, but rather were "industrial" schools teaching basic reading and math and vocational trades, they gave Indians an entry into professional sports by allowing the students to compete at the college level.

The Carlisle Indian Industrial School in Carlisle, Pennsylvania, opened in 1879 and closed in 1918. It was the first off-reservation school funded by the federal government. The Carlisle sports program gained national attention under Coach Glenn S. "Pop" Warner, who guided the football teams to numerous victories from 1899–1912. According to *American Indian Sports Heritage* by Joseph Oxendine,

Carlisle produced many outstanding Indian athletes including Lewis Tewanima, Gus Welch, and others. Carlisle's greatest athlete was Jim Thorpe, a Sac and Fox-Potawatomi from Oklahoma. While at Carlisle, from 1904 to 1912, he lettered in eleven sports: football, baseball, track, boxing, wrestling, la-crosse, gymnastics, swimming, hockey, handball, and basketball. In 1912, he won respective gold

Jim Thorpe, Sac and Fox-Potawatomi at the peak of his career, 1911–1912. Named the greatest football player of the half century in the Associated Press Mid-Century Poll and the winner of two Olympic gold medals, he was an excellent all round sportsman. Courtesy of Associated Press/Wide World Photos.

JIM THORPE WINS—AND LOSES—TWO GOLD MEDALS

In the 1912 Olympic games in Sweden, Jim Thorpe won two gold medals, one for the decathlon and one for the pentathlon. He was hailed as a hero on his return to the United States and was voted the "Greatest Athlete of the Half-Century" in 1950 by the Associated Press. He was also the subject of a seventy-year controversy over the nature of amateurism in sports. Around six months after his triumphal Olympic performance, a newspaper reported that he had received money (two dollars a day for expenses) while playing baseball for minor league teams in the summers of 1909 and 1910. The Amateur Athletic Union (AAU) stripped him of his amateur standing and the International Olympic Committee (IOC) struck his name from the record book, took back his medals, and gave them to the second-place winners. Rule 26 of the IOC forbids anyone to compete in the Olympics who has received money for playing sports. It is likely that he did not think it would hurt his standing, since it was common for other Olympic athletes to play for expenses in minor league teams, and his coach told him to do so. His innocence is also suggested in that he played under his real name, while other players used assumed names to keep their amateur standing intact. While officials probably looked the other way at this practice, his name was too big and his achievements were too great for the IOC to ignore.

Jim Thorpe was by all accounts a modest man. After winning the decathlon, when the King of Sweden congratulated him by saying, "Sir, you are the greatest athlete in the world," he reportedly replied, "Thanks, King." He did nothing to try to get his medals returned and rarely spoke of his achievements. He went on to coach college and professional teams, and he played professional football and baseball until 1928. He died in 1953 at the age of 64, but his family never gave up efforts to have his standing restored and his medals returned. In 1982, the Jim Thorpe Foundation was established to work toward restoration of his medals.

In 1973, the AAU reinstated his amateur status. In 1982, due to the discovery of a technicality that voided the earlier stand, the IOC had no choice but to return his amateur status.

Replicas of the medals were formally presented to the heirs of Jim Thorpe on January 18, 1983. In 1984, Dennis Banks, a Ojibwa militant leader, organized the Jim Thorpe Longest Run, in which teams of Indian runners left from the Onondaga Nation in upstate New York and ran in relays across the United States, ending in Los Angeles in time for the 1984 Olympics. During the Olympics, a large powwow was held to honor Jim Thorpe and the return of his medals to his family after seventy years.

Commemorative stamp of Jim Thorpe, Sac and Fox-Potawatomi from Oklahoma. Jim Thorpe won two gold medals at the 1912 Olympics, one for the pentathlon, the other for the decathlon. He was stripped of his medals by the International Olympic Committee because he accepted expense money for playing in minor league baseball. Courtesy of the U. S. Postal Service.

Runners leaving New York City on their way to the Onondaga reservation in upstate New York to take part in the Jim Thorpe Longest Run. The Longest Run began at Onondaga and ended in Los Angeles at the site of the 1984 Olympics. At a ceremony during the games, the Olympic Committee returned Jim Thorpe's gold medals to his family. Photograph by M.K. de Montaño.

medals for the pentathlon and decathlon in the Olympics and scored twenty-five touchdowns for the Carlisle football team. He went on to play professional baseball for seven years and professional football for nine years.

Carlisle began formal competition in football in 1893 with limited success in the beginning, but soon began playing the best college teams in the country with some success. The unexpected success sparked a recruitment drive for students with athletic promise. In 1899, Glen Warner, an aggressive, relentless, and hard driving football coach, was hired. He pushed the team into excessively heavy schedules and lead the team to surprising successes against Harvard, Villanova, Syracuse, and Colum-

bia. In 1906, Carlisle was ranked fifth in the nation. In 1911, Carlisle, with Jim Thorpe playing, won eleven out of twelve games, with a team that had no playing field of their own. In 1914, a former student, Gus Welsh, initiated a complaint concerning the sacrifice of academics for the sports program. The school was investigated by the Senate, which led to its closing in 1918.

Haskell Institute is located in Lawrence, Kansas, close to sizeable and diverse native communities. Haskell was created by an act of Congress in 1882 and opened in 1884. In 1971, Haskell became Haskell Indian Junior College. When Carlisle closed in 1918, Indian sports achievement was centered at Haskell, and the school gained national prominence in football and track. Probably the greatest Indian athlete from Haskell was John Levi, an Arapaho from Oklahoma. Levi, who attended Haskell from 1921 to 1924, was on the All-American football team in 1923. While at Haskell, he played football, basketball, baseball, and track. During a baseball game between Haskell and Drake University, John Levi played baseball for Haskell and, between innings, competed in a track meet against Baker University and won first place in the shotput, discus, and high jump. Other outstanding athletes who got their start at Haskell were Philip Osif and Wilson "Buster" Charles, who were both members of the 1932 United States Olympic team.

During the 1920s and 1930s, Haskell attained national prominence for its sports programs, especially in football and track. As early as 1917, Haskell was winning track meets against large universities. Haskell produced several Olympic and professional athletes before the commissioner of Indian affairs intervened so as not to repeat the mistake of Carlisle. Sports would not overshadow the real goal of the school—the assimilation of the students into mainstream culture. Haskell maintained a balance between sports and academics and still produced outstanding athletes, such as Chester Ellis, the national Golden Gloves champion in 1939, and Billy Mills, who won the gold medal for the 10,000 meters in the 1964 Olympics. Haskell celebrated its centennial in 1984 and continues to offer a wide variety of educational and vocational courses to Native Americans. Haskell also has active sports teams for men and women, but sports do not dominate the school as they once did.

Marie Kreipe swimming the butterfly in competition at the 1982 Master's Long Course swimming meet in the Woodlands, Texas. Marie, a Potawatomi from Kansas, competes in the 70- to 74-year-old group. She has won numerous medals and was awarded a Presidential Sports Award in Swimming from President Jimmy Carter in 1977. Photograph by M. K. de Montaño.

Members of the Mesquakie tribe celebrate the 135th anniversary of their return to their ancestral homelands in Iowa with a hidden ball game. The game is played by two teams, one hides a ball or a stone under a small blanket, the other tries to find it. Photograph by Doug Wells, reprinted with permission of The Des Moines Register and Tribune Company.

THE AMERICAN INDIAN ATHLETIC HALL OF FAME

The American Indian Athletic Hall of Fame was established in 1972 on the campus of Haskell Indian Junior College to honor Indian athletes who have made a national impact in sports and athletic events and to preserve records of their achievements and memorabilia. Over sixty individuals from a variety of tribes have been inducted, spanning 1890 to the 1990s. The inductees' sport achievements are in traditional native activities and modern sports.

Inductees into the American Indian Athletic Hall of Fame (1972–1991)

Name	Tribe/Nation	School(s)	Sports; Teams; Years Played	Year Inducted
Arcasa, Alexander	Coleville	Carlisle	Carlisle football and lacrosse (1909–1912); All-American Football (1912)	1972
Bender, Charles	Chippewa	Carlisle	Philadelphia Athletics (baseball) (1903–1917); Top American League pitcher (1911); Selected to Baseball Hall of Fame (1953)	1972
Charles, Wilson	Oneida	Haskell University of New Mexico	Haskell track & field, football, and basketball (1927–1931); U.S. Olympic (decathlon) team (1932)	1972
Exendine, Albert	Delaware	Carlisle	Carlislie football (1902–1907); All-American (1906, 1907)	1972
Guyon, Joseph	White Earth Chippewa	Carlisle Georgia Tech University	Carlisle football (1911–1914); Georgia Tech (1917–1918); All-American (1917–1918); Professional football (1920–1927) with Canton, Kansas City, New York Giants; Professional Football Hall of Fame (1966)	1972
Johnson, Jimmie	Stockbridge-Munsee	Carlisle Northwestern University	Carlisle football (1899–1903); All-American, (1903); Northwestern football (1904–1905)	1972
Levi, John	Arapaho	Haskell	Haskell football (1921–1924); All-American fullback (1923); New York Yankees baseball (1925)	1972
Meyers, John	Cahuilla	Dartmouth College	New York Giants baseball (1908–1912); Brooklyn Dodgers, (1916–1917); Batted .358 in 1912	1972
Reynolds, Allie P.	Creek	Oklahoma State	Baseball pitcher with Cleveland Indians (1942–1946), and New York Yankees (1947–1954); Best earned run average in the American League (1952, 1954); Led League in strikeouts and shutouts for two years; America's Professional Athlete of the year (1951)	1972
Roebuck, Theodore	Choctaw	Haskell	Haskell football and track (1923–1927); All-American track, (1926); Professional boxer and wrestler	1972

Name	Tribe/Nation	School(s)	Sports; Teams; Years Played	Year Inducted
Sanders, Reuben	Tututni-Rouge River Tribe	Chemawa Indian School Wilmette College	Chemawa Indian School football (1890s); Wilmette College football, (1890s); Legendary distinction as participant in football, baseball, track, and bike racing in Athletic Clubs in Oregon	1972
Tewanima, Louis	Hopi	Carlisle	Haskell track team (1907–1912); U.S. Olympic team (1908, 1912); Won silver medals in 5,000- and 10,000-meter runs, (1912); Held world record (ten miles) (1909)	1972
Thorpe, Jim	Sac & Fox Potawatomi	Carlisle	Carlisle football and track (1907–1912); Canton Bulldogs, New York Giants football (1920–1929); New York Giants baseball, (1913–1919); Olympic Games (winner of pentathlon and decathlon) (1912); Greatest Athlete (first half of the twentieth Century [Associated Press])	1972
Weller, Louis	Caddo	Haskell	Haskell football (1929–1931); Professional football with Boston Red Sox (NFL) and Tulsa Oilers (AFL)	1972
Brown, Ellison	Narragansett		U.S. Olympic marathon team, 1936; Boston Marathon winner, (1936, 1939)	1973
Busch, Elmer	Pomo	Carlisle	Carlisle football, 1910–1914; All-American (1913)	1973
Finger, Wallace L.	Sioux	Haskell	Haskell track (1926); Established records in Drake, Texas, and Kansas Relays	1973
Hawley, Albert	Gros Ventre-Assiniboine	Haskell Davis & Elkins College	Haskell Institute football (1922–1928); Davis & Elkins football (1928–1932); All-American (1928, 1929)	1973
Hudson, Frank	Laguna Pueblo	Carlisle	Carlisle football (1890–1900); All-American (1899)	1973

(continued)

Name	Tribe/Nation	School(s)	Sports; Teams; Years Played	Year Inducted
Jacobs, Jack	Creek	Oklahoma University	Oklahoma University football (1939–1942); Professional football with Cleveland Rams, Washington Redskins, Green Bay Packers, Winnipeg Blue Bombers (1942–1955)	1973
Johnson, Walter	Paiute	Haskell University of Redland	Haskell football (1929–1933); All-American (1931, 1932); University of Redlands football (1934–1935)	1973
Mills, William	Oglala Sioux	Haskell University of Kansas	Track and cross-country at Haskell and University of Kansas, (1955–1962); Gold medal (10,000 meters) at Olympics (establishing record), 1964	1973
Mt. Pleasant, Frank	Tuscarora	Carlisle	Carlisle football and track & field; All-American quarterback (1905); U.S. Olympic team (long jump and triple jump) (1908)	1973
Pierce, Bemus	Seneca	Carlisle	Carlisle football (1894–1898); First American Indian All-American (1896); Professional football (1900–1901); Homestead Athletic Club, Akron Pros, and Oorang Indians (1922)	1973
Renick, Jessie	Choctaw	Oklahoma A & M	Oklahoma A & M basketball (1937–1940); All-American (1939, 1940); Captain of U.S. basketball team in Olympic Games (gold medal) (1948); Coach-player with the Philips Oilers (1948–1952)	1973
Rogers, Ed	White Earth Chippewa	Carlisle University of Minnesota	Carlisle football (1896–1897); University of Minnesota football (1901–1903); All-American (1903)	1973
Rosal, Angelita	Sioux		Member of U.S. Woman's Table Tennis Team (at age 17) (1972–1973)	1973
Welsh, Gustavus	Chippewa	Carlisle	Carlisle football team quarterback and captain (1911–1914); All-American (1912); Canton Ohio Bulldogs (1915–1917)	1973

Name	Tribe/Nation	School(s)	Sports; Teams; Years Played	Year Inducted
Wolf, Jimmie	Kiowa	Panhandle State Oklahoma State	Panhandle State football (1955–1956; Oklahoma State football (1957–1958); NAIA All-American (1958); National scoring champion (1958)	1973
Ellis, Chester	Seneca	Haskell	Haskell boxing (1935–1939); International Golden Gloves champion (bantamweight) (1939)	1977
Howell, Stach	Pawnee	Murray A & M Junior College East Central College	Murray A & M Junior College basketball (1947–1948); Junior College All-American (1948); NAIA All-American basketball (1950)	1977
James, Clyde	Modoc	Missouri Southwest State College	Missouri Southwest State basketball (1924–1925); Tulsa Eagles and Tulsa Diamond Oilers (AAU basketball teams) (1927–1947)	1977
Musell, Rollie	Chickasaw	Chilocco Indian School	Missouri Valley AAU boxing champion (1935); More than 100 professional fights (1938–1942)	1977
Osif, Philip	Pima	Haskell	Haskell track & cross-country (1924–1927); Captain of two-mile relay team that was undefeated in Penn, Kansas, and Texas Relays; National AAU junior and senior six-mile champion	1977
Foster, Harold	Navajo	Central Arizona College	Central Arizona track & field; NJCAA All-American cross-country runner (1972); Fastest cross-country time in nation for junior colleges (1973)	1978
Sahmaunt, Joseph	Kiowa	Cameron State Junior College Oklahoma City University	Cameron State Junior College basketball (1957); Oklahoma City University (1958–1960); All-American (honorable mention) (1959–1960)	1978
Thornton, Joe Trindle	Cherokee	Chilocco Indian School	World archery champion (1961); Member of world champion U.S. Archery Teams, (1967, 1971); National Archery Champion (at age 54) (1970)	1978

(continued)

Inductees into the American Indian Athletic Hall of Fame (1972–1991) *(cont.)*

Name	Tribe/Nation	School(s)	Sports; Teams; Years Played	Year Inducted
Ward, Egbert B.	Yakima	Haskell Washington State College	Haskell football, basketball, baseball (1923–1926); Selected as quarterback on Haskell's All-Time team; Washington State College football, basketball, baseball (1927–1928)	1978
Smith, Elijah	Oneida	Haskell Davis & Elkins College	Haskell football, baseball, track (1923–1926); Established national record for extra points kicked; Davis & Elkins College football, baseball (1927–1929)	1980
Gawboy, Robert	Chippewa	Purdue University	World swimming record in 200-yard breaststroke (1955); Gold medal winner AAU Aquatic meet (1955)	1980
Wheelock, Martin	Oneida	Carlisle	Carlisle football (1894–1902); All-American (1901); "All-University" (Philadelphia *Inquirer*) (1902)	1980
Bray, David	Seneca	Cornell University	Cornell lacrosse, track, cross-country, basketball (1976–1977); All-American lacrosse (1977); North American Lacrosse Association All-Star (1975–1977)	1981
Levering, Nelson	Omaha-Bannock	Haskell	Midwest Golden Glove welterweight boxing champion (1947, 1948); Won 23 of 28 professional fights, 17 by knockout	1981
Tincup, Austin Ben	Cherokee	Haskell	Major league baseball player with the Philadelphia Phillies and Chicago Cubs (1914–1915); Coach and scout with Yankees, Browns, Phillies	1981
Aitson, Amos	Kiowa	Riverside Indian School	Riverside Indian School football (1944); boxing (1944–1945); National AAU boxing champion (118 class) (1945)	1982

Name	Tribe/Nation	School(s)	Sports; Teams; Years Played	Year Inducted
Levi, George	Arapaho	Haskell	Haskell football, track, and basketball (1923–1926); All-American (honorable mention) football (1926)	1982
Yarr, Thomas C.	Snohomish	Notre Dame University	Notre Dame football (1929–1933); All-American center (1931); Captain of national championship team (1931)	1982
Burd, Sampson	Blackfeet	Carlisle	Carlisle football (1909–1911, 1914–1915); All-American (1911); Lacrosse, and track & field (1909–1911)	1985
Franklin, Virgil	Arapaho-Kiowa	Chilocco Indian School Murray State College	Murray State boxing, football, baseball, and track (1947–1948); National Golden Glove and National AAU boxing champion (126 lbs.) (1945); All-Armed Forces featherweight title (1946)	1985
Holmes, Robert T.	Ottawa	Haskell Riverside Junior College Texas Technical College	Haskell, Riverside, Texas Tech football, track & field (1931–1938); Established Haskell records in 100-yard dash and javlin throw	1985
House, Gordon	Navajo-Oneida	Phoenix Indian School Ft. Wingate Indian School Albuquerque Indian School	State lightweight boxing champion in Arizona, Nevada, and Texas (1948); All-Armed Forces lightweight boxing champion, (1945); Professional Boxer (1946–1949)	1985
Abel, Clarence "Taffy"	Sault Ste. Marie Chippewa	Sault Ste. Marie High School University of Minnesota	Amateur hockey, 1920–1926; U.S. Olympic Team captain and color bearer, took the Olympic oath for all U.S. players (1924); Professional hockey with N.Y. Rangers (1926–1929) (team won the Stanley Cup in 1919); Chicago Black Hawks, (1929–1934) (team won the Stanley Cup in 1934); U.S. Hockey Hall of Fame (1973)	1989

(continued)

Name	Tribe/Nation	School(s)	Sports; Teams; Years Played	Year Inducted
Ingram, James Aron	Chickasaw	Bacone College Oklahoma Christian College	Bacone College baseball, track & field, and basketball (1958–1960); Oklahoma Christian College track & field (1961–1963); Oklahoma Christian College school record holder in the 880 run, mile run, two-mile run, sprint medley, and distance medley.	1989
Moore, Euel "Monk"	Chickasaw		Minor league baseball (1929–1934); Professional baseball with the Philadelphia Phillies (1934–1935); N.Y. Giants (1935); Philadelphia Phillies (1936–1937); Minor league baseball, (1938–1940)	1989
Williams, Alvin LeRoy	Caddo		Amateur boxer (1944–1948); Professional boxer (1944–1960); fought 94 professional bouts, won 54 (24 by knockout), 7 draws, and 33 losses; Oklahoma Athletic Hall of Fame (1973); Founded The American Indian New Life Boxing Club in Oklahoma City (1975)	1989
Allen, John Gene	Tonkawa-Sac & Fox	Oklahoma A&M College Northeastern State College	Oklahoma A&M College football (1956); Northeastern State College football, basketball, and baseball, (1957–1958); Professional football with London Lords of Canadian League (1959–1960); named "Basketball Coach of the Year," Region 3, Oklahoma Coaches Association (1981–1982)	1991
Moore, Edwin Stanton	Creek	Chilocco Indian School Oklahoma A&M College	Oklahoma A&M College football (1938–1940); awarded Department of the Interior Meritorious Service Medal upon retirement as Director of Indian Education, Muskogee, Oklahoma (1979)	1991

(continued)

Name	Tribe/Nation	School(s)	Sports; Teams; Years Played	Year Inducted
Payne, Andrew Hartley	Cherokee	Oklahoma City University	Winner of "The Great Cross-Country Marathon Race" from Los Angeles to New York City, which began on March 4, 1928 with 275 participants; finished the 3,442.3 mile race in 573 hours, 4 minutes, 34 seconds.	1991
The 1926 Haskell Indian Football Team	Various tribal affiliations	Haskell	Of 13 games, won 12 and tied 1. Highest scoring team of the year— 559 points, highest scoring player, Mayes McLain, scored 259 points.	1991

Honorary Inductees into the American Indian Athletic Hall of Fame (1972–1985)

Name	Tribe/Nation	Services Honored	Year Inducted
Bruce, Louis R.	Mohawk-Sioux	Former commissioner of the Bureau of Indian Affairs, instrumental in founding the American Indian Athletic Hall of Fame	1973
Bennett, Robert	Oneida	Former commissioner of the Bureau of Indian Affairs, instrumental in founding the American Indian Athletic Hall of Fame	1977
McDonald, Frank W.	Non-Indian	Recognized for service to Indian youth and Indian people; coach and administrator at Haskell	1978
Lavatta, George P.	Shoshone-Bannock	Continuous service to the American Indian Hall of Fame	1981
Cochran, Turner	Caddo-Chickasaw	Instrumental in developing the "Hall of Heroes" at Haskell Indian Junior College; Curator of the American Indian Athletic Hall of Fame	1982
Carney, Sidney M.	Choctaw-Creek	Instrumental in elevating Haskell Institute to Junior College status	1985

WORLD ESKIMO-INDIAN OLYMPICS

Founded in 1961, the world-famous World Eskimo-Indian Olympics are held each July in Fairbanks, Alaska. The four days of games test athletic skill, strength, endurance, concentration, and agility in sports passed down from one generation of natives to another over the centuries. In addition to the games, there are dance, art, and cultural displays as well as sewing competitions, Eskimo and Indian dance team competitions, and contests for fish cutting, seal skinning, and *muktuk* (an Inuit food treat) eating. The Native Baby Contest, for children between the ages of six and twenty-four months, grabs everyone's attention. The babies and parent (or grandparent) who wear traditional clothing win on authenticity and audience appeal. The games come complete with an Olympic flame, the lighting of seal oil lamps, and a logo with six interwoven rings representing the six major Eskimo and Indian tribes in Alaska: Aleuts, Athabascans, Eskimos (Inuits), Haidas, Tlingits, and Tsimshians.

Ancient Eskimos took their games seriously. Competition in them required toughness and stamina. To keep tough, Eskimos developed contests that left no part of the body untested. Elders of the small villages staged games to condition young men for the subzero environment of the arctic and for hunts that lasted many days. Games provided training in the strength, endurance, agility, and concentration needed for young hunters to jump across ice floes in the event the sea ice on which they traveled broke away from the shorefast ice. Young hunters needed strength to haul game, ice, and wood over long distances and to pull slippery fish from nets. Dancing, storytelling, and cultural games were also integral parts of these informal events.

EVENTS

Race of the Torch—Traditional opening event of the games. Five kilometers long, the winners of the men's and women's races carry a flaming torch around the arena, pass them to two elders who tend a traditional source of light, peat-soaked in seal oil, for the duration of the games.

Alaskan High Kick (Men and Women)—The contestants sit on the floor and with one hand grab their opposite foot. With the other hand remaining on the floor, they spring up and kick the suspended seal-fur ball with the free foot, landing on that same foot before any other part of the body touches the floor. The foot being held must remain firmly grasped throughout the attempt.

Arm Pull (Men and Women)—Two players sit on the floor facing each other and position themselves so that one leg crosses over the opposite leg of the other player. They then lock arms at the elbows, fists down, the free hand of both players is placed on the knee or ankle of the opponent. They then pull, attempting to straighten the bent arm of their opponent. There are three attempts allowed, with arms and legs switched after each attempt.

Blanket Toss or *Nalukatuk* (Men and Women)—Sport originating in the distant past by Eskimo whaling communities on the Arctic coast, *Nalukatuk* was never performed at any other time except at celebrations for successful whalers. The blanket is made from three to four *oogruk* (bearded seal) skins sewed together. The person on the blanket does not jump or bend his or her knees and avoids looking down while being tossed. The person tossed can reach heights of thirty to forty feet with a good team of pullers.

Drop the Bomb (Men and Women)—The contestants, in a horizontal iron-cross position with three men carrying them, hold their bodies rigid for as long as their strength and endurance will allow. Those going the farthest distance without permitting their body to sag wins.

Ear Pull—Sitting face-to-face with either twine or sinew looped around their ears, two athletes play tug-of-war with their heads. When the twine slips off one of the contestant's ears, he loses that round. The winner must win the best two out of three rounds.

Ear Weight—With sixteen pounds of lead weight hanging from twine looped around the ear, the contestant must walk around the arena until the weight can no longer be supported.

Eskimo Stick Pull—Two athletes sit facing each other with their feet pressed together and knees bent. They grasp a stick, their hands alternating, all hands touching. The object is to pull the opponent upright or to pull the stick out of his grasp. The stick cannot be grasped at any time during the match. Best two out of three wins, with hands alternating each match.

Four-Man Carry—The event tests strength and endurance with distance the measure of winning.

Greased Pole Walk (Men and Women)—This game originated with the Athabascan Indians of interior Alaska. A pole, about six inches in diameter and twelve feet long, is covered with grease. The object is to see who can walk or slide the farthest without falling off.

Indian Stick Pull—This contest tests strength and grip. The object is to pull a greased, tapered stick straight back out of the grasp of the opponent.

Kneel Jump (Men and Women)—The contestant kneels on the floor at the starting line with feet flat, bottoms up. From this kneeling position, he or she then jumps as far forward as possible without losing balance. No steps forward or backward are allowed. The contestants are allowed to swing their arms to gather momentum for the leap forward.

Knuckle Hop (Men and Women)—The object is to go for distance; while positioned as for push-ups, the athlete propels himself forward with only the toes and knuckles in contact with the floor. The back must remain straight and the elbows bent.

One-Foot High Kick (Men and Women)/**Two-Foot High Kick** (Men and Women)—These two events represent one of the greatest tests of athletic skill. The events are similar but in the two-foot kick both feet must remain together while making contact with the target, commonly a sealskin ball suspended at heights known to reach eight feet in the air, and then when landing on the floor. In the One-Foot High Kick, the athlete jumps from one foot, kicks the target, and then lands on that same foot.

One-Hand Reach—A test of balance and strength, the contestants must balance on their hands, elbows tucked into the lower stomach area, and the body parallel to the floor with legs stretched backward. In this position, the athlete then reaches one hand up to touch a suspended target and returns that hand to the floor before any other part of the body touches the floor.

Toe Kick (Men and Women)—The contestants jump forward, attempting to kick a stick backward with the toes of both feet, landing forward of the stick's original position. The stick is moved forward in three-inch increments, with each contestant allowed three attempts at each distance.

White Men vs. Native Women Tug-O-War—Native women have never lost this annual contest, which is held outside on the grass behind the arena.

A demonstration of the two-foot high kick, an event in the Eskimo-Indian Olympics, in which a suspended sealskin ball is kicked with both feet. Photograph by M. K. de Montaño.

DEGRADING NATIVE AMERICAN SPORTS MASCOTS

Fall and winter are the seasons when hundreds of sports fans root for professional, college, and public school teams with war-whooping mascots and team names such as "Braves," "Redskins," and "Chiefs." Many Indians and non-Indians believe cartoon Indian mascots insult and stereotype actual native people. Furthermore, they believe Indian mascots develop and perpetuate racist perceptions of Native Americans, especially when mascots are used in sports events where students may dress like Indians, war whoop, wave tomahawks, and use symbols such as feathers, headdresses, and drums that have religious and cultural significance.

For over twenty years, Indians and non-Indians have protested Indian mascots and insensitive team names. During this time, over a dozen colleges have changed either their team name or mascot or both. Scores of public schools around the nation are name-shopping as well.

A CHRONOLOGY OF THE MASCOT CONTROVERSY

1970   Dartmouth College (New Hampshire) changed its nickname from "Indians" to "Big Green."

1971   Marquette University (Wisconsin) abolished its mascot, "Willie Wampum."
Stanford University dropped its "Indians" team name and Chief Lightfoot mascot.

Mankato State College (Minnesota) dropped its Indian caricature mascot but retained its Indian nickname.

1972   The Cleveland Indian Center filed suit in Cuyahoga County Common Pleas Court, Ohio, objecting to "Chief Wahoo," the Cleveland Indians baseball team mascot.

1973   University of Oklahoma dropped "Little Red" mascot.

1978   Syracuse University (New York) dropped its "Saltine Warrior" mascot.
Pekin High School (Illinois) dropped its defamatory nickname "Chinks" and switched to "Dragons."

1988   Siena College (New York) dropped the team name "Indians" and replaced it with "Saints."
Saint John's University (New York) retired its Indian mascot but kept "Redmen" nickname.
Saint Mary's College (Minnesota) dropped its "Red Men" nickname in favor of "Cardinals."
The American Indian Registry for Performing Arts called on national Indian community to protest an ABC-TV program "Wonder Years," which presented Indians as mascots for the show's high school team.

Bradley University (Illinois) retired its costumed Indian mascot.

1989 Montclair State College (New Jersey) dropped its nickname and mascot.

1990 University of Illinois trustees voted to retain "Chief Illiniwek" mascot.

The depiction of Native Americans as sports team mascots, like this generalized drawing, anger many Native American and non-native people. Drawing by Leslie Frank McKeon.

1991 American Indians protested outside the World Series games between the Atlanta Braves and the Minnesota Twins.
National Congress of American Indians passed a unanimous resolution denouncing Indian nicknames.
Eastern Michigan University changed its nickname from "Hurons" to "Eagles."

1992 American Indians protested outside the Super Bowl XXVI. The National Coalition on Racism in Sports and the Media was formed.
William Hilliard, editor of the Portland *Oregonian*, announced he will no longer publish "Redskins," "Redmen," "Braves," and Indian team names.
Columbus, Georgia, "Indians," a minor league affiliate of the Cleveland Indians, changed its name to "Redsticks."
Michael Douglass, District of Columbia radio station manager of WTOP and WASH, announced that the stations will not use offensive names when referring to American Indians.
Don Shelton, assistant sports editor at the *Seattle Times* announced that the Redskins, Redmen, and Red Raiders will no longer appear in headlines, photo captions, or quotes larger than the story.

Artists

VISUAL ARTS

Native American art is as diverse and as up-to-date as the artists who produce it. Indian artists work with natural materials such as clay, hides, and antler as well as modern methods such as arc welding, camcorders, and computers. They produce beadwork, ceramics, quillwork, basket and textile weavings, jewelry, ribbonwork, and other "traditional" art forms, as well as beaded baseball hats, welded steel sculpture, and conceptual installations.

Many Native Americans see their art as part of an unbroken continuum, grounded in the past and incorporating influences from outside, but no less "Indian" because of the influences. Indian artists have been borrowing from outside their culture since before the arrival of Europeans. Acculturation and change in Native American cultures began in pre-Columbian times as a result of intertribal contact.

Precontact North America was criss-crossed by trade routes worn smooth by ancient Native American traders carrying raw materials, finished products, and ideas from one area to another. For centuries before Europeans arrived, North American Indians were in contact with other Native American groups who spoke different languages and whose life styles varied from their own. The effects of this contact can be seen in the artistic production of the people. About 700 years ago, in what is now the state of Oklahoma, artists carved elaborate depictions of men wearing ceremonial clothing. A favorite medium for the Oklahoma carvings was marine shells imported from the Gulf of Mexico. The ico-

nography of the carvings shows a link with the belief systems of Middle America. Painted ceramics from the Pueblos of present-day New Mexico were traded with the people in present-day Kansas. Flint, shells, feathers, copper, and paint were traded in large quantities over wide areas.

In the Southwest, the Anasazi or "ancient ones," lived in the Four Corners region, where four states, Arizona, New Mexico, Colorado, and Utah meet. They farmed the desert and produced shell and stone jewelry, cotton textiles, wood sculpture, and black-on-white pottery. Between A.D. 900–1100, they built apartment houses, called pueblos, that housed thousands of people. By A.D. 1300, the Anasazi had abandoned their dwellings and moved south, to east central Arizona–west central New Mexico. The area was inhabited by a people archaeologists call the Mogollon, who created pottery that was characteristically brown-on-red.

Through continuous contact, the two groups influenced each other, and their pottery shows the effects of this contact. The early black-on-white pottery scheme of the Anasazi, and the brown-on-red of the Mogollon merged after the Anasazi resettled with the Mogollon. The new color scheme incorporated something from each culture, resulting in a new decorative tradition of brown, black, white and red, which is the basis for much contemporary Pueblo pottery decoration.

Contact with Europeans produced changes in cultural systems that were used to change. Native Americans have a long history of adopting new elements that fit into their existing systems and mak-

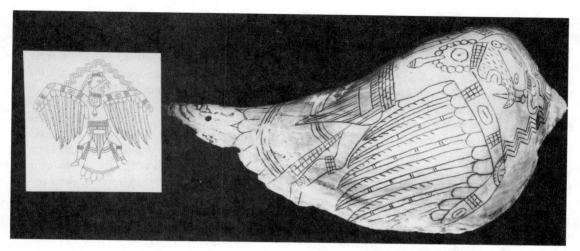

Incized conch shell from Spiro Mound, Oklahoma. Spiro Mound is the site of an ancient ceremonial center where elite families were buried in earthen mounds accompanied by ceremonial objects, such as this conch shell depicting an eagle man. The conch shell and others like it were carried from the Gulf of Mexico to northeast Oklahoma and to other sites reaching as far north as Canada. Courtesy of the National Museum of the American Indian/ Smithsonian Institution.

Right: The Anasazi, ancestors to the Pueblo people of the Southwest characteristically made black on white pottery decorated with geometric shapes and crosshatching. Courtesy of the National Museum of the American Indian/Smithsonian Institution.

Below: Polychrome bowl made in the late nineteenth century by a Zuni potter. The Zuni of western New Mexico are descendents of the Mogollon and the inheritors of the ceramic traditions of both the Anasazi and the Mogollon. Courtesy of the National Museum of the American Indian/Smithsonian Institution.

ing the new elements uniquely their own. Many of the art forms that are commonly thought of as "traditional" are a result of contact with Europeans and Native American creativity, including beadwork, ribbonwork, silversmithing, and Navajo weaving. New Indian art, whether it is "contemporary traditional" or avant guarde, has a connection to ancient beliefs and long-held values, influenced to a certain degree by others, but not necessarily less Indian because of the influence. On a basic level, the "Indianness" of Indian art is grounded in ritual and mythology and expresses a special relationship with the natural world.

Inherent in North American Indian art is a psychic projection of the relationship between humans and nature, which gives the art a presence that is beyond that of an object of beauty. There is a power underlying the aesthetic that comes from a Native American world-view that extends moral considerations to the natural world. For Native Americans, elements of the natural world possess spirits, just as humans do, and humans must have an ethical rela-

Mimbres bowl, New Mexico. The ancient people of the Mimbres valley in southwest New Mexico were related to the Mogollon. Classic Mimbres pottery, made from 1000 to 1130 A.D., consists of a white body with black painted designs depicting geometric forms and animals or human and animal transformations. Courtesy of the National Museum of the American Indian/Smithsonian Institution.

tionship with all of nature. This concept is expressed in the use of kinship terms for natural phenomena, such as Mother Earth, the Three Sisters (corn, beans, and squash), or Grandmother Moon. The Sioux have a ritual expression, or prayer, *Mitakuye oyasin*, that means "We are all related," or "All my relatives."

In tribal oral literature, humans change into animals, and animals into humans. Animals are often depicted living the same kind of life that humans do, enjoying a smoke, talking, gambling, dancing, and feasting. As a result, there is an attitude of respect and reverence for nature, an ideal that stresses reciprocity, not exploitation. These ideals are made visible in art objects. The design of an object is closely patterned on nature's own designs. What may appear to be surface decoration is rarely purely ornamental; it is most often an expression of an idea communicated through the use of design elements in a visual language.

Along the Northwest coast, from Washington state to the Alaskan panhandle, the warm Japanese current flows off shore, keeping the coastal area warm and wet. The area is covered by a rich rain forest with a thick growth of trees and abundant food from the sea and the forests. Surrounded by a bountious natural setting, the people developed a sophisticated system of social privilege and a distinct artistic tradition expressed most forcefully in carvings of animal figures on wooden totem poles, masks, rattles, spoons, bowls, and other objects. The carvings of animals represent spiritual founders of lineages among the people, and they are used to validate the privilege of different lineages. Animal masks and their associated songs and dances are considered to be the private property of different families or of societies, and one must belong to the family, or be a member of the society, to have the right to wear the masks and to sing their songs. Masks are worn in dances that retell ancient mythologies and reinforce the rights and privileges of the wearer. Totem poles are erected in front of homes and proclaim for all to see the lineage and privilege of the household.

The extraordinary carvings conform to a distinct style that seems to re-create animals from stylized

Top: *Haida rattle from Queen Charlotte Island, Canada. Sometimes called a "chief's rattle," it depicts a raven, a frog, and a shaman. Courtesy of the National Museum of the American Indian/Smithsonian Institution. Bottom: Bella Coola eagle mask from the Northwest Coast. Masks like this are worn in dances. Courtesy of the National Museum of the American Indian/Smithsonian Institution.*

Tlingit tunic woven of mountain goat hair and shredded spruce bark. The technique of depicting animals from stylized depictions of their parts can be seen in this example of Northwest Coast Chilkat weaving. Courtesy of the National Museum of the American Indian/Smithsonian Institution.

depictions of their parts. Eyes, noses, mouths, legs, and tails are abstracted and reformed into bilaterally symmetrical representations of animals that inhabit a metaphysical forest or ocean just beyond our world. The Northwest coast artists are also renowned for painting on wood and paper, weaving Chilkat blankets from mountain goat hair and shredded spruce bark, weaving basketry hats, and creating jewelry in silver and gold.

At one time, the people of the Northwest coast were forbidden to practice their religion, and their masks and other objects used in ceremonial occasions were confiscated by the government. Today, Northwest coast artists have added artistic forms of Euroamerican traditions, such as printmaking, painting on canvas, and photography to their repertory, and traditional arts have been re-energized and handed down to the next generation.

In Alaska, Native American artists continue ancient traditions that include fine carvings in wood and ivory, basketmaking, leather work, and textile

Fearon Smith, a member of the Lelooska family, carving a cedar mask. Lelooska is the name given to a Cherokee family who live in Washington state. The family was adopted by Chief James Sewid of the Kwakiutl because of their dedication to preserving and promoting the arts of the Kwakiutl. Photograph by M.K. de Montaño.

weaving. Wood is often used to carve imaginative masks that are used in dances by the Eskimo. Masked dances are meant to influence the mythological being, animal, or spirit that is depicted by the mask. The masks were at one time an integral part of life and though less central to today's livelihood, some masks are still made and worn in dances.

Eskimo men, inheritors of an ancient carving tradition, create small carvings in wood and ivory from walrus and narwhal tusks. The carvings are of animals and people. At one time, the lifelike carvings of seals, polar bears, and walruses adorned finely crafted hunting tools. Some figures were illustrations of animal-human transformation, reflecting the con-

Seal mask, made by the Inuit (Eskimo) of Good News Bay, Alaska. The soul of an animal is often depicted by a human face, as in this mask. Courtesy of the National Museum of the American Indian/Smithsonian Institution.

cept of the possibility of the close relationship between humans and animals. Human figures were used as toys for children and as amulets. Since the dawn of time, Eskimo girls have learned from their mothers to create luxurious fur clothing for their families. In an environment where the winter temperature averages 30 degrees below zero (Fahrenheit), a tear in clothing can be fatal. Warm clothing is a necessity. Not only is Eskimo clothing functional, it is an art form. Today, carvings in wood and ivory are sold to museums and collectors. Eskimo artists also participate in artistic traditions introduced by Europeans, including painting on canvas, jewelrymaking, and printmaking.

The Eastern Woodlands cover the eastern part of the United States, stretching from west of the Great Lakes south through the eastern third of Kansas to Louisiana and east to the Atlantic. The area was once covered by a huge forest, coniferous trees in the north and mangrove swamps in the south. The landscape between was—and to some extent still is today—composed of a deciduous forest with rivers, lakes, and streams. Before the arrival of Europeans, the forests were full of game—deer, wood bison, beaver, otters, bears; the rivers and streams were full of fish and waterfowl. The people depended on the animals and plants and honored them for their important role in the cycle of life.

The people recognize a multitude of spirits that animate the forests. Animals possess a powerful spiritual force that is used to augment the power of humans. Art of the woodlands often refers to and utilizes an animal's mythic power through design and symbols, as well as the use of materials from parts of animals. Quills, claws, fur, hide, feathers and tails from animals involves the spiritual power that comes from these animals. In much the same way, a floral pattern worked on a pouch may not be an exact replica of a certain flower, but neither is it merely surface decoration. It may represent the blossoms of flowers that grow nearby, or it may be an intricate arrangement of circles and lines referring to and invoking the cycle of life and eternity.

In the northern part of the woodlands, porcupine quills are used to decorate many items, including

Delaware moccasins made of buckskin decorated with porcupine quillwork, horse hair, and tin cones. The Delaware, or Lenape, originated in the Northeast Woodlands of southern New York, New Jersey, Delaware, and parts of Pennsylvania. Most of the Delaware were forced to leave their ancestral homes over time and are widely scattered—only a few remain in their homeland. Courtesy of the National Museum of the American Indian/Smithsonian Institution.

birch bark boxes, clothing, pouches, burden straps, and hair ornaments. Pre-contact designs tend to be geometric, and newer designs often include more or less realistic depictions of animals, flowers, and humans. The northern woodland people, particularly around the Great Lakes, also have a tradition of birch bark basketry. Designs on birch bark containers are often bilaterally symmetrical, reflecting a view of the landscape in the Great Lakes, where the still waters of the lakes mirror the earth and sky.

About 200 years ago, in the Great Lakes area the art of ribbonwork was first developed. Ribbonwork is a decorative technique that uses European materials (silk ribbons) but yet something distinctively Indian is created. The ribbonwork designs are similar to designs in birch bark containers and to designs used in earlier quillwork embroidery. Today, ribbonwork is often created with sewing machines, but some is still made by hand. The technique involves tacking two or more layers of different colored ribbons together, one on top of the other. The top layer is cut into an abstract floral or geometric design and it is sewn with tiny cross stitches around the edges of the design to the contrasting base color. The finished strips of ribbonwork are then sewn to clothing.

Woven reed matmaking is a little known art that was once practiced widely throughout the eastern forests, from the Atlantic coast to the eastern plains. These multipurpose reed mats were once used in Native-American homes as cushions, as covering for winter lodges, and as wrapping for household belongings and medicine bundles. The mats are not only functional, but beautiful. The reeds, which grow near water, are dyed beautiful rich colors, vibrant greens, rusty orange, dark blue, and deep purple. They are then attached to a frame and kept pliable with water, while they are woven into mats of various sizes. The designs are geometric—diamonds, stripes, and losenges predominate. Very few mats are made today. Among the most beautiful

are the mats made by the Mexican band of Kickapoo, a group who fled the United States in 1830 and settled on both sides of the U.S.–Mexican border in Eagle Pass, Texas and in Nacimiento, Mexico. The Mexican Kickapoo, who were recently given federal recognition, have preserved many traditional aspects of woodland culture.

The Choctaw were forced westward from their homes in the Southeast in the 1830s. Prior to their exile, they had adopted many white ways, including farming, housing, and clothing. The people kept many of their traditions, which are visible in their clothing. Choctaw women created a distinct beadwork style that incorporates ancient designs featuring double curved scrolls and other elements from

This dance shawl was made in the 1970s by Sioux artist Patricia Bird. The shawl is made from polyester and is decorated with a felt "box and border" design. The materials and the sewing technique are new, but the design is an ancient one that is often seen on buffalo robes from the plains. Photograph by M. K. de Montaño.

Sarah Keahna, Mesquakie (Sac and Fox) from Iowa, making a ribbonwork panel. Ribbonwork panels are made of several layers of different colored ribbons with cut-out floral or geometric motifs. Photograph by M. K. de Montaño.

This 1850 Cheyenne buffalo robe is decorated with a "box and border" design, which is a common motif for nineteenth-century women's robes. Courtesy of the National Museum of the American Indian/Smithsonian Institution.

Refugia Suke, of the Texas Traditional Band of Kickapoo, making a woven mat in 1977. When a band of Kickapoo, whose homelands are in the Great Lakes, moved to the Texas–Mexico border, they took their knowledge of matmaking with them. Once common over much of the Eastern Woodlands, very few of these reed mats are woven today. Photograph by M. K. de Montaño.

prehistoric ancestral ceramics and incized shells. The women's dresses are Choctaw versions of the clothing white women were wearing at the time.

In the eighteenth century, different groups of Muscogee (Creeks) and Hitchiti, with remnants of the Yamassee and Yuchi along with escaped African slaves, moved south to take refuge in present-day Florida. Today, they live in Florida and Oklahoma and are known collectively as the Seminole. The Seminole, like Native Americans everywhere, adopted what they wanted from the whites and interpreted the new materials and techniques in a way that fit their world-view. Cloth, sewing machines, and sewing techniques from the whites were combined with native sensibilities, and a unique, enduring clothing tradition was created. Seminole patchwork came into being around the early twentieth century, with the introduction of sewing machines.

Patchwork differs from ribbonwork in that small pieces of cloth are cut to shape and then sewn to-

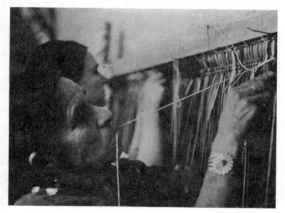

This Choctaw family of the late nineteenth century is wearing clothing adapted from non-Indian fashions of the day, but the beadwork designs of their sashes reach back to pre-contact Southeastern designs found on pottery and engraved shells. Courtesy of the National Museum of the American Indian/Smithsonian Institution.

Seminole family with a missionary in the Everglades of Florida. The family members are wearing distinctive Seminole patchwork clothing. Courtesy of the National Museum of the American Indian/Smithsonian Institution.

gether edge to edge, making up the body of the work. In ribbonwork, cloth strips or ribbons are cut to shape and sewn on to a foundation strip, which is then stitched to a garment. Patchwork designs have evolved from simple stripes into elaborate diamond, square, cross, and zigzag shapes and, today, usually include accents of ric-rac. The tradition continues today, and women's dresses, men's jackets, aprons, pot holders, little girl's pinafores are popular articles of clothing sold at gift shops, museums, and pow-wows.

The Great Plains is the ancient homeland of the sedentary horticultural tribes, who lived in earth lodges and, after about 1740, to the mobile buffalo-hunting tribes. The people of the Plains have an ancient spiritual relationship with the buffalo and with the food crops that sustain them. There is also an enduring tradition of respect for generosity and bravery. On the Plains, as elsewhere, the people wore their art. Clothing was highly decorated, and the designs reflected the people's values. The beaded pictorial vest celebrated the bravery of a warrior. He carried a feathered lance, an emblem of honor in a warrior's society. The hoofprints at the bottom of the vest probably indicated that the wearer stole horses from the enemy, an act of bravery. His horse wore scalp locks on its bridle, and its tail was bound up for battle. Above his head flies the eagle, the most powerful of birds. The vest shown at right was most likely made by a woman to depict the military status of the man for whom it was made.

Quillwork is an ancient art form in North America, and North American Indians are the only people in the world who have developed a refined art form using porcupine quills. Quillwork probably originated in the Eastern Woodlands and was taken out onto the plains by woodlands tribes, such as the Sioux and Cheyenne, when they moved onto the plains to follow the buffalo in the early eighteenth century. Quillwork extends beyond the habitat of porcupines as quills have long been traded to other areas. The range of porcupines in the United States, however, extends into the Great Lakes region and eastward to the Atlantic coast, south into Pennsylvania, in and near the Rocky Mountains across the

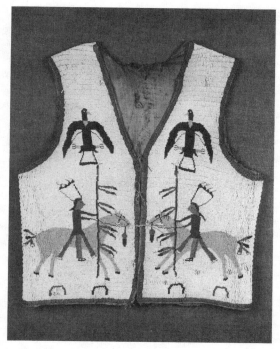

Late nineteenth-century, fully beaded Sioux vest from North or South Dakota. In the late nineteenth century, Sioux women, confined to reservations, continued to create beautiful clothing for their families. Beadwork of this period is often elaborate and tiny glass beads often filled large areas of the garments. This vest probably depicts the war honors of the wearer. Courtesy of the National Museum of the American Indian/ Smithsonian Institution.

northwest part of Colorado, the southeast part of Utah, and across Arizona to the western edge of California. Porcupine habitat includes a strip along the Cascade Mountains of Washington, Oregon, and into northern California. There are many ways to use quills, including embroidery, weaving, wrapping, plaiting, and folding. There are also many variations and combinations of each technique. The quills must be sorted first according to size and then washed and dyed. They are softened in the mouth and drawn through the teeth to flatten them before being worked.

Some quillwork and beadwork designs are created

THE SACRED ORIGIN OF LAKOTA (SIOUX) QUILLWORK

The sacred origin of quillwork is told in Lakota history as the story of Double Woman. They say there was a young woman who was visited in a dream by a woman who was really twins. At this time, no one had ever considered using porcupine quills for anything. Double Woman instructed the young Lakota woman on how to pluck the porcupine quills and select and arrange them according to lengths and how to die them. She then taught her sacred designs and how to work the quills. The young woman stayed isolated for days during this spiritual initiation while she learned the art of quillwork. When she emerged from her tipi she shared her secret with a friend and then, with the women of the dream societies, they, in turn, sought only other women to whom Double Woman had appeared in a dream. Double Woman often favored women who were also twins. Since it was a great honor to have been visited and taught by Double Woman, the making of quillwork was regarded as very sacred work.

With the arrival of the white people came an influx of their goods, such as beads, cloth, and metals. At first, many of the native people, particularly the holy men and women, resented and resisted these goods. Beads were "dead;" they had never been alive. Quills came from living creatures, usually porcupines, although sometime from birds as well, and carried sacred powers from those animals. It was feared that beads and other white products might destroy sacred power.

There was a lot of controversy surrounding the adoption of beads by some native artists. The first glass beads to be used came from glass factories in Venice in the early 1800s. They were large beads called "pony" beads, because they had been delivered by pony pack trains. These early pony beads were large opaque glass beads, usually black, white, red, and sky blue, which were the same colors used in quillwork designs. After an initial rejection, the beads were accepted, and in the 1820s, a group of women started a beadworkers guild. No one knows whether this was originally a religious or a social organization, but whatever their intention, the beadworker's guild became a sacred society similar to the quillworker's guild.

It became apparent that some divine power was influencing the women who worked the sacred designs in beads and inspiring their work. The beadwork created by members of the guild was like quillwork, made in fulfillment of a vow and carried with it a blessing. Although the beads themselves did not come from a sacred source and did not have the power of quills, the designs were also revealed through inspiration in dreams. The process of beadwork was eventually strictly regulated by certain ordained traditions.

simply because they are aesthetically pleasing. However, on the Great Plains, much of the traditional bead and quillwork was sacred. Only select women were allowed to do this work as members of special guilds, and among those guilds, only certain ones were endowed with the power to carry out this supernaturally ordained art. The execution of this work was a distinguished accomplishment as valued and as valid as recognition of a man's bravery. It was a sacred honor to be a member of the guild, and with this honor, came blessings, both for the woman who made the object and for whomever wore, owned, or used it. Quillwork was and is considered more of a ritual than merely a production. A quillwork artist would ask the powers to give a blessing for the object she was quilling, whether it was a cradle, a pipestem, or moccasins. In return for this blessing, she would vow to quill a buffalo robe for a holy man, a medicine man, or a warrior. When she had completed the process, she would offer her work to the sacred powers and present the holy man with the promised robe.

The beadwork that we think of today as synonomous with traditional Indian art did not come into existence until Europeans brought glass beads to the Americas. The first glass beads were brought by Columbus who, after landing on an island in the Caribbean on October 12, 1492, gave the curious Taino strings of beads, which they wore around their necks. These were relatively large beads, made in glass factories in Venice. Beads eventually became an important trade item and, by 1840, were spread widely over North America in a variety of sizes. Distinct tribal designs, worked with tiny "seed" beads, began to appear by the 1860s.

The southwestern United States is also famous for its artistic traditions. Today, as in the past, the towns of Santa Fe and Taos are centers for exchanging art and inspiring artists. Since at least the eleventh century, traders have set out from the Southwest toward distant trading centers carrying sea shells, feathers, red ocher, woven products, and small ceramic vessels that were traded for local products. The Southwest people are justly famous for their artistic products, including jewelry of silver, stone and shell; ceramics; textile and basket weavings; painting; featherwork; and leatherwork.

The Pueblo tradition of making and wearing disc-shaped shell beads and creating turquoise inlaid marine shell ornaments began centuries ago. Sea shells are associated with water, a precious commodity to horticulturalists in the arid Southwest. They were laboriously imported from the Pacific coast by traders who traveled aboriginal trade routes in prehistoric times. The shell ornaments were worn, then and now, in ceremonies designed to bring rain. The wearing of shell necklaces expresses a desire for water for the crops and illustrates the belief that humans can, and must influence the natural phenomena; humans have a part to play in the timely occurrence of rain.

Pueblo men have been weaving with cotton since at least 800 A.D.. The Hopi cultivate a species of cotton, *Gossypium hopi*, that has been adapted to their environment. Indications of the vertical loom

(the type still used by Pueblo and Navajo weavers) have been found in kiva floors dating after 1100. Kivas are underground ceremonial chambers, so weaving may have been developed as a kiva activity. To this day, textiles remain an important part of ceremonial clothing among the pueblo dwellers in the Southwest.

Navajo women probably learned weaving techniques from intermarriage with Pueblo refugees who lived among the Navajo in the aftermath of the Pueblo Revolt against the Spanish in 1680. By 1750, Navajo women were weaving two-piece dresses and striped blankets with wool which was introduced by the Spanish late in the sixteenth cen-

These stamps depict Navajo rugs, woven from wool that was first introduced by the Spanish. Courtesy of the U. S. Postal Service.

tury. Early Navajo blankets were based on the Pueblo woman's *manta* design, which was composed of broad stripes, and are indistinguishable from Hopi striped blankets. Navajo weavers soon developed an elaboration of the striped blanket design, which was often traded to Ute and Apache middlemen in the native trade system. Navajo blankets were found on the site of the Wounded Knee massacre in South Dakota in 1890. In fact, many of these blankets reached the plains, where their high price earned them the name "Chief's Blanket."

The design elements found in most Navajo textiles were largely the result of suggestions by white trading post owners, who knew the market and provided weavers with examples of designs that they thought would sell, but the result was unmistakenly Navajo. The resulting designs have become so thoroughly identified with Navajos (and because of stereotyping, with all Indians) that some commercial textile mills began to copy and adapt Navajo designs for their blankets. Many of these blankets were sold to Indian consumers who wore them in place of buffalo, deer, and elk hide robes, and by 1900, factory-made blankets were worn in place of hide robes. Pendleton blankets, made in Oregon, feature adaptations of Navajo designs and are popular gift items among Indians everywhere.

The Pueblo people of the Southwest are inheritors of a long tradition of decorated ceramics. As with all Native Americans, artistic production and the quality of life deteriorated rapidly with continued contact with Europeans. Some art forms dissapeared, some adapted, and some ancient forms have experienced a renaissance. The twentieth century has witnessed a growing awareness and respect for Native American art. This modern renaissance, which is, in part, responsible for a small measure of economic security of the Pueblos, ultimately affects all Native American art. An important person in the renaissance is Maria Martinez of San Ildefonso Pueblo, the Tewa village located on the Rio Grande about twenty miles from Santa Fe, New Mexico. The Spanish invaded the pueblos searching for gold. They stayed to exploit the people and the land and were firmly established by 1598. A decline of Pueblo culture and population began with Spanish rule. The Spanish suppressed the exercise of Pueblo religion and forced it into secrecy. Indian men were compelled by the invaders to work in mines and women to work in Spanish households. A smallpox epidemic killed half of the population in the 1700s. The skilled potters of the Pueblo were put to work making plain kitchen ware for the Spanish. Potterymaking as a fine art declined, and old designs were forgotten.

Maria Martinez (*Poveka*) was born about 1881, forty years after the United States took control of the area. During this time the assimilation policy was at its height in the United States; Indian children were

THE INDIAN ARTS AND CRAFTS ACT OF 1990

Title I of Public Law 101-644 of November, 1990 makes it unlawful to offer or display for sale or sell any good, with or without a Government trademark, in a manner that falsely suggests it is Indian produced, an Indian product, or the product of a particular Indian or Indian tribe or Indian arts and crafts organization, resident within the United States. According to the law, a person must be a member of a Federal or State recognized Indian tribe to be considered an Indian artist or, for those who are not members of a Federal or State recognized tribe, they must be certified as an Indian artisan by an Indian tribe.

Those who are members of a recognized tribe need to be able to present a copy of an official tribal document that acknowledges them as members. Those who are not members will need to be formally certified as an Indian artisan by their tribe of ancestry. A copy of the law can be obtained by contacting the Indian Arts and Crafts Board (IACB).

Maria Martinez, from the Pueblo of San Ildefonso in New Mexico, is famous for revitalizing ceramic production in the Southwest Pueblos. Ralph T. Coe, curator of the exhibition Sacred Circles: 2,000 Years of North American Indian Art, admires a Maria Martinez pot before installing it in the exhibition. Maria Martinez (center) and her sister Sara, look on. Photograph by M. K. de Montaño.

routinely taken from their homes and sent to schools where the teachers tried to substitute Euro-american culture for Native American cultures. Maria went to school, but also learned potterymaking from her aunt. Most of the pottery at the pueblo was made for kitchen use at this time.

In 1907, the School of American Research began several archaeological excavations in ancestral home sites of the Pueblo people, and Maria's husband, Julian, was employed at the site. The director of the expedition brought a pottery sherd to Maria and asked her to create a whole pot from the fragment. Maria created a whole pot from studying the sherd, and her husband painted it with a design based on painted fragments of the pottery of their ancestors. While making pottery based on recently uncovered ancient examples, Maria and Julian accidently produced some pots that were completely black. The reddish body of the pottery can be chemically altered by a procedure induced during firing called oxidation, wherein the fire is smothered. This process was known and practiced in ancient times, but Maria and Julian accidentally rediscovered it, and the black pottery became popular with museum shops and tourists. By the 1920s, ceramic production was an

economic factor in the pueblo, not only to Maria's family, but to the pueblo as a whole, and the revival of ceramic production spread to other pueblos. Julian experimented with the firing and decorating process, developing a "black on black" technique that became famous, which is characterized by a shiny black body with matt black decorations. The effect is a beautifully elegant creation. Maria's ceramics eventually sold for thousands of dollars and are collector's pieces today.

The artistic renaissance profoundly affected the economic security and posterity of the Pueblos and promoted the recognition of all forms of Native American art. The ownership of a "Maria" piece is an economic investment; a piece that sold for from three to twelve dollars in the 1920s is now worth over a thousand dollars. The work of Maria and Julian can be found in many museums here and abroad, and famous potters from around the world have visited her shop in San Ildefonso. Although she died in 1980, the presence of Maria is evident everywhere in the pueblo. Many pueblo residents sell ceramics from their homes, and there is a museum dedicated to her work in San Ildefonso.

On the plateau, the artistic traditions are in some

The Wampanoag of Massachusetts know you cannot keep taking without giving something back. This small openwork splint basket with a cornmeal dumpling, was made to be left in the forest as an offering by people gathering wild fruits. Courtesy of the National Museum of the American Indian/Smithsonian Institution.

This elaborately constructed Pomo basket from California was made between 1875 and 1890. Baskets like this one, with tiny feathers woven into it, are called "gift" baskets because they were often given away. Courtesy of the National Museum of the American Indian/Smithsonian Institution.

ways similar to Plains traditions. Beadwork is often geometric, but artists have also developed a realistic pictorial style of beadwork, and there is a continuing tradition of woven fiber bags, hats, and baskets. In California, the art of basketry has the same importance as ceramics and textile weaving for the Southwest. The Pomo of California create finely woven exquisite baskets. Some Pomo baskets are enriched by having beads woven into them; others feature marine shell ornaments. There is a special kind of Pomo basket that is called a "gift" basket, as they are often given away. The gift baskets have small feathers, such as iridescent green from mallard ducks, red from woodpeckers, and the black topknot of quails woven into them.

When an aspiring basketmaker sits at the foot of an elder and learns weaving techniques and traditional motifs, she learns much more than how to make a basket. The masters of all the artistic traditions are culture bearers who also preserve and share values, spiritual connections, and attitudes that are perhaps invisible but important to maintaining the heart of the culture. They see that the next generation understands that the people must have a relationship with the plants, animals, and the land that

sustains them. Part of making beautiful and meaningful things, whether it is called art, craft, or seen as a part of life, entails knowing its cultural and, often, its spiritual context. Many Native American artists who consciously create art in traditions introduced by Europeans carry these same values and attitudes into their work.

Painting on canvas and paper, sometimes refered to as "easel art," is an idea that was introduced by Europeans. Native Americans have decorated functional items with painted designs for centuries. Some of the things that were imbued with meaning by painting were ceramics; rawhide containers; tanned buffalo, deer, and elk hides; totem poles; tipis; the walls of ceremonial chambers; altars, rattles; masks; drums; and shields. Contact with Europeans added new elements and influenced painterly techniques. Cloth and paper were added to hides and other natural materials as a surface to paint on, and crayons and colored pencils were adopted for use in painting and drawing. In the late nineteenth century, the U.S. government imprisoned a group of Indian men from the Plains, without the formality of a trial to determine any wrongdoing, in order to force their relatives to remain on reservations. While the men were incarcerated in the prison at Fort Marion, Florida, they were given instruction in English, reading, and writing. They were also given paper and colored pencils with which to draw. The prisoners at Fort Marion took the opportunity to express themselves in the medium. The drawings were reminiscent of paintings on buffalo hides, which often depicted a man's adventures. Their drawings were collected and sold as curiosities. Out of this beginning on the Plains, a tradition of painting on paper and later, on canvas was begun.

In the late nineteenth century in the Southwest, anthropologists influenced Pueblo and Navajo men to paint scenes of their dances on paper. These first paintings were bought by museums and collectors but were considered ethnography and curios, not art. In 1933, the Santa Fe Indian School opened an art department and the Southwest became another focus for painting on paper and canvas. Early paintings relate in subject matter and style to painting of the past. Before contact with Europeans, men often painted scenes of their activities, especially hunting and warfare, on tipi liners, shields, shirts and other articles made of tanned hides. Now these subjects were painted on the "new" mediums of paper and canvas.

The Buffalo Hunt by Ma Pe Wi, Zia Pueblo, New Mexico. The indigenous tradition of painting on hides and ceramics was applied to a new medium—paper—by Native American artists. Courtesy of the National Museum of the American Indian/Smithsonian Institution.

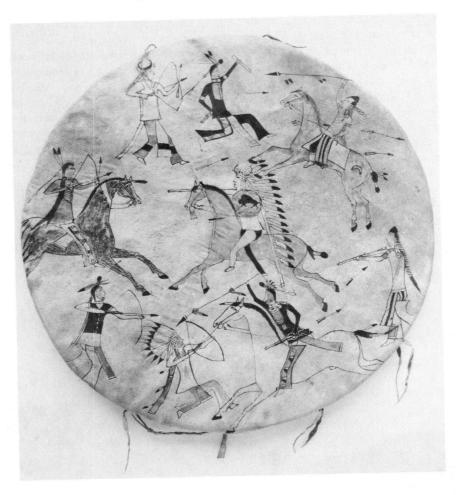

As Native American artists increasingly use the techniques and conventions of western art, they are caught in a conundrum. Ethnocentric bias has kept "traditional" Indian art from being considered "fine art," and Indian artists who create works that do not look like Indian art of the past are considered assimilated. This view does not acknowledge the reality that Indian culture has always changed. Painters like T. C. Cannon, who used contemporary pop art to express a deeply felt Indian philosophy, did what Native American people have always done: adopted those things that are useful to them in order to keep alive that which is most important.

At the Institute of American Indian and Alaska Native Culture and Arts Development in Santa Fe, the topic of contemporary artistic expression and its relationship to tradition is a lively and perennial subject. The school, initially called the Institute of American Indian Art, was established in 1962 as a Bureau of Indian Affairs school for artistically talented American Indians, and now has a well deserved reputation for developing Native American artists. Many of the best known contemporary artists attended and/or teach or have taught at the Institute. In 1988, the Institute severed its ties to the BIA and is now run by a board that reports directly to Congress.

Opposite: Painted hide shield, Dakota (Sioux), late nineteenth century. Hide paintings from the Plains were characterized by a flat (without modeling) painting style, with little or no background. Men often painted scenes from their visions or representations of their experiences in hunting or warfare. Courtesy of the National Museum of the American Indian/Smithsonian Institution.

Today, Native American artists produce work that has obvious origins in Indian art of the past, as well as art that incorporates western artistic traditions. Some Native American artists prefer to be considered artists who happen to be Indian, others consciously follow a Native American artistic tradition. All artwork produced by Native Americans can be considered Indian art. While there are artistic traditions, there is no one acceptable definition of what constitutes traditional art. At one time glass beads were considered non-traditional. Today's beaded baseball caps and tennis shoes are tomorrow's tradition. Indian artists are free to express themselves in any and all mediums, from avant-garde performances to porcupine quill work. Indian art does not depend on adherence to forms and techniques of the past any more than being Indian depends on living an anachronistic life.

More information on Indian art and artists can be obtained from the following:

Atlatl

402 West Roosevelt
Phoenix, Arizona 85003
(602) 253-2731

The name comes from a prehistoric wooden tool used to throw spears with more force and accuracy. Atlatl is a nonprofit Native American arts service organization. Their mission is to promote the vitality of contemporary Native American arts to the general public while providing technical assistance to those artists. Established in 1977, Atlatl emphasizes service and provides a traveling exhibit service, distribution of audiovisual materials, publishes *Native Arts Update*, a quarterly newsletter, and provides workshops, technical as-

sistance and consultation services. Atlatl maintains a national *Registry of Native American Artists* and provides a research and referral service to locate Native American artists for cultural centers and museums. Artists do not pay to be listed in the registry, users pay service fees in accordance with their need.

Indian Arts and Crafts Board

Mail Stop 4004-MIB
U.S. Department of the Interior
Washington, D.C. 20240
(202) 208-3773

The Indian Arts and Crafts Board (IACB) was established as an independent agency within the Department of the Interior in 1935 in order to promote the development of Native American arts and crafts. The IACB provides business and personal professional advice, information, fund raising assistance, and promotion of Native American artists and craftsmen and cultural organizations. It has helped establish over 200 tribally-owned crafts marketing enterprises and cooperatives that are owned by the artists themselves. The board also assists crafts enterprises to provide training for individual artists. It administers three museums, the Southern Plains Museum in Anadarko, Oklahoma; The Sioux Indian Museum in Rapid City, South Dakota; and the Museum of the Plains Indian, in Browning, Montana. As an informational service the board publishes a number of informational and exhibit catalogs including *Source Directory of Native Owned and Operated Arts and Crafts Businesses*, with listings by state (available from the IACB at the above address, free of charge).

Heard Museum

22 Monte Vista Road
Phoenix, Arizona 85003
(602) 252-8840

The Heard is an anthropology and art museum, with permanent exhibits on the Southwest, travelling exhibitions, and a library/archives. In addition to books, pamphlets, sound recordings, and a film and video collection, the library contains the Native American Artists Resource Collection which documents over 10,000 individual artist's achievements. All forms of information are included in the Native American Artists Resource Collection, including business cards, journal and newspaper articles, resumes, exhibition catalogs, artists' papers and correspondence, documented interviews, and gallery announcements.

Huntington Free Library

9 Westchester Square
Bronx, New York 20461
(718) 829-7770

The Huntington is the library for the Museum of the American Indian/Heye Foundation (now the National Museum of the American Indian Smithsonian Institution). The library maintains a Native American artists file.

National Museum of the American Indian

Smithsonian Institution
Broadway at 155th Street
New York New York 10032
(212) 283-2420

The National Museum of the American Indian (NMAI) was created in 1989 by an Act of Congress, which transferred the collections of the Museum of the American Indian/Heye Foundation to the Smithsonian Institution. The NMAI is an institution of living culture dedicated to the preservation, study and exhibition of the life, languages, literature, history, and arts of the Native Peoples of the Western Hemisphere. The NMAI will be built on the last available space on the National Mall in Washington, D. C., across the street from the National Air and Space Museum and near the U. S. Capitol. In addition to the Washington, D. C. site, the museum will operate a significant exhibition and education facility in lower Manhattan in the Alexander Hamilton U. S. Custom House. It will be known as the George Gustav Heye Center of the NMAI. A cultural resource center for collections research will be located at the Smithsonian's Museum Support Center in Suitland, Maryland.

The George Gustav Heye Center in New York is scheduled to open in 1994. The museum's cultural resources facility at the Museum Support Center in Maryland is expected to open in 1997. Its public exhibition facility on the National Mall in Washington, D. C., is expected to open by the end of the decade. When the Custom House facility opens, the museum will vacate its current premises at 155th Street and Broadway.

PERFORMING ARTS

Native Americans have a rich history of expressing spirituality, values, and tribal identity through performance. In traditional Native American societies, most celebrations, whether they are sacred or social occasions, involve music and dance. Although they are not meant for entertainment, these events often include theatrical elements such as lighting, masks, and pantomime. Despite government and missionary suppression, Native Americans continue to express themselves through music and dance performances that are based on performances of past generations. Native Americans have also adopted Euroamerican forms of performance including ballet and modern dance, rock, opera, and country and western singing. Native artists are also creating new forms of performance by blending the traditional with introduced aspects of music and dance.

In Inupiat and Yupik (Eskimo) celebrations of Alaska, one or more communities often gather for an evening of song and dance. In the old days, people gathered in the *karigi* (community house), today the local school gym often serves as a communal performance arena. In Alaska, as in other areas of Native America, the people are experiencing a renaissance of their cultural expressions, and many traditional songs and dances have been revived. A gathering today might be similar to a performance witnessed by a Russian Naval officer in 1842. Lt. Zagoskin, visiting a community on the lower Yukon River over

THE RAVEN DANCE

Among the repertoire of the King Island Inupiat is a Raven dance, performed by a dancer wearing a carved wooden raven mask. The dancer's arms imitate the wings of the bird as it soars in flight and the chorus sings:

Man down below
I see you from above
As I fly and hover.
Where are your friends?

The song tells the story of a man who went out hunting and became separated from his partners. A hunter, lost and alone, is in danger in the Arctic. As he was pondering what to do, a shadow passed over him and he looked up to see a raven hovering overhead, looking at him. The man eventually found his way back to the village and composed the song to tell the story of his brush with death. The story is told from the perspective of the raven.

Raven mask made by the Inuit (Eskimo) of Anvik, Yukon River, Alaska. Masks like this one are worn in the Raven Dance. Courtesy of the National Museum of the American Indian/Smithsonian Institution.

100 years ago, described a dimly lit communal house filled by the entire population of two villages. The drummers were seated on a bench along one side of the room. All were packed around the small dance arena, anxiously waiting for the dance to begin. Suddenly a man wearing a raven mask swung into the arena on a rope tied to the ceiling. As he let go of the rope the drums accentuated his landing with a tremendous boom. Without missing a beat the dance began. The dancer pantomimed the story of an unlucky hunter, then he took the part of the raven, while the chorus told the story in song. There are many Inupiat stories about Raven, and they are still dramatized in masked dances.

On the Northwest Coast, the Native people make the most out of elaborate staging, complex costuming, dramatic lighting, and masks to create an otherworldly ambiance for their celebrations. Northwest Coast ceremonies and social occasions are often held in a large communal house lit by firelight. Some participants wear blankets decorated with abalone shell buttons that flash in the flickering light. Others wear masks representing spiritual founders of lineages, personages in oral traditions, or the spirits of natural and supernatural beings. The masks often feature moving parts—mouths or beaks that open and close, or eyes that roll. some masks are hinged and involve transformation by opening to reveal a

INDIAN STUDENTS AT HASKELL INSTITUTE PERFORM HIAWATHA

For several years in the early twentieth century the students at Haskell Institute performed a stage version of Henry Wadsworth Longfellow's epic poem, *Hiawatha*. Haskell was an off-reservation government boarding school designed to eradicate the Indian traditions of its students and teach them white ways. They were not allowed to speak their Indian languages or participate in traditional customs, yet they were encouraged to perform in *Hiawatha*. Longfellow based his poem on oral traditions of the Anishnabah or Chippewa of the Great Lakes. Many elements of the authentic stories are ribald and the hero is both a demigod and a fool. These elements and others did not seem appropriate to Longfellow and were left out of his retelling. In addition, he appropriated the name of a cultural hero of the Six Nations (Iroquois) and erroneously placed him as the protagonist of his whitewashed version of Anishnabah literature. For performances the students were dressed in painted and fringed muslin in imitation of buckskin. Turkey feathers were worn in their headbands in place of eagle feathers. The cast travelled to Denver in 1908 and performed for enraptured audiences there and perhaps in other cities as well. *Hiawatha*, a white idea of Indian culture, was the only way the students could be acceptably Indian.

The 1913 cast of Hiawatha, *performed by students of Haskell Institute. Courtesy of M. K. de Montaño.*

different being inside. Puppets are used as well as masks—all to help make the invisible world visible. Puppets are used in many areas. In Alaska, Eskimo puppets fly through the air on strings invisible in the firelight, hand puppets in the Southwest are part of ceremonies meant to induce rain, the Northwest Coast uses puppets to help tell the story.

Long ago on the plains, men reenacted their hunting and military adventures through song and dance. Men and women belonged to one or more societies and participated in the society's dances. Dance clothing reflected social status, membership in a society, individual artistry, and tribal identity. Some of the dance forms, most notably the war dance, along with the songs and clothing, have endured, evolved, and spread from tribe to tribe over the United States and Canada in the form of the powwow. The powwow is a unifying social event for diverse Native American communities. There are hundreds of powwows every year and powwow music is the basis for a lively recording industry, with several popular labels. Good powwow singers are in demand, and their recordings are sold to an appreciative, mostly Native American audience.

There are also many traditional tribal performance groups that are formed in response to a request for dancers to accompany a museum exhibit, or to participate in a multicultural festival. When the exhibit or festival is over, the group dissolves as an entity, perhaps another group from the same community will form for a different occasion. There are some groups that become institutionalized, adopt a name, have a leader, and travel, sharing the traditions of their community.

Most Native Americans are able to follow paths in both the native and the non-native worlds. Today Native American artists continue to perform age old ceremonial songs and dances. Many of these traditional songs and dances have been adapted to fit today's circumstances. The Inupiat have songs about experiences with airplanes and television. War dances honor soldiers who participated in Desert Storm, Vietnam, or other wars. New forms are created by integrating traditional with introduced forms. Dancers combine traditional steps and themes

with modern dance expression. Singers combine traditional rhythms, structure, and themes, with folk or rock instrumentation. Other artists excel in introduced genres, such as ballet and opera. Whatever the genre, Native American performance art is alive and well, enriching us all.

The list that follows gives a sampling of Native American contributions to the performing arts.

PERFORMING ARTISTS

Bands

Kinrawk, Blackfoot. Native American rock. Recordings include "Red, Raw, & Ready."

Redbone, rock and roll band. Albums include "Message from a Drum," "Beaded Dreams Through Turquoise Eyes," and "Wovoka."

XIT, Navajo rock and roll band organized in 1970. Albums include "Plight of the Redman," "Silent Warriors," "Relocation," and "Entrance."

Comedians

Charlie Hill, Oneida. Comedian who performs around United States and on television. Debut album "Born Again Savage."

Dance

Belinda James, San Juan Pueblo. Modern and ballet dancer, founded the dance company, Divi Shadende (they are dancing). Choreographed "Stringling," "Chinook," and "Metamorphoses."

Rosalie Jones, Blackfeet-Pembina Chippewa from Montana. Modern dancer and choreographer. Blends traditional dance with classical and modern dance. Studied at Juilliard, founder of Daystar Classical Dance-Drama of Indian America. Professor of dance at the Institute of American Indian Art.

Moscelyne Larkin (Little Running Turtle), Shawnee/Peoria. Classical ballerina from Oklahoma.

THE POWWOW

The word "powwow" came into the English language from an Eastern Algonquian language. In the Massachuset language, *pauwau* literally means "he uses divination." It refers to a shaman or medicine man, who could divine the future from information and power received while dreaming. A shaman, accompanied by a rattle or drum and surrounded by well wishers, would often sing during a healing or a divining ceremony. English Colonists took the name for the shaman and applied it to the event. Today, "powwow" is sometimes used to refer to an important meeting, but to Native Americans it refers to a gathering of Indian people to visit, feast, sing, and dance together.

Powwows, in the Native American sense of the word, probably started in the last decades of the nineteenth century as Indian people adapted to new conditions. The majority of powwow dances were war dances, which originated with the warrior societies of the plains. When Indian people were confined to reservations, the war dances became social dances. But they did not lose their connection to warriors. People who are in the armed service today or are veterans are today's equivalent of the warriors of old, and powwows often recognize and honor them. In addition, much of the powwow clothing for men has evolved from insignia worn by warriors. The roach headdress, feathered bustles, and eagle feathers worn by men in powwows were once worn only by proven warriors. Today they are worn by Indian men and boys as a symbol of Indian identity. Women's powwow clothing are contemporary versions of traditional clothing, usually made from buckskin or cloth.

Powwows are held outside in grassy areas or inside, often in gymnasiums, when weather dictates. The center of a powwow is the drum, which refers to the instrument and to the singers who play the drum and sing at the same time. On the northern and southern Plains, some powwow traditions differ. For example, on the southern Plains, a single drum is placed in the

A fancy dancer waits for the powwow to begin. Note the American flag design on his beaded headband. Photograph by M. K. de Montaño.

center of the dance arena, while in the north, one or more drums are placed at its edge. Spectators sit in bleachers or on folding chairs. Participants dance either sunwise (clockwise), or counterclockwise around the drum. In the northern tradition, men and women usually dance in opposite directions.

Powwows are not so much a performance for an audience as they are a way of sharing, reinforcing, and expressing Indian heritage. Since many powwows are held every year, and most are open to the public, a powwow is a good way to learn about American Indian heritage. The details of a powwow vary with the location, but in general, they begin with the Grand Entry, in which all dancers, dressed in their finest regalia, enter the powwow arena dancing slowly in a parade around the drum. Intertribal War dances follow, interspersed with Honor dances and other special dances such as the Two-step, Round dance, or Crow Hop.

Contests draw dancers from far away to compete for prize money. Dancers compete in gender and in age groups. For example, there are often junior and senior divisions as well as "tiny tots." Within age groups, there are categories based on styles of dancing and types of regalia worn while dancing. Dancers are judged for their dancing, their regalia, and the extent of their participation. In general, men compete in "traditional," "fancy dance," and "grass dance" categories. Popular women's dance categories are "traditional," "northern shawl," and "jingle dress."

For both men and women the categories refer to dance styles and to the type of regalia worn while dancing. The men's traditional dance style is sedate and dignified. It is directly related to an older style where war deeds were pantomimed. The regalia of a traditional dancer is based on tribal dress of the nineteenth century or earlier. The fancy dance is characterized by exuberant and strenuous high stepping footwork, with turns and spins. Fancy dancers wear brightly colored feather bustles, elaborate beadwork, and bells. Fancy dancers do not follow a tribal style of dress, as much as a fancy dance intertribal style. Grass dancers look similar to fancy dancers, except they do not wear bustles but wear thick fringe on a yoke and their aprons. Grass dancers dance like fancy dancers,

but with a rhythmic rocking gait. All male dancers wear moccasins.

Women's traditional dancing is characterized by a kind of stylized gliding with a gentle knee bend and an upright posture. Buckskin dancers generally wear white buckskin dresses decorated with long fringe and intricate beadwork. Cloth dresses are of several kinds. In the midwest, women often wear elaborate ribbonwork skirts with cloth blouses. Many women also wear cloth dresses patterned after buckskin dresses, and there are many tribal styles, such as Navajo velvet dresses and long full-skirted Cherokee dresses. All female dancers wear moccasins and wear or carry hand made shawls with long fringe. The dance step of women's traditional dance makes the long fringe on the dresses and shawls sway to the beat of the drum.

Women who dance the Northern shawl style wear cloth dresses with a beaded yoke and moccasins. Their dance steps are more like the men's fancy dance steps, with high bouncing steps and twirls, which cause their shawls to spread out like wings. Northern shawl dancers move over the floor like birds circling on an updraft. Women's Jingle dresses are cloth dresses covered with many small tin cones. Their dance steps are similar to the Northern shawl dancers, athletic and high stepping. When jingle dress dancers enter the arena, thousands of tin cones on their dresses add another layer of sound keeping time to the beat of the drum.

Each dancer interprets the dance individually within the canons of their particular dance category. Most dances do not have coordinated choreography, every dancer chooses steps as a way to express his or her own Indian identity. As the dancers circle the drum, from communities far and near, with different customs, each one dancing a personal interpretation, all are united by the heartbeat of Mother Earth expressed through the drum.

Kevin Locke, Standing Rock Sioux. Hoop dancer.

Maria Tallchief, Osage. Prima ballerina with George Balanchine's Ballet Society, now the New York City Ballet, in 1954 and 1955. Best known for her performance in Stravinsky's "The Fire Bird."

Marjorie Tallchief, Osage. The premiere *danseuse etoile* (star) of the Paris Opera Ballet, she danced with the Ballet Theater and the Grand Ballet du Marquie de Cuevas.

Juan Valensuela, Yaqui. Taught at the Institute of American Indian Art. A recipient of a National Endowment for the Arts grant to teach dance workshops to reservation and urban Native Americans.

Dance Groups

American Indian Dance Theater, troupe headquartered in New York with dancers from the Plains, Southwest, and Canada performing traditional and social dances staged and directed by Hanay Geiogamah, Kiowa/Delaware, from Oklahoma.

Cape Fox Dancers, a family of Tlingit dancers originally from Saxman, Alaska, performing ceremonial dances in traditional Tlingit regalia accompanied by narratives.

Chilkat (Tlingit) Indian Dancers housed at the Chilkat Center for the Performing Arts in Haines, Alaska. Renowned for elaborately decorated regalia, carved wood masks, button blankets, and other ceremonial clothing.

Coastal Pomo Indian Dancers, from Point Arena, California, performing traditional Pomo singing and dancing.

Haskell Singers and Dancers, students of Haskell Indian Junior College in Lawrence, Kansas, perform traditional Native American dances and songs. Dances include fancy, traditional, and hoop dances.

King Island Inupiat Dancers, Inupiat. Forced off of their small island off the Alaskan coast in the 1960s and relocated to several Alaskan cities, this dance group keeps the traditions and identity of the King Island Inupiat alive.

Nathan Leader Charge, Sioux, at Rosebud Fair on the Rosebud Sioux reservation, South Dakota. Photograph by Gary Galante.

Jim Sky Iroquois Dancers, a troupe from Ontario, Canada, in existence for many years. Goal is to educate audiences about native people and to dispel stereotypes.

Thunderbird American Indian Dancers, a troupe headquartered in New Jersey, performing music and dance in full regalia from Northwest coast, Northeast, Plains, and Southwest. Choreography by Hanay Geiogamah.

Musicians/Composers

Athabascan Old-Time Fiddlers from Alaska, play fiddles, mandolins, and guitars in public performances.

Louis Ballard, Quapaw/Cherokee. composer, musician, educator whose works are performed regularly by major American orchestras, bands, choral societies, chamber music ensembles, ballet companies, and soloists throughout the world. His "Desert Trilogy" was nominated for the Pulitzer Prize in Music

Southern Plains buckskin dresses are made in two parts: the top is constructed like a poncho, with the bottom as a skirt. The top fits loosely over the skirt and is belted at the waist. The long fringes on the dress sway rhythmically in time with the drum. Photograph by M. K. de Montaño.

Jingle dress dancers enter the arena during the grand entry of a powwow in Milwaukee, Wisconsin in 1990. The tin cones that cover the dresses are often made from the lids of snuff cans. Photograph by M. K. de Montaño.

169

John Keel, a Comanche from Oklahoma, dances at a 1992 powwow sponsored by the National Museum of the American Indian in New York City. Photograph by Georgetta Stonefish.

As the singers begin the grand entry song, dancers enter the arena in single file, slowly dancing around the drum. Traditional men dancers often lead the grand entry at the powwow. Photograph by M. K. de Montaño.

Chibon Whitecloud (Oto), a traditional Southern Plains dancer, at a 1976 powwow sponsored by the Native American Alliance, an Indian club at the University of Kansas. Photograph by M. K. de Montaño.

Fancy dancers wear two bustles: one at the shoulders and one at the waist. Here the bustles almost obscure a dancer at a powwow on the Rosebud Reservation in South Dakota. Photograph by Gary Galante.

The elegant Southern Plains buckskin dress compliments the natural poise and grace of this dancer at rest during a powwow at Haskell Indian Junior College in Lawrence, Kansas. Photograph by M. K. de Montaño.

Stanley Pretty Paint, Crow from Montana, at a North Battleford, Saskatchewan powwow. Photograph by Gary Galante.

in 1972. He wrote the first modern American Indian ballet "Koshare," which premiered in Barcelona in 1960.

Jack Frederick Kilpatrick, Cherokee. Composer. Composed symphony for Oklahoma Semicentennial in 1957.

Robert Mirabel, Taos Pueblo. Composer, double-chambered flute music.

Russell Moore, Pima. Jazz trombonist. Performed at White House and at inaugural balls for presidents John F. Kennedy and Lyndon B. Johnson. Soloed in many jazz bands across country as well as having own band at various points in his career.

R. Carlos Nakai, Ute/Navajo. Composer. Performer who integrates traditional music with original interpretations for the Native American flute. Albums include "Changes," "Cycles," and "Journeys."

Doc Tate Nevaquaya, Comanche. Plays nearly extinct music for the wooden flute.

Jim Pepper, Kansa (Kaw). Jazz musician and composer. Recordings include the album "Goin' and Comin'." His composition "Witchi Tai To" is a jazz classic which made the Top-40 pop chart.

Performance Artists

James Luna, Luiseño. His installations and performances are satirical and humorous commentaries on contemporary Indian issues.

Singers/Singing Groups

Akwesasne Mohawk Singers, from St. Regis Reservation in New York, sing social songs during public performances.

Ashland Singers, Northern Cheyenne. Traditional powwow singers, their recordings include "Northern Cheyenne War Dance."

Assiniboine Junior, Assiniboine. Traditional powwow singers, their recordings include Pow Wow Songs" and "Intertribal Songs."

Badland Singers of Fort Peck, Montana. Organized in 1972, perform for dancers in powwow circuits.

Bala-Sinem Choir ("red people" in Hopi), organized in 1970 by Mark Romancito, a Fort Lewis College student from Zuni Pueblo.

James Bilagody, Navajo. A traditional and contemporary singer whose recordings include "Beauty Ways."

Gordon Bird, Mandan-Hidatsa-Arikara. A flutist who plays traditional and modern songs. His recordings include "Music of the Plains."

Black Lodge Singers. A family group of powwow singers. Their recordings include "Pow-Wow Highway Songs."

Calf Robe Singers, Blackfoot. A family of powwow singers. Recordings include "Family Pow Wow."

Cathedral Lake Singers. Powwow singers. Their recordings include "Pow-Wow Songs."

Fernando Cellicion, Zuni. A traditional flutist, his recordings include "The Traditional Indian Flute of Fernando Cellicion," "Traditional & Contemporary Flute of Fernando Cellicion," and "Buffalo Spirit."

Chinle Swingin' Echoes, Navajo. a traditional song and dance group. their recordings include "Voices from Canyon De Chelly" and "Making Memories."

Ned Tsosie Clark, Navajo. A traditional singer whose recordings include, "King of the Navajo Song & Dance."

Vincent Craig, Navajo. Songwriter and singer of traditional songs as well as contemporary pieces he has composed. Honored his father, a code talker during World War II, with a single recording "Code Talker Man."

Johnny Curtis, Apache. A Gospel singer whose recordings include "Somebody Cares."

Dik Darnell, Lakota. Recordings include "Following the Circle."

Bobby Eagle. Recordings include "Heros, Warriors, & Saints," a tribute to Vietnam (and other) veterans.

Fort Oakland Ramblers, Includes Ponca, Otoe, and Tonkawa members. Traditional powwow singers. Their recordings include "Oklahoma Intertribal & Contest Songs."

Guy & Allen. Recordings include "Peyote Canyon."

William Horncloud, Lakota. An old time singer, renowned on the plains for his singing. He has many recordings on Canyon Records, including "Sioux Favorites."

Harold Littlebird, song writer/singer and recording artist from Pueblos of Laguna and Santo Domingo, New Mexico, who sings traditional and contemporary songs. Albums include "A Circle Begins" and "The Road Back In."

Lupton Valley Singers, Navajo. A woman's group of traditional singers. Their recordings include "Summer Memories."

Mandaree Singers, Mandan, Hidatsa, Arikara. Traditional powwow singers. Their recordings include "Mandaree Singers: Live at New Town, North Dakota."

Davis Mitchell, Navajo. A traditional singer whose recordings include "Navajo Singer Sings for You," "The Navajo Kid Rides Again" and "A Good Year for the Rose."

Ned Morris, Navajo. A traditional singer. His recordings include "The Singing Navajo Songwriter."

Navajo Nation Swingers, Navajo. Traditional singers/dancers. Their recordings include "Navajo Style."

Billie Nez, Navajo. Navajo and intertribal Peyote songs. His recordings include "Peyote Songs from Navajoland."

D.J. Nez, Navajo. A former Marine and rodeo cowboy with songs about Native American cowboys, veterans, and others. His recordings include: "My Heros Have Always Been Indians," "Navajo in Paris" and "Peyote Voices," an album of traditional Navajo and intertribal Peyote songs, recorded with Ricky Yazzie.

A. Paul Ortega, Apache. Sings traditional and contemporary songs accompanying himself with drums and guitar.

Bonnie Patton, Sioux. Opera Singer.

Cornel Pewewardy, Comanche-Kiowa. Sings traditional and contemporary songs accompany-

ing himself with flute and drum. Recordings include "Spirit Journey."

Pura Fe, Native American musical vocal group specializing in traditional and contemporary pieces.

Buddy Red Bow, Lakota. Contemporary country-rock. Recordings include "Journey to the Spirit World."

Red Earth Singers, Mesquakie. Traditional powwow singers.

Sage Point Singers. Powwow singers. Their recordings include "Pow-Wow Cookin."

Buffy Sainte-Marie, Cree from Canada raised in New England. Folk singer, composer, musician (guitar), recording artist. Performs internationally and in all major U.S. cities. Albums include "The Best of Buffy St. Marie," "I'm Gonna Be a Country Girl Again," and "It's My Way."

Keith Secola, Bois Fort Ojibwa. Recording artist. Albums include "Indian Cars," "Circle," and "Time Flies Like an Arrow. . . Fruit Flies Like a Banana."

Joanne Shenandoah, Oneida. Musician, performer, and recording artist. Albums include "Loving Ways" co-produced with A. Paul Ortega.

Southern Thunder, includes members from several Oklahoma tribes. Traditional powwow singers. Recordings include "Intertribal Songs of Oklahoma."

Douglas Spotted Eagle. Flutist; traditional and new age music. His recordings include "Sacred Feelings," "Legend of the Flute Boy" and "Canyon Speak."

Thunder Mountain, Ojibwa. Powwow singers/drummers. Their recordings include "Pow Wow Songs Recorded Live at White Swan, Washington."

John Trudell, Santee Sioux. Poet, musician, recording artist, and Indian rights activist. Albums include "Tribal Voices," "AKA Graffiti Man" and "Heart Jump Bouquet."

Mitch Walking Elk, Cheyenne/Arapaho. Singer, song writer, recording artist. Albums include "Dreamer" and "Indians."

Floyd Red Crow Westerman, Sisseton-Wahpeton Sioux. Folksinger, recording artist, Indian rights activist. Albums include "Custer Died For Your Sins," "Indian Country," and "The Land Is Your Mother."

Whippoorwill Singers, Navajo. A group of traditional singers. Their recordings include "Brother to Brother."

White Eagle, Rosebud Sioux. Tenor opera singer. Soloist at a pre-presidential inaugural gala for George Bush aired on Columbia Broadcasting System.

Chesley Goseyun Wilson, Apache. Traditional singer and storyteller who has performed all over the United States. Received the 1989 National Heritage Fellowship Award for his skill in handcrafting traditional apache violins.

Storytellers

M. Cochise Anderson, Chickasaw. Musician and storyteller based in New York.

Joe Bruchac, Abenaki descent from New York. Draws on traditions of Abenakis and Six Nations (Iroquois) in his program of traditional stories from the northeastern woodlands.

Chille Pop, Intertribal. An ensemble of musicians and performers who flavor traditional music with contemporary perspectives and styles. Based in New York City.

Joe Cross, Caddo-Potawatomi and Donna Couteau, Sac and Fox. Originally from Oklahoma, and based in New York City, the pair combines music, dance and storytelling.

Geri Keams, Navajo. Presents the songs and stories of her people in dramatic staged performances.

Medicine Story, Wampanoag from Massachusetts. Shares the traditional stories of his people and other nations.

Naa Kahidi Theater. From Alaska, they perform authentic renditions of traditional literature.

North American Indian Traveling College, Mohawk. Based in Canada, the group performs storytelling, music, and dance of the Six Nations (Iroquois).

Henry Real Bird, Crow from Montana. Shares his tribe's stories; has been the featured poet at the Cowboy Poetry Gathering for several years.

Will Rogers, Cherokee. Not only an actor and humorist, he was also a newspaper publisher and a Congressman from California.

Theater Actors/Groups

Jane Lind, Aleut. Theater, film, and television actor, and singer. Trained in New York and Paris, France. Appearances include the daytime television shows, "Ryans Hope" and "Days of our Lives" and voiceover for the PBS Nature segment, "Land of the Eagles."

Spiderwoman Theater, Kuna-Rappahannock. A professional Native American company founded around 1975 by sisters Muriel Miguel, Gloria Miguel and Lisa Mayo who write, direct, produce, and act in pieces such as "Winnie-too's Snake Oil Show From Wigwam City."

Recording Companies

There are several labels that specialize in Native American music. Most carry LPs, compact disks, and cassettes. Some also have music videos. The following are companies that include, or are totally devoted, to Native American music.

Archive of Folk Culture

American Folklife Center
Library of Congress
Washington, D.C. 20540-8100
(202) 287-5510

The Archive has a large collection of Native American music, including the earliest field recordings made anywhere in the world. The recordings are accessible in a public reading room in Washington, D. C. Many selections can also be purchased from the American Folklife Center and some have been issued by commercial recording companies. Information is available by calling (202) 707-2076; FAX: (202) 707-2076. Finding aids are available free of charge at the above address.

Jane Lind, Aleut theater, film, and television actor.
Photograph by Thomas O. Kriegsmann.

Canyon Records & Indian Arts

4143 North 16th Street
Phoenix, Arizona 85016
(602) 266-4823

They have powwow and contemporary Native American music. Canyon sells its own as well as other company's recordings.

Indian House

P.O. Box 472
Taos, New Mexico 87571
(505) 776-2953

A catalog of their powwow and contemporary Native American music is available from the above address.

Indian Records, Inc.

Box 47
Fay, Oklahoma 73646
(405) 887-3316

They specialize in powwow and contemporary Native American music.

Rounder Records

c/o Roundup Distribution
P. O. Box 154
North Cambridge, Massachusetts 02140
(800) 443-4727

They sell remastered recordings of Smithsonian/Folk titles issued on CD and cassette (see below).

SOAR

Sounds of America Records
P. O. Box 8606
Albuquerque, New Mexico 87198
(505) 268-6100

SOAR, which includes the new sub-labels, Natural Visions and Warrior, features traditional and contemporary music on cassette and CD.

Smithsonian/Folkways Recordings

Office of Folklife Programs
955 L'Enfant Plaza, Suite 2600
Smithsonian Institution
Washington, D.C. 20560
(202) 287-3262
FAX: (202) 287-3699

In 1987, the Smithsonian Institution acquired Folkways Recording, a collection of more than 2,100 folk music recordings from around the world. The recordings include Native American music from North and South America and are available by contacting Smithsonian/Folkways at the above address to request an order form and catalog of titles. Some titles are also available on Rounder Records through Roundup Distribution (see above).

FILM AND VIDEO ARTS*

Millions of people around the world get their ideas about Native Americans from the movies. Screen images pervade our society and influence our perception of Indians. Too many generations of movie-goers have received a misleading impression, often mired in the worst stereotypes and frequently obscuring the great diversity of Native American cultures. By the late nineteenth century, the image of the Plains and Apache Indians, who greatly resisted white domination at this time, were most represented in the popular entertainment of the time. The fact that they lived in hundreds of distinct groups with equally distinct cultures and history has been blurred by the movies and television into a "seen one Indian, seen 'em all" stereotype.

The foundation for these images of Native Americans descended from the early written accounts by explorers and travelers of the "new world." Captivity narratives of the late seventeenth and eighteenth century reinforced the Puritan image of Indians as inspired by the devil ("Good fetch'd out of evil"—captivity account of Rev. John Williams, 1706). Nineteenth- and early twentieth-century paintings of well-known artists such as George Catlin, Karl Bodmer, Alfred Miller, Charles Schreyvogel, Frederic Remington, and Charles Russell, and the noble and ignoble savages of James Fenimore Cooper's *Leatherstocking Tales* also helped reinforce a false image. The Beadles dime novels that appeared in 1860 depicted Indians as bloodthirsty savages. The wild west shows of Buffalo Bill, Annie Oakley, and over 100 more medicine and wild west shows employing Indian actors staged mock battles between white settlers and savage Indians. By the beginning of the

twentieth century, the popular image of Indians as savage feathered horsemen was firmly fixed.

By 1894, Thomas Alva Edison recognized the high entertainment value of Indians in wild west variety acts and filmed them in the earliest motion pictures. Edison invented the kinetoscope, a peep-hole viewing box where people lined up to see the magic of moving pictures, which showed forty to ninety second flickerings such as *Sioux Ghost Dance* (1894), *Moki Snake Dance* (1901), and scenes from the Eskimo pavilion at the 1893 World's Columbian Exposition. These motion pictures showing Indian ceremonial dances and Eskimo lifestyle provided men, women, and children with their first images of American Indians.

During the silent film era 1903–1929, the film stereotype of Indians was forming as hundreds of films were made. Between 1910 and 1913 alone, one hundred or more films about Indians appeared each year, according to Michael Hilger in *The American Indian in Film*. What eventually developed were serials with the classic western ingredients of settlers and frontiersmen struggling with nature and villainous Indians, usually played by non-Indian performers, on horses. Movement replaced action, sets were inexpensive, captions were simple. White American producers and directors pictured Indian life as savage and at a lower stage of development than white civilization. Film Indians were depicted as being doomed to extinction (either through extermination or assimilation) by the relentless western drive of civilization. Serials continued to be popular and major American studios shot forty different Western serials featuring Indians between 1930 and 1956, such as *Custer's Last Stand* (1936), *Overland with Kit Carson* (1939), and *Blackhawk, Son of Geronimo* (1952), all with ten to fifteen episodes. By the mid-twentieth century, Indians were a "staple" in Saturday afternoon movie serials and necessary in the formation of the myth of the West.

When sound came in 1927, Indians, who were rarely given speaking lines, became adversaries for white heroes. Always shown shrieking, pillaging, abducting, scalping, and whooping, Indians were not treated as people but rather as props for advanc-

* The section "Film and Video Arts" is by Elizabeth Weatherford, Department Head of the Film and Video Center of the National Museum of the American Indian/Smithsonian Institution. She is the senior author of *Native Americans on Film and Video*, a selective catalog of independent and tribal media productions, and is currently Research Associate in the Program for Ethnographic Film and Video at New York University.

JUST LIKE THE MOVIES

The media—radio, television, film—is powerful. The messages dominate our thinking, particularly when the viewer has little or no opportunity for firsthand observation. How many Americans see "Indians" anywhere but on the screen? And either way, who is able to distinguish fact from fiction? There is a story told about the shooting in Monument Valley of one of the epic Westerns directed by the renowned John Ford. The cameras stop. The Navajo actors dismount and take off their Sioux war bonnets. One of the film crew says to the Indians, "That was wonderful, you did it just right." An Indian actor replies, "Yeah, we did it just like we saw it in the movies." Without question, the American view of the "Indian" is "just like we saw it in the movies."

Rennard Strickland (1989)
Professor of Law and Director, Center for
Study of American Indian Law and Policy,
University of Oklahoma

ing the plot. They were as necessary to western action films—over 2,000 of them filmed since 1913—as horses, forts, stage coaches, and guns. Their function was to die at the hands of soldiers, settlers, ranchers or whatever whites happened to be featured in the film at the time. Between 1951 and 1970, at least eighty-six Indian-versus-Army films appeared depicting proud, bloodthirsty Indians. In 1992, Hollywood still churned out movies with these recurring images.

One of the persistent problems in all the westerns and other movies produced about Indians has been the use of non-Indians in acting roles as Indians. Indian actors were rarely given leading roles, although exceptions like *Eskimo* (1933), a film adaptation of a Peter Freuchen book with an all-native cast, were produced by Hollywood studios.

American Indians were active in the early film industry since 1909, when James Young Deer and his wife Red Wing became the first Indian actors to portray Indians in *The True Heart of an Indian* released by Pathé Western. The silent film era used Indian extras and reservation settings as backdrops. Cherokee actor Victor Daniels, or Chief Thunder Cloud, used as a prop with evil expressions in *Geronimo* (1939), never received credit under either of his names. Star billing went to Andy Devine, Preston Foster, and Ellen Drew—all whites. Chief John Big

Tree, who made the transition from silent films to sound, appeared in films produced by John Ford, a director who had used Navajo extras in his movies since *Stagecoach* (1939). Mona Darkfeather, Jim Thorpe, Iron Eyes Cody, and dozens of other Indian actors had movie roles, although roles that never portrayed an accurate or positive image for Native American people.

From the beginning, Native Americans have been major critics of the movie industry's treatment of their people. On March 18, 1911, *Moving Picture World* reported that a delegation of Indians from northwest and western reservations registered their objections with the BIA charging that "the moving pictures of wild western life used white men costumed as Indians in depicting scenes that are not true pictures of the Indians, and are in fact grossly libelous." Indian commissioner Robert G. Valentine, also displeased by the popular Indian pictures, promised to help the Indians "to eliminate the objectionable features of Indian life portrayals." On October 7, 1911, *Moving Picture World* reported that Native Americans were greatly disturbed to be so unjustly pictured in films. In 1914, Native actors threatened to strike. That same year, Chauncey Yellow Robe, Sioux, after viewing *The Indian Wars Refought* (1914), protested in a speech to the Society of American Indians about the film's reenactment of

NON-INDIAN ACTORS AS INDIANS

When was the last time in arts film & tv
No, count on my fingers
The last 500 times
Indians/Red Nations
Played Themselves.
History ain't no necessity
People—it is Reality.

M. Cochise Anderson
Chickasaw poet, storyteller, actor

Hollywood has churned out hundreds of movies since the turn of the twentieth century. Surely no group has ever been so misrepresented in so many movies for so long. Many Indians and non-Indians feel that in casting, native actors have occupied a singular niche because, until recently, Indians usually were not cast to play Indians. Bankable non-Indian stars got major Indian roles. The following selected non-Indian actors landed parts as Indians.

Dame Judith Anderson played Buffalo Cow Head in *A Man Called Horse* (1970).

Robby Benson played Billy Mills, Sioux Olympic champion in long distance running in *Running Brave* (1983).

Joey Bishop played Kronk in *Texas Across the River* (1966).

Robert Blake played Willie Boy in *Tell Them Willie Boy is Here* (1969).

Charles Bronson played Captain Jack in *Drum Beat* (1954).

Yul Brynner played Black Eagle in *Kings of the Sun* (1963).

Jeff Chandler played Cochise in *Broken Arrow* (1963).

Cyd Charisse played an Indian girl in *The Wild North* (1952).

Buster Crabbe played Magua in *Last of the Redmen* (1947).

Tony Curtis played Ira Hayes, Pima, one of the soldiers who raised the flag on Iwo Jima in *The Outsider* (1961).

Linda Darnell played Dawn Starlight in *Buffalo Bill* (1944).

Kevin Dillon played Skitty Harris in *War Party* (1989).

Yvonne DeCarlo played Wah 'Tah in *Deerslayer* (1943).

Trevor Howard played Windwalker in *Windwalker* (1980).

Rock Hudson played Taza in *Taza, Son of Cochise* (1954).

Buster Keaton played Chief Rotten Eagle in *Pajama Party* (1964).

Burt Lancaster played Jim Thorpe, Sac and Fox athlete who won the pentathlon and decathlon in the 1912 Olympics in *Jim Thorpe, All American* (1951).

Victor Mature played Crazy Horse in *Chief Crazy Horse* (1955).

Ricardo Montalban played Little Wolf in *Cheyenne Autumn* (1964).

J. Carrol Naish played Sitting Bull in *Annie Get Your Gun* (1950).

Leonard Nimoy played Black Hawk in *Old Overland Trail* (1953).

Jack Palance played Toriano in *Arrowhead* (1953).

Lou Diamond Phillips played Eskimo Agaguk in *Shadow of the Wolf* (1993).

Elvis Presley played Joe Lightcloud in *Stay Away Joe* (1968).

Anthony Quinn played Osceola in *Seminole* (1953) and Inuk in *Savage Innocents* (1960).

Burt Reynolds played Yaqui Joe in *100 Rifles* (1969).

Jennifer Tilly played Igiyook in *Shadow of the Wolf* (1993).

Loretta Young played Ramona in *Ramona* (1936).

NATIVE AMERICAN ACTORS

Indians have acted in films since the silent film era. According to Michael Hilger in *American Indians in Film*, over 140 Indians played Indians in silent and sound films between 1903 and 1984. Indians were used primarily as extras and in bit parts, enough to keep them marginally employed. A few Indian actors, however, managed to attain stardom.

Since the 1970s, several Native Americans have been cast in leading roles and have gained star recognition in Hollywood and television movies.

Chief John Big Tree, Seneca—*The Primitive Lover* (1922); *The Huntress* (1923); *The Iron Horse* (1924); *The Red Rider* (1925); *The Frontier Trail* (1926); *The Frontiersmen* (1927); *Winners of the Wilderness* (1927); *Spoilers of the West* (1928); *Sioux Blood* (1929); *Red Fork Range* (1931); *Custer's Last Stand* (1936); *Drums Along the Mohawk* (1939); *Stagecoach* (1939); *Western Union* (1941); *She Wore a Yellow Ribbon* (1949); *Devil's Doorway* (1950)

Monte Blue, Cherokee—*Told in the Hills* (1919); *Ride, Ranger, Ride* (1936); *The Outcasts of Poker Flat* (1937); *Hawk of the Wilderness* (1938); *The Iroquois Trail* (1950); *Apache* (1954)

Tantoo Cardinal, Cree—*War Party* (1989); *Dances with Wolves* (1990); *Black Robe* (1991)

George Clutesi, Nootka—*I Heard the Owl Call My Name* (1973); *Nakia* (1974); *Dreamspeaker* (1979); *Nightwing* (1979); *Spirit of the Wind* (1982)

Iron Eyes Cody, Cherokee—*Broken Arrow* (1950); *Custer's Last Stand* (1936); *Texas Pioneer* (1932); *The Senator Was Indiscreet* (1947); *Indian Agent* (1948); *The Paleface* (1948); *Massacre River* (1949); *Cherokee Uprising* (1950); *Fort Defiance* (1951); *Son of Paleface* (1952); *Sitting Bull* (1954); *Westward Ho the Wagons!* (1957); *Gun Fever* (1958); *Great Sioux Massacre* (1965); *El Condor* (1970); *A Man Called Horse* (1970); *Gray Eagle* (1977)

Victor Daniels, a.k.a. Chief Thunder Cloud, Cherokee—*Laughing Boy* (1934); *Rustlers of Red Dog* (1935); *Custer's Last Stand* (1936); *Ride, Ranger, Ride* (1936); *Riders of the Whistling Skull* (1937); *Flaming Frontiers* (1938); *The Great Adventures of Wild Bill Hickok* (1938); *The Lone Ranger* (1938); *Geronimo* (1940); *Young Buffalo Bill* (1940); *Western Union* (1941); *Overland Mail* (1942); *Daredevils of the West* (1943); *Buffalo Bill* (1944); *Outlaw Trail* (1944); *The Phantom Rider* (1946); *Romance of the West* (1946); *The Prairie* (1947); *The Senator was Indiscreet* (1957); *Blazing Across the Pecos* (1948); *Ambush* (1950); *Colt 45* (1950); *Davy Crockett, Indian Scout* (1950); *I Killed Geronimo* (1950); *Ticket to Tomahawk* (1950); *The Traveling Saleswoman* (1950); *Santa Fe* (1951)

Chief Darkcloud (a.k.a. Elijah Tahamont), Sioux or Abenaki—*Song of the Wildwood Flute* (1910); *The Squaw's Love* (1911); *What Am I Bid?* (1919)

Dove Eve Darkcloud, Algonquin—*Desert Gold* (1919)

Mona Darkfeather, Seminole—*At Old Fort Dearborn* (1912)

William Eagleshirt, Sioux—*Last of the Line* (1914); *The Conqueror* (1917)

Gary Farmer, Six Nations Mohawk—*Powwow Highway* (1989); television series *Forever Knight* (1993)

Chief Dan George, Salish—*Smith!* (1969); *Little Big Man* (1970, nominated for Oscar, Best Supporting Actor in 1971); *Cancel my Reservation* (1972); *Alien Thunder* (1973); *Harry and Tonto* (1974); *The Outlaw Josey Wales* (1976); *Spirit of the Wind* (1982)

Rodney A. Grant, Omaha—*Powwow Highway*

(1989); *War Party* (1989); *Dances with Wolves* (1990); *Son of Morning Star* (1991)

Graham Greene, Oneida—*Dances with Wolves* (1990, nominated for Oscar, Best Supporting Actor in 1991); *Thunderheart* (1992); *Clearcut* (1992); *Last of His Tribe* (1992); *Cooperstown* (1993)

Charlie Hill, Oneida—*Harold of Orange* (1983)

Michael Horse, Apache/Zuni—*The Legend of the Lone Ranger* (1981); *Passenger 57* (1992)

Geraldine Keams, Navajo—*The Outlaw Josey Wales* (1976)

Jane Lind, Aleut—*Salmonberries* (1990)

Eddie Little Sky, Sioux—*Apache Warrior* (1957); *Revolt at Fort Laramie* (1957); *Gun Fever* (1958); *Sergeants 3* (1962); *Duel at Diablo* (1966); *The Way West* (1967); *A Man Called Horse* (1970); *Run Simon Run* (1970); *Journey Through Rosebud* (1972); *Breakheart Pass* (1976)

Ray Mala, Eskimo—*The Great Adventures of Wild Bill Hickok* (1938); *North West Mounted Police* (1940); *Red Snow* (1952)

Chief Many Treaties (a.k.a. Bill Hazlette), Blackfeet—*The Pioneers* (1941); *Overland Mail* (1942); *Deer Slayer* (1943); *The Law Rides Again* (1943); *Buffalo Bill* (1944); *Buffalo Bill Rides Again* (1947)

Elaine Miles, Umatilla—"Marilyn" in television series *Northern Exposure* (1991)

Anthony Nukema, Karok-Hopi—*Pony Soldier* (1952); *Westward Ho the Wagons!* (1957)

Lois Red Elk, Sioux—*A Man Called Horse* (1970); *Joe Panther* (1976); *Ishi: The Last of His Tribe* (1978)

Princess Red Wing, Winnebago—*Red Wing's Gratitude* (1909); *The Squaw Man* (1914); *The Thundering Herd* (1914)

Rodd Redwing, Chickasaw—*Apache Chief* (1949); *Buffalo Bill in Tomahawk Territory* (1952); *Son of Geronimo* (1952); *Conquest of Cochise* (1953);

The Pathfinder (1953); *Saginaw Trail* (1953); *Cattle Queen of Montana* (1954); *Flaming Star* (1960); *Shalako* (1968)

Will Rogers, Cherokee—*Laughing Bill Hyde* (1918); *The Story of Will Rogers* (1952)

Joanelle Romero, Apache—*Powwow Highway* (1989)

Frank Salsedo, Wintu—*I Will Fight No More Forever* (1975)

Will Sampson, Creek—*One Flew Over the Cuckoo's Nest* (1975); *Buffalo Bill and the Indians or Sitting Bull's History Lesson* (1976); *The Outlaw Josie Wales* (1976); *The White Buffalo* (1977); *Old Fish Hawk* (1979)

Jay Silverheels (a.k.a. Harry Smith), Six Nations Mohawk—*The Prairie* (1947); *Laramie* (1949); *Broken Arrow* (1950); *Battle at Apache Pass* (1951); *Brave Warrior* (1952); *The Nebraskan* (1953); *The Pathfinder* (1953); *War Arrow* (1954); *The Vanishing American* (1955); *The Lone Ranger* (1956); *Indian Paint* (1963); *Smith!* (1969); *Santee* (1973); co-starred as "Tonto" in the television series *The Lone Ranger*; became the first American Indian to have his star set in Hollywood's Walk of Fame along Hollywood Boulevard (1979).

Chief Luther Standing Bear, Lakota—*White Oak* (1921); *Santa Fe Trail* (1930); *The Conquering Horde* (1931); *Texas Pioneers* (1932); *The Miracle Rider* (1935)

Charles Stevens, Apache—*Tom Sawyer* (1930); *Winners of the West* (1940); *My Darling Clementine* (1946); *Buffalo Bill Rides Again* (1947); *The Cowboy and the Indians* (1949); *Ambush* (1950); *Indian Territory* (1950); *Ticket to Tomahawk* (1950); *Wagons West* (1952); *The Vanishing American* (1955)

Nipo T. Strongheart, Yakima—*Young Daniel Boone* (1950); *Pony Soldier* (1952)

(continued)

NATIVE AMERICAN ACTORS (cont.)

Wes Studi, Cherokee—*Dances With Wolves* (1990); *Last of the Mohicans* (1992)

Jim Thorpe, Sac and Fox—*Battling with Buffalo Bill* (1931); *Behold My Wife* (1935); *Rustlers of Red Dog* (1935); *Treachery Rides the Range* (1936); *Prairie Schooners* (1940); *Wagonmaster* (1950)

Chief Thunderbird, Cherokee—*Battling with Buffalo Bill* (1931); *Rustlers of Red Dog* (1935); *Wild West Days* (1937); *North West Mounted Police* (1940)

Sheila Tousey, Menominee—*Thunderheart* (1992)

Ray Tracey, Navajo—*Joe Panther* (1976)

John Trudell, Santee Dakota—*Thunderheart* (1992)

John War Eagle, Yankton Sioux—*Broken Arrow* (1950); *Ticket to Tomahawk* (1950); *The Last Outpost* (1951); *Tomahawk* (1951); *Laramie Mountains* (1952); *Pony Soldier* (1952); *The Wild North* (1952); *The Great Sioux Uprising* (1953); *Last of the Comanches* (1953); *Saginaw Trail* (1953); *The Black Dakotas* (1954); *They Rode West* (1954); *Dragoon Wells Massacre* (1957); *Westward Ho the Wagons!* (1957); *Tonka* (1958); *Flap* (1970); *When the Legends Die* (1972)

Floyd Red Crow Westerman, Sisseton–Wahpeton Sioux—*Dances With Wolves* (1990); *Clearcut* (1992); television series *L.A. Law* (1991) and *Northern Exposure* (1992)

Chauncey Yellow Robe, Sioux—*The Silent Enemy* (1930)

James Young Deer, Winnebago—*The Mended Lute* (1909); *The True Heart of an Indian* (1909); *Yaqui Girl* (1911)

Chief Yowlachie, Yakima—*War Paint* (1926); *The Red Raiders* (1927); *Sitting Bull at the "Spirit Lake Massacre"* (1927); *The Glorious Trail* (1928); *Hawk of the Hills* (1929); *Santa Fe Trail* (1930); *North West Mounted Police* (1940); *Winners of the West* (1940); *White Eagle* (1941); *Canyon Passage* (1946); *The Prairie* (1947); *The Senator was Indiscreet* (1947); *The Dude Goes West* (1948); *The Paleface* (1948); *Red River* (1948); *The Cowboy and the Indians* (1949); *Ma and Pa Kettle* (1949); *Mrs. Mike* (1949); *Annie Get Your Gun* (1950); *Cherokee Uprising* (1950); *Ticket to Tomahawk* (1950); *Son of Geronimo* (1952); *The Pathfinder* (1953)

---

the 1890 Battle of Wounded Knee which, at the time, was widely promoted for use in U.S. schools. Yellow Robe attacked the film for promoting a falsified version of the event as a noble battle rather than a tragic massacre. In 1936, Natives organized to try to stop Hollywood from misrepresenting them. William Hazlette, a Blackfeet, formed a Native American affiliation of the Screen Actor's Association that lasted until World War II. In June 1939, a New York *Herald Tribune* article reported that a California group called the Indian Actors' Association tried to place its members in theater jobs by encouraging them to study traditions and re-learn forgotten skills so they could become experts at the studios. Forty

years later, in 1979, the *Hollywood Reporter* stated that the American Indian Talent Guild had "seen little progress in its demand for more roles for Indians in both theatrical and TV films."

During the 1960s and 1970s, groups organized to combat the distorted "Hollywood" Indian image and more whites were willing to listen. When *A Man Called Horse* opened in 1970, members of the American Indian Movement (AIM) handed out leaflets at theaters charging that "every dollar going into the box office is a vote for bigotry." AIM criticized the movie's desecration of Indian religion, its use of non-Indian actors, and technical errors. One Sioux reviewer pointed out that traditional Sioux did not desert their elderly and were not routinely cruel. The film also incorrectly drew on Catlin paintings of the Mandans to portray Lakota culture. In 1980, Choctaw Phil Lucas coproduced with Robert Hagopian a five-part series *Images of Indians*, (available in video format for sale or rental from the Native American Public Broadcasting Corporation in Lincoln, Nebraska) which examined the stereotypes drawn by the movies and questioned what the effects of the Hollywood image has been on the Indians' own self-image.

Despite the existence of hundreds of highly trained and talented American Indian performers in Los Angeles, New York, and on virtually all of the nation's reservations, non-Indians continued to play Indian roles on screen and stage. In 1960, Harry Preston Smith, better known as Jay Silverheels, a Mohawk from the Six Nations Reserve in Ontario, Canada, who portrayed Tonto in the 1950's "Lone Ranger" episodes, spoke out against the way in which Indians were pictured on television, and even wrote his protests in strong letters to President Dwight Eisenhower. With the help of other Indians such as Buffy Sainte-Marie, Iron Eyes Cody, and Rodd Redwing, he formed in 1966 an Indian Actors' Workshop at the Los Angeles Indian Center as a vehicle by which to get Native American people on the screen and to try and change the image of Indian people. The Workshop promoted the use of native people in native roles, trained Indians in trick riding and other horse riding skills, and taught dramatic skills to Indians. Over fifteen years later in 1983, Indians organized the Los Angeles-based, non-profit American Indian Registry for the Performing Arts to act as a liaison between Indian performers and producers and casting directors. Each year the registry publishes a directory of Native American actors, directors, producers, and technicians that is made available to the entertainment industry. Kevin Costner, producer and director of *Dances With Wolves* (1990), worked with the registry and found twelve Native American actors who were given roles in his film. The registry was not contacted by Robert Redford, however, who cast Lou Diamond Phillips as a Navajo police officer in his film version of the Tony Hillerman novel, *The Dark Wind*.

In the 1960s, Hollywood began to address the reality of harsh federal government policies and U.S. Army extermination of Indians. Sympathetic portrayals of Indians, albeit with non-Indians in leading Indian roles, appeared that broke down the traditional celluloid stereotypes. In *Cheyenne Autumn* (1964), director John Ford depicted the heroic flight of Cheyennes from Oklahoma to their homeland in northern Montana. The Cheyenne characters speak in ersatz Cheyenne and white characters appear to respect the native people. To be sure *Cheyenne Autumn*, not completely devoid of cinematic clichés, is peopled with "good" and "bad" Indians. In 1970, Hollywood released *Little Big Man* with its sympathetic portrayals of Indian characters and depiction of traditional heroes like Wild Bill Hickok and Custer as mentally unstable. Filmmaker Arthur Penn cast Chief Dan George, a Salish elder and elected chief from British Columbia who became an actor in middle age as Old Lodge Skins, the elderly chief of the Cheyennes and the hero's surrogate father. For his role, Chief Dan George won the New York Critics and National Society of Film Critics awards in 1971. Although he did not win the Oscar for his Best Supporting Actor nomination, he put his people in the limelight. As Michael Hilger pointed out in *American Indian in Film*, although there was a growth of awareness in the 1960s and into the 1970s, "sympathy doesn't give way to real empathy until the contemporary period."

The history of Hollywood's treatment of Indians in film can be seen as inauthentic with occasional attempts to be accurate, sometimes by showing native material culture or portraying the devastating after-effect and moral dilemmas caused by colonialist intrusion. From the beginning of filmmaking, starting with Edison's kinetoscope productions, directors were determined to go to native locations and to document the lifestyles of the people. By 1918, missionaries, tourism developers, anthropologists, cartographers, and even Hollywood directors had shot footage of Yuman, Alaska Eskimo, Winnebago, Blackfeet, Crow, and many Pueblo peoples. A general interest in views of authentic Native American cultures, in part fueled by dissatisfaction with the

INDEPENDENT NATIVE FILM AND VIDEO MAKERS

Within the past twenty years, Native Americans have had significant control over their own images. The following independent film and video makers have been active in producing or directing films and videos that document experiences of Native peoples in their own and the dominant culture.

Maggi Banner, Hopi/Tewa—*Coyote Goes Underground* (1989); *Tiwa Tales* (1991)

Dean Curtis Bear Claw, Crow—*Warrior Chiefs in a New Age* (1991)

Roy Bigcrane, Salish—*The Place of Falling Waters* (1991)

Arlene Bowman, Navajo—*Navajo Talking Picture* (1986)

Frank Brown, Bella Bella—*Voyage of Rediscovery* (1990)

George Burdeau, Blackfeet—*The Real People* (8 parts) (1976); *Pueblo Peoples: First Contact* (1991); *Surviving Columbus* (1990)

Gil Cardinal, Metis—*Foster Child* (1986); *The Spirit Within* (1988–91); *Tikinagan* (1991); *My Partners, My People* (14 parts) (1991–92)

Larry Cesspooch, Ute—*Ute Indian Tribe Video* (130 productions) (1979 to present)

Greg Coyes—*My Partners, My People* (14 parts) (1991–92)

Willie Dunn—*The Ballad of Crowfoot* (1968); *The Other Side of the Ledger* (1972)

Joseph Fisher, Blackfeet—*Transitions* (with Darrell Kipp) (1991)

Independent filmmaker Darrell Kipp, Blackfeet. Photograph by Beverly Singer.

Carol Geddes, Tlingit—*Doctor, Lawyer, Indian Chief* (1986)

Ava Hamilton, Arapaho—*Everything Has a Spirit* (1992)

Bob Hicks, Creek/Seminole—*Return of the Country* (1984)

George P. Horse Capture, Gros Ventre—*I'd Rather Be Powwowing* (1983)

Alexie Isaac, Yupik Eskimo—*Yupiit Yuraryarait* (1983); *Eyes of the Spirit* (1984)

Darrell Kipp, Blackfeet—*Transitions* (with Joseph Fisher) (1991)

Carol Korb, Yurok—*Shenandoah Films* (12 productions) (1983–present)

Nettie Kuneki, Klickitat—*. . . And Woman Wove it in a Basket* (1990)

---

melodrama and stereotyping in movies, created an audience for a new form. This was first realized by a geologist and filmmaker, Robert J. Flaherty, who traveled to Canada's Hudson Bay area to make *Nanook of the North* (1922), This motion picture would ultimately be labeled as the first of a new genre, a "documentary." The film's success is tied to its apparent authenticity, and all-Eskimo cast to re-enact the rigors of living in the harsh Arctic environment.

The 1960s saw a remarkable outpouring of documentaries by and about natives in the United States and Canada. In the summer of 1966, Sol Worth, a film communication scholar, and John Adair, a cul-

Zacharias Kunuk, Inuit—*Qaggig/The Gathering Place* (1989); *Nunaqpa/Going Inland* (1991); *Saputi/Fish Weir* (1993)

Larry Littlebird, Santo Domingo Pueblo—*The Real People* (8 parts) (with George Burdeau) (1976); *I'd Rather Be Powwowing* (1983)

Phil Lucas, Choctaw—*Images of Indians* (5 parts) (1980); *The Honor of All* (3 parts) (1985–86); *Voyage of Rediscovery* (1990)

Catherine Martin, Micmac—*Kwa'nu'te* (1991); *Shirley Bear: Reclaiming the Balance* (1991)

Victor Masayesva, Jr., Hopi—*Hopiit* (1982); *Itam Hakim Hopiit* (1984); *Ritual Clowns* (1988); *Pott Starr* (1990); *Siskyavi: A Place of Chasms* (1991); *Imagining Indians* (1992)

Nellie Moore, Inupiat—*Inupiat Eskimo Healing* (1985)

Fidel Moreno, Yaqui/Huichol—*Wiping the Tears of Seven Generations* (1990); *Peyote Road* (1992)

Alanis Obomsawin, Abenaki—*Mother of Many Children* (1977); *Incident at Restigouche* (1984); *Poundmaker's Lodge: A Healing Place* (1987); *Cry from a Diary of a Metis Child: Richard Cardinal* (1986); *No Address* (1989); *Kanahsetake: 270 Years of Resistance* (1993)

Sandra Johnson Osawa, Makah—*The Native Americans* (10 parts) (1975); *I Know Who I Am* (1979); *In the Heart of Big Mountain* (1988); *The Eighth Fire* (1992)

Russell Peters, Mashpee Wampanoag—*People of the First Light* (7 parts) (1979); *Appanaug* (1992)

Judy Peterson, Aleut—*Our Aleut History: Alaska Natives in Progress* (1987)

David Poisey, Inuit—*Starting Fire with Gunpowder* (1991)

Randy Red Road, Cherokee—*Cowtipping* (1992); *Haircuts Hurt* (1992)

Duke Redbird, Cree—*Charley Squash Goes To Town* (1959)

Diane Reyna, Taos Pueblo—*Surviving Columbus* (1992)

Gary Robinson, Cherokee—*Creek Nation Video* (7 parts) (1982–86)

Beverly R. Singer, Santa Clara Pueblo—*The Powwow: Coming Together of Many Tribes* (1979); *Solar Energy* (1981); *Looking Back: Institute of American Indian Arts* (1988); *Indigenous People and the Land* (1990); *Mondo's Story* (1991); *One Mind, Body, and Spirit* (1993)

Mona Smith, Navajo—*Her Giveway: A Spiritual Journey with AIDS* (1988); *Honored by the Moon* (1990); *That Which Is Between* (1991)

Ruby Sootkis, Northern Cheyenne—*The Season of Children* (1992)

Chris Spotted Eagle, Houma—*Do Indians Shave?* (1974); *Wyld Ryce* (4 parts) (1979–80); *The Great Spirit Within the Hole* (1983); *Our Sacred Land* (1984)

Christine Welch, Metis—*Women in the Shadows* (1992)

Raymond Yakeleya, Dene—*We Remember* (1979)

tural anthropologist, introduced 16mm filmmaking to the Navajo community of Pine Springs, Arizona. None of the Navajo men and women had had experience making films, although most had seen Hollywood films and television. Encouraged to choose their own subjects, most of the participants filmed objects or rituals that were important to Navajo people. *Navajo Film Themsleves* consists of seven short documentaries.

In 1967, the National Film Board of Canada sponsored its Challenge for Change project to "promote citizen participation in the solution of social problems." Several Indian filmmakers were trained and equipped under this program, including Mike

Mitchell (Mohawk), who was project director for *You Are On Indian Land* (1969), a film report about protests by New York Mohawk Indians against the refusal of the government to enforce the Jay Treaty—which guarantees the Mohawks unhampered movement across the Canadian–U.S. border.

The 1970s was the decade of change for the native media. At the beginning of the decade, when only a handful of Indians were active in the media, native people recognized its value as a political and social tool. They trained themselves in production techniques so they could provide accurate reporting about important legal and cultural issues facing native peoples. But the 1990s, more than 200 Native American people have produced film, video, and audio works. Hundreds of documentaries testify to native dedication and determination to succeed in spite of funding difficulties, crew problems, and too few places to show the films. In 1983, the first television documentary produced by an all-Indian crew, *I'd Rather Be Powwowing*, was aired on public television. Produced by George Horse Capture, (Gros Ventre), directed by Larry Littlebird (Santo Domingo Pueblo), with sound by Larry Cesspooch (Ute), the film follows Al Chandler, a Gros Ventre from the Fort Berthold Indian Reservation in North Dakota, who observes Indian traditions by frequently taking part in powwows.

Tribes and native organizations also have funded media projects to record tribal traditions and important events. Since 1979, the Ute Indian Tribe of Fort Duchesne, Utah, has been making video documentaries about Ute traditions. Many of the tapes are in the Ute language, others in Ute and English. In 1979 and early 1980s, the Ojibwa and Cree Cultural Centre in Timmins, Ontario, Canada produced over twenty-five videotapes portraying traditional craft techniques, stories, and profiles of elders. Since the early 1980s, the Muscogee Creek Nation Communications Center in Okmulgee, Oklahoma produced videotapes to present accurate and contemporary views of the Creek Nation. In Alaska, two organizations have produced videos. KYUK-TV, located in Bethel, Alaska and begun in 1972, has produced works on the lifestyles and native culture of the

Yukon–Kuskokwim Delta, both for local broadcast and for the general public. It produces radio and television programs in both English and Yupik that focus on the Yupik Eskimo way of life and the people's viewpoints on contemporary events and the continuation of their cultural traditions. The station has provided opportunities for community members to be involved as production consultants and spokespeople in the documentaries and also has employed native producers, cinematographers, narrators, and on-camera interviewers. In Lincoln, Nebraska, the Native American Public Broadcasting Consortium (NAPBC), established in 1977, develops and produces public television and radio programs and educational programs, supports and distributes programs by, for, and about Native Americans, for Native American and general audiences. The NAPBC, based at the Nebraska Educational Telecommunications Center and funded in part by the Corporation for Public Broadcasting, also acts as consultant for film, video, and radio productions, awards scholarships to native communications students, and provides technical assistance to tribal and community operations.

Since 1972, the Canadian Broadcasting Corporation (CBC) has beamed commercial programming by satellite into most Inuit villages in the Arctic for eighteen hours each day. Television competed with community activities. Men stopped hunting and women stopped visiting friends in order to watch soap operas, white detective stories, superheroes, and advertisements that exposed Inuit audiences to alien forms of violence and consumerism. And worse, English invaded homes, the last refuge of the Inuktitut language. In 1980, the Inuit Tapirisat (Inuit Brotherhood) was granted access to a CBC satellite channel and given money to establish Inukshuk, an experimental television network to provide regionally oriented programs and to offset the "southern" programming CBC provides. The Inuit organization used satellite time to broadcast throat-singing concerts, firefighter training sessions, and homemade hunting movies.

Since Inukshuk successfully demonstrated that there were audiences for Inuit programs and professional staffs were able to produce them, the Canadian government licensed a permanent Inuit network in 1981 called the Inuit Broadcasting Corporation (IBC). It began producing and broadcasting by satellite over five hours per week of original programming in Inuktitut and English on the CBC Northern Television band. Seven communities across the central and western Arctic became production sites and receive the programs. Programs concerned with language and cultural survival dramatize ancient Inuit stories while others tackle difficult social problems like alcoholism and wife-beating, far too common in the Arctic. Inuit children now watch *Super Shamou*, a Inuit-styled caribou hunter who straps on a cape and flies off to rescue Inuit children in trouble. The IBC is currently the only Native American broadcast network in North America.

Professional organizations now provide training in producing, broadcasting and cinematography. Since the late 1960s, the National Film Board (NFB) of Canada has recruited native producers. Building on NFB's Challenge for Change project which brought native Canadians into media production, NFB opened Studio One in Edmonton in 1990. Under the leadership of Carol Geddes, Tlingit, its outreach programs tries to attract native Canadians to pursue media careers.

In the United States, there has been no national production initiatives focused specifically on Native Americans. However, the independent media community's support of underrepresented media makers have included major attention to Native American producers, including the Independent Television Service, the Rockefeller Foundation Intercultural Media Fellowships, and the Public Broadcasting System. One regional project has offered an interesting model. At Montana State University the Native Voices Public Television Workshop, directed by Dan Hart, trains and supports Indian producers in the Northwest region between Washington State and the Dakotas. The Workshop provides funding, personnel, and facilities and has stressed developing tools, including archival image research, for re-visioning history from tribal perspectives.

While Native-made films and video offer a fresh perspective, access to viewing them has been limited to special contexts—film and video festivals, university courses, conferences, and local public television broadcasts. Several national organizations and festivals have been founded to showcase the works of these media makers and to extend access to audiences.

In 1975, the American Indian Film Institute was founded in Culver City, California under the leadership of Choctaw Michael Smith. Its American Indian Film Festival is presented annually in San Francisco, and winners are celebrated with American Indian Motion Picture Awards in various categories, with some emphasis on Hollywood films and the work of prominent Native American actors who have been honored in special showcases.

In 1979, the biennial Native American Film and Video Festival was launched in New York City. Its purpose is to showcase the works of independent and tribal community film, video, and audio makers, and it focuses on productions about First Nations people from throughout the hemisphere. It has premiered such native directors as Victor Masayesva, Jr., Gil Cardinal, Chris Spotted Eagle, Zacharias Kunuk, and Sandra Osawa, and has shown large audiences works from Northern Native Broadcasting Yukon, the Inuit Broadcasting Corporation, Ute Indian Tribe Audio-Visual, the Media Department of the Creek Nation of Indians, and the Kayapo of Brazil. The Festival is sponsored by the Film and Video Center, located in the new National Museum of the American Indian, which is the national center for information about native productions and services to independent media makers in this field.

Since 1991, a number of new Native-organized festivals—Dreamspeakers Festival of Indigenous Film and Video in Edmonton, Canada and the Two Rivers Native Film and Video Festival in Minneapolis—have resulted in wider opportunities for Native producers not only to gain audiences, but to organize their own forums. In 1993, the Deadwood Film Festival in South Dakota became the setting for the formation of the first national organization of Native American independent film and television producers. Headquartered in Denver, Col-

On location interview with Alan Houser, renowned Apache sculptor, and Beverly Singer, independent video and filmmaker, in Santa Fe, New Mexico, in 1988. Photograph by Andrew Gardner.

orado, the producer's organization intends to address the continuing problems for Native producers to gain access to production funding and to help insure the integrity of productions about native people by involving Native Americans in key professional positions.

The phenomenal commercial success of *Dances With Wolves* (it garnered eight Academy Awards out of twelve nominations) indicates American curiosity about real-life Indians. But as George Burdeau, Blackfeet producer and founding director of the Communications Arts Department at the Institute of American Indian Arts in Santa Fe, New Mexico, pointed out at the 1991 Native American Film and Video Festival in New York City: "The image of Indians has been so erroneous for so many years that the only way it can be changed is for Native Americans to produce films themselves." Today, Native Americans are doing just that. They are producing films that portray Indians in realistic situations, often using Indian actors in contemporary roles. And they are challenging Hollywood's make-believe Indian screen images. In addition, since *Dances With Wolves*, Hollywood producers seem to be making sincere efforts to cast Indian people in Indian parts. Ironically, even if Indian actors are found, union rules require that they compete with non-Indian actors for Indian roles. As Gary Farmer, Mohawk actor from the Six Nations Reserve in Ontario, Canada, argued at the New York City 1991 film festival: ". . . there are some amazing native image makers out there. They have embraced the new technology and bring a whole new approach to filmmaking. There's a lot of future for Indian films." Clearly, Native Americans are now filming the real stories of their cultures.

Voices of Communication

NATIVE AMERICAN MEDIA

From 1826 to the present, over 2,000 newspapers and periodicals have been published by tribes, Indian organizations, Indian schools, urban Indian centers, prison groups, and scholars. Formats have varied from several mimeographed news-sheets and offset journals to full-fledged newspapers printed on standard newsprint running over forty pages. Some publications were ephemeral, their publishing lives ending with the first or second issue, while others folded after thirty years; still others have endured for decades and circulate widely around the world. These papers are intended for tribal, intertribal, regional, urban, national, or international audiences, and appear weekly, biweekly, monthly, every other month, quarterly, or unpredictably. While most circulations are small, the large number of publications on many reservations suggests the appetite Indian people have for news and information by and about themselves.

People eager to learn about Indians and their communities should read the native press. With a native point of view, these papers cover current events, economics, law, health issues, arts, history of respective constituencies, natural resource issues, literature, education, and social issues in contemporary American Indian and Alaska Native communities. Poetry, story-telling, traditional food recipes, movie and book reviews, and opinion pieces round out the contents.

A CHRONOLOGY OF NATIVE AMERICAN JOURNALISM

February 21, 1828–1834—The *Cherokee Phoenix* edited by Elias Boudinot in the Cherokee Nation, New Echota, Georgia. The first tribal paper and the first paper to publish news in an American Indian language. Published in English and the Cherokee syllabary. Weekly.

In 1826, Cherokee Elias Boudinot, chosen by the Cherokee Nation to raise funds to buy printing equipment, made a speech to whites in Philadelphia in which he stressed the need for a tribal press. After the funds were raised, the Cherokee Nation named him editor of the proposed newspaper, called *The Cherokee Phoenix*, a position he held from 1828 to 1832.

"To obtain a correct and complete knowledge of these people, there must exist a vehicle of Indian intelligence, altogether different from those

which have heretofore been employed. Will not a paper published in Indian country . . . have the desired effect? I do not say that Indians will produce learned and elaborate dissertations in explanation and vindication of their own character; but they may exhibit specimens of their intellectual efforts, of their eloquence, of their moral, civil and physical advancement, which will do quite as much to remove prejudice and to give profitable information."

The Cherokee Phoenix, *first published in 1828, was the first tribal paper in the United States. It published news in the Cherokee syllabary and in English. Courtesy Georgia Historical Commission.*

September 26, 1844–1906—The *Cherokee Advocate* first edited by William Potter Ross in the Cherokee Nation, Tahlequah, Indian Territory. Published in English and the Cherokee syllabary. Weekly.

April 1916–November 1922—*Wassaja: Freedom's Signal for the Indians* edited by Carlos Montezuma in Chicago. Monthly.

1956–present—*Tribal Tribune* first edited by B. J. Covington. Published by Colville Confederated Tribes in Nespelem, Washington. Monthly.

November 1959–present—*Navajo Times* (formerly the *Navajo Times Today*) first edited by Dillon Platero. Published by the Navajo Tribe in Window Rock, Arizona. At one time, the only daily Indian newspaper in the United States. Weekly.

June 6, 1962–present—*Fort Apache Scout* first edited by W. Cavanaugh. Published by the White Mountain Apache Tribe in Whiteriver, Arizona. Biweekly.

1962–present—*Jicarilla Chieftain* first edited by Beatrice Kemm. Published by the Jicarilla Apache Tribal Council in Dulce, New Mexico. Biweekly.

October 1, 1962–present—*Tundra Times* first edited by Howard Rock. Independently published. Temporarily out of circulation from December 1991 to October 1992. Weekly.

1963–present—*Americans Before Columbus* first edited by Ansel Carpenter, Fran Poafybitty, Tillie Walker. Published by National Indian Youth Council in Albuquerque, New Mexico. Bimonthly.

1964–1992—*Native Nevadan* (formerly *Inter-*

tribal Council of Nevada Newsletter) first edited by John Dressler. Published by Intertribal Council of Nevada, Reno, Nevada. Monthly.

1964–1980—*Wassaja* first edited by Rupert Costo and Jeannette Henry. Published by American Indian Historical Society. Bimonthly.

January 1968–present—*Cherokee One Feather* first edited by Alvin Smith, Tom Bradley, and Calvin Lossiah. Published by the Eastern band of Cherokees in Cherokee, North Carolina. Weekly.

1969–present—*Akwesasne Notes* first edited by Gerald Gambill (Rarihokwats). Now published by the Mohawk Nation in Rooseveltown, New York. Six times per year.

May 1969–present—*Southern Ute Drum* first edited by John E. Baker. Published by the Southern Ute Tribe at Ignacio, Utah. Biweekly.

December 5, 1969–present—*Choctaw Community News* first edited by Robert Benn. Published by Choctaw Community Action Agency in Philadelphia, Mississippi. Monthly.

1970–present—*Sho-Ban News* first edited by Lorraine Edmo. Published by Shoshone-Bannock Tribes in Fort Hall, Idaho. Weekly.

Fort Apache Scout *office, Fort Apache Indian Reservation, in Whiteriver, Arizona. Photograph by Karen Warth.*

Navajo Times *office in Window Rock, Navajo Nation, Arizona. Photograph by Karen Warth.*

SELECTED NATIVE AMERICANS IN THE MEDIA

"Communications provide a means by which we can interpret our own reality, define our identity and in turn express these to the world community. To those of us who have chosen this path the responsibilities are numerous. We are the present day story tellers. We are the messengers between villages and nations. We are the carriers of the word. In many ways we are today's tribal historians."

Gordon Regguinti, Leech Lake Ojibwe
Executive Director
Native American Journalists Association, 1992

The following selected Native American newspaper editors and publishers, television, video, and radio producers, and heads of media organizations have been among the "present day storytellers."

Peggy Berryhill, Muskogee. Producer of *Spirits of the Present*, a series for public radio.

Frank M. Blythe, Sioux-Cherokee. Executive director of Native American Public Broadcasting Consortium (Lincoln, Nebraska) since 1977.

Elias Boudinot, Cherokee. The first Native American editor in U.S. history. Edited *Cherokee Phoenix* from 1828 until 1832.

Rupert Costo, Cahuilla. Publisher and editor. Founder of *Indian Historian*, *Wassaja*, and *Weewish Tree* (children's journal). Died in 1989.

Paul DeMain, Wisconsin Oneida-White Earth Chippewa. Managing editor of *News from Indian Country* (Hayward, Wisconsin).

Gary Fife, Creek-Cherokee. Producer/host of National Native News (Anchorage, Alaska), since 1987 aired on over 160 public radio stations across the country.

Tom Giago, Oglala Lakota. Founder in 1981 of *Lakota Times*, now *Indian Country Today* (Rapid City, South Dakota), the largest independently owned American Indian newspaper. Giago's syndicated column appears in some twenty papers in Arizona, Colorado, Nebraska, New Mexico, and South Dakota.

Hattie Kauffman, Nez Percé. National correspondent for *CBS This Morning*, 1990; former feature reporter for ABC's *Good Morning America* program. Winner of four Emmy Awards.

Richard V. LaCourse, Yakima. Assistant editor, *Yakima Nation Review* in Washington State. Former news director of the American Indian Press Association in Washington, D.C. (1970–1975), and former editor of *Confederated Umatilla Journal*, *Manitoba Messenger*, and *CERT Report*.

Carlos Montezuma, Yavapai Apache. Founder of *Wassaja*, a monthly publication, in 1916.

Rose Robinson, Hopi. Founding member of American Indian Press Association, 1970–1975. Editor of *Exchange* (Phelps-Stokes Fund).

Howard Rock, Point Hope Inuit. Editor of *Tundra Times*, nominated for a Pulitzer Prize in 1975. Died in 1976.

Mark Trahant, Shoshone-Bannock. News editor of *Salt Lake Tribune*. Became editor in 1983 of *Navajo Times Today*, at one time the only daily newspaper published for an American Indian audience. Honored in 1985 by the National Press Foundation, with a special citation for "an inspiring display of individual journalistic initiative" in remaking the tribal weekly into a daily.

Charles Trimble, Oglala Lakota. Founder and executive director of the American Indian Press Association (1970–1975).

The office of Indian Country Today (*formerly known as* Lakota Times) *in Rapid City, South Dakota. Photograph by Karen Warth.*

June 1972–present—*NARF Legal Review* (formerly *Announcements*) first edited by Joan L. Carpenter. Published by Native American Rights Fund in Boulder, Colorado. Biannual.

1974–present—*Speaking of Ourselves* first edited by Betty Blue, Larry Aitken, and Todd LeGarde. Published by Minnesota Chippewa Tribe in Cass Lake, Minnesota. Monthly.

August 1977–present—*Lac Courtes Oreilles Journal* first edited by Paul DeMain. Published by Lac Courtes Oreilles Chippewa Tribe in Hayward, Wisconsin. Bimonthly. Since 1987, *News from Indian Country*. Published independently. Twice a month.

1978–1989—*Native Self-Sufficiency* first edited by Paula Hammett. Published by Seventh Generation Fund in Forestville, California. Quarterly.

February 1978–present—*USET Calumet* first edited by Gloria Wilson. Published by the United South and Eastern Tribes in Nashville, Tennessee. Bimonthly.

August 1979–present—*The Circle* first edited by Marcia McEachron. Published by Minneapolis Indian Center in Minneapolis, Minnesota. Largest urban Indian newspaper in the United States. Monthly.

July 9, 1981–present—*Lakota Times* first edited by Tim Giago. Published independently in Rapid City, South Dakota. Renamed *Indian Country Today* in October 1992. Weekly.

1981–present—*The Eagle*, formerly *Eagle Wing Press*, first edited by Jim Roaix. Published independently in Naugatuck, Connecticut. Monthly.

1982–present—*AFN Newsletter* published by Alaska Federation of Natives in Anchorage, Alaska. Quarterly.

1982–present—*Vietnam Era Veterans Intertribal Association Newsletter* first edited by Harold Barse in Oklahoma City, Oklahoma. Quarterly.

1983–present—*Seminole Tribune* first edited by Glory Wilson. Published by the Tribal Council and Seminole Tribe of Florida. Biweekly.

1985–present—*Native Arts Update* first edited by Erin Younger. Published by Atlatl in Phoenix, Arizona. Quarterly.

NATIVE AMERICAN AUTOBIOGRAPHIES

Native people have always painted and narrated their personal life histories. Using pictographs, or picture drawing, men painted their war exploits on animal-hide robes, skins, shields, tipis, and cloth for everyone to "read." Later, warriors used sketch books, called "bragging biographies" by nineteenth-century ethnographer Garrick Mallery, to record personal feats. The renowned Lakota religious visionary Short Bull preserved his life record with pencil, ink, watercolors, and crayon, as did legendary Sitting

Bull, Lakota visionary, leader, and warrior. He used pencil, ink, and watercolors to create autobiographical pictographs of his military feats. Warriors returning from battles also narrated "coup tales," which spoke about their accomplishments to the community. Personal history took other forms as well. Prominent Kiowa and Kiowa-Apache tribal leaders, who obtained designs and colors through visions and dreams, decorated their tipis with a "narration" of their spiritual experiences. Plains Indian men also painted their clan relationships and spiritual and warrior experiences on personal shields. In the Southeast, some native warriors and chiefs chose to tattoo their heroic exploits onto their bodies. Women expressed personal characteristics as well in artistic autobiographical forms. Their quill and beadwork on clothing and parfleches (folded hide containers) expressed clan and family affiliations.

Traditional native names were autobiographical as well. Throughout their lives, native people acquired new names which documented personal achievements, transitions, and events. In Plains Indian traditions, proper names embodied personal or family stories. In *Indian Boyhood*, Dr. Charles Alexander Eastman explained that his first Dakota name, "Hakadah," meant "the pitiful last" because his mother died shortly after his birth. Several years later, Eastman became known as "Ohiyesa" or "winner" when a medicine man renamed him after a victory in a lacrosse game. Names might describe

Around 1875, Wo-haw, a young Kiowa, used traditional Plains hide painting to convey his personal thoughts about his identity after months of wearing army clothing, speaking, reading, and writing English and studying the Bible while imprisoned at Fort Marion in Florida. Courtesy of Missouri Historical Society.

NATIVE AMERICAN JOURNALISTS ASSOCIATION
Boulder, Colorado 80309

The perception of Native Americans is largely shaped by what people read, see, and hear in the media. Unfortunately, most of what has been communicated in the past 500 years has been through the eyes of non-native journalists for non-natives. Recognizing the need for a greater native presence at all levels of communications, in both native and non-native communities, the Native American Journalists Association (formerly the Native American Press Association) was formed in 1984 to support and increase the involvement of Native Americans in the media. There are more than 450 native media organizations and approximately 700 native journalists in the United States and Canada. Only a handful of native journalists are employed by publications and radio and TV stations which serve the general public.

---

appearance, High Back Bone, Left Handed Big Nose, or Squint Eyes, or a family's wish for the child's future. Plenty Coups, a famed Crow warrior, felt obliged to live up to his name, given him by his grandfather who dreamed he saw his grandson count many coups—touching a live enemy and getting away without being harmed.

With the advent of English settlements in New England, natives educated in eighteenth-century English and scripture wrote and published occasional works in English. During the 1760s and 1770s, several Dartmouth-educated, Christianized Indians, under Eleazar Wheelock's tutelage, wrote letters in English discussing their own conversions as well as their attempts to convert other Indians. Over sixty years later, William Apes, a Pequot born in 1798, penned what is believed to be the first Indian autobiography, *A Son of the Forest*, published in 1829. "As-told-to" autobiographies (dictating stories to translators and writers who put spoken words into print) soon followed (Black Hawk, one of the first, dictated his life story in 1833), as well as more autobiographies written by Indians who mastered English.

During the nineteenth and early twentieth centuries, with native people confined to reservations, Euro-american missionaries, military figures, anthropologists, and historians eagerly collected "as-told-to" personal stories, creating a collaborative autobiography—a Native American oral narrator and Euro-american editor working together to produce an autobiography that usually mixed oral history; traditional stories; and personal, family, and tribal experiences. Anthropologists especially recognized the value of life histories as a means to understanding tribal cultures and collected hundreds of autobiographical narratives. They also understood that personal reminiscences permitted "outsiders" to see through the eyes of medicine men and women, warriors, and farmers. Today, native people write autobiographies in English or continue to narrate their stories to translators and collaborators who record, edit, and revise them. Contemporary writers such as N. Scott Momaday, Kiowa, and Leslie Silko, Laguna Pueblo, have created autobiographies combining precontact native oral and artistic traditions with the Euro-american literary traditions.

Following is a selected list of notable Native American autobiography.

Nineteenth Century

Apes, William, Pequot. *A Son of the Forest. The Experience of William Apes, a Native of the Forest. Comprising a Notice of the Pequot Tribe of Indians* (1829).

Bear's Heart, Cheyenne. *Bear's Heart: Scenes from*

NATIVE AMERICAN RADIO BROADCASTING

Since 1972, these selected Native American radio stations have broadcast programs in English and Native languages throughout the United States.

1972—KTDB-FM in Ramah, New Mexico. The first Indian-owned and operated noncommercial station in the nation. Broadcasts local, state, and national news in Navajo and English. Call letters from Te'ochini Dinee Bi-Radio ("Radio Voice of the People"). Now broadcasts from Pine Hill, New Mexico.

1975—KRNB-FM broadcasts to Makah from Neah Bay, Washington. KEYA-FM broadcasts to Turtle Mountain Chippewa at Belcourt, North Dakota.

1976—KSUT-FM broadcasts to the Southern Ute at Ignacio, Colorado. WOJB-FM broadcasts from Hayward, Wisconsin, to Lac Courte Oreilles people.

1977—KMDX-FM begins broadcasting in Parker, Arizona—the first native-owned commercial radio station in the country. Owned by Gilbert Leivas from the Colorado River Tribe. KINI-FM broadcasts from St. Francis on Rosebud Sioux Reservation, South Dakota. KILI broadcasts from Porcupine on Oglala Sioux Pine Ridge Reservation, South Dakota. KNDN-AM broad-

casts from Farmington, New Mexico where it is "All Navajo, All the Time." From 1957 to 1977, the station broadcast some programs in Navajo under KWYK-AM; today broadcasts are almost entirely in the Navajo language except for some music.

1978—KSHI-FM begins broadcasting at Zuni Pueblo, New Mexico. KNCC-FM begins broadcasting at Tsaile, Arizona, making the Navajo Reservation the first reservation with two radio stations. KIDE-FM begins broadcasting at Hoopa Reservation in California.

1982—KNNB-FM broadcasts from Whiteriver, Arizona, to the White Mountain Apaches.

1984—CKON-FM began broadcasting from Rooseveltown on the St. Regis Mohawk Reservation in New York.

1986—KTNN-AM signed on the air in Window Rock, Arizona. The radio station, owned and operated by the Navajo Nation, airs 20 percent of the station's programs in Navajo, Hopi, Apache, Pueblo, and Ute languages.

1987—National Native News, beamed by satellite from Anchorage, Alaska began broadcasting—the country's first and only daily radio news service cover-

the Life of a Cheyenne Artist of One Hundred Years Ago With Pictures By Himself (1977).

Black Elk, Oglala Lakota. *Black Elk Speaks* (1932).

Black Hawk, Sak. *Life of Ma-ka-tai-me-she-kia-kiak-, or Black Hawk* (1833).

Blackbird, Andrew J., Ottawa. *History of the Ottawa and Chippewa Indians of Michigan; A Grammar of Their Language, and Personal Family History of the Author* (1887).

Blacksnake, Seneca, *Chainbreaker: The Revolutionary War Memoirs of Governor Blacksnake as Told to*

Benjamin Williams (1989). Born about 1749, dictated after Blacksnake's 90th birthday.

Brown, Catherine, Cherokee. *Memoirs of Catherine Brown, a Christian Indian of the Cherokee Nation* (1924).

Cohoe, William, Cheyenne. *A Cheyenne Sketchbook* (1964). Contains late-nineteenth-century autobiographical drawings.

Copway, George (Kah-ge-ga-gah-bowh), Chippewa. *The Life, History, and Travels of Kah-ge-ga-gah-bowh* (1847).

Eastman, Charles Alexander, Santee Dakota. *From*

ing Native American issues. From the original thirty stations using the service, primarily in Alaska, the number has grown in 1992 to 165 public and tribal radio stations nationwide airing National Native News. Produced by Alaska Public Radio Network, NNN has been recognized by the Alaska State legislature for its contributions to public radio. NNN which has had an impressive history of national and regional awards and honors is produced and hosted by Gary Fife.

1991—KGHR-FM, the first Indian high school radio station in the country signed on the air in Tuba City, Arizona. It became this small town's second radio station and third public broadcasting station based on the Navajo Reservation.

Signs for radio stations KNNB-FM located at Whiteriver, Arizona, and KINI-FM located at St. Francis, South Dakota. Photographs by Karen Warth.

the Deep Woods to Civilization: Chapters in the Autobiography of an Indian (1916) and Indian Boyhood (1902).

En-me-gah-bowh (John Johnson), Chippewa. En-me-gah-bowh's Story: An Account of the Disturbances of the Chippewa Indians at Gull Lake in 1857 and 1862 and Their Removal in 1868 (1904).

Geronimo, Apache. Geronimo's Story of His Life (1906).

Grayson, Chief G. W., Creek, A Creek Warrior for the Confederacy. The Autobiography of Chief G. W. Grayson (1988).

Griffis, Joseph, Osage. Tahan: Out of Savagery into Civilization (1915).

Hopkins, Sarah Winnemucca, Paiute. Life Among the Piutes: Their Wrongs and Claims (1883).

Howling Wolf, Southern Cheyenne. Howling Wolf: A Cheyenne Warrior's Graphic Interpretation of His People (1968). Contains late-nineteenth-century autobiographical drawings. (See Zo-Tom.)

Jacobs, Peter (Pah-tah-se-ga), Chippewa. Journal of the Reverend Peter Jacobs, Indian Wesleyan Missionary from Rice Lake to the Hudson's Bay Territory, and Returning, Commencing May,

1852. With a Brief Account of His Life . . . (1853).

Jones, Reverend Peter, Chippewa. *Life and Journals of Kah-ke-wa-quo-na-by (Rev. Peter Jones) Wesleyan Missionary* (1860) and *History of the Ojebway Indians with Especial Reference to Their Conversion to Christianity . . . with a Brief Memoir of the Writer* (1861).

Joseph, Chief, Nez Percé. *Chief Joseph's Own Story* (April 1879 *North American Review* article).

LaFlesche, Francis, Omaha. *The Middle Five: Indian Schoolboys of the Omaha Tribe* (1963). Reprint of 1900 edition.

Maxidiwiac, Hidatsa. *Wa-Hee-Nee: An Indian Girl's Story, Told by Herself* (1921).

Owens, Narcissa, Cherokee. *Memoirs of Narcissa Owens* (1907).

Plenty-Coups, Crow. *American: The Life Story of a Great Indian, Plenty-Coups, Chief of the Crows* (1930).

Pretty-Shield, Crow. *Red Mother* (1932).

Sitting Bull, Hunkpapa Lakota. *Three Pictographic Autobiographies of Sitting Bull* (1938).

Standing Bear, Luther, Oglala Lakota. *My Indian Boyhood* (1928), *My People the Sioux* (1931), and *Land of the Spotted Eagle* (1933).

Tubbee, Okah (William Chubbee), Choctaw. *A Thrilling Sketch of the Life of the Distinguished Chief Okah Tubbee, Alias William Chubbee, Son of the Head Chief, Mosholeh Tubbee, of the Choctaw Nation of Indians* (1848).

Two Leggings, Crow. *Two Leggings: The Making of a Crow Warrior* (1967).

White Bull, Chief Joseph, Lakota. *The Warrior Who Killed Custer: The Personal Narrative of Chief Joseph White Bull* (1968). Contains traditional pictographs and written text.

White Calf, Chief (Running Wolf, James Jacob), Blackfeet. *Piegan: A Look from Within at the Life, Times, and Legacy of an American Indian* (1966).

Whitewolf, Jim, Kiowa Apache. *Jim Whitewolf: The Life of a Kiowa Apache* (1969).

Wooden Leg, Cheyenne. *Wooden Leg: A Warrior Who Fought Custer* (1931).

Yellow Wolf, Nez Percé. *Yellow Wolf: His Own Story* (1940).

Zo-Tom, Kiowa. *Plains Indian Sketch Books of Zo-Tom and Howling Wolf* (1969). Contains late-nineteenth-century autobiographical drawings.

Twentieth Century

Alford, Thomas Wildcat, Shawnee. *Civilization, as Told to Florence Drake* (1936).

Allen, Elsie, Pomo. *Pomo Basketmaking: A Supreme Art for the Weaver* (1972).

Bennett, Kay, Navajo. *Kaibah: Recollection of a Navajo Girlhood.* (1964).

Betzinez, Jason, Apache. *I Fought with Geronimo* (1959).

Black Elk, Wallace, Lakota. *The Sacred Ways of a Lakota* (1990).

Blowsnake, Sam (Big Winnebago), Winnebago. *Autobiography of a Winnebago Indian* (1920).

Brown, Emily Ivanoff (Tecasuk), Inupiat. *The Roots of Tecasuk: An Eskimo Woman's Family Story* (1974).

Bullchild, Percy, Blackfeet. *The Sun Came Down: The History of the World as My Blackfeet Elders Told It* (1985).

Chona, Maria, Tohono O'odham. *The Autobiography of a Papago Woman* (1936).

Cody, Iron Eyes, Cherokee. *Iron Eyes Cody: My Life as a Hollywood Indian* (1982).

Crashing Thunder, Winnebago. "Personal Reminiscenses of a Winnebago Indian" (1913).

Crow Dog, Mary, Lakota. *Lakota Woman* (1990).

Crying Wind, Kickapoo. *Crying Wind* (1977).

Cuero, Delfina, Diegueno. *The Autobiography of Delfina Cuero* (1970).

Davidson, Florence Edenshaw, Haida. *During My Time: Florence Edenshaw Davidson, A Haida Woman* (1987).

Dudley, Joseph Iron Eyes, Yankton Dakota. *Chocteau Creek: Sioux Remembrance* (1992).

Fredson, John, Gwich'in Athabascan. *Stories Told by John Fredson to Edward Sapir* (1982).

Goodbird, Hidatsa. *Goodbird the Indian: His Story* (1914).

Greene, Alma, Mohawk. *Forbidden Voice: Reflections of a Mohawk Indian* (c. 1971).

Henry, Chief, Athabascan. *The Stories that Chief Henry Told* (1979).

Herbert, Belle, Athabascan. *Shandaa: In My Lifetime* (1982).

Highwalking, Belle, Northern Cheyenne. *Belle Highwalking: The Narrative of a Northern Cheyenne Woman* (1979).

Huntington, James, Athabascan. *On the Edge of Nowhere* (1966).

James, Allen, Kashia Pomo. *Chief of the Pomos: Life Story of Allen James* (1972).

Johnston, Basil, Chippewa. *Ojibway Heritage* (1990).

Kakianak, Nathan, Inuit. *Eskimo Boyhood: An Autobiography* (1974).

Kaywaykla, James, Apache. *In the Days of Victorio: Recollections of a Warm Springs Apache* (1970).

Kegg, Maude (Naawakamigookwe), Chippewa. *Gabekanaansing/At the End of the Trail: Memories of Chippewa Childhood in Minnesota, with Texts in Ojibwa and English* (1978). Also *Portage Lake: Memories of an Ojibwe Childhood* (1991).

Lame Deer, John (Fire), Oglala Lakota. *Lame Deer: Seeker of Visions* (1972).

Least Heat Moon, William (William L. Trogden), Osage. *Blue Highways: A Journey into America* (1982).

Leevier, Annette, Chippewa. *Psychic Experiences of an Indian Princess* (1920).

Left Handed, Navajo. *Son of Old Man Hat: A Navajo Autobiography* (1938).

Lone Dog, Louise, Mohawk/Delaware. *Strange Journey: The Vision Life of a Psychic Indian Woman* (1964).

Louis, Sammy, Micmac. *Sammy Louis: The Life History of a Young Micmac* (1956).

Lowry, Annie, Paiute. *Karnee: A Paiute Narrative* (1966).

McCarthy, James, Tohono O'odham. *A Papago Traveler: The Memories of James McCarthy* (1985).

Mathews, John Joseph, Osage. *Talking to the Moon* (1945).

Mitchell, Emerson Blackhorse, Navajo. *Miracle Hill: The Story of a Navajo Boy* (1967).

Mitchell, Frank, Navajo. *Navajo Blessingway Singer: The Autobiography of Frank Mitchell, 1881–1967* (1978).

Modesto, Ruby, Cahuilla. *Not for Innocent Ears: Spiritual Traditions of a Cahuilla Medicine Woman* (1980).

Moises, Rosalio, Yaqui. *The Tall Candle: The Personal Chronicle of a Yaqui Indian* (1971).

Momaday, N. Scott, Kiowa/Cherokee. *The Way to Rainy Mountain* (1969) and *The Names* (1976).

Mountain Wolf Woman, Winnebago. *Mountain Wolf Woman, Sister of Crashing Thunder: The Autobiography of a Winnebago Indian* (1961).

Mourning Dove (Hum-ishu-ma, Christine Quintasket, Cristal McLeod Galler), Okanogan. *Mourning Dove: A Salishan Autobiography* (1990).

Nowell, Charles James, Kwakiutl. *Smoke from Their Fires: The Life of a Kwakiutl Chief* (1941).

Nunez, Bonita (Wa Wa Calachaw), Luiseno. *Spirit Woman* (1980).

Old Mexican, Navajo. *A Navajo Autobiography* (1947).

Oliver, Simeon, Inuit. *Son of the Smokey Sea* (1941) and *Back to the Smokey Sea* (1946).

Paquin, Ron, Chippewa. *Not First in Nobody's Heart: The Life Story of a Contemporary Chippewa* (1992).

Patencio, Chief Francisco, Cahuilla. *Stories and Legends of the Palm Springs Indians* (1943).

Paytiamo, James, Acoma Pueblo. *Flaming Arrow's People: By an Acoma Indian* (1932).

Pelletier, Wilfred, Ottawa. *No Foreign Land: The Biography of a North American Indian* (1973).

Peter, Katherine, Athabascan. *Neets'aii Gwindaii: Living in Chandalar* (1981).

Potts, Marie, Maidu. *The Northern Maidu* (1977).

Qoyawayma, Polingaysi (Elizabeth Q. White), Hopi. *No Turning Back: A True Account of a Hopi Girl's Struggle to Bridge the Gap between the World of Her People and the World of the White Man* (1964).

Rickard, Clinton, Tuscarora. *Fighting Tuscarora: The Autobiography of Chief Clinton Rickard* (1973).

Rogers, John (Chief Snow Cloud), Chippewa. *A Chippewa Speaks* (1957).

Sanapia, Comanche. *Sanapia, Comanche Medicine Woman* (1972).

Savala, Refugio, Yaqui. *The Autobiography of a Yaqui Poet* (1980).

Sekaquaptewa, Helen, Hopi. *Me and Mine: The Life Story of Helen Sekaquaptewa* (1969).

Senungetuk, Joseph, Inuit. *Give or Take a Century: An Eskimo Chronicle* (1971).

Sewid, James, Kwakiutl. *Guests Never Leave Hungry: The Autobiography of James Sewid, a Kwakiutl Indian* (1969).

Shaw, Anna Moore, Pima. *A Pima Past* (1974).

Silko, Leslie, Laguna Pueblo. *Storyteller* (1981).

Stands in Timber, John, Cheyenne. *Cheyenne Memories* (1967).

Stewart, Irene, Navajo. *A Voice in Her Tribe: A Navajo Woman's Own Story* (1980).

Swan, Madonna, Lakota. *Madonna Swan: A Lakota Woman's Story* (1991).

Sweezy, Carl, Arapaho. *The Arapaho Way: A Memoir of an Indian Boyhood* (1966).

MEDIA ORGANIZATIONS

The growth of Native American presses and telecommunications by, for, and about Native Americans has been tremendous in the past decade. Native public radio programming, newspaper publishing, video and public television production are in full swing covering historical, cultural, political, and economic issues. The following experienced media organizations are dedicated to the development of Native American print and telecommunications.

American Native Press Archives
University of Arkansas
Stabler Hall 502, 2801 S. University Avenue
Little Rock, Arkansas 72204–1099

The American Native Press Archives, founded in 1983, houses over 1,000 native newspapers and periodicals from the United States, Canada, Mexico, and Central and South America. The archives acts as a clearinghouse for information about U.S. American Indian and Alaska Native newspapers and periodicals published from 1826 to the present. Publishes *American Native Press* newsletter.

Migizi Communications
3123 E. Lake Street, Suite 200
Minneapolis, Minnesota 55406

Founded in 1977, Migizi provides a national Indian news service. Produces First Person Radio, a weekly half-hour program of American Indian news information, and public affairs programming, that is nationally distributed to over fifty stations in twenty-three states. Also produces a weekly local television public affairs program, "Madagimo," for WUSA-TV and produces live radio programs, video documentaries, and publications.

Native American Public Broadcasting Consortium
P.O. Box 83111
Lincoln, Nebraska 68501

The Native American Public Broadcasting Consortium, Inc. (NAPBC), established in 1977, encourages the creation, production, promotion, and distribution of quality public telecommunications programming by, for, and about Native Americans. NAPBC, which develops and produces its own pro-

Talayesva, Don (Sun Chief), Hopi. *Sun Chief: The Autobiography of a Hopi Indian* (1942).

Thompson, Lucy, Yurok. *To the American Indian: The Reminiscenses of a Yurok Woman* (1991). Reprint of 1916 edition.

Vizenor, Gerald, Chippewa. *Interior Landscapes: Autobiographical Myths and Metaphors* (1990).

Walters, Anna Lee. *Talking Indian: Reflections on Survival and Writing* (1992).

Webb, George, Pima. *A Pima Remembers* (1959).

Williams, Ted, Tuscarora. *The Reservation* (1976).

Winnie, Lucille "Jerry," (Sah-gan-de-oh), Seneca-Cayuga. *Sah-gan-de-oh, the Chief's Daughter* (1968).

Yava, Albert, Hopi-Tewa. *Big Falling Snow: A Tewa-Hopi Indian's Life and Times and the History and Traditions of His People* (1978).

Yellowtail, Crow. *Yellowtail, Crow Medicine Man and Sun Dance Chief: An Autobiography* (1991).

Young Bear, Ray, Mesquakie. *Black Eagle Child* (1992).

Zitkala-Sa (Gertrude Bonnin), Yankton Dakota. *American Indian Stories* (1921).

grams for television, radio broadcasting, and educational purposes, maintains a Native American film and video library and publishes a catalog listing programs for rental and sale.

The American Indian Registry For the Performing Arts
1717 North Highland Avenue, Suite 614
Hollywood, California 90028
(213) 962-6594

Organized to improve access to employment opportunities in the film and television industries for American Indian performers and related creative and technical professionals. Maintains a registry of Native American performers.

Anthropology Film Center Foundation
P.O. Box 493
Santa Fe, New Mexico 87594
(505) 983-4127

Founded to promote scholarship, research, and practice in visual anthropology. Provides research services, consultation, seminars, publications, instruction, equipment and facilities.

CONTEMPORARY NATIVE AMERICAN WRITERS

For countless generations, creating poetry and telling stories have always been important in Native American life. Long ago, however, the Native American poetry that graced every occasion—healing, mourning, planting crops, praying for rain and a good harvest, hunting, welcoming friends—was spoken, sung, or chanted in hundreds of native languages. Native peoples told tens of thousands of stories in their own languages to explain how the world was created, how the first people of the tribe originated, and how the sun, moon, stars, lakes and mountains came to be. They explained the origin of every landmark, plant, and animal in each tribe as well as the correct ways for people to treat one another and other beings in the world. Native Americans have always admired people who delivered a good story and valued the imagination necessary to communicate through spoken words.

By the late eighteenth century, primarily non-Indians tried to put these Indian oral traditions in writing. By the late nineteenth century, anthropologists sought the assistance of Indian informants in transcribing and translating ritual narratives, poetic chants, songs, incantations, origin stories, and "tales." Soon after, Native Americans wrote down their own stories in English. Today, American Indian and Alaska Native poets and novelists draw much of their power from the oral literary tradition, still a viable component of present-day native life, and use all the resources of the English language to write in western genres—poetry, short fiction, and novels—that tell about the efforts of Indians to combine different lifestyles, beliefs, cosmologies, and world views. Many Native American writers use their own tribal world views and cultural traditions as a vehicle to present modern themes about the Indian experience. In the process, they give new form to traditional oral literature by incorporating it into modern novels. Themes and plots relate the writers' experiences in native and non-Indian societies while reflecting tribal identity and traditions.

Native writers tell us about the power of old beliefs and identity and the survival of Native American homelands despite the forces threatening to devour more and more ancestral lands for electric and gas lines, highways, cable television, and satellite dishes. They tell of the importance of family and community, cultural rituals, and the despair of living in two worlds—Indian and non-Indian. Their works make readers witness "raw existence side by side with a refusal to cave in, often with hints of renewal through connection with tradition," writes Brian Swann in *Harper's Anthology of 20th Century Poetry*. Readers witness bitter conflicts between Indians and non-Indians and confront assimilationist federal and state policies that vie with the Indians' efforts to retain pride, dignity, and cultural traditions both on reservations and in cities. Native writers tell stories about their people's struggles with alcohol and heroin addiction, logging companies that strip timber on mountains, dams that flood traditional fishing places, displacement from homelands, child abuse, tourist invasions of sacred sites, termination of tribal identity, spiteful government bureaucrats, and destruction of people by law. The writers tell stories and write poetry about Indians struggling with "who-am-I" questions in a world that rejects and attacks their Native identities. They tell about mountains, hills, and rocks, lakes and timeless rivers, waterfalls and ponds. The writings of dozens of authors bear testimony to their relationship and reverence for land.

Prior to the 1960s, there was little interest in Native American poetry and prose, but after Kiowa writer N. Scott Momaday won the Pulitzer Prize for *House Made of Dawn* in 1969, considerable attention focused on written Native American literature. Native writers still remain something of a literary secret and their literature still fights for acceptance and inclusion in the curricula of U.S. schools and colleges. The following is a selected list including titles of works and the names of some of the Native American poets and fiction writers practicing their art today.

Sherman Alexie, Spokane/Coeur D'Alene, born 1966 in Willpinit, Washington.

   The Business of Fancydancing: Stories and Poems (1992). Poetry and stories.

Old Shirts & New Skins (1993). Poetry.

Paula Gunn Allen, Laguna–Lakota, born 1939 near Cubero, New Mexico.

The Blind Lion (1974). Poetry.
Coyote's Daylight Trip (1978). Poetry.
A Cannon Beneath My Knees (1981). Poetry.
Star Child (1981). Poetry.
Shadow Country (1982). Poetry.
The Woman Who Owned the Shadows (1983). Novel.
Studies in American Indian Literature (1983). Critical essays.
The Sacred Hoop: Recovering the Feminine in American Indian Traditions (1986). Essays.
Spider Woman's Granddaughters (1989). Short stories; winner Before Columbus Foundation American Book Award.
Grandmothers of the Light: A Medicine Woman's Sourcebook (1992). Stories.

Carroll Arnett (Gogisgi), Cherokee, born 1927 in Oklahoma City, Oklahoma.

Then (1965) poetry.
Not Only That (1967). Poetry.
Tsalagi (1976). Poetry.
South Line (1979). Poetry.
Rounds (1982). Poetry.
Engine (1988). Poetry.
Night Perimeter: New and Selected Poems, 1958–1990 (1991).

Jim Barnes, Choctaw, born 1933 near Poteau, Oklahoma.

This Crazy Land (1980). Poetry.
The Fish on Poteau Mountain (1980). Poetry.
Summons and Signs: Poems by Dagmar Nick (1980). Poetry.

Denton R. Bedford, Munsee, born 1907.

Tsali (1972). Novel.

Peter Blue Cloud (Aroniawenrate), Mohawk, born 1927 in Quebec, Canada.

Alcatraz Is Not An Island (1972). Prose and poetry.
Coyote & Friends (1976). Poetry.
Turtle, Bear and Wolf (1976). Poetry.

Back Then Tomorrow (1978). Poetry.
White Corn Sister (1977). Poetry.
Elderberry Flute Song: Contemporary Coyote Tales (1982). Stories.
Sketches in Winter, With Crows (1984). Poetry.
The Other Side of Nowhere: Contemporary Coyote Tales (1990). Poetry and stories.

Beth Brant, Mohawk, born 1941 in Detroit, Michigan.

Mohawk Trail (1985). Prose and poetry.
Food and Spirits (1991). Short stories.

Joseph Bruchac, Abenaki, born 1942 in Saratoga Springs, New York.

Indian Mountain and Other Poems (1971). Poetry.
The Good Message of Handsome Lake (1979). Poetry.
Translator's Son (1980). Poetry.
Iroquois Stories (1984). Stories.
Survival This Way: Interviews with American Indian Poets, editor (1987). Essays.
Near the Mountains (1987). Poetry.
The White Moose (1988). Stories.
Turtle Meat: And Other Stories (1992). Stories.
Dawn Land (1993). Novel.

Barny Bush, Shawnee, born 1946 in Saline County, Illinois.

My Horse and a Jukebox (1979). Poetry.
Petroglyphs (1982). Poetry.
Inherit the Blood (1985). Poetry.

Dallas Chief Eagle, Rosebud Sioux, born 1925 in Rosebud, South Dakota; died 1978.

Winter Count (1967). Novel.

Robert J. Conley, Cherokee, born 1940 in Cushing, Oklahoma.

The Witch of Goingsnake and Other Stories (1988). Stories.
Mountain Windsong: A Novel of the Trail of Tears (1992). Novel.
Nickjack (1992). Western.

Elizabeth Cook-Lynn, Crow Creek Sioux, born 1930 at Fort Thompson, South Dakota.

Then Badger Said This (1977). Poetry.

Seek the House of Relatives (1983). Poetry.

The Power of Horses: And Other Stories (1990). Stories.

From the River's Edge (1991). Novel.

Nora Marks Dauenhauer, Tlingit, born 1927 in Juneau, Alaska.

The Droning Shaman (1988). Poetry.

Ella Deloria, Dakota, born 1889 on Standing Rock Reservation, South Dakota.

Waterlily (1988, written in 1940s). Novel.

Vine Deloria, Jr., Dakota, born 1933 in Martin, South Dakota.

Custer Died for Your Sins (1969). Nonfiction.

God Is Red (1973). Nonfiction.

Metaphysics of Modern Existence (1979). Nonfiction.

Michael Dorris, Modoc, born 1945 in Dayton, Washington.

A Guide to Research on North American Indians with Arlene Hirschfelder and Mary Lou Byler (1983). Nonfiction.

A Yellow Raft on Blue Water (1987). Novel.

The Broken Cord (1989). Study of fetal alcohol syndrome; 1990 Heartland Prize, 1989 Christopher Award, 1989 National Book Critics Circle Award.

Crown of Columbus, with Louise Erdrich (1991). Novel.

Morning Girl (1992). Children's fiction.

Anita Endrezze, Yaqui, born 1952 in Long Beach, California.

Burning the Fields (1983). Poetry.

The North People (1983). Poetry.

Louise Erdrich, Turtle Mountain Chippewa/German, born 1954 at Little Falls, North Dakota.

Jacklight (1984). Poetry.

Love Medicine (1984). Novel; National Book Critics Circle Award and 1985 Los Angeles Times Book Award.

Beet Queen (1986). Novel.

Tracks (1988). Novel.

Baptism of Desire: Poems (1990). Poetry.

Crown of Columbus, with Michael Dorris (1991). Novel.

Hanay Geiogamah, Kiowa/Delaware, born 1945 in Oklahoma.

Body Indian (1980). Play.

Fog Horn (1980). Play.

49 (1980). Play.

Diane Glancy, Cherokee, born 1941 in Kansas City, Missouri.

Traveling On (1982). Poetry.

What People Do West of the Mississippi (1982). Poetry.

Brown Wolf Leaves the Res (1984). Poetry; 1985 Pegasus Award from Oklahoma Federation of Writers.

One Age in a Dream (1986). Poetry.

Offering: Poetry and Prose (1988). Poetry and prose.

Iron Woman (1990). Poetry; 1989 Capricorn Award.

Trigger Dance (1990). Short stories; 1990 Nilon Minority Award.

Lone Dog's Winter Count (1991). Poetry.

Claiming Breath (1992). Poetry.

Firesticks (1993). Stories.

Rayna Green, Cherokee, born 1942 in Dallas, Texas.

Native American Women: A Contexual Bibliography (1983). Nonfiction.

That's What She Said: Contemporary Poetry and Fiction by Native American Women (1984), editor.

Women in American Indian Society (1992). Nonfiction.

Janet Campbell Hale, Coeur d'Alene/Kootenai, born 1946 in Los Angeles, California.

The Owl's Song (1974). Novel.

Custer Lives in Humboldt County (1978). Poetry.

The Jailing of Cecelia Capture (1985). Novel.

Bloodlines: Odyssey of a Native Daughter (1993). Novel.

Joy Harjo, Creek, born 1951 in Tulsa, Oklahoma.

The Last Song (1975). Poetry.

What Moon Drove Me to This? (1979). Poetry.

She Had Some Horses (1983). Poetry.
Secrets from the Center of the World (1989). Poetry.
In Mad Love and War (1990). Poetry.

Lance Henson, Cheyenne, born 1944 in Washington, D.C.

Keeper of Arrows: Poems for the Cheyenne (1972). Poetry.
Naming the Dark: Poems for the Cheyenne (1976). Poetry.
Mistah (1978). Poetry.
Buffalo Marrow on Black (1980). Poetry.
In a Dark Mist (1982). Poetry.
Selected Poems, 1970–1983 (1985). Poetry.
A Cheyenne Sketch Book: Selected Poems 1970–1991 (1992).

Linda Hogan, Chickasaw, born 1947 in Denver, Colorado.

Calling Myself Home (1978). Poetry.
Daughters, I Love You (1981). Poetry.
A Piece of Moon (1981). Play.
Eclipse (1983). Poetry.
Seeing Through the Sun (1985). Poetry; winner Before Columbus Foundation American Book Award.
Savings: Poems (1987). Poetry.
Mean Spirit (1990). Novel. 1990 Oklahoma Book Award and Mountain and Plains Booksellers Association, Fiction Award.
Red Clay: Poems and Stories (1991). Poetry and stories.
The Book of Medicines (1993). Poetry.

Hum-Ishu-Ma (Mourning Dove), Okanogan/Colville, born 1888(?) in Bonner's Ferry, Idaho; died 1936.

Co-Ge-We-A, The Half-Blood: A Depiction of the Great Montana Cattle Range, by Hum-ishu-ma, "Mourning Dove," . . . Given through Sho-pow-tan. (1927). Novel.

Maurice Kenny, Mohawk, born 1929 in Watertown, New York.

North: Poems of Home (1977). Poetry.
Dancing Back Strong the Nation (1979). Poetry.

I am the Sun (1979). Poetry.
Blackrobe: Isaac Jogues (1982). Poetry.
Boston Tea Party (1982). Poetry.
The Mama Poems (1984). Winner 1984 Before Columbus Foundation American Book Award.
Is Summer This Bear? (1985). Poetry.
Rain and Other Fictions (1985). Poetry.
Between Two Rivers: Selected Poems (1987). Poetry.
Last Mornings in Brooklyn (1991). Poetry.

Thomas King, Cherokee, born 1943 in Roseville, California.

Medicine River (1990). Novel; PEN Oakland/Josephine Miles Award for Excellence in Literature.
All My Relations: An Anthology of Contemporary Canadian Native Fiction (1992), editor.
Green Grass, Running Water (1993). Novel.

Harold Littlebird, Laguna and Santo Domingo Pueblos, born 1951 in Albuquerque, New Mexico.

On Mountain's Breath (1982). Poetry.

Adrian C. Louis, Paiute, born 1946 in Lovelock, Nevada.

Muted War Drums (1977). Poetry.
Sweets for the Dancing Bear (1979). Poetry.
Fire Water World (1989). Poetry.
Among the Dog Eaters (1992). Poetry.

D'Arcy McNickle, Confederated Salish/Kootenai, born 1904 in St. Ignatius, Montana; died 1977.
The Surrounded (1936). Novel.
Runner in the Sun: The Story of Indian Maize (1954). Novel.
Native American Tribalism: Indian Survivals and Renewals (1973). Nonfiction.
Wind from an Enemy Sky (1978). Novel.
The Hawk is Hungry: And Other Stories (1992). Stories.

John Joseph Mathews, Osage, born 1895 in Pawhuska, Oklahoma Territory; died 1979.
Wah' Kon-Tah: The Osage and the White Man's Road (1932). Book-of-the-Month Club award.
Sundown (1934). Novel.
Talking to the Moon (1945). Memoir.

The Osages: Children of the Middle Waters (1961). History.

N. Scott Momaday, Kiowa/Cherokee, born 1934 in Lawton, Oklahoma.

House Made of Dawn (1968). Novel; Pulitzer Prize in 1969.

The Way to Rainy Mountain (1969). Memoir.

Angle of Geese and Other Poems (1974). Poetry.

The Names: A Memoir (1976). Memoir.

The Gourd Dancer: Poems (1976). Poetry.

Ancient Child (1989). Novel.

In the Presence of the Sun: Stories and Poems (1993). Stories and Poems.

Nasnaga (Roger Russell), Shawnee, born 1941 in Dayton, Ohio.

Indians' Summer (1975). Novel.

Duane Niatum, Klallam, born 1938 in Seattle, Washington.

After the Death of an Elder Klallam (1970). Poetry.

Taos Pueblo and other Poems (1973). Poetry.

Ascending Red Cedar Moon (1974). Poetry.

Digging out the Roots (1977). Poetry.

Songs for the Harvester of Dreams (1981). Poetry; winner Before Columbus Foundation American Book Award.

Drawings of the Song Animals: New and Selected Poems (1990). Poetry.

William Oandasan, Yuki, born 1947 in Santa Rosa, California.

A Sequence of Contraries in Haiku (1976). Haiku.

A Branch of California Redwood (1981). Poetry.

Round Valley Songs (1984). Poetry; 1985 Before Columbus Foundation American Book Award.

Louis (Littlecoon) Oliver, Creek, born 1904 in Oklahoma. Died 1990.

The Horned Snake (1982). Poetry.

Caught in a Willow Net (1983). Poetry.

Chasers of the Sun: Creek Indian Thoughts (1990). Poetry.

Simon Ortiz, Acoma Pueblo, born 1941 in Acoma Pueblo, New Mexico.

Going for the Rain (1976). Poetry.

Howbah Indians (1977). Short stories.

A Good Journey (1977). Poetry.

The People Shall Continue (1977). Epic story. All ages.

Fight Back: For the Sake of the People, for the Sake of the Land (1980). Poetry and nonfiction.

From Sand Creek (1981). Pushcart Prize for Poetry.

Fightin': New and Collected Stories. (1983). Short stories.

Earth Power Coming (1983), editor. Short stories.

Woven Stone (1992). Poetry.

John Milton Oskison, Cherokee, born 1874 in Vinita, Indian Territory; died 1947.

Wild Harvest (1925). Novel.

Black Jack Davy (1926). Novel.

Brothers Three (1935). Novel.

Louis Owens, Choctaw-Cherokee, born 1948 in Lompoc, California.

Wolfsong (1991). Novel.

Other Destinies: Understanding the American Indian Novel (1992). Nonfiction.

The Sharpest Sight (1992). Novel.

Chief George Pierre, Okanogan, born 1926 in Washington State.

Autumn's Bounty (1972). Novel.

Simon Pokagon, Potawatomi, born 1830 in Michigan; died 1899.

O-Gi-Maw-Kwe Mit-I-Gwa-Ki, Queen of the Woods (1899). Novel.

Carter Revard, Osage, born 1931 in Pawhuska, Oklahoma.

My Right Hand Don't Leave Me No More (1970). Poetry.

Ponca War Dancers (1980). Poetry.

Cowboys and Indians (1992). Poetry.

Christmas Shopping (1992). Poetry.

Wendy Rose, Hopi/Miwok, born 1948 in Oakland, California.

Hopi Roadrunner Dancing (1973). Poetry.

Long Division: A Tribal History (1976). Poetry.

Academic Squaw: Reports to the World from the Ivory Tower. (1977). Poetry.

SELECTED JOURNALS

The following journals offer a unique opportunity to study various aspects of American Indian and Alaska Native history and culture. The contents of most present a native perspective.

Akwe:kon Journal (formerly *Northeast Indian Quarterly*), Cornell College, Ithaca, New York. Agriculture, community health, economic development, arts, land rights, education, environmental issues, oral history, poetry, book reviews. Quarterly.

American Indian and Culture and Research Journal, Los Angeles, California. Scholarly essays, book reviews. Quarterly.

American Indian Quarterly, Berkeley, California. Scholarly essays, book reviews. Quarterly.

Honor Digest, Milwaukee, Wisconsin. Treaty rights and discrimination. Bimonthly.

Indigenous Thought, Gainesville, Florida: Human rights issues. Quarterly.

Medium Rare, Minneapolis, Minnesota. Native journalism. Quarterly.

Native Peoples, Phoenix, Arizona. Arts and culture, book reviews. Quarterly.

News from Native California, Berkeley, California. California native arts, culture, history, language, book reviews. Quarterly.

SAIL: Studies in American Indian Literature, Richmond, Virginia. Critical essays, book reviews. Quarterly.

Smithsonian Runner, Washington, D.C. Arts. Quarterly.

Tribal College, Chestertown, Maryland. Activities at tribal community colleges. Quarterly.

Turtle Quarterly, Niagara Falls, New York. Cultural arts. Quarterly.

Wicazo Sa Review, Cheney, Washington. Native American studies, scholarly essays. Quarterly.

Winds of Change, Boulder, Colorado. Science and mathematics education, book reviews. Quarterly.

Builder Kachina: A Home-Going Cycle (1979). Poetry.

Lost Copper (1980). Poetry; nominated for Pulitzer Prize.

What Happened When the Hopi Hit New York (1982). Poetry.

The Halfbreed Chronicles and Other Poems (1985). Poetry.

Going to War with All My Relations (1993). Poetry.

Norman H. Russell, Cherokee, born 1921 in Big Stone Gap, Virginia.

Night Dog and Other Poems (1971). Poetry.

Ecosystem of Love (1972). Poetry.

Indian Thoughts: The Small Songs of God (1972). Poetry.

Russell, the Man, the Teacher, the Indian (1974). Poetry.

Ralph Salisbury, Cherokee, born 1926 in northeast Iowa.

Going to the Water: Poems of a Cherokee Heritage (1983). Poetry.

A Nation Within (1983). Poetry.

Carol Lee Sanchez, Laguna Pueblo/Sioux, born 1934 near Cubero, New Mexico.

Conversations from the Nightmare (1975). Poetry.

Time Warps (1976). Poetry.

Message Bringer Woman (1976). Poetry.

Morning Prayer (1977). Poetry.

Leslie Marmon Silko, Laguna Pueblo/Mexican/white, born 1948 in Albuquerque, New Mexico.

Laguna Woman: Poems by Leslie Silko (1974). Poetry.

Ceremony (1977). Novel.

Storyteller (1981). Autobiography/prose.

Almanac of the Dead (1992). Novel.

Virginia Driving Hawk Sneve, Brule Sioux, born 1933 in Rosebud, South Dakota.

High Elk's Treasure (1972). Children's novel.

Jimmy Yellow Hawk (1972). Children's novel.

When Thunder Spoke (1973).

Betrayed (1974). Children's novel.

The Chichi Hoohoo Bogeyman (1975). Children's novel.

Mary TallMountain, Koyukon Athabascan, born 1918 in Nulato, Alaska Territory.

Nine Poems (1977). Poetry.

There Is No Word for Goodbye (1982). Poetry; Pushcart Prize 1982–1983.

Continuum (1988). Poetry.

A Light on the Tent Wall: A Bridging (1990). Poetry.

Luci Tapahonso, Navajo, born 1953 in Shiprock, New Mexico.

One More Shiprock Night (1981). Poetry.

Seasonal Woman (1982). Poetry.

A Breeze Swept Through (1987). Poetry.

Gail Tremblay, Onondaga/Micmac, born 1945 in Buffalo, New York.

Indians Singing in 20th-Century America (1990). Poetry.

Gerald Vizenor, White Earth Chippewa, born 1934 in Minneapolis, Minnesota.

The Everlasting Sky: New Voices from the People Named the Chippewa (1972). Nonfiction.

Darkness in Saint Louis Bearheart (1978). Novel. Reprinted as *Bearheart: The Heirship Chronicles.*

Wordarrows: Indians and Whites in the New Fur Trade (1978). Fiction.

Earthdivers: Tribal Narratives on Mixed Descent (1981). Fiction.

Harold of Orange (1983). Screenplay.

The People Called the Chippewa: Narrative Histories (1984). Nonfiction and fiction.

Griever: An American Monkey King in China (1987). Novel; 1987 Fiction Collective—Illinois State University Award and Before Columbus Foundation American Book Award.

The Trickster of Liberty: Tribal Heirs to a Wild Baronage at Petronia (1988). Novel.

Interior Landscapes: Autobiographical Myths and Methaphors (1990). Memoir.

The Heirs of Columbus (1991). Novel.

Landfill Meditations: Crossblood Stories (1991). Fiction.

Dead Voices: Natural Agonies in the New World (1992). Novel.

Anna Lee Walters, Pawnee/Otoe, born 1946 in Pawnee, Oklahoma.

The Sacred: Ways of Knowledge, Sources of Life (1977). Textbook.

The Sun Is Not Merciful (1985). Short stories; 1986 Before Columbus Foundation American Book Award.

Ghost Singer (1988). Novel.

The Spirits of Native America: Beauty and Mysticism in American Indian Art (1989). Essays.

Talking Indian: Reflections on Survival and Writing (1992). Memoir.

James Welch, Blackfeet/Gros Ventre, born 1940 in Browning, Montana.

Riding the Earthboy 40 (1971). Poetry.

Winter in the Blood (1974). Novel.

Death of Jim Loney (1979). Novel.

Fools Crow (1986). Novel.

Indian Lawyer (1990). Novel.

Roberta Hill Whiteman, Oneida, born 1947 in Baraboo, Wisconsin.

Star Quilt: Poems (1984). Poetry.

Elizabeth Woody, Wasco/Navajo, born 1959 on Navajo Reservation.

Hand into Stone (1988). Poetry; winner 1990 Before Columbus Foundation American Book Award.

Ray A. Young Bear, Mesquakie, born 1950 in Tama, Iowa.

Winter of the Salamander: The Keeper of Importance (1980). Novel.

The Invisible Musician (1990). Poetry.

Black Eagle Child (1992). Memoir.

Zitkala-Sa (Gertrude Bonnin), Yankton Sioux, born 1875 on Yankton Reservation, South Dakota; died 1938.

American Indian Stories (1921). Essays and short stories.

Old Indian Legends (1901).

Employment, Income, and Economic Development

NATIVE EMPLOYMENT

In the twentieth century, employment is defined as an economic benefit, or wages, for a service or labor performed. This was not always so for society in this country and most certainly not for Native Americans. Traditional Native American societies had occupations or jobs that were performed. Depending upon the tribal society, the occupations or jobs were performed by individuals or by specially trained groups for the benefit of the tribe. Examples are the Dog Soldier societies of the Cheyenne, who served as civil policemen, camp movers, and so on, in rotation with other warrior societies. Often, there were exchanges of services or jobs in which an individual who was particularly skilled in a task traded those services with those who were skilled in another. For women of the plains, there were quilling guilds, which were societies of women who were expert quill workers and who took on apprentices to teach them the art of quill work. A woman was not permitted to create certain designs in quills unless she was a full member of the quilling guild. The guild had sacred origins, which imbued the products they made with a spiritual quality. It is said that blessings flowed from the designs that belonged to the quilling guilds.

After European contact, tribal peoples were militarily defeated and placed on reservations. Most occupations and jobs that were essential to the survival of the people were no longer needed. For example, an individual who was skilled in training horses for the buffalo hunt was no longer able to continue this service. Some occupations were continued, albeit in a different form. The quilling societies, for example, became beading societies, and the women wove the sacred designs in beadwork. Many men of the Six Nations (Iroquois) whose name for themselves, *Hotinonshonni,* means "people who built longhouses," transferred their love of building into careers in high steel construction work, an occupation that has adapted to modern times. But for many Native Americans, the "new world order" brought by whites left native people impoverished on ever smaller and less productive land bases. Although Indians have been employed throughout the twentieth century, they have been the most underemployed and poorest ethnic group in America.

Despite the fact that the Bureau of Indian Affairs schools had programs of vocational training, most Native Americans did not participate in the Industrial Revolution, which changed the economic and social basis of this country. Native American children and youth were sent to schools far away from their homes and families to learn English and vocational occupations. Some of the vocations that were taught, like harness making and blacksmithing for the boys, had little future in an increasingly industrial society. For women and girls, training was focused on domestic service. The curriculum was designed to produce servants and laborers for whites, a policy that was condemned by the authors of the 1928 *Meriam Report* "not because these employments are in themselves objectionable but because they represent standards of life too low to be sought as a goal for any race."

The education offered in government schools did not equip the students to compete with whites. Most of the teachers were not qualified to teach vocational courses and the training did not enable the students to become skilled. In response to criticisms pointed out in the *Meriam Report*, reforms were made in the bureau's programs for education and employment. School curriculum was changed to be more useful, restrictions on the expression of Indian culture were somewhat relaxed, and efforts were made to place Indians in jobs in major cities near reservation communities. A Guidance and Placement division was created in the BIA and employment agencies were set up in Minneapolis, Minnesota, Phoenix, Arizona, and Salt Lake City, Utah. By 1932, almost one thousand Indian workers were placed in off-reservation jobs.

In accordance with the Indian Reorganization Act of 1934, which contained a provision for Indian preference in government jobs, Indians began to work for the BIA. By the end of 1934, of 5,325 classified positions in the BIA, 1,785 were held by Indians. When Congress established the Civilian Conservation Corps (CCC) in 1933, President Franklin D. Roosevelt authorized the creation of a separate Indian CCC—the Indian Emergency Conservation Work (IECW) program—which was administered by the BIA. The IECW employed 85,000 Indians in a variety of jobs related to conservation of natural resources. These job experiences raised the income level of the workers and gave Indians experience in skills that were useful on or off the reservations such as the maintenance and operation of machinery, construction work, and conservation techniques.

World War II profoundly affected Native Americans. At the end of World War II, approximately 65,000 men and women returned to their reservation communities with new skills learned in the service, and with experience in living and working alongside non-Indians. This familiarity with non-Indian society prepared the way for a measure of integration into the social and economic life of the white world. "Should economic conditions after the war continue to offer employment opportunities in industry" noted Indian commissioner John Collier in his Annual Report for 1942, "many Indians will undoubtedly choose to continue to work away from the reservations. Never before have they been so well prepared to take their places among the general citizenry and to become assimilated into the white population." In 1940, less than five percent of Native Americans lived in cities, by 1950 approximately twenty percent of Native Americans lived in cities.

The eighty percent who stayed on the reservations were living in poverty. Most reservations were located in isolated areas (on lands the whites did not want) and there were few job opportunities on or near reservations. In the 1950s, the government began an organized program of relocating Indians from reservations to cities. In 1950, Dillon S. Meyer, the former director of the War Relocation Authority, was sworn in as Commissioner of Indian Affairs. Commissioner Meyer used his experience in placing Japanese-Americans in internment camps during World War II to carry out the BIA's relocation of Native Americans.

Field relocation offices were opened in major cities in the west and midwest and between 1952 and 1957, around 13,000 Native Americans were relocated. Those with education and/or job skills fared best. Many found it difficult to adjust. Low paying jobs and job insecurity resulted in Indians living in slum areas. Racism and difficulty adjusting to the white system prompted many to return home. The government claimed that only around thirty percent of the relocatees returned. Some independent researchers estimated that seventy-five percent returned to the reservations.

The program was unable to find enough jobs for all those who relocated, and many of the jobs it did find were insecure and low-paying jobs, such as those in seasonal agriculture. Indian people often expressed their dislike of the relocation program, which was seen as an individual form of termination. A terminated tribe was no longer considered an Indian tribe by the federal government. Some Indians felt the government was trying to force individual Indians into giving up their identity by placing them in non-Indian settings. They preferred a placement program that would focus on job opportunities near reservations. In 1956, vocational training became part of the relocation plan and in 1957 the Indian Vocational Training Act was responsible for establishing training centers near reservations and in cities. The act also authorized new loan regulations that permitted tribes to borrow from their trust accounts to improve industrial development on their reservations. Trust accounts are monies held by the federal government for the benefit of a tribe. As such, they have restrictions on their use.

In 1962, the BIA changed the name of the relocation program to the Employment Assistance program, and directed employment assistance resources to reservations. Since the self-determination policy of the 1970s, tribes have been able to focus on economic development on reservations themselves, but progress is slow. The challenge for the 1990s in Indian communities continues to be the attraction of economic development to reservations so Indian people can live and work on their land base.

The current economic status of the Native American workforce can be found in *Local Estimates of Resident Indian Population and Labor Force Estimates, January 1991*, published by the Bureau of Labor Statistics. The study is confined to Indians living on federal reservations or in areas or communities adjacent or contiguous to reservations that are considered part of the service population of the BIA. As defined by the Bureau of Labor Statistics, the "potential labor force" is composed of all individuals sixteen years old and over, excluding students and those who either must care for children, are retired, or are disabled. Only twenty-five percent of this group earn over $7,000 annually. The official estimate of Native American unemployment is forty-five percent, while the average unemployment rate for the United States is eight percent. Judging from the Bureau of Labor Statistics' figures, the unemployment problem for American Indians seems severe. However, since the Bureau of Labor Statistics' estimate does not include those who are discouraged from seeking work, the real unemployment rate for Native Americans may be much higher. In 1985, the Full Employment Action Council reported that Native American un-

employment may in fact be as high as eighty-seven percent on some reservations. Some of the most commonly cited reasons for high unemployment for Native Americans are poor education, discrimination, and the lack of industry on and near reservations.

The profile of occupations of Native Americans is in many respects similar to that of white Americans, however, Indians are twice as likely to have blue collar jobs than whites, and are much more likely to have skilled blue collar jobs than African Americans, perhaps because of the prevalence of vocational training opportunities for Indians. Indians are different in that they, more than any other ethnic group, are dependent on the federal government for jobs, especially the BIA which has Indian preference, and tribal governments. Also, while traditional occupations such as jewelry making, weaving, and pottery making have a significant economic impact on some reservation communities, for most American Indians, these occupations are not self-supporting.

Native Americans have had little control over many of the changes in their economic lives that have occurred since contact with Europeans. The Indian land base shrunk as the United States grew and the process has left Native Americans an impoverished minority in the land of their ancestors. Perhaps, after five hundred years of paternalism, it is time to compensate for the past with a commitment to honor treaties, respect the sovereignty of tribal nations and allow Indians to make their own decisions about their economic future.

WATER

There has been a lot said about the sacredness of our land which is our body; and the values of our culture which is our soul; but water is the blood of our tribes, and if its life-giving flow is stopped, or it is polluted, all else will die and the many thousands of years of our communal existence will come to an end.

Frank Tenorio, Governor
San Felipe Pueblo, 1978.
*From: Indian Water Policy in a
Changing Environment*, 1982.

Santa Clara Canyon, Fourth Pond, Santa Clara Pueblo, New Mexico. The pond is part of the irrigation network that nourishes Santa Clara village. Photograph by Beverly Singer.

Land and water lead the list of those items deemed essential for the present livelihood and future economic survival of Indians—especially in the American West where water is scarce. The survival of Indian tribes as economic units in the arid and semi-arid western states requires the protection of Indian rights to water on, under, and adjacent to Indian land. The development of viable agricultural systems, grazing economies, industrial ventures, municipal, mining, or recreation depends on adequate, reliable delivery of water from customary sources. Without water, reservation lands would be virtually uninhabitable, and irrigated farming, fishing resources, and other water-dependent industries would be nonexistent.

A formidable body of law favorable to Indian

people has been developed, which, if properly administered and applied, would protect Indians against divestiture of their water rights. Indian water rights are inherent and reserved to tribes through treaties and agreements and are not derived from federal grant, appropriation, or purchase. The federal government, however, whose trust responsibility includes protecting Indian rights to the use of water, has until recently ignored Indian water rights established under the Winters Doctrine and failed to protect them from infringement by non-Indian individuals and the states. During the last five to ten years, however, the government has increased its efforts to protect and quantify Indian water rites.

Besides the Winters Doctrine, other court rulings

have further defined the nature of tribal reserved water rights. Indian water rights are property rights based on federal law and are not dependent on state law nor on other doctrines used in establishing non-Indian water rights. Indian water rights are "prior and paramount," meaning that the priority date of Indian rights goes back to the establishment of their reservations or earlier. Indian water rights are not lost if they are not used (a tribe whose reservation was created in 1830 but who began using its reserved water rights in 1930 has a prior right to all others whose rights were established after 1830). Indian water rights include all sources of water—lakes, rivers, streams, springs, and groundwaters that cross, border, or underlie Indian reservations.

In the West where the demand for water outweighs the supply, tribes in Arizona, California, Idaho, Montana, Nevada, New Mexico, Oregon, Utah, Washington, Wyoming, and Colorado constantly have to negotiate, litigate, and fight state governments, miners, ranchers, farmers, municipalities, and federal land management agencies to protect their water rights. Increasing demands on the western river systems, expanding corporate agribusiness enterprises in the Columbia Basin, growing industrial and municipal needs of the Southwest, demands for water for energy production in the northern Plains, and other demands throughout the West compete with tribal uses. Indeed, entire economies of some states depend on water from streams

WINTERS DOCTRINE

In 1908, the U.S. Supreme Court recognized Indian water rights in the landmark case of *Winters v. United States* (from which emanates the body of law commonly referred to as the Winters doctrine), which became the cornerstone of Indian water rights and established that Indian water rights are a matter of federal law.

The case involved the Gros Ventre and Assiniboine tribes of the Fort Belknap Reservation in Montana. In 1877, traditional leaders of these two tribes signed an agreement that reduced the reservation and established the Milk River in 1888 as the northern boundary of the diminished reservation. In 1904, a severe drought occurred. Henry Winters and other individuals who were issued patents to establish farms upstream from the tribes on the Milk River and who had been using water since 1900 began drying up the river before it reached the reservation. An insufficient quantity of water came down to the tribes and finally their water dried up altogether.

When disaster threatened the tribes, the U.S. Justice department asked for a court order restraining Henry Winters and others from diverting water (which was

valid under state law) needed by the tribes. The settlers, ordered to respect Indian water rights, contested the injunction. There was insufficient water to meet the needs of the upstream farmers and the Indian reservation. Finally, in 1908, the case reached the Supreme Court, which decided for the Indian tribes in an eight-to-one decision. The Court found that Indians had reserved their water rights for the lands they did not cede in treaties with the U.S. government. Therefore the Court ruled that the Indians had a "prior and paramount right" to water resources in the amount necessary to satisfy the present and future needs [a homeland for Indians, hunting, fishing, mining, timber, farming, industry, and recreation] of the Indian reservation. The Court held that the rights of Indians would not be governed by Montana state doctrine of prior appropriation but by federal law. Priority of a tribe's water rights generally dates from the date of creation of the reservation. The waters already lawfully appropriated by others prior to the creation of the reservation are generally not available to the reservation. The Court left unsettled what quantity of water was reserved for the tribe.

and underground aquifers in which Indian tribes have extensive rights. In over fifty lawsuits filed during the 1970s and 1980s, tribes who have prior and paramount rights to water have challenged urban municipalities, state governments, farmers, and energy and industrial companies alike. The conflicts are sharpest in the water-poor Southwest where water diverted from rivers and streams is overappropriated for agricultural, mining, municipality, and industrial purposes. The water table has declined severely because the withdrawal of ground water exceeds the precipitation. In some areas of Arizona, the water table has declined from 50 feet forty years ago to more than 400 feet.

Many water fights end up in state and federal courts for twenty to forty years and others are settled by Congress after extensive negotiations between tribes and local water users, a process that may last five to ten years. In some congressional settlements, the federal government is required to deliver water annually to replace the tribal surface and ground water supplies that have been irretrievably lost to cities, mines, and agri-business owing to the past failure of the federal government to protect Indian water rights. In water settlements, if the federal government fails to keep its promise, it must pay damages whenever it fails to deliver the required water supply. The tribes can sue the United States for millions of dollars in damages for every year the federal government fails to discharge its legal obligation to them.

MINERALS, OIL, GAS, COAL, AND OTHER RESOURCES

Many tribes possess substantial land bases with oil, gas, coal, and other minerals that provide significant sources of wealth for Indian tribes and individuals if developed. Those tribes planning to develop natural resources endorse intensive use of these resources as necessary for the tribe's future. Other tribes who advocate subsistence endeavors and resist exploiting the land through economic development argue that commercial exploitation of resources clashes with environmental concerns and with traditional religious views. Great debates take place in Indian communities over whether and how to develop natural resources. Indian people vary in their opinions concerning the effect of resource development on a tribe's social structure and traditional, religious, and environmental beliefs.

Historically, through congressional acts and judicial decisions, a tangle of federal agencies managed tribal energy resources. So many agencies were involved that a predictable diffusion of responsibility occurred among them, resulting in ineffective resource management. In recent years with disclosures about federal government mismanagement of their natural resources, tribes have recognized the need to direct the development of tribal resources. Today, tribes are gaining control of their resources. They are protecting, managing, and developing—or choosing not to develop—their lands consistent with their own priorities and traditions.

Indian reservations contain about 5 to 6 percent of the proven reserves of U.S. oil and gas, 30 percent of the strippable low-sulfur coal, and 50 to 60 percent of uranium, and depended on federal institutions to protect their interests. However, federal agencies violated their trust duties. The Department of the Interior often failed to make timely deposits of royalty payments to Indians and the government concluded substandard mineral leases at below market value rates without tribal consent. Mineral development resulted in meager economic returns and plenty of environmental and social disruption.

During the 1970s, when the United States experienced an energy crisis prompting new interest in reservation resources, tribes resolved not to be exploited. Twenty-five tribes organized the Council of Energy Resource Tribes, which championed fair evaluation of Indian energy resources, resolved to correct inequitable agreements between tribes and energy corporations, and brought technical knowledge to tribes so they could skillfully negotiate resource management with government agencies and the industrial community.

A turning point in Indian resource management was the passage of two laws in 1982 that guaranteed

Indian people an active role in the development of their resources: the Indian Mineral Development Act and the Federal Oil and Gas Royalty Management Act. The 1982 Indian Mineral Development Act authorizes tribes to negotiate directly with mining companies. The act empowers tribal governments to enter into any joint venture, operating, production sharing, managerial, leasing, and any other agreement providing for the exploration, extraction, processing, other development, and sale of oil, gas, uranium, coal, geothermal resources, or other energy or non-energy mineral resources in which tribes own a beneficial or restricted interest. Since all terms (rents, royalties, exploration rights, length of term, and so on) are negotiable under the act, tribes can determine the type of agreement that best suits them. The act also provides that allotted Indian lands can be included in a tribal mineral agreement under certain conditions. Tribes, however, cannot negotiate royalty regulations of the U.S. Minerals Management Service.

Today, tribes have become active in resource management decisions. They have renegotiated coal leases, made oil and gas agreements joint ventures, and included provisions for tribal employment, training, and scholarships. Tribes now negotiate using sophisticated economic valuation criteria so tribal resource development nets millions of dollars.

Mineral production and mineral resource development can also provide significant income and employment to tribes and individual Indians who have chosen to develop their resources. The economic return to the Indian mineral owner from mineral production historically has been between 75 to 80 percent of the total income generated on Indian trust lands. On some Indian lands, the mineral income has been over 95 percent of the total income generated.

Oil and gas leasing activities on Indian lands have been declining steadily since 1983. As a result, income from leasing of oil and gas on Indian lands has decreased significantly since 1983. Oil wells have been plugged and abandoned regularly and very few new wells have been drilled to replace them. This has caused oil production to drop significantly in the last several years. According to the U.S. Min-

erals Management Service, in 1983 the total income for oil and gas on Indian lands was over $140 million. In 1990, the combined oil and gas income was $81.96 million. Decreases in the mineral income often mean economic hardship for the Indian mineral owner and Indian tribe. In 1991, declining mineral revenues forced the Wind River and Uintah and Ouray Reservation tribal governments to go to four-day work weeks. The decline severely strained tribal social, health care, and law enforcement programs.

While oil and gas are declining, coal production is steadily increasing, and revenues from coal production continue to increase. Arizona and New Mexico continue to be the top states for Indian coal production. Coal income for 1990 was $60,791,496. The figure represented an increase in income of over 160 percent since 1985. Renegotiated coal leases and higher coal prices accounted for the increase.

Mineral assessment programs have disclosed the presence of other minerals—base metals (copper, lead, zinc, molybdenum, tungsten) and precious metals (gold, silver, platinum) on Indian lands. At this time, gold exploration outpaces exploration for other minerals. During the 1980s, gold production was at record levels with activity generally centered in Nevada, California, Montana, and Washington State. Since world production of gold is projected to peak by 1995 and then decline substantially, gold prices are expected to increase. On reservations where gold potential is high, tribes are in strategic positions to make agreements for exploration and development if they choose to do so.

It is the policy of the interior secretary and the BIA to promote mineral development on Indian lands as a source of income and employment. The BIA encourages Indian tribes and individual Indians to enter into mineral agreements on their trust and restricted lands for mineral development with the aim of obtaining a maximum economic recovery and reasonable compensation for the development of their resources.

From the nineteenth century, surface land leases have also added revenues to tribal and individual

Indian coffers. Agriculture, business, and other leases (for residential and other nonagricultural and nonbusiness purposes) constitute surface, as opposed to mining, leases. Because of the federal trust relationship by which the federal government holds trust title to Indian lands and natural resources, such land cannot be sold, conveyed, or mortgaged without federal approval. Leasing, however, permits tribal economic development of trust lands.

Three U.S. government agencies participate in administering Indian mineral agreements, leases, and permits. The BIA must approve mineral agreements, leases, and permits (along with the Indian mineral owner and the mining company) and can also cancel them. The Bureau of Land Management (BLM), which assists in approving mineral agreements, provides presale and postsale evaluation and technical assistance to the BIA. The BLM approves all exploration, reclamation, and mining plans involving Indian lands except for coal. The BLM's Office of Surface Mining approves reclamation plans on strip mining operations. The U.S. Minerals Management Service collects rents and royalties for monies owed and paid to Indian mineral owners on producing leases.

AGRICULTURE

Land-based agricultural resources are vital to the economic and social welfare of many Native American tribes. In a state such as Nevada, agriculture is the backbone of the reservation economy. The management of these valuable and renewable natural resources not only provides sustenance, income, and employment opportunities for native people, but also affects native lives in other ways. The harmony of people, soil, water, air, vegetation, and wildlife, collectively comprising the agricultural community, influences native emotional and spiritual well-being. A strong agricultural base improves an individual's or a tribe's tie to the land, a bond that often helps preserve tribal heritage and customs.

As in the past, native people gather agricultural resources for food, ceremonial use, or medicine. Native Americans and Alaska Native tribes own and utilize cultivated crops; livestock; garden produce; uncultivated, naturally occuring items; and the lands from which these products are grown. Of the more than 54 million acres of land held in trust for Indian people, over 80 percent, or 46 million acres, are used for agriculture. Farming and ranching generated $450 million in gross revenues in 1985 and about $410 million in gross revenues in 1990, making agriculture a large contributor to the reservation economy. Some 34,000 Indian families and organizations earned their living through farming or ranching in 1985 and 46,200 Indian families and organizations in 1990. But less than 35 percent of Indian-owned farmlands are used by Indians. Indian use of grazing land is higher, about 83 percent nationwide in 1985, but down from 92 percent achieved in 1983.

On many reservations, rangeland and livestock operations provide considerable employment and income. Constituting 5 percent of the nation's pasture and rangeland and covering 44 million acres, most Indian rangelands are located in the western states. Nearly three-fourths of the land used by Indians is almost exclusively tribally owned on reservations in Arizona, New Mexico, Utah, and Nevada. A majority of productive Indian rangelands are leased and used by non-Indians on reservations in the northern Plains and northwestern states where land ownership is a composite of intermixed tribally and individually owned allotted Indian land, fee patent non-Indian owned land, and state and federal land.

Indian lands provide farming opportunities but because off-reservation financial institutions deny credit to many Indian farmers and because of droughts and a host of other problems, opportunities are not what they should be. There are roughly 9.2 million acres of Indian-owned cropland, which composes about 1.7 percent of the nation's total.

In 1987, the Intertribal Agriculture Council (IAC) was established to pursue and promote the conservation, development, and use of agricultural resources to better native lives. The IAC represents

Harvesting lettuce in the Lehi District of the Salt River Reservation, Arizona. Courtesy of the Bureau of Indian Affairs.

member tribes which control 43 million of the 54 million acres of Indian lands in the contiguous United States and approximately half of the 44 million acres in Alaska. An independent body, the IAC is a conduit of information between the BIA and the tribes.

TIMBER

Forests provided timber for shelter and transportation and offered sustenance for Native Americans in the pre-European contact period. During the nineteenth century, non-Indian loggers sought timber from Indian lands as they extended their operations across the upper Midwest. With the emergence of a Division of Forestry in the BIA and the initiation of large-scale timber harvest operations on Indian forest lands after 1910, some tribal governments west of the Mississippi River came to rely on stumpage

revenue as a major source of income. Later, as forest development work was initiated, the tribes looked to Indian timberlands for jobs and business opportunities.

Nationally, Indian timber represents only a small fraction (2 percent) of the 740 million acres of forest land. In the Pacific Northwest states of Washington, Oregon, and Montana and in the Southwest states of Arizona and New Mexico, Indian timberlands are significant to the overall forest economy. The national importance of Indian timber is seen in the marketing of Navajo and Fort Apache timber from the Southwest, and logging and marketing of Indian forest products in the Pacific Northwest. Indian sawmills supply a considerable volume of raw materials annually to the national wood products industry.

Indian forests in many areas of the country have played a major role in the economic lives of Indian tribes. In 1940, most of the sawmills located on Indian reservations were small units operated princi-

COUNCIL OF ENERGY RESOURCE TRIBES

In 1975, leaders of twenty-five energy-resource own-ing tribes forged a coalition called the Council of Energy Resource Tribes (CERT). CERT enables mem-bers to speak in a unified voice on energy matters to federal government officials and provides them with information, technical assistance, links to financial institutions, and market services. From the beginning, CERT wanted tribes to gain control of their mineral resources. The council today, with a membership of fifty-three tribes, is governed by the elected leadership of its member tribes and works to attain self-sufficiency and self-government. Recognizing that trained and experienced Indian people are an impor-tant prerequisite to attaining these goals, CERT educa-tion programs prepare young Native Americans for careers in resource management.

CERT MEMBER TRIBES—KNOWN AND POTENTIAL RESOURCES

Acoma Pueblo, New Mexico—coal, geothermal, natural gas

Blackfeet, Montana—coal, natural gas, oil

Chemehuevi, California—hydroelectric, oil, ura-nium

Cherokee, Oklahoma—coal, natural gas, oil

Cheyenne–Arapaho, Oklahoma—gas, oil

Cheyenne River Sioux, South Dakota—coal, gas, oil

Chippewa Cree, Montana—coal, gas, lignite, oil, uranium

Coeur D'Alene, Idaho—hydroelectric, uranium

Crow, Montana—coal, natural gas, oil

Fort Belknap Indian Reservation, Montana (Gros Ventre and Assiniboine)—geothermal, lignite, natural gas, oil

Fort Hall Indian Reservation, Idaho (Shoshone–Bannock)—geothermal, hydroelectric, natural gas

Fort Peck Indian Reservation, Montana (Assini-boine–Sioux)—geothermal, lignite, natural gas, oil

Hopi, Arizona—coal, natural gas, oil, uranium

Hualapai, Arizona—hydroelectric, natural gas, oil, uranium

Jemez Pueblo, New Mexico—hydroelectric, natu-ral gas, oil, uranium

Jicarilla Apache, New Mexico—coal, geothermal, natural gas, oil

Kaibab Paiute, Arizona—coal, natural gas, ura-nium

Kalispel, Washington—hydroelectric, uranium

Laguna Pueblo, New Mexico—coal, natural gas, oil, uranium

pally to provide building materials for tribal mem-bers. Only on the Menominee Indian Reservation in Wisconsin and the Red Lake Indian Reservation in Minnesota were large sawmills processing timber for off-reservation markets. The Menominee sawmill, established in 1908 at Neopit, Wisconsin, and the Red Lake sawmill, established in 1924 (and closed in 1984) at Redby, Minnesota, were locally significant commercial enterprises that operated throughout the

twentieth century. By 1980, there were five major Indian-owned forest enterprises: the Navajo Forest Products Industries, Fort Apache Timber Company, Warm Springs Forest Products Industries, and the Menominee and Red Lake sawmills. The Colville Indian sawmill began operation in 1986. These saw-mills not only have returned revenue to Indian tribes, they also have provided employment and vo-cational training to tribal members.

Menominee, Wisconsin—hydroelectric

Muckleshoot, Washington—coal, hydroelectric, natural gas, oil

Navajo, Arizona, New Mexico, Utah—coal, geothermal, natural gas, oil, uranium

Nez Percé, Idaho—hydroelectric

Northern Cheyenne, Montana—coal, natural gas, oil

Northern Ute, Utah—coal, natural gas, oil, oil shale, tar sand

Oglala Sioux, South Dakota—natural gas, oil, uranium

Paiute, Utah—coal, gas, oil, oil shale, uranium

Pauma, California—hydroelectric

Pawnee, Oklahoma—gas, oil

Penobscot, Maine—hydroelectric

Pojoaque Pueblo, New Mexico—sand and gravel, uranium

Ponca, Oklahoma—gas, oil

Pyramid Lake Paiute, Nevada—geothermal

Rosebud Sioux, South Dakota—geothermal, natural gas, oil, oil shale

Sac and Fox, Oklahoma—gas, oil

Saginaw Chippewa, Michigan—gas, oil.

Salish and Kootenai Confederated Tribes of Flathead Indian Reservation, Montana—hydro-electric, natural gas

San Juan Pueblo, New Mexico—gas, oil

Santa Ana Pueblo, New Mexico—geothermal

Seminole, Florida—natural gas, uranium

Southern Ute, Colorado—coal, natural gas, oil

Spokane, Washington—coal, hydroelectric, uranium

St. Regis Mohawk, New York—hydroelectric

Standing Rock Sioux, North Dakota/South Dakota—coal, gas, oil

Three Affiliated Tribes of the Fort Berthold Indian Reservation, North Dakota (Mandan, Hidatsa, Arikara)—geothermal, lignite, natural gas, oil

Tule River, California—hydroelectric

Turtle Mountain Band of Chippewa Indians, North Dakota—coal, natural gas, oil

Umatilla Indian Reservation, Oregon—geothermal, hydro

Ute Mountain Ute, Colorado—coal, natural gas, oil, uranium

Walker River Paiute, Nevada—geothermal, hydroelectric, uranium

Wichita, Oklahoma—natural gas, oil

Yakima, Washington—hydroelectric, natural gas, oil

Zia Pueblo, New Mexico—geothermal, natural gas, oil

The development of more scientific and accurate inventory and mapping techniques have resulted in an increase in the volume of commercial Indian timber. Significantly, this knowledge and application of intensive forest management principles to Indian forests have resulted in an increase in the allowable annual cut (AAC) from many reservations.

The Pacific Northwest is the major commercial producer of Indian-owned timber. The Portland area, which includes the states of Oregon, Washington, Idaho, parts of Montana, and southeast Alaska contained almost 24 billion board feet of commercial timber in 1985. The Southwest, composed of the Navajo, Phoenix, and Albuquerque Area Offices, trailed a distant second to the Portland Area Office in 1985, with a total commercial volume of roughly 7.7 billion board feet.

Applying intensive forest management—

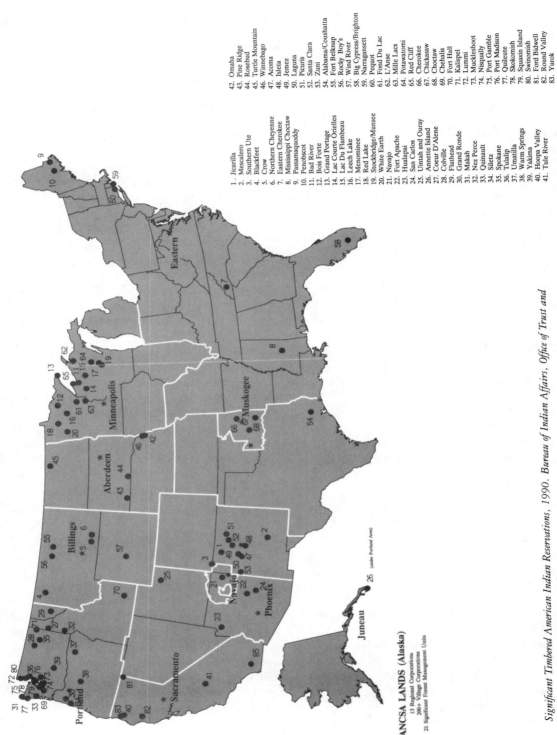

1. Jicarilla
2. Mescalero
3. Southern Ute
4. Blackfeet
5. Crow
6. Northern Cheyenne
7. Eastern Cherokee
8. Mississippi Choctaw
9. Passamaquoddy
10. Penobscot
11. Bad River
12. Bois Forte
13. Grand Portage
14. Lac Courte Oreilles
15. Lac Du Flambeau
16. Leech Lake
17. Menominee
18. Red Lake
19. Stockbridge/Munsee
20. White Earth
21. Navajo
22. Fort Apache
23. Hualapai
24. San Carlos
25. Uintah and Ouray
26. Annette Island
27. Coeur D'Alene
28. Colville
29. Flathead
30. Grand Ronde
31. Makah
32. Nez Perce
33. Quinault
34. Siletz
35. Spokane
36. Tulalip
37. Umatilla
38. Warm Springs
39. Yakima
40. Hoopa Valley
41. Tule River

42. Omaha
43. Pine Ridge
44. Rosebud
45. Turtle Mountain
46. Winnebago
47. Acoma
48. Isleta
49. Jemez
50. Laguna
51. Picuris
52. Santa Clara
53. Zuni
54. Alabama/Coushatta
55. Fort Belknap
56. Rocky Boy's
57. Wind River
58. Big Cypress/Brighton
59. Narragansett
60. Pequot
61. Fond Du Lac
62. L'Anse
63. Mille Lacs
64. Potawatomi
65. Red Cliff
66. Cherokee
67. Chickasaw
68. Choctaw
69. Chehalis
70. Fort Hall
71. Kalispel
72. Lummi
73. Muckleshoot
74. Nisqually
75. Port Gamble
76. Port Madison
77. Quileute
78. Skokomish
79. Squaxin Island
80. Swinomish
81. Ford Bidwell
82. Round Valley
83. Yurok

ANCSA LANDS (Alaska)

13 Regional Corporations
200+ Village Corporations
21 Significant Forest Management Units

Significant Timbered American Indian Reservations, 1990. Bureau of Indian Affairs, Office of Trust and Economic Development, Division of Forestry.

thinning, forestation, improved fire management, forest inventory—contributed to an increase in the annual harvest from Indian timberlands. Labor-intensive forestry operations also provided Indians with jobs and income.

Founded in 1976, the Intertribal Timber Council, with fifty-five member tribes located from Maine to Alaska to New Mexico, provides a forum for communicating between tribes and the BIA on matters relevant to the pursuit and development of timber resources for the benefit of Indian people.

OUTDOOR RECREATION ON INDIAN LANDS

Indian tribes and tribal lands in the United States offer public outdoor recreation and related tourist-oriented opportunities. Growing numbers of tribes stock and manage big game herds to attract non-Indians to the reservations for recreation.

The following chart includes tribes that responded to a BIA questionnaire on outdoor recreation on Indian lands. The exclusion of a particular tribe or reservation may represent nothing more than a lack of completed forms. The inclusion of a tribe does not necessarily mean a commitment to continued development of tourism and public-use programs.

Activities designated with a dash indicate either a lack of information or no current program.

BUSINESS

Many tribal leaders say only jobs can solve severe problems of unemployment, poverty, and alcoholism on and off reservations. Since more Indians see self-employment as a viable opportunity, numbers of individually Indian-owned, reservation-based businesses increased during the 1980s. Tribally owned businesses also keep people working on the reservation.

In 1987, the U.S. Department of Commerce's Bureau of the Census surveyed minority-owned business enterprises and found 1,143 Aleut-owned firms, 2,353 Eskimo-owned firms, and 17,884 American Indian-owned businesses. Native people own everything from brokerages, construction companies, food stores, hotels, manufacturing plants, to printing and publishing companies, public utilities, restaurants, textile mills, and trucking companies.

The following industry groups generated the largest sales in declining order for Native American business owners in 1987: special trade contractors, miscellaneous retail, agricultural services, forestry and fishing, automotive dealers and service stations, food stores, business services, eating and drinking places, construction, trucking and warehousing, and personal services.

GAMING

Across the country, resource-poor reservations with few other economic opportunities have turned high stakes bingo parlor and gambling operations into major money-makers for tribal programs and the means to economic independence. Moreover, gaming revenues have replaced the drastic federal budget cuts of the 1980s that nourished reservation economies. More than 100 tribes in over twenty states have gambling operations that generate an estimated $2.5 billion a year. In some areas where tribal games are major sources of jobs for tribal members and non-Indians, gaming employment lowers Indian unemployment rates and reduces welfare loads of state and federal governments.

Because gaming operations are on Indian land, where tribes are not subject to local and state rulings, they can offer activities not permitted off-reservation. States with bingo cannot regulate these games on Indian reservations. Since state limits do not apply to Indian reservations, their games offer top prize money. Casinos, some with million dollar prizes, and bingo parlors, however, attract spenders who bring sorely needed revenues that spur social and other economic development projects. Monies

Outdoor Recreation Opportunities/Programs on Indian Lands

Tribe/Reservation	PUBLIC USES/MANAGEMENT PROGRAMS							
	Fish	Hunt	Camp	Bike	Boat	Hike	Snow	Tour
ABERDEEN AREA								
Cheyenne River, SD	●	●	●	—	●	—	—	—
Crow Creek, SD	●	●	●	—	●	●	—	—
Devils Lake, ND	●	●	●	—	●	—	●	—
Flandreau, SD	—	—	●	—	—	—	—	—
Fort Berthold, ND	●	●	●	—	●	—	—	●
Lower Brulé, SD	●	●	●	—	●	—	—	—
Omaha, NE	●	●	●	—	—	—	—	—
Pine Ridge, SD	●	●	—	—	●	—	—	—
Rosebud, SD	●	●	●	—	●	—	—	—
Santee Sioux, NE	●	●	●	—	—	—	—	—
Sisseton-Wahpeton, SD	●	●	—	—	●	—	—	—
Standing Rock, ND	●	●	●	—	●	—	—	—
Turtle Mountain, ND	●	●	●	—	●	—	—	—
Winnebago, NE	●	●	—	—	—	—	—	—
Yankton Sioux, SD	●	●	●	—	●	—	—	—
ALBUQUERQUE AREA								
Acoma, NM	—	●	—	—	—	—	—	●
Isleta, NM	●	—	●	—	—	—	—	●
Jemez, NM	●	●	—	—	—	—	—	—
Jicarilla, NM	●	●	●	—	●	—	●	●
Laguna, NM	—	●	●	—	—	—	—	—
Mescalero, NM	●	●	●	—	●	●	●	●
Nambe, NM	●	—	●	—	●	—	—	—
Picuris, NM	●	—	●	—	—	—	—	—
Pojoaque, NM	—	—	●	—	—	—	—	—
Sandia, NM	●	—	—	—	—	—	—	—
San Ildefonso, NM	●	●	●	—	—	●	—	—
San Juan, NM	●	—	—	—	—	—	—	●
Santa Clara, NM	●	—	●	—	—	—	●	—
Southern Ute, NM	●	●	●	—	—	—	—	●
Taos, NM	—	—	—	—	—	—	—	●
Tesuque, NM	—	—	●	—	—	●	—	—
Ute Mountain Ute, CO	●	—	●	—	—	●	—	—
Zia, NM	●	—	—	—	—	—	—	—
Zuni, NM	●	●	●	●	—	●	—	—

(continued)

Tribe/Reservation	PUBLIC USES/MANAGEMENT PROGRAMS							
	Fish	*Hunt*	*Camp*	*Bike*	*Boat*	*Hike*	*Snow*	*Tour*
ANADARKO AREA								
Alabama–Coushatta, TX	•	–	•	–	•	–	–	•
Citizen Potawatomi, OK	–	–	•	–	–	–	–	•
Kickapoo, KS	–	–	•	–	–	–	–	•
Prairie Potawatomi, KS	•	•	•	–	–	–	–	–
BILLINGS AREA								
Blackfeet, MT	•	•	•	•	•	•	•	•
Crow, MT	•	•	•	–	•	–	•	•
Fort Belknap, MT	•	•	•	–	•	–	•	•
Fort Peck, MT	•	•	•	–	•	–	–	–
Northern Cheyenne, MT	–	–	•	–	–	–	–	–
Rocky Boy's, MT	•	–	•	–	–	–	•	–
Wind River, WY	•	–	•	–	•	•	–	–
EASTERN AREA								
Cherokee, NC	•	–	•	•	–	•	–	–
Choctaw, MS	•	•	•	–	•	–	–	•
Miccosukee, FL	•	•	•	–	•	–	–	–
Penobscot, ME	•	•	–	–	•	–	–	•
Seminole, FL	•	–	•	–	•	–	–	–
Seneca, NY	•	–	•	–	•	–	•	–
MINNEAPOLIS AREA								
Bay Mills, MI	–	–	•	–	•	–	•	–
Bois Forte, MN	•	•	–	–	•	–	•	–
Grand Portage, MN	•	•	•	–	•	–	–	–
Grand Traverse, MI	–	–	•	•	•	•	•	•
Keweenaw Bay, MI	•	•	•	–	–	–	–	–
Lac Courte Oreilles, WI	•	–	•	–	•	–	•	–
Lac du Flambeau, WI	•	•	•	–	•	–	•	•
Leech Lake, MN	•	•	•	•	•	•	•	•
Menominee, WI	•	•	–	–	•	–	–	–
Mille Lacs, MN	•	•	•	–	•	•	•	•
Mole Lake, WI	–	–	•	–	–	–	–	–
Oneida, WI	•	•	–	–	–	•	•	–
Red Cliff, WI	•	•	•	–	•	–	–	–

(continued)

Outdoor Recreation Opportunities/Programs on Indian Lands (*continued*)

Tribe/Reservation	PUBLIC USES/MANAGEMENT PROGRAMS							
	Fish	Hunt	Camp	Bike	Boat	Hike	Snow	Tour
Red Lake, MN	●	●	–	–	–	–	–	–
Saginaw, MI	●	●	●	–	●	●	●	–
Sault Ste. Marie, MI	–	–	–	–	–	●	●	–
St. Croix, WI	–	–	–	–	●	–	–	–
Stockbridge-Munsee, WI	●	●	–	–	–	●	–	–
White Earth, MN	●	●	●	–	–	–	–	–
MUSKOGEE AREA								
Cherokee, OK	–	–	–	–	–	–	–	●
NAVAJO AREA								
Navajo, AZ	●	●	●	–	●	●	–	●
PHOENIX AREA								
Camp Verdi, AZ	–	–	●	–	–	●	–	●
Chemehuevi, CA	●	●	●	–	●	–	–	●
Cocopah, AZ	●	●	●	–	●	●	–	●
Colorado River, AZ	●	●	●	–	●	–	–	●
Duck Valley, NV	●	–	●	–	–	–	–	–
Fort Apache, AZ	●	●	●	–	●	●	●	●
Fort McDermitt, NV	–	–	●	–	–	–	–	–
Fort McDowell, AZ	●	–	●	–	●	–	–	–
Fort Mojave, CA	●	–	●	–	●	–	–	–
Fort Yuma, AZ	●	●	●	–	●	–	–	–
Gila River, AZ	–	–	●	–	●	–	–	●
Havasupai, AZ	–	–	●	–	–	●	–	●
Hopi, AZ	–	–	●	–	–	●	–	●
Hualapai, AZ	●	●	●	–	●	●	–	–
Kaibab, AZ	–	●	●	–	–	●	–	–
Pyramid Lake, NV	●	–	●	–	●	–	–	–
Salt River, AZ	●	–	●	–	●	–	–	–
San Carlos, AZ	●	●	●	–	●	●	–	–
Uintah & Ouray, UT	●	●	●	–	●	–	–	–
Walker River, NV	●	–	●	–	●	–	–	–
Washoe, NV	●	–	●	–	●	–	–	–
Yomba, NV	●	–	●	–	–	–	–	–

(continued)

Outdoor Recreation Opportunities/Programs on Indian Lands (*continued*)

Tribe/Reservation	PUBLIC USES/MANAGEMENT PROGRAMS							
	Fish	Hunt	Camp	Bike	Boat	Hike	Snow	Tour
PORTLAND AREA								
Coeur d' Alene, ID	●	●	●	–	●	●	–	–
Colville, WA	●	●	●	–	●	–	–	●
Flathead, MT	●	●	●	●	●	●	●	●
Fort Hall, ID	●	●	–	–	●	–	–	●
Makah, WA	●	–	●	–	●	●	–	●
Metlakatla, AK	●	●	●	–	●	●	–	●
Quileute, WA	●	–	●	–	●	●	–	–
Skokomish, WA	–	–	●	–	●	●	–	–
Spokane, WA	●	–	●	–	●	–	–	–
Tulalip, WA	●	–	–	–	●	–	–	–
Umatilla, WA	●	●	●	–	–	–	–	–
Warm Springs, OR	●	–	●	●	●	●	–	●
Yakima, WA	●	●	●	–	●	●	●	●
SACRAMENTO AREA								
Aqua Caliente, CA	–	–	●	–	–	●	–	–
La Jolla, CA	●	–	●	–	–	–	–	●
Yurok, CA	●	–	●	–	–	–	–	–

● = yes; – = no

acquired through bingo, casino, and other gaming enterprises provide college tuitions, fund private health clinics, offer retirement benefits and housing for tribal elders, add classrooms and dorms at tribal community colleges, finance new business enterprises, and build new houses for tribal members. While, to some, gambling may be an objectionable way to earn income, it is the survival straw of the 1990s for a desperate people. According to the October 16, 1991 issue of the *Lakota Times*, the Indian nations are clutching at this straw in order to survive. When the Indians have a strong economic base, perhaps they can turn from gambling to other economic ventures.

Some state governments, suspicious of this new independent source of tribal income, have tried to control tribal gaming and claimed tribes have become havens for organized crime. The Cabazons, a small tribe in southern California that operated a casino north of Palm Springs, won court cases against state and county governments that tried to shut down the gambling casino. The U. S. Supreme Court finally upheld, in 1987, the sovereign right of a federally recognized tribe to conduct gambling enterprises on its reservation despite state objections that California gambling laws applied on Indian reservations. Congress followed in 1988 by passing the Indian Gaming Regulatory Act, strengthening the BIA responsibility to oversee Indian gambling, and establishing in the Interior Department the National Indian Gaming Commission, with rule making and regulatory powers. There also is a National Indian Gaming Association, a voluntary association of members representing federally recognized tribal governments, gaming tribes, rancherias, pueblos, and businesses involved in gaming in Indian country.

The Indian Gaming Regulatory Act created three classes of gaming: Class I—social gaming with prizes of minimal value or traditional forms of Indian gaming connected with tribal ceremonies or celebrations; Class II—Bingo and other similar games, and Class III—dog and horse racing, and casino-style games. Under the 1988 act, tribes can conduct Class II and Class III gaming in states that permit similar forms of gaming for non-Indians or if the tribe negotiated an exemption with state officials. The tribe and National Indian Gaming Commission regulate Class II games, and Class III casino-type games require a compact between a tribe and a state. New 1992 federal rules bar Indian casinos from running electronic slot machines or keno without state approval. By the end of 1992, there were fifty tribal–state compacts approved by the interior secretary in sixteen states that operate Class III casino-type operations. Arizona had 2 casinos, California, 5; Colorado, 2; Connecticut, 1; Iowa, 2; Louisiana, 2; Minnesota, 11; Montana, 1; Nebraska, 1; Nevada, 1; North Dakota, 2; Oklahoma, 1; Oregon, 1; South Dakota, 5; Washington, 2; and Wisconsin, 11.

Native Americans and Military Service

American Indians have a long history of supporting the U. S. military. They fought loyally in every one of the American wars, long before Congress granted them citizenship in 1924. During the American Revolution, the Oneida and Tuscarora nations, members of the Six Nations (Iroquois) Confederacy, sided with the Americans. During the Civil War, the loyalties of Indians were divided, as were those of white people. Some Indians fought for the Union, others for the Confederacy. The Confederacy enjoyed the support of the Cherokees, Creeks, Chickasaws, Choctaws, and Seminoles in Indian Territory (now Oklahoma). Colonel Stand Watie, who commanded two regiments of Cherokee Mounted Rifles and three battalions of Cherokee, Seminole, and Osage infantry reportedly fought more battles west of the Mississippi River than any other unit. The last general in the Confederate army to give up, Watie surrendered to the Union in June 1865, at Doakville, Choctaw Nation, Indian Territory.

Indians fought in the Spanish-American War, some joining Teddy Roosevelt's Rough Riders in the charge at San Juan Hill. In World War I, 12,000 Indian men and women served, nearly all volunteers. The number in the military doubled in World War II. Indians served in all branches of the service, and many were cited and decorated for distinguished service.

American Indians have joined the armed services of the United States to serve their country and community and to protect the rights, lands, and dignity of their tribe. In the tradition of Indian cultures, the way to manhood and an honored position in the Indian community was to serve in warrior societies or armed services where ceremonial status was earned.

Indian communities support their men and women warriors regardless of the policy that sends them to battle. Relatives who sponsor ceremonies send soldiers into war armed with eagle feathers, sacred bundles, prayers of protection, and ceremonial sweats to prepare them for battle.

The Stars and Stripes and Feathered Staff (representing Indian people) "lead the way" at Indian cere-

Navajo Nation honored its veterans with a plaque placed at Window Rock, Navajo Nation, Arizona. Photograph by Karen Warth.

227

INDIAN PARTICIPATION IN TWENTIETH-CENTURY WARS

Native Americans have served loyally in every branch of the military during the twentieth century. As *News from Indian Country* reported in a mid-February 1991 lead story titled "American Indians Proud of Service Record": "In some tribal communities across the country, you can find families in which every single son, and in some cases the daughters, have served in the armed forces of one branch or another."

World War I (1917–1918)	12,000 served, nearly all volunteers.
World War II (1941–1945)	25,000 served (21,767 in Army, 1,910 in Navy, 874 in Marines, 121 in Coast Guard).
Vietnam (1965–1975)	42,500 served (10,829 in Army, 24,000 in Navy, 2,450 in Marines, and 5,237 in Air Force).
Persian Gulf (Desert Storm) (1991)	3,000 served.

Veterans carrying the flags in the Grand Entry of a powwow, Milwaukee, Wisconsin, 1990. Photograph by M. K. de Montaño.

monies and powwows (year-round festive Indian gatherings where tribal dancers, singers, crafts-people, families, friends, and Indian visitors come together to celebrate with their time-honored traditional dances and songs). Since American troops carried flags into battle, special war powers are attributed to the flags, believed to guarantee success and special military service to the owner. During the grand entry, the opening ceremony of a powwow, Indian veterans, honored for their patriotism, carry the American, Veterans of Foreign Wars, Vietnam Indian, and Canadian flags into the arena, followed by guests and dancers. Honoring songs follow. Some tribes sing a war victory song followed immediately

MEDALS OF HONOR

American Indians have played prominent roles in the military history of this country since its very beginning. The number of Indians receiving Medals of Honor attests to this. Created in 1861, the Medal of Honor is given to candidates whose acts "far exceeded any just demand of duty."

	Date Earned	Awarded Medal
Alchesay, *Apache*	1872–1873	April 12, 1875
Barfoot, Van T., *Choctaw*	May 23, 1944	October 4, 1944
Blanquet, *Apache*	1872–1873	April 12, 1875
Childers, Ernest, *Oklahoma Creek*	September 22, 1943	April 8, 1944
Chiquito, *Apache*	1872–1873	April 12, 1875
Co-Rux-Te-Chod-Ish (Mad Bear), *Pawnee*	July 8, 1869	August 24, 1869
Elsatsoosu, *Apache*	1872—1873	April 12, 1875
Evans, Ernest E., *Pawnee* (?)	October 25, 1944	November 24, 1945
Factor, Pompey, *Seminole*	April 25, 1875	May 28, 1875
George, Charles, *Eastern Band of Cherokees*	November 30, 1952	March 18, 1954
Harvey, Raymond (?)	March 9, 1951	August 2, 1951
Jim, *Apache*	1872–1873	April 12, 1875
Kelsay, *Apache*	1872–1873	April 12, 1875
Kosoha, *Apache*	1872–1873	April 12, 1875
Machol, *Apache*	1872–1873	April 12, 1875
Montgomery, Jack, *Oklahoma Cherokee*	February 22, 1944	January 15, 1945
Nannasaddie, *Apache*	1872–1873	April 12, 1875
Nantaje, *Apache*	1872–1873	April 12, 1875
Paine, Adam, *Seminole*	September 26–27, 1874	October 13, 1875
Payne, Isaac, *Seminole*	April 25, 1875	May 28, 1875
Red Cloud, Mitchell, *Winnebago*	November 5, 1950	April 25, 1951
Reese, John N., *Oklahoma Creek*	February 9, 1945	October 19, 1945
Rowdy, *Apache*	March 7, 1890	May 15, 1890
Ward, John, *Seminole*	April 25, 1875	May 28, 1875

by the national anthem of the host Indian nation. On the powwow dance circuit, honor and personal war songs for World War I, World War II, Congressional Medal holders, Korean and Vietnam veterans are sung. In recent years, nearly every tribe has com-posed a flag song dedicated to men and women who served in the armed forces. Tribal flag songs speak of special war deeds in defense of the American flag. The equivalent of the national anthem, people stand quietly while flag songs are sung.

NATIVE AMERICAN VETERANS MEMORIAL

On November 1, 1986, the first national memorial honoring Native American veterans was dedicated at Arlington National Cemetery near the grave of Ira Hayes, Pima, one of the Marines who raised the flag on Iwo Jima in World War II. At the base of the memorial, a cottonwood tree is planted as a living memorial to those who served, on which rests a bronze plaque that proclaims: "Dedicated To Our Indian Warriors and Their Brothers Who Have Served Us So Well—The Viet-Nam Era Veterans—We Are Honored To Remember You—The Indigenous People of America."

The idea for a memorial for Indian veterans origi-nated with Mr. Bob Kelly from the Crow Nation, who designed the 2-foot by 3-feet plaque and had it cast in 1979. Known as the "Grandfather" plaque because it predates "The Wall," the Vietnam Memorial in Wash-ington, D.C., the plaque was shuffled through bureau-cracy, lost, and eventually found in the BIA where it had been donated. Arlington National Cemetery offi-cials, responding to native veteran appeals, agreed to establish the memorial. Frederick E. Hart's bronze statue entitled "Three Fighting Men" that uses Cauca-sian-, Hispanic-, and African-American servicemen to suggest the diversity of the combatants at Iwo Jima arguably neglected native soldiers who fought val-iantly in every war that this country has fought. The first national memorial to native veterans corrects this omission.

The gravesite of Ira Hayes in Arlington National Cemetery, Washington, D.C. Photograph by Karen Warth.

First national memorial honoring Native American veterans in Arlington National Cemetery, Washington, D.C. Photograph by Karen Warth.

CODE TALKERS

WORLD WAR I AND II—CHOCTAW CODE TALKERS

In the closing days of World War I, fourteen Choctaw Indian men in the Army's Thirty-Sixth Division trained to use their language helped the American Expeditionary Force win several key battles in the Meuse-Argonne Campaign in France, the final big German push of the war. The fourteen Choctaw code talkers were Albert Billy, Mitchell Bobb, Victor Brown, Ben Caterby, James Edwards, Tobias Frazer, Ben Hampton, Solomon Louis, Pete Maytubby, Jeff Nelson, Joseph Oklahombi, Robert Taylor, Calvin Wilson, and Walter Veach.

With at least one Choctaw man placed in each field company headquarters, they handled military communications by field telephone, translated radio messages into the Choctaw language, and wrote field orders to be carried by "runners" between the various companies. The Germany army, which captured about one out of four messengers, never deciphered the messages written in Choctaw.

During the annual Choctaw Labor Day Festival in 1986, Chief Hollis E. Roberts presented posthumous Choctaw Nation Medals of Valor to the families of the code talkers. This was the first official recognition the Choctaw Code Talkers had been given. On November 3, 1989, in recognition of the important role the Choctaw Code Talkers played during World War I, the French government presented Chief Roberts with the "Chevalier de l'Ordre National du Merite" (the Knight of the National Order of Merit), the highest honor France can bestow.

A January 23, 1919, memorandum from the commanding officer of the 142nd Infantry headquarters to the commanding general of the Thirty-Sixth Division revealed some of the code: "The Indian for 'Big Gun' was used to indicate artillery. 'Little Gun shoot fast' was substituted for machine gun, and the battalions were indicated by one, two, or three grains of corn."

The Choctaws were recognized as the first to use their native language as an unbreakable code in World War I. The Choctaw language was again used in World War II. Choctaws conversed in their language over field radios to co-ordinate military positions, giving exact details and locations without fear of German interception.

WORLD WAR II—COMANCHE CODE TALKERS

After induction into the army, seventeen Comanche men were selected for the Signal Corps because of their unique language. The Comanche Signal Corp included Charles Chibitty, Haddon Codynah, Robert Holder, Forrest Kassanavoid, Wellington Mihecoby, Edward Nahquaddy, Perry Noyabad, Clifford Otitovo, Simmons Parker, Melvin Permansu, Elgin Red Elk, Roderick Red Elk, Larry Saupitty, Morris (Sunrise) Tabbyetchy, Tony Tabbytite, Ralph Wahnee, and Willie Yackeschi. Trained in all phases of communication, these members of the army's Fourth Signal Division used the Comanche language to relay important messages that could not be understood or decoded by the enemy during World War II. The Comanche phrase *posah-tai-vo* meaning "crazy white man" was used for Adolph Hitler. Since the Comanches had a word for airplane but not for bomber, the code talkers came up with the Comanche phrase for "pregnant airplane."

Working in teams with regiments in the field, these men coded messages back to division headquarters where another member of the Signal Corps received and decoded the message.

On September 12, 1944, the commanding general commended the Fourth Signal Corp for outstanding service between June 6, 1944, and September 1944.

The French government honored the Signal Corps, along with the Choctaw Code Talkers, on November 3, 1989, by presenting the "Chevalier de L'Ordre National du Merite" to the Comanche tribal chief. Three surviving Comanche code talkers, Charles Chibitty, Roderick Red Elk, and Forrest Kassanavoid attended the ceremony.

WORLD WAR II—NAVAJO CODE TALKERS

The Navajo code played a crucial role in the U.S. victory in the Pacific during World War II. Breaking codes as fast as they were worked out, Japanese cryptographers never broke the code based on Navajo, virtually an unwritten language in 1942. The idea originated with Philip Johnston, an engineer raised on the Navajo Reservation where his father had been a missionary. Worried about U.S. military setbacks because of communication leaks and confident that few people in the world understood the complex syntax and tonal qualities of Navajo, he suggested that the marines use the language as the basis for a code. One word, spoken in four different alterations in pitch or tone of voice, had four different meanings. After staging a demonstration in which several Navajo friends transmitted English into Navajo and back into English, the Marine Corps authorized an official program to develop and implement the code. Twenty-nine Navajos fluent in Navajo and English, some only fifteen years old, constructed and mastered the Navajo code, which they transmitted in simulated battles. Twenty-seven code talkers were shipped to Guadalcanal, while two remained behind to train more code talkers.

The code talkers devised an alphabet to spell out words for which no code terms could be devised.

They used words, many taken from nature, that had logical associations with military terms and names of places. Thus, the code word for observation plane became ne-ahs-jah, or "owl" in Navajo; besh-lo or "iron fish" was the word for submarine. The Navajo word for potato meant grenade and a whale signified a battleship. The Navajo word for America (Ne-he-mah) meant "our mother" and clan names were used for military units. By the end of the war, 411 terms baffled Japanese cryptographers who were unable to decipher a single syllable from thousands of transmitted messages.

Eventually, some 400 Navajos served in the code-talker program. Assigned to the Third, Fourth, and Fifth Divisions of the U.S. Marines, they served in many campaigns in the Pacific theater, usually in two-men teams conversing by field telephones and walkie-talkie to call in air strikes and artillery bombardments, direct troop movements, report enemy locations, direct fire from American positions, and transmit sensitive military information. At Iwo Jima, the code talkers immortalized themselves. The entire military operation to capture the island was directed by orders communicated by the Navajo code talkers. During the first forty-eight hours, while the marines landed and consolidated their shore positions, six Navajo radio nets operated around the clock. They sent and received more than 800 messages without error. When the marines raised the flag on Mount Suribachi, the code talkers relayed the message in the Navajo code: "sheep-uncle-ram-ice-bear-ant-cat-horse-itch."

In 1992, the Pentagon honored the Navajo code talkers with an exhibit that documents the history of the code. Back in the Gallup-McKinley Chamber of Commerce, a "permanent home" houses historic photos, posters, trophies, radios, and other valuable

(continued)

CODE TALKERS (*cont.*)

items. Phoenix, Arizona, boasts the nation's first permanent tribute to the code talkers, a fourteen-foot sculpture by Doug Hyde of a young Indian boy holding a flute in his hand. Called on to participate in public ceremonies and parades country-wide, the Navajo code talkers have been honored in books, films, curriculum materials, and by a beautiful recording "Code Talkers" sung by Vincent Craig, the son of Bob Craig, a code talker in the Marine Fifth Division.

Tribute to Navajo Code Talkers, *a sculpture by Doug Hyde, was dedicated March 2, 1989 in Phoenix, Arizona. Photograph by Karen Warth.*

Navajo Code

A	Wol-la-chee	Ant
B	Shush	Bear
C	Moasi	Cat
D	Be	Deer
E	Dzeh	Elk
F	Ma-e	Fox
G	Klizzie	Goat
H	Lin	Horse
I	Tkin	Ice
J	Tkele-cho-gi	Jackass
K	Klizzie-yazzie	Kid
L	Dibeh-yazzie	Lamb
M	Na-as-tso-si	Mouse
N	Nesh-chee	Nut
O	Ne-ahs-jah	Owl
P	Bi-sodih	Pig
Q	Ca-yeilth	Quiver
R	Gah	Rabbit
S	Dibeh	Sheep
T	Than-zie	Turkey
U	No-da-ih	Ute
V	A-keh-di-glini	Victor
W	Gloe-ih	Weasel
X	Al-an-as-dzoh	Cross
Y	Tsah-as-zih	Yucca
Z	Besh-do-gliz	Zinc

"Saipan" was thus spelled: *Dibeh* ("sheep"), *Wol-la-chee* ("ant"), *Tkin* ("ice"), *Bi-sodih* ("pig"), *Wol-la-chee* ("ant"), *Nesh-chee* ("nut"). Code talkers chose alternative words for e, t, a, o, i, n, the six most frequently used letters in the English language. Instead of using "ant" for "A" to spell out a code word, they also used "apple" or "axe."

TWENTIETH-CENTURY VETERANS IN NATIVE AMERICAN LITERATURE

During the twentieth century, native people served in the U.S. armed services far exceeding their percentage of the population. Native fiction writers explore the impact and legacy of World War II and Vietnam on native people.

Joy, Harjo, Creek. "Northern Lights." Short fiction about Whirling Soldier, Vietnam veteran in *Talking Leaves: Contemporary Native American Short Stories* (1991).

Duane Niatum, Klallam. "Crow's Sun." Short fiction about young Thomas, enlisted in the navy at seventeen, who is sentenced to the brig in *Talking Leaves: Contemporary Native American Stories* (1991).

Simon Ortiz, Acoma Pueblo. "Kaiser and the War." Short fiction about "Kaiser," from one of the pueblos, who refused to join the U.S. army in *The Man to Send Rain Clouds: Contemporary Stories by American Indians* (1974).

Simon Oritz, Acoma Pueblo. *From Sand Creek* (1981). Poetry about war-shocked ex-soldiers at the Veterans Hospital on Arkansas River, Colorado.

Robert L. Perea, Oglala Lakota. "Dragon Mountain." Short fiction about army life in Vietnam in *The Remembered Earth: An Anthology of Contemporary Native American Literature* (1979).

Leslie Silko, Laguna Pueblo. *Ceremony* (1977). Novel about a World War II veteran.

AMERICAN NAVAL FIGHTING SHIPS

Distinguished native men and women and native names for tribes, villages, places, geographic features, plants, and other words from Indian languages provided hundreds of names for ocean-going tugboats, steamers, gunboats, sloop-of-wars, tankers, oilers, mine layers, monitors, patrol boats, battleships, frigates, cutters, rams, cruisers, landing ships, cargo ships, tenders, and many other kinds of naval vessels. The following ships with Indian names were drawn from the eight-volume *Dictionary of American Naval Fighting Ships*.

Battleship (BB)

Delaware VI (BB-28)—Indian tribe in United States and Canada

Illinois (BB-7)—French rendition of Algonquian word *Illini* meaning "men" or "warriors"

Indiana I (BB-1) and Indiana II (BB-58)—State named because it had been home of Indians

Iowa II (BB-4) and Iowa III (BB-61)—State named for a Siouan Indian tribe originally inhabiting the Missouri Territory

Minnesota II (BB-22)—State named for a Sioux Indian word meaning "sky-tinted water"

Missouri III (BB-11) and Missouri IV (BB-63)—State named for Missouri River, Indian name meaning "muddy waters"

Oklahoma (BB-37)—state name; in Choctaw means "red man."

Tennessee V (BB-43)—Word derived from Cherokee Indian term which referred to several Cherokee settlements

(continued)

AMERICAN NAVAL FIGHTING SHIPS (cont.)

Frigate (FR) (Patrol Boat or Frigate—PF)

Delaware I—Indian tribe in United States and Canada

Mohawk I—North American Indian tribe, part of Six Nations (Iroquois) Confederacy

Woonsocket I (PF-32)—Town that takes its name from Indian word meaning "at the place of the mist"

Coast Guard Cutter (CGC)

Modoc II (WPG-46)—Small tribe of Lutuanian Indians

Mohave II (WPG-47)—Indians of the Yuman tribe

Mohawk V (WPG-78)—North American Indian tribe, part of the Six Nations (Iroquois) Confederacy

Tahoma II (WPG-60)—Salishan Indian word meaning "snow peak"

Light Cruiser (CL)

Spokane (CL-120)—Indian tribe; word means "children of the sun"

Store Ship (AF)

Pontiac IV (AF-20)—Ottawa Indian chief

Aircraft Carrier (CV)

Ticonderoga IV (CV-14)—Iroquois Indian term meaning "between two lakes"

Schooner (Sch)

Chippewa I—Tribe living around Lake Superior

Ticonderoga I—Iroquois Indian term meaning "between two lakes"

Zaca—Probably a Chumash word meaning "village" or "chief"

Landing Ship Vehicle (LSV)

Osage II (LSV-3)—Branch of Siouan Indian tribe in Missouri

Ozark III (LSV-2)—Indian tribe of Quapaw Confederacy

Submarine or Merchant Steamship (SS)

Mingo II (SS-261)—Iroquois term of reproach applied to neighboring Indians

Moccasin II (SS-5)—Word of Algonquian origin meaning "shoe"

Attack Cargo Ship (AKA)

Ottawa II (AKA-101)—Indian tribe of southern Ontario and Michigan

Seminole IV (AKA-104)—member of the tribe of Muskogen Indians who live in Florida

Attack Transport or Animal Transport (APA)

Oneida V (APA-221)—Name originates from Six Nations (Iroquois) Indian tribe

Armored Cruiser (ACR)

Tennessee IV (ARC-10)—Word derived from a Cherokee Indian word which referred to several Cherokee settlements

Brig

Chippewa II—Tribe of Indians living around Lake Superior

APPENDIX I
Native American Tribes by State

The list of tribes shown here was compiled from several sources, the most important being the *Federal Register*, which publishes an annual list of tribes that are recognized by the federal government, and the "List of petitioners by date of initial petition" from the Bureau of Indian Affairs Branch of Acknowledgement and Research. Additional information was found in the *Atlas of North American Indian Tribes* by Carl Waldman, the *Reference Encyclopedia of the American Indian*, by Barry Klein, *The Indian Tribes of North America* by John Swanton, and the *Handbook of North American Indians*, edited by William Sturtevant. The addresses in the list are of the tribal councils and were taken from the *Tribal Leaders Directory* from the Division of Tribal Government Services of the BIA, and from the sources cited above.

The BIA's Branch of Acknowledgement and Research was created in 1978 to standardize criteria for establishing that an American Indian group exists as an Indian tribe. In 1978, there were forty petitioners for acknowledgement on hand. Since then, ninety-two new groups have petitioned.

A group may seek acknowledgement or recognition for several reasons; acknowledgement by the federal government instills a sense of identity and pride. It allows for a government to government relationship between the tribe and the federal government, and it usually makes a tribe eligible for government services. The services are similar to those usually provided by municipalities for their citizens such as education, health care, and fire protection. Recognition may include establishing a trust for the land and resources, which helps protect the tribal land base.

Key

(F)   = has federal recognition
(P)   = has petitioned for federal recognition
(PD) = petition for federal recognition denied
(R)   = federal recognition restored
(S)   = has state recognition
(I)   = determined ineligible to petition

ALABAMA

Cherokee

Cherokees of Jackson County, Alabama (P)
P.O. Box 41
Higdon, AL 35979

Cherokees of Southeast Alabama (P)
510 South Park Avenue
Dothan, AL 36301

Tuscola United Cherokee Tribe of Florida and
    Alabama, Inc. (P)
P.O. Box S
Geneva, FL 32732

Mowa Band of Choctaw Indians (P)

P.O. Box 268
McIntosh, AL 36553
(205) 944-2242

Creek

MaChis Lower Alabama Creek Indian Tribe (PD)
708 South John Street
New Brockton, AL 36351
(205) 894-6039

Poarch Band of Creek Indians of Alabama (F)
Route 3, Box 243-A
Atmore, AL 36502
(205) 368-9136

Principal Creek Indian Nation East of the
   Mississippi (P)
P.O. Box 201
Florala, AL 36442
(904) 834-2728

ALASKA

Ahtna, Incorporated (F)

P.O. Drawer G
Copper Center, AK 99573
Copper River Native Association
Two Athabascan Native Villages
Copper Center
Gulkana

Aleut Corporation (F)

2550 Denali Street
Anchorage, AK 99501
Aleut League

Thirteen Aleut Native Villages

Akutan	Pauloff Harbor
Atka	St. George
Belkofsky	St. Paul
False Pass	Sand Point
King Cove	Squaw Harbor
Nelson Lagoon	Unalaska
Nikolski	

Annette Island Reserve (F)

Tsimshian Tribe
Metlakatla Indian Community Council (F)
P.O. Box 8
Metlakatla, AK 99926
(907) 886-4441

Arctic Slope Regional Corporation (F)

P.O. Box 129
Barrow, AK 99723
Arctic Slope Native Association

Five Eskimo Native Villages

Anaktuvak Pass
Barrow
Kaktovik (Barter Island)
Point Hope
Wainwright

Bering Straits Native Corporation (F)

P.O. Box 1008
Nome, AK 99762
Bering Straits Native Association

Sixteen Eskimo Native Villages

Brevig Mission	Savoonga
Diomede (Inalik)	Shaktoolik
Elim	Shishmaref
Gambell	Stebbins
Glovin	Teller
Koyuk	Unalakleet
Nome	Wales
St. Michael	White Mountain

Bristol Bay Native Corporation (F)

P.O. Box 189
Dillingam, AK 99576
Bristol Bay Native Association

Twenty-four Eskimo and Aleut Native Villages

Chignik	Clark's Point
Chignik Lagoon	Dillingham
Chignik Lake	Egegik

Ekuk
Ekwok
Igiugig
Ivanof Bay
Koliganek
Lake Aleknagik
Levelock
Manokotak
Newhalen
New Stuyahok

Nondalton
Pedro Bay
Perryville
Pilot Point
Port Heiden
  (Meshik)
South Naknek
Togiak
Twin Hills

Calista Corporation (F)

516 Denali Street
Anchorage, AK 99501
Yupiktak Bista Association

Forty-four Eskimo and Athabascan Native Villages

Akiachak
Akiak
Akolmuit
  (Nunapitchuk
  and Kasigluk)
Alakanuk
Artiak
Bethel
Chefornak
Chevak
Crooked Creek
Eek
Emmonak
Goodnews Bay
Holy Cross
Hooper Bay
Kipnuk
Kongiganak
Kotlik
Kwethluk
Kwigillingok
Kwinhagek
  (Quinhagek)
Lime Village
Lower Kalskag
Marshall
  (Fortuna Ledge)

Mekoryuk
Mountain Village
Napakiak
Napaskiak
Newtok
Nightmute
  (Nightmuit)
Oscarville
Pilot Station
Pitkas Point
Platinum
Russian Mission
  (Yukon)
St. Mary's
Scammon Bay
Sheldon's Point
Steetmute
Stony River
Tanunak
Toksook Bay
Tuluksak
Tuntutuliak
Upper Kalskag
  (Kalskag)

Chugach Natives, Inc. (F)

903 Northern Lights Boulevard
Fairbanks, AK 99501
Chugach Native Association

Four Aleut and Athabascan Native Villages

English Bay
Port Graham
Seldovia (Indian Possessions)
Tatilek

Cook Inlet Region, Inc. (F)

2525 C Street
Anchorage, AK 99503
Cook Inlet Native Association

Three Athabascan Native Villages

Eklutna
Ninilchik
Tyonek

Doyon, Limited (F)

Doyon Building
201 First Avenue
Fairbanks, AK 99701
Tanana Chiefs Conference

Thirty-two Athabascan and Eskimo Native Villages

Alatna
Allakaket
Anvik
Arctic Village
Beaver
Cantwell
Chalkyitsik
Circle
Dot Lake
Eagle Village
  (Eagle)
Fort Yukon
Galena
Grayling
Hughes
Huslia
Kaltag
Koyukuk

McGrath
  (McGrath Native Village)
Mentasta Lake
  (Mentasta)
Minto
Nenana Addition
  (Nenana)
Nikolai
Northway
Nulato
Rampart
Ruby
Shageluk
  Stevens Village
Tanacross
Tanana
Tetlin
Venetie

Koniag, Inc. (F)

P.O. Box 746
Kodiak, AK 99615
Kokiak Area Native Association

Seven Aleut Native Villages

Akhiok   Old Harbor
Karluk   Ouzinkie
Kodiak   Port Lions
Larsen Bay

NANA Regional Corporation (F)

P.O. Box 49
Kotzebue, AK 99752
Northwest Alaska Native Association

Ten Eskimo Native Villages

Ambler   Kotzebue
Buckland   Noatak
Deering   Noorvik
Kiana   Selawik
Kivalina   Shungnak

Sealaska Corporation (F)

1 Sealaska Plaza, Suite 400
Juneau, AK 99801
Tlingit-Haida Central Council

Eleven Tlingit and Haida Native Villages

Angoon   Kake
Craig   Klawok
Hoonah   Klukwan
Hydaburg   Saxman
Juneau (Juneau   Sitka Village
   Indian Village)   Yakutat

Thirteenth Regional Corporation (F)

4241 21st West
Seattle, WA 95109

Tsimshian Tribal Council (P)

1067B Woodland Avenue
Ketchikan, AK 99901
(907) 225-2961

ARIZONA

Apache

San Carlos Apache Tribe of the San Carlos
   Reservation *(F)*
San Carlos Tribal Council
P.O. Box 0
San Carlos, AZ 85550
(602) 475-2361

Tonto Apache Tribe of Arizona (F)
Tonto Apache Tribal Council
Tonto Reservation #30
Payson, AZ 85541
(602) 474-5000

White Mountain Apache Tribe of the Fort Apache
   Reservation *(F)*
White Mountain Apache Tribal Council
P.O. Box 700
Whitewater, AZ 85941
(602) 338-4346

Cocopah Tribe of Arizona (F)

Cocopah Tribal Council
Box 9C
Somerton, AZ 85350
(602) 627-2102

Havasupai Tribe of the Havasupai Reservation (F)

Havasupai Tribal Council
P.O. Box 10
Supai, AZ 86435
(602) 448-2961

Hopi Tribe of Arizona (F)

Hopi Tribal Council
P.O. Box 123
Kykotsmovi, AZ 86039
(602) 734-2445

Hualapai Tribe of the Hualapai Indian Reservation (F)

Hualapai Tribal Council
P.O. Box 168
Peach Springs, AZ 86434
(602) 769-2216

Colorado River Indian Tribes of the Colorado River Indian Reservation, Arizona and California (F)
(Mohave and Chemehuevi)

Colorado River Tribal Council
Route 1, Box 23-B
Parker, AZ 85344
(602) 669-9211

Fort McDowell Mohave-Apache Indian Community of the Fort McDowell Indian Reservation (F), *(Mohave, Apache, and Yavapai)*

Mohave-Apache Community Council
P.O. Box 17779
Fountain Hills, AZ 85268
(602) 990-0995

Navajo Tribe of Arizona, New Mexico, and Utah (F)

Navajo Tribal Council
P.O. Box 308
Window Rock, AZ 86515
(602) 871-4941

Paiute

Kaibab Band of Paiute Indians of the Kaibab Indian Reservation (F)
Kaibab Paiute Tribal Council
Tribal Affairs Building
HC 65, Box 2
Fredonia, AZ 86022
(602) 643-7245

San Juan Southern Paiute (P)
P.O. Box 2656
Tuba City, AZ 86045
(602) 526-7143

Pima-Maricopa

Gila River Pima-Maricopa Indian Community of the Gila River Indian Reservation of Arizona (F)
P.O. Box 97
Sacaton, AZ 85247
(602) 562-3311

Salt River Pima-Maricopa Indian Community of the Salt River Reservation (F)
Salt River Pima-Maricopa Indian Community Council
Route 1, Box 216
Scottsdale, AZ 85256
(602) 941-7277

Quechan Tribe of the Fort Yuma Indian Reservation (F)

Quechan Tribal Council
P.O. Box 11352
Yuma, AZ 85364

Tohono O'odham (Papago)

Ak Chin Indian Community of Papago Indians of the Maricopa, AK Chin Reservation (F)
Ak Chin Indian Community Council
Route 2, Box 27
Maricopa, AZ 85239
(602) 568-2227

Tohono O'odham Nation of Arizona (F) (Formerly known as the Papago Tribe of the Sells, Gila Bend, & San Xavier Reservation)
Tohono O'odham Council
P.O. Box 837
Sells, AZ 85634
(602) 383-2221

Pascua Yaqui Tribe of Arizona (F)

Pascua Yaqui Tribal Council
7474 South Camino De Oesta
Tucson, AZ 85746
(602) 883-2838

Yavapai-Apache Indian Community of the Camp Verde Reservation (F)

Yavapai-Apache Community Council
P.O. Box 1188
Camp Verde, AZ 86301
(602) 445-8790

Yavapai-Prescott Tribe of the Yavapai Reservation (F)

Yavapai-Prescott Board of Directors
P.O. Box 348
Prescott, AZ 86301
(602) 445-8790

ARKANSAS

Chicamauga Cherokee of Arkansas and Missouri (P)

217 Forest Lane
Republic, MO 65738
Arkansas number: (501) 856-2772

Revived Ouachita Indians of Arkansas and America (P)

P.O. Box 34
Story, AR 71970

CALIFORNIA

Berry Creek Rancheria (F)

1779 Mitchell Avenue
Oroville, CA 95965
(916) 534-3859

Blue Lake Rancheria of California (F)

P.O. Box 428
Blue Lake, CA 95525
(707) 668-5005

Cahto Indian Tribe of Laytonville Rancheria (F)

P.O. Box 1239
Laytonville, CA 95454
(707) 984-6197

Cahuilla

Agua Caliente Band of Cahuilla Indians of the Agua Caliente Indian Reservation (F)
Agua Caliente Tribal Council
960 East Tahquitz Way, #106
Palm Springs, CA 92262
(619) 325-5673 or -7685

Augustine Band of Cahuilla Mission Indians of the Augustine Reservation (F)
Thermal, CA 92274

Cabazon Band of Cahuilla Mission Indians of the Cabazon Reservation (F)
84-245 Indio Spring Drive
Indio, CA 92201
(619) 342-2593

Cahuilla Band of Mission Indians of the Cahuilla Reservation (F)
P.O. Box 860
Anza, CA 92306
(714) 763-5549 or (619) 926-3319

Los Coyotes Band of Cahuilla Mission Indians of the Los Coyotes Reservation (F)
P.O. Box 249
Warner Springs, CA 92086
(619) 782-3269

Morongo Band of Cahuilla Mission Indians of the Morongo Reservation (F)
11581 Potrero Road
Banning, CA 92220
(714) 849-4697 or -4698

Ramona Band or Village of Cahuilla Mission Indians of California (F)
P.O. Box 26
Anza, CA 92306

Santa Rosa Band of Cahuilla Mission Indians of the Santa Rosa Reservation (F)
325 North Western
Hemet, CA 92343

Santa Rosa Indian Community of the Santa Rosa
  Rancheria (F)
16835 Alkali Drive
Lemoore, CA 93245
(209) 924-1278

Torres-Martinez Band of Cahuilla Mission Indians of
  California (F)
66-725 Martinez Road
Thermal, CA 92274
(619) 397-0300

Costanoan of Carmel Mission Indians (P)
P.O. Box 1657
Monrovia, CA 91016

*Chemehuevi Indian Tribe of the Chemuhuevi
Reservation (F)*
Chemehuevi Tribal Council
P.O. Box 1976
Chemehuevi Valley, CA 92363
(619) 858-4531

Choinumni Tribe (P)
Choinumni Council
2428 South Cedar Avenue
Fresno, CA 93725

Indian Canyon Band of Costanoan/Mutsun Indians
  of California (P)
P.O. Box 48
Hollister, CA 95024

Chukchansi
Picayune Rancheria of Chukchansi Indians of
  California (F)
P.O. Box 708
Coarsegold, CA 93614
(209) 683-6633

Chukchansi Yokotch Tribe (P)
P.O. Box 329
Coarsegold, CA 93653
(209) 689-3318

Chumash
Coastal Band of Chumash Indians (P)
c/o Santa Barbara Urban Indian Health
610 Del Monte Avenue
Santa Barbara, CA 93101
(805) 965-0718

Santa Ynez Band of Chumash Mission Indians of the
  Santa Ysabel Reservation (F)
P.O. Box 517
Santa Ynez, CA 93460
(805) 688-7997

*Covelo Indian Community of the Round Valley
Reservation (F) (Yuki, Pit River, Little Lake, Konkau,
Wailaki, Pomo, Nom-Laka, and Wintun Tribes)*
Covelo Indian Community Council
P.O. Box 448
Covelo, CA 95428
(707) 983-6126

Diegueño
Barona Group of the Barona Reservation,
  California (F)
Barona General Business
1095 Barona Road
Lakeside, CA 92040
(619) 443-6612 or -6613

Capitan Grande Band of Diegueño Mission Indians
  of California (F)
Alpine, CA 92001

Campo Band of Diegueño Mission Indians of the
  Campo Indian Reservation (F)
1779 Campo Truck Trail
Campo, CA 92006
(619) 478-9046

Cuyapaipe Community of Diegueño Mission Indians
  of the Cuyapaipe Reservation (F)
4390 La Posta Trucktrail
Pine Valley, CA 92062
(619) 478-5289

Inaja Band of Deigueño Mission Indians of the Inaja
and Cosmit Reservation (F)
739 A Street, Apt. 9
Ramona, CA 92065
(619) 789-0381

La Posta Band of Diegueño Mission Indians of the La
Posta Indian Reservation (F)
1064 Barona Road
Lakeside, CA 92040
(619) 782-9294

Manzanita Band of Diegueño Mission Indians of the
Manzanita Reservation (F)
P.O. Box 1302
Boulevard, CA 92005
(619) 766-4930

Mesa Grande Band of Diegueño Mission Indians of
the Mesa Grande Reservation (F)
P.O. Box 270
Santa Ysabel, CA 92070
(619) 782-3835

Santa Ysabel Band of Diegueño Mission Indians of
the Santa Ysabel Reservation (F)
P.O. Box 130
Santa Ysabel, CA 92070
(619) 765-0845

Sycuan Band of Diegueño Mission Indians of
California (F)
5459 Dehesa Road
El Cajon, CA 92021
(619) 445-2613

Viejas Group of the Viejas Reservation (F)
P.O. Box 908
Alpine, CA 92001
(619) 445-3810

Hoopa Valley Tribe of the Hoopa Valley Reservation (F)
Hoopa Valley Indian Rancheria
P.O. Box 1348
Hoopa, CA 95546
(916) 625-4211

Kern Valley Indian Community (P)
P.O. Bin DD
Kernville, CA 93238
(609) 376-3761

Jamul Indian Village of California (F)
P.O. Box 612
Jamul, CA 92035
(619) 669-0301

Karok

Karok Tribe of California (F)
P.O. Box 1016
Happy Camp, CA 96039
(916) 493-5305

Quartz Valley Rancheria of Karok, Shasta & Upper
Klamath Indians of California (F)
P.O. Box 94
Etna, CA 96027
(916) 467-3307 or -5407

Luiseño

La Jolla Band of Luiseño Mission Indians of the La
Jolla Reservation (F)
Star Route, Box 158
Valley Center, CA 92082
(619) 742-3771

Pala Band of Luiseño Mission Indians of the Pala
Reservation (F)
P.O. Box 43
Pala, CA 92059
(619) 742-3784

Pauma Band of Luiseño Mission Indians of the
Pauma and Yuima Reservation (F)
P.O. Box 86
Pauma Valley, CA 92061
(619) 742-1289

Pechanga Band of Luiseño Mission Indians of the
Pechanga Reservation (F)
P.O. Box 1477
Temecula, CA 92390
(714) 676-2768

Rincon Band of Luiseño Mission Indians of the
Rincon Reservation (F)
P.O. Box 68
Valley Center, CA 92082
(619) 749-1051

Soboba Band of Luiseño Mission Indians of the
Soboba Reservation (F)
P.O. Box 487
San Jacinto, CA 92383
(714) 654-2765

Twenty-Nine Palms Band of Luiseño Mission Indians
of California (F)
1150 East Palm Canyon Drive, #75
Palm Springs, CA 92262

United Lumbee Nation of North Carolina and America
(PD)
P.O. Box 911
Exeter, CA 93221

Maidu

Enterprise Rancheria of Maidu Indian of
California (F)
Oroville, CA 95965

Greenville Rancheria of Maidu Indians of
California (F)
P.O. Box 237
Greenville, CA 95947
(916) 284-6446

Mooretown Rancheria of Maidu Indians of
California (F)
1900 Oro Dam Boulevard, #8
Oroville, CA 95965
(916) 533-3625

Susanville Indian Rancheria of Paiute, Maidu, Pit
River & Washoe Indians of California (F)
P.O. Drawer U
Susanville, CA 96130
(916) 257-6264

Rohnerville Rancheria of Bear River or Mattole Indians
of California (F)
P.O. Box 108
Eureka, CA 95502
(707) 442-3931

Me-Wuk (also spelled Miwok)

Buena Vista Rancheria of Me-Wuk Indians of
California (F)
4650 Calmine Road
Ione, CA 95640

Chicken Ranch Rancheria of Me-Wuk Indians of
California *(F)*
P.O. Box 1699
Jamestown, CA 95237
(209) 984-3057

Ione Band of Miwok Indians (P)
Route 1, Box 191
Ione, CA 95649
(916) 274-2559

Jackson Rancheria of Me-Wuk Indians of
California (F)
1600 Bingo Way
Jackson, CA 95642
(209) 223-3931

Sheep Ranch Rancheria of Me-Wuk Indians of
California (F)
Sheep Ranch, CA 95250

Shingle Springs Band of Miwok Indians, Shingle
Springs Rancheria (Verona Tract) (F)
P.O. Box 1340
Shingle Springs, CA 95682
(619) 676-8010

Tuolumne Band of Me-Wuk Indians of the
Tuolumne Rancheria of California (F)
P.O. Box 696
Tuolumne, CA 95379
(209) 928-4277

Mission

Juaneno Band of Mission Indians (P)
31742 Via Belardes
San Juan Capistrano, CA 92675
(714) 493-4933

San Luis Rey Band of Mission Indians (P)
c/o Mission Indian Bands Paralegal Consortium
360 North Midway, Suite 301
Escondido, CA 92027
(619) 741-5211

Mohave Tribe (F)

Fort Mohave Tribal Council
500 Merriman Avenue
Needles, CA 92363
(619) 326-4591

Colorado River Indian Tribes of the Colorado River Indian Reservation, Arizona and California (F)
(Mohave and Chemehuevi)

Colorado River Tribal Council
Route 1, Box 23-B
Parker, AZ 85344
(602) 669-9211

Mono

Big Sandy Rancheria of Mono Indians of
   California (F)
P.O. Box 337
Auberry, CA 93602
(209) 855-4003

Cold Springs Rancheria of Mono Indians of
   California (F)
P.O. Box 209
Tollhouse, CA 93667
(209) 855-2326

Dunlap Band of Mono Indians (P)
P.O. Box 126
Dunlap, CA 93621
(209) 338-2842

Mono Lake Indian Community (P)
P.O. Box 237
Lee Vining, CA 93541

Northfolk Rancheria of Mono Indians of
   California (F)
3027 Clement Street, #2
San Francisco, CA 94121

North Fork Band of Mono Indians (P)
P.O. Box 49
North Fork, CA 93643
(209) 299-3729

Ohlone/Costanoan

Amah Band of Ohlone/Costanoan Indians (P)
789 Canada Road
Woodside, CA 94062

Ohlone/Costanoan Mukwekma Tribe (P)
31 Fountain Valley, Suite 2B
San Jose, CA 95113

Paiute

Bridgeport Paiute Indian Colony of California (F)
P.O. Box 37
(619) 932-7083

Cedarville Rancheria of Northern Paiute Indians of
   California (F)
P.O. Box 142
Cedarville, CA 96104

Fort Bidwell Indian Community of Paiute Indians of
   the Fort Bidwell Reservation (F)
Fort Bidwell Community Council
P.O. Box 127
Fort Bidwell, CA 96112
(916) 279-6310

Fort Independence Indian Community of Paiute Indians of the Fort Independence Reservation (F)
P.O. Box 67
Independence, CA 93526
(619) 878-2126

Susanville Indian Rancheria of Paiute, Maidu, Pit
River & Washoe Indians of California (F)
P.O. Drawer U
Susanville, CA 96130
(916) 257-6264

Utu Utu Gwaitu Paiute Tribe of the Benton Paiute
Reservation (F)
Star Route 4, Box 56-A
Benton, CA 93512
(619) 933-2321

Paiute-Shoshone

Big Pine Band of Owens Valley Paiute and Shoshone
Indians of the Big Pine Reservation, California (F)
P.O. Box 700
Big Pine, CA 93513
(619) 938-2121

Paiute-Shoshone Indians of the Bishop Community
of the Bishop Colony (F)
Bishop Indian Tribal Council
P.O. Box 548
Bishop, CA 93514
(619) 873-3584

Paiute-Shoshone Indians of the Lone Pine Community of the Lone Pine Reservation (F)
Star Route 1-1101, South Main Street
Lone Pine, CA 93545
(619) 876-5414

Pit River (Achomawi)

Alturas Rancheria of Pit River Indians of
California (F)
P.O. Box 1035
Alturas, CA 96101

Antelope Valley Paiute Tribe (P)
P.O. Box 119
Coleville, CA 96107
(916) 266-3126

Susanville Indian Rancheria of Paiute, Maidu, Pit
River & Washoe Indians of California (F)
P.O. Drawer U
Susanville, CA 96130
(916) 257-6264

Pit River Tribe of California (including Big Bend,
Lookout, Montgomery Creek and Roaring Creek
Rancheries and XL Ranch) (F)
Pit River Tribal Council
P.O. Drawer 1570
Burney, CA 96013
(916) 335-5421

Pomo

Cloverdale Rancheria of Pomo Indians of
California (F)
285 Santana Drive
Cloverdale, CA 95424
(707) 894-5773

Coyote Valley Band of Pomo Indians of California (F)
P.O. Box 39
Redwood Valley, CA 95470
(707) 485-8723

Dry Creek Rancheria of Pomo Indians of
California (F)
P.O. Box 607
Geyserville, CA 95441
(707) 431-8232

Elem Indian Colony of Pomo Indians (F)
Sulphur Bank Rancheria
P.O. Box 618
Clearlake Oaks, CA 95423
(707) 998-3314

Hopland Band of Pomo Indians of the Hopland
Rancheria (F)
P.O. Box 610
Hopland, CA 95449
(707) 744-1647

Kashia Band of Pomo Indians of the Stewarts Point
  Rancheria (F)
P.O. Box 54
Stewarts Point, CA 95480
(707) 784-2594

Manchester Band of Pomo Indians of the Manchester-
  Point Arena Rancheria (F)
P.O. Box 623
Point Arena, CA 95468
(707) 882-2788

Middletown Rancheria of Pomo Indians of
  California (F)
P.O. Box 292
Middletown, CA 95461

Pinoleville Rancheria of Pomo Indians of
  California (F)
367 North State Street, Suite 2-4
Ukiah, CA 95482
(707) 463-1454

Potter Valley Rancheria of Pomo Indians of
  California (F)
P.O. Box 94
Potter Valley, CA 95469
(707) 743-1649

Redding Rancheria of Pomo Indians of California (F)
1786 California Street
Redding, CA 96001
(916) 241-1871

Redwood Valley Rancheria of Pomo Indians of
  California (F)
P.O. Box 499
Redwood Valley, CA 95470
(707) 485-0361

Robinson Rancheria of Pomo Indians of
  California (F)
P.O. Box 1119
Nice, CA 95464
(707) 275-0527

Sherwood Valley Rancheria of Pomo Indians of
  California (F)
2141 South State Street
Ukiah, CA 95482
(707) 468-1337

Upper Lake Band of Pomo Indians of Upper Lake
  Rancheria of California (F)
P.O. Box 20272
Sacramento, CA 95820
(916) 371-2576

*Big Valley Rancheria of Pomo and Pit River Indians of
California (F)*
P.O. Box 153
Finley, CA 95435

Salinan Nation (P)
P.O. Box 610546
San Jose, CA 95161

*San Manual Band of Serrano Mission Indians of the
San Manual Reservation (F)*
5438 North Victoria Avenue
Highland, CA 92346
(714) 862-8509

San Pasqual General Council (F)
P.O. Box 365
Valley Center, CA 92082
(619) 749-3200

Shasta
Shasta Nation (P)
P.O. Box 1054
Yreka, CA 96097
(916) 842-5654

Quartz Valley Rancheria of Karok, Shasta & Upper
  Klamath Indians of California (F)
P.O. Box 94
Etna, CA 96027
(916) 467-3307 or -5407

Death Valley Timbi-Sha Shoshone Band of California (F)

P.O. Box 206
Death Valley, CA 95682
(619) 676-8010

Smith River

Big Lagoon Rancheria of Smith River Indians of California (F)
P.O. Drawer 3060
Trinidad, CA 95570
(707) 826-2079

Smith River Rancheria of California (F)
P.O. Box 239
Smith River, CA 95567
(707) 487-9255

Table Mountain Rancheria (F)

P.O. Box 243
Friant, CA 93626
(209) 822-2125

Tolowa

Elk Valley Rancheria of Smith River Tolowa Indians of California (F)
P.O. Box 1042
Crescent City, CA 95531
(707) 464-4680

Tolowa Nation (P)
P.O. Box 131
Fort Dick, CA 95538
(707) 464-2259

Cher-Ae Heights Indian Community of the Trinidad Rancheria (F)

P.O. Box 630
Trinidad, CA 96112
(707) 677-0211

Tule River Indian Tribe of the Tule River Reservation (F)

P.O. Box 589
Porterville, CA 93258
(209) 781-4271

Quartz Valley Rancheria of Karok, Shasta & Upper Klamath Indians of California (F)
P.O. Box 94
Etna, CA 96027
(916) 467-3307 or -5407

Washoe

Washoe Tribe of Nevada and California (F) (Carson Colony, Dresslerville & Washoe Ranches)
Woodfords Community Council
Route 1, Markleeville, CA 96120
(916) 694-2170

Susanville Indian Rancheria of Paiute, Maidu, Pit River & Washoe Indians of California (F)
Susanville Rancheria
P.O. Drawer U
Susanville, CA 96130

Wintun

Cachil DeHe Band of Wintun Indians of the Colusa Indian Community of the Colusa Rancheria (F)
P.O. Box 8
Colusa, CA 95932
(916) 458-8231

Cortina Indian Rancheria of Wintun Indians of California (F)
P.O. Box 41113
Sacramento, CA 95841
(916) 726-7118

Grindstone Indian Rancheria of Wintun-Wailaki Indians of California (F)
P.O. Box 63
Elk Creek, CA 95939
(916) 968-5116

Hayfork Band of Nor-El-Muk Wintu Indians (P) (also known as Nor-E-Muk Band of Wintu Indians of Northern California)
P.O. Box 673
Hayfork, CA 96041
(916) 628-5175

Rumsey Indian Rancheria of Wintun Indians of
    California (F)
P.O. Box 18
Brooks, CA 95606
(916) 796-3400

Wintoon Indians (P)
c/o Wintu Education & Cultural Council
8450 Riverland Drive, Unit 42
Redding, CA 96002
(916) 365-9063

Wintu Indians of Central Valley, California (P)
P.O. Box 835
Central Valley, CA 96109
(916) 223-4262

Table Bluff Rancheria of California (F) (Wiyot)
P.O. Box 519
Loleta, CA 95551
(707) 733-5583

Wukchumni Council (P)
1420 North Encino Street
Visalia, CA 93291
(209) 625-2449

Yokayo Tribe of Indians (P)
1114 Helen Avenue
Ukiah, CA 94518
(707) 462-4074

Yurok
Coast Indian Community of Yurok Indians of the
    Resighini Rancheria (F)
P.O. Box 529
Klamath, CA 95548
(707) 482-2431

Yurok Indian Tribe
Yurok Indians Reservation
c/o Klamath Field Office
P.O. Box 789
Klamath, CA 95548

Big Lagoon Rancheria (F) (Yurok and Tolowa)
P.O. Box 3060
Trinidad, CA 95570
(707) 826-2079

*American Indian Council of Mariposa County (also
known as Yosemite)* (P)
P.O. Box 1200
Mariposa, CA 95338
(209) 966-3918

COLORADO

Munsee Thames River Delaware (P)
P.O. Box 587 / 601 Manitou Avenue
Manitou Springs, CO 80911

Ute
Southern Ute Indian Tribe of the Southern Ute
    Reservation (F)
Southern Ute Tribal Council
P.O. Box 737
Ignacio, CO 81137
(303) 563-4525

Ute Mountain Tribe of the Ute Mountain Reserva-
    tion, Colorado, New Mexico, Utah (F)
Ute Mountain Ute Tribal Council
General Delivery
Towaoc, CO 81344
(303) 565-3751

CONNECTICUT

*The Mohegan Tribe of Indians of the State of
Connecticut* (P)
1841 Norwich, New London Turnpike
Uncasville, CT 06382
(203) 527-5216

Golden Hill Paugusset Tribe (P)
Box 126
Trumbull, CT 06611
(203) 377-4410

Golden Hill Pequot and Mohegan Tribes (S)
Trumbull, CT 06611

Pequot

Paucatuck Eastern Pequot Indians of
  Connecticut (P) (S)
939 Lantern Hill Road
Ledyard, CT 06339
(203) 445-8521

Mashantucket Pequot Tribe of Connecticut (F)
Mashantucket Pequot Tribal Council
P.O. Box 160
Ledyard, CT 06339
(203) 536-2681

Schaghticoke Indian Tribe (P)
626 Washington Road
Woodbury, CT 06798

DELAWARE

Nanticoke Indian Association (P)
Route 4, Box 107-A
Millsboro, DE 19966
(302) 945-3400

FLORIDA

*Tuscola United Cherokee Tribe of Florida and
Alabama, Inc. (P)*
P.O. Box S
Geneva, FL 32732

Creek

Florida Tribe of Eastern Creek Indians (P)
P.O. Box 28
Bruce, FL 32455
(904) 835-2078

Creeks East of the Mississippi (PD)
P.O. Box 123
Molino, FL 32577
(904) 587-2116

Miccosukee Tribe of Indians of Florida (F)
Miccosukee Business Committee
P.O. Box 440021, Tamiami Station
Miami, FL 33144
(305) 223-8380

Seminole

Oklewaha Band of Seminole Indians (P)
P.O. Box 521
Orange Springs, FL 32682
(904) 546-1386

Seminole Nation of Florida (P)
c/o Indian Law Resource Center
601 E Street Southeast
Washington, D.C. 20003
(202) 547-2800

Seminole Tribe of Florida, Dania, Big Cypress &
  Brighton Reservations (F)
Seminole Tribal Council
6073 Stirling Road
Hollywood, FL 33024
(305) 583-7112

GEORGIA

Cherokee

Cane Break Band of Eastern Cherokees (P)
Route 3, Box 750
Dahlonega, GA 30533
(404) 864-6010

Cherokee Indians of Georgia, Inc. (P)
1516 14th Avenue
Columbus, GA 31901
(404) 327-3914

Georgia Tribe of Eastern Cherokees, Inc. (P)
P.O. Box 993
Dahlonega, GA 30533
(404) 864-3805

Southeastern Cherokee Confederacy, Inc. (PD)
Route 1, Box 111
Leesburg, GA 31763
(912) 436-9040

*Lower Muskogee Creek Tribe—East of the Mississippi,
Inc. (PD)*
Route 1, Tama Reservation
Cairo, GA 31728
(904) 736-1935

IDAHO

*Coeur D'Alene Tribe of the Coeur D'Alene
Reservation (F)*
Coeur D'Alene Tribal Council
Plummer, ID 83851

Delawares of Idaho, Inc. (P)
3677 North Maple Grove Road
Boise, ID 83704
(208) 377-1984

Kootenai Tribe of Idaho (F)
Kootenai Tribal Council
P.O. Box 1269
Bonners Ferry, ID 83805
(208) 267-3519

Nez Perće Tribe of Idaho (F)
Nez Percé Executive Committee
P.O. Box 305
Lapwai, ID 83540
(208) 843-2253

*Shoshone-Bannock Tribes of the Fort Hall Reservation of
Idaho (F)*
Fort Hall Business Council
P.O. Box 306
Fort Hall, ID 83203
(208) 238-3700

INDIANA

*Miami Nation of Indians of the State of Indiana,
Inc. (P)*
P.O. Box 41
Peru, IN 46970
(317) 473-9631

IOWA

Sac & Fox Tribe of the Mississippi in Iowa (F)
Sac & Fox Tribal Council
Route 2, Box 56C
Tama, IA 52339
(515) 484-4678

KANSAS

Delaware-Muncie (P)
Box 274
Pomona, KS 66076

Iowa Tribe of Kansas and Nebraska (F)
Executive Committee
Route 1, Box 58A
White Cloud, KS 66094
(913) 595-3258

*Kickapoo Tribe of Indians of the Kickapoo Reservation in
Kansas (F)*
Tribal Council
Route 1, Box 157A
Horton, KS 66439
(913) 486-2131

Prairie Band of Potawatomi Indians of Kansas (F)

Tribal Council
Route 2, Box 50A
Mayetta, KS 66509
(913) 966-2255 or -2771

Sac & Fox Tribe of Missouri in Kansas and Nebraska (F)

Tribal Council
P.O. Box 38
Reserve, KS 66434
(913) 742-7471

LOUISIANA

Choctaw

Choctaw-Apache Community of Ebarb (P)
Route 1, Box 347
Zwolle, LA 71486
(318) 645-4103

Clifton-Choctaw Indians (P)
P.O. Box 32
Gardner, LA 71431
(318) 793-8796

Jena Band of Choctaws (P)
P.O. Box 14
Jena, LA 71342
(318) 992-2717

Chitimacha Tribe of Louisiana (F)

Chitimacha Tribal Council
P.O. Box 661
Charenton, LA 70523
(318) 923-4973

Coushatta Tribe of Louisiana (F)

Coushatta Tribal Council
P.O. Box 818
Elton, LA 70532
(318) 923-4973

United Houma Nation, Inc. (P)

Star Route, Box 95-A
Golden Meadow, LA 70357
(504) 475-6640

Tunica-Biloxi Indian Tribe of Louisiana (F)

P.O. Box 311
Mansura, LA 71351
(318) 253-9767

MAINE

Houlton Band of Maliseet Indians of Maine (F)

Houlton Maliseet Band Council
P.O. Box 576
Houlton, ME 04730
(207) 532-4273

Aroostook Band of Micmacs (P)

8 Church Street / P.O. Box 844
Presque Isle, ME 04769
(207) 622-4731

Passamaquoddy Tribe of Maine (F)

Indian Township Passamaquoddy Reservation
P.O. Box 301
Princeton, ME 04668
(207) 796-2301

Pleasant Point Passamaquoddy Reservation
P.O. Box 343
Perry, ME 04667
(207) 853-2551

Penobscot Tribe of Maine (F)

Community Building
Indian Island
Old Town, ME 04468
(207) 827-7776

MARYLAND

Piscataway-Conoy Confederacy and Sub-Tribes, Inc. (P)
P.O. Box 48
Indian Head, MD 20640

MASSACHUSETTS

Nipmuc
Hassanamisco-Nipmuc Tribe (S)
Grafton, MA 01519

Nipmuc Tribe of Massachusetts
  (Chaubunagungamaug Band) (P)
Nipmuc Tribal Council
117 Garden City
Dudley, MA 01570
(617) 943-4569

Nipmuc Tribe of Massachusetts (Hassanamisco
  Band) (P)
Nipmuc Tribal Council
2 Longfellow Road
Northborough, MA 01532

Wampanoag
Gay Head Wampanoag Indians of Massachusetts (F)
Wampanoag Tribal Council of Gay Head, Inc.
State Road
Gay Head, MA 02535
(617) 645-9265

Mashpee Wampanoag (P)
Route 130
Mashpee, MA 02649
(617) 477-1825

MICHIGAN

Chippewa
Bay Mills Indian Community of the Sault Ste. Marie
  Band of Chippewa Indians, Bay Mills Reservation
  (F)
Bay Mills Executive Council
Route 1
Brimley, MI 49715
(906) 248-3241

Keweenaw Bay Indian Community of L'Anse and
  Ontonagon Bands of Chippewa
Indians of the L'Anse Reservation (F)
Keweenaw Bay Tribal Council
Center Building
Route 1, Box 45
Baraga, MI 49908
(906) 353-6623

Lac Vieux Desert Band of Lake Superior Chippewa
  Indians of Michigan (F)
P.O. Box 446
Watersmeet, MI 49969
(906) 358-4722

Lake Superior Chippewa of Marquette, Inc. (P)
P.O. Box 1071
Marquette, MI 49855

Saginaw Chippewa Indian Tribe of Michigan,
  Isabella Reservation (F)
Saginaw Chippewa Tribal Council
7070 East Broadway Road
Mt. Pleasant, MI 48858
(517) 772-5700

Sault Ste. Marie Tribe of Chippewa Indians of
  Michigan (F)
Sault Ste. Marie Chippewa Tribal Council
206 Greenough Street
Sault Ste. Marie, MI 49783
(906) 635-6050

Consolidated Bahwetig Ojibwas and Mackinac Tribe (P)
P.O. Box 697
Sault St. Marie, MI 49783
(906) 635-9521

Little River Band of Ottawa Indians (P)
238 Parkdale Avenue
Manistee, MI 49660

Ottawa and Chippewa

Burt Lake Band of Ottawa and Chippewa Indians, Inc. (P)
4371 Indian Road
Brutus, MI 49716

Grand Traverse Band of Ottawa and Chippewa Indians of Michigan (F)
Route 1, Box 135
Suttons Bay, MI 49682
(616) 271-3538

Potawatomi

Hannahville Indian Community of Wisconsin Potawatomi Indians of Michigan (F)
Hannahville Indian Community Council
Hannahville Route 1, Road N14910
Wilson, MI 49896
(906) 466-2342

Huron Potawatomi Band (aka Nottawaseppi Band of Huron Potawatomis) (P) (S)
2221 1½ Mile Road
Fulton, MI 49052
(616) 729-5151

Pokagon Band of Potawatomi Indians (P)
53237 Town Hall Road
Dowagiac, MI 49057
(616) 782-6323

Upper Kispoko Band of the Shawnee Nation (P)
617 South Washington Street
Kokomo, IN 46901
(317) 457-5376

MINNESOTA

Chippewa

Kah-Bay-Kah-Nong (Warroad Chippewa) (P)
Box 336
Warroad, MN 56763

Minnesota Chippewa Tribal Executive Committee
Box 217
Cass Lake, MN 56633
(218) 335-2252

Minnesota Chippewa Tribe (F) (Six component reservations)
Bois Forte Band
Nett Lake Reservation Business Committee
P.O. Box 16
Nett Lake, MN 55772
(218) 757-3261

Fond du Lac Band
Fond du Lac Reservation Business Committee
150 University Road
Cloquet, MN 55720
(218) 879-4593

Grand Portage Band
Grand Portage Reservation Business Committee
P.O. Box 428
Grand Portage, MN 55605
(218) 475-2277 or -2279

Leech Lake Band
Leech Lake Reservation Business Committee
Route 3, Box 100
Cass Lake, MN 56633
(218) 335-2208

Mille Lac Band
Mille Lac Reservation Business Committee
Star Route
Onamia, MN 56359
(612) 532-4181

White Earth Band
White Earth Reservation Business Committee
P.O. Box 418
White Earth, MN 56591
(218) 983-3285

Red Lake Band of Chippewa Indians of the Red Lake
    Reservation (F)
Red Lake Tribal Council
P.O. Box 550
Red Lake, MN 56671
(218) 679-3341

Little Traverse Bay Bands of Odawa Indians (P)

P.O. Box 130
Cross Village, MI 49723
(616) 263-7141

Sioux

Lower Sioux Indian Community of Minnesota
    Mdewakanton Sioux Indians of the Lower Sioux
    Reservation in Minnesota (F)
Lower Sioux Indian Community Council
R.R. 1, Box 308
Morton, MN 56270
(507) 697-6185

Mdewakanton Sioux Community of Minnesota (Prior
    Lake) (F)
Shakopee Sioux Community Council
2330 Sioux Trail Northwest
Prior Lake, MN 55372
(612) 445-8900

Prairie Island Indian Community of Minnesota
    Mdewakanton Sioux Indians of the Prairie Island
    Reservation (F)
Prairie Island Indian Community Council
5750 Sturgeon Lake Road
Welch, MN 55089
(612) 388-8889

Upper Sioux Indian Community of the Upper Sioux
    Reservation (F)
Upper Sioux Board of Trustees
P.O. Box 147
Granite Falls, MN 56241
(612) 564-2360 or -2550

MISSOURI

Cherokee

Chickamauga Cherokee of Arkansas and Missouri (P)
217 Forest Lane
Republic, MO 56738
Missouri number: (417) 732-1339

Northern Cherokee Nation of the Old Louisiana
    Territory (P)
1502 East Broadway, Suite 201
Columbia, MO 65201

Northern Cherokee Tribe of Indians (P)
P.O. Box 1061
Columbia, MO 65202

MISSISSIPPI

Mississippi Band of Choctaw Indians (F)

Choctaw Tribal Council
Route 7, Box 21
Philadelphia, MS 39350
(601) 656-5251

MONTANA

*Assiniboine and Sioux Tribes of the Fort Peck Indian
Reservation* (F)

Fort Peck Executive Board
P.O. Box 1027
Poplar, MT 59255
(406) 768-5311 or -5155

Blackfeet Tribe of the Blackfeet Indian Reservation of Montana (F)

Blackfeet Tribal Business Council
P.O. Box 850
Browning, MT 59417
(407) 338-7276

Little Shell Tribe of Chippewa Indians of Montana (P)

P.O. Box 347
Havre, MT 59501
(406) 265-2741

Chippewa-Cree Indians of the Rocky Boy's Reservation (F)

Chippewa-Cree Business Committee
Box Eldar, MT 59521
(406) 395-4282

Crow Tribe of Montana (F)

Crow Tribal Council
Box 159
Crow Agency, MT 59022
(406) 353-2205

Fort Belknap Indian Community of the Fort Belknap Reservation of Montana (F) (*Gros Ventre and Assiniboine*)

Fort Belknap Community Council
Box 249
Harlem, MT 59526
(406) 353-2205

Northern Cheyenne Tribe of the Northern Cheyenne Indian Reservation (F)

Northern Cheyenne Tribal Council
P.O. Box 128
Lame Deer, MT 59043
(406) 477-6284

Confederated Salish and Kootenai Tribes of the Flathead Reservation (F)

Confederated Salish and Kootenai Council
Box 278
Pablo, MT 59855
(406) 675-2700

NEBRASKA

Iowa Tribe of Kansas and Nebraska (F)

Executive Committee
Route 1, Box 58A
White Cloud, KS 66094
(913) 595-3258

Omaha Tribe of Nebraska (F)

Omaha Tribal Council
P.O. Box 368
Macy, NE 68039

Sac & Fox Tribe of Missouri in Kansas and Nebraska (F)

Sac & Fox Tribal Council
P.O. Box 38
Reserve, KS 66434
(913) 742-7471

Santee Sioux Tribe of the Santee Reservation of Nebraska (F)

Santee Sioux Tribal Council
Route 2
Niobrara, NE 68760
(402) 857-3302

Winnebago Tribe of Nebraska (F)

Winnebago Tribal Council
Winnebago, NE 68071
(402) 878-2272

NEVADA

Confederated Tribes of the Goshute Reservation, Nevada and Utah (F)

Goshute Business Council
P.O. Box 6104
Ibapah, UT 84034
(801) 234-1138

Shoshone

Duckwater Shoshone Tribe of the Duckwater
  Reservation (F)
Duckwater Shoshone Tribal Council
P.O. Box 68
Duckwater, NV 89314
(702) 289-3013

Ely Indian Colony of Nevada (F)
Ely Colony Council
16 Shoshone Circle
Ely, NV 89301
(702) 289-3013

Te-Moak Tribe of Western Shoshone Indians of
  Nevada (F)
Tribal Council of the Te-Moak Western Shoshone
  Indians of Nevada
525 Sunset Street
Elko, NV 89801
(702) 738-9251

Constituent Bands of the Te-Moak Tribe of Western
  Shoshone Indians (F)
Battle Mountain Band Council
35 Mountain View Drive, #138-13
Battle Mountain, NV 89820
(702) 635-2004

Elko Band Council
P.O. Box 478
Elko, NV 89801
(702) 738-8889

South Fork Band Council
Box B-13
Lee, NV 89829
(702) 744-4273

Wells Indian Colony Band Council
P.O. Box 809
Wells, NV 89835
(702) 752-3045

Yomba Shoshone Tribe of the Yomba Reservation (F)
Yomba Tribal Council
Route 1, Box 24
Austin, NV 89310
(702) 964-2463 or 423-6919

Paiute

Las Vegas Tribe of Paiute Indians of the Las Vegas
  Indian Colony (F)
Las Vegas Colony Council
1 Paiute Drive
Las Vegas, NV 89106
(702) 386-3926

Lovelock Paiute Tribe of the Lovelock Indian
  Colony (F)
Lovelock Tribal Council
Box 878
Lovelock, NV 89419
(702) 273-7861

Moapa Bank of Paiute Indians of the Moapa River
  Indian Reservation (F)
Moapa Business Council
P.O. Box 56
Moapa, NV 89025
(702) 865-2787

Pahrump Band of Paiutes (P)
P.O. Box 73
Pahrump, NV 89041
(702) 486-5211

Pyramid Lake Paiute Tribe of the Pyramid Lake
  Reservation (F)
Pyramid Lake Paiute Tribal Council
P.O. Box 256
Nixon, NV 89424
(702) 574-0140

Summit Lake Paiute Tribe of Nevada (F)
P.O. Box 1958
Winnemucca, NV 89445
(702) 623-5151

Yerington Paiute Tribe of the Yerington Colony and
     Campbell Ranch (F)
Yerington Paiute Tribal Council
171 Campbell Lane
Yerington, NV 89447
(702) 463-3301 or 883-3895

Walker River Paiute Tribe of the Walker River
     Reservation (F)
Walker River Paiute Tribal Council
P.O. Box 220
Schurz, NV 89427
(702) 773-2306

Paiute and Shoshone

Fort McDermitt Paiute and Shoshone Tribes of the
     Fort McDermitt Indian Reservation (F)
P.O. Box 457
McDermitt, NV 89421
(702) 532-8259

Paiute-Shoshone Tribe of the Fallon Reservation and
     Colony (F)
Fallon Business Council
8955 Mission Road
Fallon, NV 89406
(702) 423-6075

Shoshone-Paiute Tribes of the Duck Valley
     Reservation (F)
Shoshone-Paiute Business Council
P.O. Box 219
Owyhee, NV 89832
(702) 757-3161

Winnemucca Indian Colony of Nevada (F)
Winnemucca Colony Council
Winnemucca, NV 89445

Washoe

Washoe Tribe (F)
Washoe Tribal Council
Route 2, 919 Highway 395 South
Garnerville, NV 89410
(702) 265-4191 or 883-1446

Communities of the Washoe Tribe (F)
Carson Colony Community Council
502 Shoshone Street
Carson City, NV 89701
(702) 883-6431 or 265-4191

Dresslerville Community Council
1585 Watasheamu
Gardnerville, NV 89410
(702) 838-6431 or 265-4191

Reno-Sparks Indian Colony (Washoe and Paiute) (F)
Reno-Sparks Indian Council
98 Colony Road
Reno, NV 89502
(702) 329-2936

NEW JERSEY

Nanticoke Lenni-Lenape Indians (P)
P.O. Box 544 / 18 East Commerce Street
Bridgeton, NJ 08302

Ramapough Mountain Indians, Inc. (P)
40 Malcolm Road
Mahwah, NJ 07430
(201) 529-1171

NEW MEXICO

Apache

Jicarilla Apache Tribe of the Jicarilla Apache Indian
     Reservation (F)
Jicarilla Apache Tribal Council
P.O. Box 147
Dulce, NM 87528
(505) 759-3242

Mescalero Apache Tribe of the Mescalero
     Reservation (F)
Mescalero Apache Tribal Council
P.O. Box 176
Mescalero, NM 87340
(505) 671-4495

Navajo

Canoncito Band of Navajos (P)
P.O. Box 498
Canoncito, NM 87026
(505) 836-7141

Navajo Tribe of Arizona, New Mexico and Utah (F)
Navajo Tribal Council
P.O. Box 308
Window Rock, AZ 86515
(602) 871-4941

Ramah Navajo Chapter (F)
P.O. Box 267
Ramah, NM 81137
(505) 867-3317

Pueblo

Pueblo of Acoma (F)
P.O. Box 309
Acomita, NM 87034
(505) 552-6604

Pueblo of Cochiti (F)
P.O. Box 70
Cochiti, NM 87041
(505) 465-2244

Pueblo of Isleta (F)
P.O. Box 317
Isleta, NM 87022
(505) 869-3111 or -6333

Pueblo of Jemez (F)
P.O. Box 78
Jemez Pueblo, NM 87024
(505) 834-7359

Pueblo of Laguna (F)
P.O. Box 194
Laguna, NM 87026
(505) 552-6654

Pueblo of Nambe (F)
Route 1, Box 117-BB
Santa Fe, NM 87501
(505) 455-7752 or -7905

Pueblo of Picuris (F)
P.O. Box 127
Penasco, NM 87553
(505) 587-2519

Pueblo of Pojoaque (F)
Route 11, Box 71
Santa Fe, NM 87501
(505) 455-2278 or -2279

Pueblo of San Felipe (F)
P.O. Box A
San Felipe Pueblo, NM 87001
(505) 867-3381

Pueblo of San Ildefonso (F)
Route 5, Box 315-A
Santa Fe, NM 87501
(505) 455-2273

Pueblo of San Juan (F)
P.O. Box 1099
San Juan Pueblo, NM 87566
(505) 852-4400 or -4210

Pueblo of Sandia (F)
P.O. Box 6008
Bernalillo, NM 87004
(505) 867-3317

Pueblo of Santa Ana (F)
P.O. Box 37
Bernalillo, NM 87004
(505) 867-3301

Pueblo of Santa Clara, (F)
P.O. Box 580
Española, NM 87532
(505) 753-7316 or -7330

Pueblo of Santo Domingo (F)
P.O. Box 99
Santo Domingo Pueblo, NM 87052
(505) 465-2214

Pueblo of Taos (F)
P.O. Box 1846
Taos, NM 87571
(505) 758-9593

Pueblo of Tesuque (F)
Route 11, Box 1
Santa Fe, NM 87501
(505) 983-2667

Pueblo of Zia (F)
General Delivery
San Ysidro, NM 87053
(505) 867-3304

Zuni Tribe of the Zuni Reservation (F)
P.O. Box 339
Zuni, NM 87327
(505) 782-4481

Tiwa Indian Tribe (P)

(also known as the San Juan de Guadalupe Tiwa)
4028 San Ysidro Road
San Ysidro, NM 88005
(505) 526-0790

*Ute Mountain Tribe of the Ute Mountain Reservation,
Colorado, New Mexico & Utah* (F)

Ute Mountain Ute Tribal Council
General Delivery
Towaoc, CO 81344
(303) 565-3751

NEW YORK

Six Nations (Iroquois)
Cayuga Nation of New York (F)
P.O. Box 11
Versailles, NY 14168
(716) 532-4847

St. Regis Band of Mohawk Indians of New York (F)
St. Regis Mohawk Council Chiefs
St. Regis Reservation
Hogansburg, NY 13655
(518) 358-2272

Oneida Nation of New York (F)
Tribal Council
Route 2, West Road
Oneida, NY 13424

Onondaga Nation of New York (F)
P.O. Box 319B
Nedrow, NY 13120
(716) 469-7810

Seneca Nation of New York (F)
P.O. Box 231
Salamanca, NY 14779
(716) 945-1790

Tonawanda Band of Seneca Indians of New York (F)
Council of Chiefs
7027 Meadville Road
Basom, NY 14013
(716) 542-9942

Tuscarora Nation of New York (F)
2006 Mt. Hope Road
Lewiston, NY 14092
(716) 297-4990

Poosepatuck Tribe (S)
Mastic, Long Island, NY 11950

Shinnecock Tribe (P) (S)

P.O. Box 59
Southampton, Long Island, NY 11968
(516) 283-6143

NORTH CAROLINA

Cherokee

Cherokee Indians of Hoke County, Inc. (I)
Route 1, Box 129-C
Lumber Bridge, NC 28357
(919) 323-4848

Cherokee Indians of Robeson and Adjoining
    Counties (I)
Route 2, Box 272-A
Red Springs, NC 28377

Cherokee-Powhattan Indian Association (P)
P.O. Box 3265
Roxboro, NC 27573
(919) 599-6448

Eastern Band of Cherokee Indians of North
    Carolina (F)
P.O. Box 455
Cherokee, NC 28719
(704) 497-2771

Coharie Intra-Tribal Council, Inc. (P)

Route 3, Box 356-B
Clinton, NC 18318
(191) 564-6901

Coree (also known as Faircloth Indians) (P)

P.O. Box 161
Atlantic, NC 28511

Haliwa-Saponi Indian Tribe, Inc. (P)

P.O. Box 99
Hollister, NC 27844
(191) 486-4017

Hattadare Indian Nation (P)

Route 1, Box 85-B
Bunnlevel, NC 28323
(919) 893-2512

Kaweah Indian Nation, Inc. (PD)

Route 1, Box 99
Oriental, NC 28571

Lumbee Regional Development Association, Inc. (I)

East Main Street / P.O. Box 68
Pembroke, NC 28372
(919) 521-2401

Meherrin Indian Tribe (P)

P.O. Box 508
Winton, NC 27986

Tuscarora

Hatteras Tuscarora Indians (I)
Route 1, Box 385
Maxton, NC 28364
(919) 521-2426

Tuscarora Indian Tribe (I)
Route 2, Box 108
Maxton, NC 28364
(919) 844-3827

Tuscarora Nation of North Carolina (I)
P.O. Box 565
Pembroke, NC 28372
(919) 521-2655

Waccamaw Siouan Development Association, Inc. (I)

P.O. Box 221
Bolton, NC 28423

NORTH DAKOTA

Chippewa

Christian Pembina Chippewa Indians (P)
P.O. Box 727
Dunseith, ND 58329

Turtle Mountain Band of Chippewa Indians of North
 Dakota (F)
Turtle Mountain Tribal Council
Belcourt, ND 58316
(701) 477-6451

Little Shell Band of North Dakota (P)
Dunseith, ND 58329

Three Affiliated Tribes of the Fort Berthold Reservation
(F) (Mandan Hidatsa, and Arikara)
Fort Berthold Tribal Business Council
P.O. Box 220
New Town, ND 58763
(701) 627-4781

Sioux
Devils Lake Sioux Tribe of the Devils Lake Sioux
 Reservation (F)
Devils Lake Sioux Tribal Council
Sioux Community Center
Fort Totten, ND 58335
(701) 766-4221

Standing Rock Sioux Tribe of North & South
 Dakota (F)
Standing Rock Sioux Tribal Council
Fort Yates, ND 58538
(701) 854-7231

OHIO

Alleghenny Nation (Ohio Band) (P)
2239 Mahoning Road Northeast
Canton, OH 44705
(216) 453-6224

North Eastern U.S. Miami Inter-Tribal Council (P)
1535 Florencedale
Youngstown, OH 44505
(216) 746-4956

Shawnee
Shawnee Nation United Remnant Band (P)
P.O. Box 162
Dayton, OH 45401
(513) 275-6685

Piqua Sept of Ohio Shawnee Indians (P)
Bancohio Building, Suite 828
4 West Main Street
Springfield, OH 45502

OKLAHOMA

Apache
Apache Tribe of Oklahoma (F)
Apache Business Committee
P.O. Box 1220
Anadarko, OK 73005
(405) 347-9493

Fort Sill Apache Tribe of Oklahoma (F)
Fort Sill Apache Business Committee
Route 2, Box 121
Apache, OK 76006
(405) 588-2298

Caddo Indian Tribe of Oklahoma (F)
Caddo Tribal Council
P.O. Box 487
Binger, OK 73009
(405) 656-2344

Cherokee
Cherokee Nation of Oklahoma (F)
P.O. Box 948
Tahlequah, OK 74465
(918) 456-0671

United Keetoowah Band of Cherokee Indians (F)
2450 South Muskogee Avenue
Tahlequah, OK 74464
(918) 456-5491

Cheyenne-Arapaho Tribes of Oklahoma (F)

Cheyenne-Arapaho Business Committee
P.O. Box 38
Concho, OK 73022
(405) 262-0345

Chickasaw Nation of Oklahoma (F)

P.O. Box 1548
Ada, OK 74820
(405) 436-2603

Choctaw Nation of Oklahoma (F)

P.O. Drawer 1210
16th & Locust Streets
Durant, OK 74701
(405) 924-8280

Comanche Indian Tribe of Oklahoma (F)

Comanche Tribal Business Committee
P.O. Box 908
Lawton, OK 73502
(405) 247-3444

Creek

Alabama-Quassarte Tribal Town of the Creek Nation
    of Oklahoma (F)
P.O. Box 404
Eufaula, OK 74432
(918) 689-9570

Creek Nation of Oklahoma (F)
P.O. Box 580
Okmulgee, OK 74447
(918) 756-8700

Kialegee Tribal Town of the Creek Indian Nation of
    Oklahoma (F)
928 Alex Noon Drive
Wetumka, OK 74883

Thlopthlocco Tribal Town of the Creek Nation of
    Oklahoma (F)
Route 2, Box 204
Wetumka, OK 74883
(405) 452-3529

Delaware Tribe of Western Oklahoma (F)

Delaware Executive Committee
P.O. Box 825
Anadarko, OK 73005

Iowa Tribe of Oklahoma (F)

Iowa of Oklahoma Business Committee
Iowa Veterans Hall
P.O. Box 190
Perkins, OK 74059
(405) 547-2403

Kaw Indian Tribe of Oklahoma (F)

Kaw Business Committee
Drawer 50
Kaw City, OK 74641
(405) 269-2552

*Kickapoo Tribe of Oklahoma (including the Kickapoo
Traditional Tribe of Texas)* (F)

Kickapoo of Oklahoma Business Committee
P.O. Box 58
McLoud, OK 74851
(405) 964-2075

Kiowa Indian Tribe of Oklahoma (F)

Kiowa Business Committee
P.O. Box 369
Carnegie, OK 73015
(405) 654-2300

Miami Tribe of Oklahoma (F)

P.O. Box 636
Miami, OK 74355
(918) 540-2890

Modoc Tribe of Oklahoma (F)

P.O. Box 939
Miami, OK 74354
(918) 540-1190

Osage Tribe of Oklahoma (F)

Tribal Administration Building
Pawhuska, OK 74056
(918) 287-4622

Otoe-Missouria Tribe of Oklahoma (F)

Otoe-Missouria Tribal Council
P.O. Box 68
Red Rock, OK 74058

Ottawa Tribe of Oklahoma (F)

Ottawa Business Committee
P.O. Box 110
Miami, OK 74355
(918) 540-1536

Pawnee Indian Tribe of Oklahoma (F)

Pawnee Business Council
P.O. Box 470
Pawnee, OK 74058
(918) 762-3624

Peoria Tribe of Oklahoma (F)

P.O. Box 1527
Miami, OK 74355
(918) 540-2535

Ponca Tribe of Indians of Oklahoma (F)

Ponca Business Committee
P.O. Box 2, White Eagle
Ponca City, OK 74601

Citizen Band Potawatomi Indian Tribe of Oklahoma (F)

Citizen Band Potawatomi Business Committee
P.O. Box 151
Shawnee, OK 74801
(405) 275-3125 or 3128

Quapaw Tribe of Oklahoma (F)

Quapaw Tribal Business Committee
P.O. Box 765
Quapaw, OK 74363
(918) 542-1853

Sac & Fox Tribe of Oklahoma (F)

Sac & Fox of Oklahoma Business Committee
Route 2, Box 246
Stroud, OK 66529
(918) 986-3526 or (405) 275-4270

Seminole Nation of Oklahoma (F)

P.O. Box 1498
Wewoka, OK 74884
(405) 257-6287

Seneca-Cayuga Tribe of Oklahoma (F)

P.O. Box 1283
Miami, OK 74355
(918) 542-6609

Shawnee

Absentee-Shawnee Tribe of Indians of Oklahoma (F)
Absentee-Shawnee Executive Committee
P.O. Box 1747
Shawnee, OK 74801
(405) 275-4030

Eastern Shawnee Tribe of Oklahoma (F)
P.O. Box 350
Seneca, MO 64865
(918) 666-2435

Tonkawa Tribe of Oklahoma (F)

Tonkawa Business Committee
P.O. Box 70
Tonkawa, OK 74653
(405) 628-2561

Wichita Indian Tribe of Oklahoma (F)

Wichita Executive Committee
P.O. Box 729
Anadarko, OK 73005
(405) 247-2425

Wyandotte Tribe of Oklahoma (F)

P.O. Box 250
Wyandotte, OK 74370
(918) 678-2297 or -2298

Yuchi Tribal Organization (P)

30 North Water Street
Sapulpa, OK 74067

OREGON

Confederated Tribes of the Umatilla Reservation (F)
(*Umatilla, Cayuse and Wallawalla*)

Umatilla Board of Trustees
P.O. Box 638
Pendleton, OR 97801
(503) 276-3165

Northwest Cherokee Wolf Band (PD)

Southeastern Cherokee Confederacy, Inc.
P.O. Box 592
Talent, OR 97540
(503) 535-5406

Confederated Tribes of the Coos, Lower Umpqua and Siuslaw Indians of Oregon (R)

P.O. Box 660
Coos Bay, OR 97420
(503) 267-5454

Coquille Tribe of Oregon (F)

250 Hull Street
Coos Bay, OR 97420
(503) 888-4274

Confederated Tribes of the Grand Ronde Community of Oregon (F)

P.O. Box 38
Grande Ronde, OR 97347
(503) 879-5215

Klamath Indian Tribe of Oregon (F)
Klamath General Council
Box 436
Chiloquin, OR 97624
(503) 783-2219

Burns Paiute Indian Colony (F)

Burns-Paiute General Council
HC 71, 100 Pasigo Street
Burns, OR 97720
(503) 573-2088

Confederated Tribes of the Siletz Reservation (F)

Siletz Tribal Council
P.O. Box 549
Siletz, OR 97380
(503) 444-2532

Tchinouk Indians (PD)

5621 Altamont Drive
Klamath Falls, OR 97601
(503) 884-3844

Cow Creek Band of Umpqua Indians of Oregon (F)

1376 Northeast Walnut
Roseberg, OR 97347
(503) 672-9696

Confederated Tribes of the Warm Springs Reservation of Oregon (F) (*Warm Springs, Northern Paiute, and Wasco*)

Warm Springs Tribal council
P.O. Box C
Warm Springs, OR 97761
(503) 553-3333

RHODE ISLAND

Narragansett Indian Tribe of Rhode Island (F)

P.O. Box 268
Charleston, RI 02813
(401) 792-9700

SOUTH CAROLINA

Four Hole Indian Organization (P)

Edisto Tribal Council
Route 3, Box 42F
Ridgeville, SC 29472
(803) 871-2126

Santee Tribe, White Oak Indian Community (P)

Route 1, Box 200
Holly Hill, SC 29059
(803) 496-3246

SOUTH DAKOTA

Sioux

Cheyenne River Sioux Tribe of the Cheyenne River
    Reservation (F)
Cheyenne River Sioux Tribal Council
P.O. Box 590
Eagle Butte, SD 57625
(605) 964-4155

Crow Creek Sioux Tribe of the Crow Creek
    Reservation (F)
Crow Creek Sioux Tribal Council
P.O. Box 658
Fort Thompson, SD 57339
(605) 245-2221 or -2222

Flandreau Santee (Sioux) Tribe of South Dakota (F)
Flandreau Santee Sioux Executive Committee
Flandreau Field Office
Box 283
Flandreau, SD 57028
(605) 997-3891

Lower Brulé Sioux Tribe of the Lower Brule
    Reservation (F)
Lower Brule Sioux Tribal Council
Lower Brule, SD 57548
(605) 473-5561

Oglala Sioux Tribe of the Pine Ridge Reservation (F)
Oglala Sioux Tribal Council
Pine Ridge, SD 57548

Rosebud Sioux Tribe of the Rosebud Indian
    Reservation (F)
Rosebud Sioux Tribal Council
Rosebud, SD 57570
(402) 837-5391

Sisseton-Wahpeton Sioux Tribe of the Lake Traverse
    Reservation (F)
Sisseton-Wahpeton Sioux Tribal Council
Route 2
Agency Village
Sisseton, SD 57262
(605) 698-3911

Standing Rock Sioux Tribe of North & South
    Dakota (F)
Standing Rock Sioux Tribal Council
Fort Yates, ND 58538
(701) 854-7231

Yankton Sioux Tribe of South Dakota (F)
Yankton Sioux Tribal Business & Claims Committee
Box 248
Marty, SD 57361
(605) 384-3641

TENNESSEE

Cherokee

Etowah Cherokee Nation (P)
P.O. Box 5454
Cleveland, TN 37320

Red Clay Inter-Tribe Indian Band (PD)
Southeastern Cherokee Confederacy, Inc.
7703 Georgetown Road
Ooltewah, TN 37363
(615) 238-9346

TEXAS

Alabama and Coushatta Tribes of Texas (F)

Route 3, Box 640
Livingston, TX 77351
(409) 563-4391

Kickapoo Traditional Tribe (F)
P.O. Box 972
Eagle Pass, TX 78853
(512) 773-2105

Ysleta Del Sur Pueblo of Texas (F) (Tigua)
119 South Old Pueblo Road
P.O. Box 17579
El Paso, TX 79907
(915) 859-7913 or -7914 or -7918

UTAH

Goshute
Confederated Tribes of the Goshute Reservation,
    Nevada and Utah (F)
Goshute Business Council
P.O. Box 6104
Ibapah, UT 84034
(801) 234-1138

Skull Valley Band of Goshute Indians of Utah (F)
Skull Valley Executive Committee
% Uintah & Ouray Agency
P.O. Box 130
Fort Duchesne, UT 84026
(801) 722-2406

Navajo Tribe of Arizona, New Mexico and Utah (F)
Navajo Tribal Council
P.O. Box 308
Window Rock, AZ 86515
(602) 871-4941

Paiute Indian Tribe of Utah (F)
Tribal Council of the Paiute Indian Tribe of Utah
600 North 100 East Paiute Drive
Cedar City, UT 84720
(801) 586-1111

*Northwestern Band of Shoshoni Indians of Utah
(Washakie) (F)*
660 South 200 West
Brigham City, UT 84302

Ute
Ute Indian Tribe of the Uintah Ouray
    Reservation (F)
Uintah & Ouray Tribal Business Committee
P.O. Box 130
Fort Duchesne, UT 84026
(801) 722-5141

Ute Mountain Tribe of the Ute Mountain Reserva-
    tion, Colorado, New Mexico & Utah (F)
Ute Mountain Ute Tribal Council
General Delivery
Towaoc, CO 81344
(303) 565-3751

VERMONT

St. Francis/Sokoki Band of Abenakis of Vermont (P)
Abenaki Tribal Council
Box 276
Swanton, VT 05488
(802) 868-2559

VIRGINIA

*The Upper Mattaponi Indian Tribal Association, Inc.
(P) (S)*
Box 12-A
St. Stephens Church, VA 23148
(804) 769-2248

United Rappahannock Tribe, Inc. (P)
Indian Neck, VA 23077
(804) 769-3128

WASHINGTON

Confederated Tribes of the Chehalis Reservation (F)
Chehalis Community Council
P.O. Box 536
Oakville, WA 98568
(206) 273-5911

Chinook Indian Tribe, Inc. (P)

P.O. Box 228
Chinook, WA 98614
(206) 777-8303

Clallam

Lower Elwha Tribal Community of the Lower Elwha
  Reservation (F)
Lower Elwha Community Council
1666 Lower Elwha Community Center
Port Angeles, WA 98362
(206) 452-8471

Jamestown Clallam (F)
150 South 5th Avenue, Suite 2
Sequim, WA 98382
(206) 683-1106

Port Gamble Indian Community of the Port Gamble
  Reservation (F)
Port Gamble Community Council
P.O. Box 280
Kingston, WA 98346
(206) 297-2646

Confederated Tribes of the Colville Reservation (F)
(Colville, Okanogan, Lakes, San Poil, Methow,
Nespelem, Entiat, Wenatchee, Moses, Nez Percé, and
Palouse)

Colville Business Committee
P.O. Box 150
Nespelem, WA 99155
(509) 634-4711

Cowlitz Tribe of Indians (P)

12812 101 Avenue Court East
Puyallup, WA 98373
(206) 840-3247

Duwamish Indian Tribe (P)

15507 First Avenue South
Seattle, WA 98148
(206) 244-0606

Hoh Indian Tribe of the Hoh Indian Reservation (F)

Hoh Tribal Business Committee
HC 80, Box 917
Forks, WA 98331
(206) 374-6582

Kalispel Indian Community of the Kalispel
Reservation (F)

Kalispel Business Committee
Box 39
Usk, WA 99180
(509) 445-1147

Jamestown Klallam Tribe of Washington (F)

305 Old Blyn Highway
Sequim, WA 98382
(206) 683-1109

Lummi Tribe of the Lummi Reservation (F)

Lummi Business Council
2616 Kwina Road
Bellingham, WA 98226
(206) 734-8180

Makah Indian Tribe of the Makah Indian
Reservation (F)

Makah Tribal Council
P.O. Box 115
Neah Bay, WA 98357
(206) 645-2205

Muckleshoot Indian Tribe of the Muckleshoot
Reservation (F)

Muckleshoot Tribal Council
29015 172nd Street Southeast
Auburn, WA 98002
(206) 939-3311

Nisqually Indian Community of the Nisqually
Reservation (F)

Nisqually Indian Community Council
4820 She-Nah-Num Drive Southeast
Olympia, WA 98503
(206) 456-5221

Nooksack Indian Tribe of Washington (F)

Nooksack Tribal Council
P.O. Box 157
Deming, WA 98244

Puyallup Tribe of the Puyallup Reservation (F)

Puyallup Tribal Council
2002 East 28th Street
Tacoma, WA 98404
(206) 597-6200

Quileute Tribe of the Quileute Reservation (F)

Quileute Tribal Council
P.O. Box 279
LaPush, WA 98350
(206) 374-6163

Quinault

Quinault Tribe of the Quinault Reservation
Quinault Business Committee
P.O. Box 189
Taholah, WA 98587
(206) 276-8211

Shoalwater Bay Tribe of the Shoalwater Bay Indian Reservation (F)

(Quinault, Chichinook, and Chehalis)
Shoalwater Bay Tribal Council
P.O. Box 130
Tokeland, WA 98590
(206) 267-6766

Samish Tribe of Indians (PD)

P.O. Box 217
Anacortes, WA 98221
(206) 293-6404

Sauk-Suiattle Indian Tribe of Washington (F)

Sauk-Suiattle Tribal Council
5318 Chief Brown Lane
Darrington, WA 98241
(206) 435-8366

Skokomish Indian Tribe of the Skokomish Reservation (F)

Skokomish Tribal Council
No. 80 Tribal Center Road
Shelton, WA 98584
(206) 426-4232

Snohomish

Snohomish Tribe of Indians (P)
1422 Rosario Road
Anacortes, WA 98221
(206) 293-7716

Tulalip Tribes of the Tulalip Reservation (F)
   (Snohomish)
Tulalip Board of Directors
6700 Totem Beach Road
Marysville, WA 98270

Snoqualmie Indian Tribe (P)

18525 Novelty Hill Road
Redmond, WA 98052
(206) 885-7464

Snoqualmoo Tribe of Whidbey Island (P)

540 Linder Street
Friday Harbor, WA 98250
(206) 378-5734

Spokane Tribe of the Spokane Reservation (F)

Spokane Business Council
P.O. Box 100
Wellpinit, WA 99040
(509) 258-4581

Squaxin Island Tribe of the Squaxin Island Reservation (F)

Squaxin Island Tribal Council
SE 70, Squaxin Lane
Shelton, WA 98584
(206) 426-9781

Steilacoom Tribe (P)

P.O. Box 419
Steilacoom, WA 98388
(206) 847-6448

Stillaguamish Tribe of Washington (F)

Stillaguamish Board of Directors
3439 Stoluckquamish Lane
Arlington, WA 98223
(206) 652-7362

*Suquamish Indian Tribe of the Port Madison
Reservation (F)*

Suquamish Tribal Council
P.O. Box 498
Suquamish, WA 98392
(206) 598-3311

Swinomish Indians of the Swinomish Reservation (F)

Swinomish Indian Tribal Community
P.O. Box 817
LaConner, WA 98257
(206) 466-3163

Upper Skagit Indian Tribe of Washington (F)

Upper Skagit Tribal Council
2284 Community Plaza
Sedro Wooley, WA 98284
(206) 856-5501

*Confederated Tribes of the Bands of the Yakima Indian
Nation of the Yakima Reservation (F)*

Yakima Tribal Council
P.O. Box 151
Toppenish, WA 98948

WISCONSIN

Brotherton Indians of Wisconsin (P)

AV 2848 Witches Lake Road
Woodruff, WI 54568
(715) 542-3913

Chippewa

Bad River Band of the Lake Superior Tribe of Chippewa Indians of the Bad River Reservation (F)
Bad River Tribal Council
P.O. Box 39
Odanah, WI 54861
(715) 682-4212

Lac Courte Oreilles Band of Lake Superior Chippewa
Indians of the Lac Courte Oreilles Reservation of
Wisconsin (F)
Lac Courte Oreilles Tribal Council
Route 2, Box 2700
Hayward, WI 54843

Lac du Flambeau Band of Lake Superior Chippewa
Indians of the Lac du Flambeau Reservation of
Wisconsin (F)
Lac du Flambeau Tribal Council
P.O. Box 67
Lac du Flambeau, WI 54538
(715) 588-3303 or -3306

Red Cliff Band of Lake Superior Chippewa Indians of
Wisconsin (F)
Red Cliff Tribal Council
P.O. Box 529
Bayfield, WI 54814
(715) 779-5805

St. Croix Chippewa Indians of Wisconsin, St. Croix
Reservation (F)
St. Croix Council
P.O. Box 287
Hertal, WI 54845
(715) 349-2195

Sokoagon Chippewa Community of the Mole Lake
Band of Chippewa Indians (F)
Sokoagon Chippewa Tribal Council
Route 1, Box 625
Crandon, WI 54520
(715) 478-2604

Menominee Indian Tribe of Wisconsin (F)

P.O. Box 397
Keshena, WI 54135
(715) 799-3341

Stockbridge-Munsee Community of Mohican Indians of Wisconsin (F)

Stockbridge-Munsee Tribal Council
Route 1
Bowler, WI 54416
(715) 793-4111

Forest County Potawatomi Community of Wisconsin Potawatomi Indians (F)

General Council
P.O. Box 346
Crandon, WI 54520
(715) 478-1903

Wisconsin Winnebago Indian Tribe of Wisconsin (F)

Wisconsin Winnebago Business Council
P.O. Box 311
Tomah, WI 54660
(608) 372-4147

WYOMING

Arapahoe Tribe of the Wind River Reservation (F)

Arapahoe Business Council
P.O. Box 396
Fort Washakie (also known as the Wind River Reservation), WY 82514
(307) 255-8394

Shoshone Tribe of the Wind River Reservation (F)

Shoshone Business Council
P.O. Box 538
Fort Washakie (also known as the Wind River Reservation), WY 82514
(307) 332-3532

APPENDIX II

Reservations, Rancherias, Colonies, and Historic Indian Areas

When the first white man came over the wide waters, he was but a little man . . . very little. His legs were cramped by sitting long in his big boat, and he begged for a little land . . . When he came to these shores the Indians gave him land, and kindled fires to make him comfortable . . . But when the white man had warmed himself at the Indian's fire, and had filled himself with the Indian's hominy, he became very large. He stopped not at the mountain tops, and his foot covered the plains and the valleys. His hands grasped the eastern and western seas. Then he became our Great Father. He loved his red children, but he said: 'you must move a little farther, lest by accident I tread on you.'

> Speckled Snake, Creek chief in 1829.
> From: Armstrong (1970)

Some of our chiefs make the claim that the land belongs to us. It is not what the Great Spirit told me. He told me that the lands belong to Him, that no people owns the land; that I was not to forget to tell this to the white people when I meet them in council.

> Kennekuk, the Kickapoo prophet in 1827.

The development of a list of reservations is very complex. The sources of information on Indian land contain different kinds of information and no one source is exactly the same as any other. Some list only land that is linked to a tribe that has federal recognition, some include state recognized reservations, and other sources list land that is not recognized by either state or federal governments but is sometimes referred to as reservation land by its inhabitants.

The size of reservations is not static. Over the years, Indian land holdings have been eroded by the actions of government. Some tribes have managed to add acreage to their land base as a result of purchases, court cases, or other kinds of settlements. Some reservation land is owned by individual Indians, some by whites, and some is owned by the tribe as a whole. One or a combination of these types of ownership can occur on one reservation. Some Indian land is held in trust by the federal government for individuals and some in trust for tribes. Some land is held in trust, but is not considered a reservation.

Federal reservations are considered to be land with boundaries established by treaty, statute, and/or executive or court order, and recognized by the federal government as territory in which American Indian tribes have jurisdiction, except where Congress has expressly stated otherwise. Land held in trust is property associated with a particular American Indian reservation or tribe, held in trust by the federal government. The trust relationship involves federal protection of the land and its resources.

Between 1887 and 1907, all the reservations in

Oklahoma were dissolved in a series of laws and agree-ments. Although it is home to nearly thirty tribal nations, the only reservation in Oklahoma today is the Osage. The former reservations of Oklahoma are sometimes referred to as historic Indian areas.

The following list of reservations is not meant to be definitive, but an informational source to help identify Indian country and who lives there.

Information for this section was compiled from several sources (see the bibliography for a complete listing).

Key

Name of the reservation

(F)=Federal reservation,

(S)=State reservation

(U)=Unrecognized by federal or state governments but considered reservations by people living there

(The name of the people who live there)

When established or recognized (The dates when some reservations were established are not avail-able. "NA" designates this missing information)

Size in acres

ALABAMA

Poarch Band of Creeks Reservation (F)
(Poarch Band of Creeks Tribe)
Established: 1984
213 acres

ALASKA

Annette Island Reserve (F)
(Tsimshian Tribe)
Established: 1891
86,471 acres

ARIZONA

Maricopa (Ak Chin) Reservation (F)
(Papago Tribe)
Established: 1912
21,840 acres

Camp Verde Reservation (F)
(Yavapai-Apache Tribe)
Established: 1914
653 acres

Cocopah Reservation (F)
(Yuma Tribe)
Established: 1917
6,009 acres

Colorado River Reservation (F)
(Mojave and Chemehuevi Tribes)
Established: 1865
225,995 acres

Fort Apache Reservation (F)
(White Mountain Apache Tribe)
Established: 1871
1,664,972 acres

Fort McDowell Reservation (F)
(Mojave, Apache and Yavapai Tribes)
Established: 1903
24,680 acres

Gila River Indian Community (F)
(Pima and Maricopa Tribes)
Established: 1859
371,933 acres

Havasupai Reservation (F)
(Havasupai Tribe)
Established: 1880
188,077 acres

Hopi Reservation (F)
(Hopi Tribe)
Established: 1882
1,561,213 acres

Hualapai Reservation (F)
(Hualapai Tribe)
Established: 1883
992,463 acres

Kaibab Reservation (F)
(Paiute Tribe)
Established: NA
120,413 acres

Navajo Reservation (F)
(Navajo Tribe)
Established: 1868
13,989,222 acres

Pascua Yaqui Reservation (F)
(Pascua Yaqui Tribe)
Established: NA
895 acres

Payson Community of Yavapai-Apache Indians (F)
(Yavapai-Apache Tribe)
Established: 1972
85 acres

Salt River Reservation (F)
(Pima and Maricopa Tribes)
Established: 1879
50,506 acres

San Carlos Reservation (F)
(Apache Tribe)
Established: 1871
1,826,541 acres

Tohono O'Odham (Papago) Reservation (F)
(Tohono O'Odham Tribe)
Established: 1874
2,774,450 acres

Yavapai Reservation (F)
(Yavapai Tribe)
Established: 1935
1,398 acres

CALIFORNIA

Agua Caliente Reservation (F)
(Agua Caliente Band of Mission
　Indians)
Established: 1896
23,173 acres

Alturas Rancheria (F)
(Pit River Tribe)
Established: 1906
20 Acres

Augustine Reservation (F)
(Augustine Band of Mission
　Indians)
Established: 1893
502 acres

Barona Reservation (F)
(Barona Group of Capitan
　Grand Band of Mission
　Indians)
Established: 1875
5,181 acres

Berry Creek Rancheria (F)
(Maidu Tribe)
Established: 1916
33 acres

Big Bend Rancheria (F)
(Pit River Tribe)
Established: 1916
40 acres

Big Lagoon Rancheria (F)
(Yurok Tribe)
Established: 1918
20 acres

Big Pine Reservation (F)
(Paiute and Shoshone Tribes)
Established: 1939
279 acres

Bishop Reservation (F)
(Paiute and Shoshone Tribes)
Established: 1912
875 acres

Cabazon Reservation (F)
(Cabazon Band of Mission
　Indians)
Established: 1876
1,382 acres

Cahuilla Reservation (F)
(Cahuilla Band of Mission
　Indians)
Established: 1875
18,884 acres

Campo Reservation (F)
(Campo Community Band of
　Mission Indians)
Established: 1893
15,480 acres

Capitan Grande Reservation (F)
(Capitan Grande Band of Mis-
　sion Indians)
Established: 1875
15,753 acres

Cedarville Rancheria (F)
(Paiute Tribe)
Established: 1914
20 acres

Chemehuevi Reservation (F)
(Chemehuevi Tribe)
Established: 1907
30, 654 acres

Cold Springs Rancheria (F)
(Mono Tribe)
Established: NA
155 acres

Colusa Rancheria (F)
(Cachil Dehe Band of Wintun
　Indians)
Established: 1907
273 acres

Cortina Rancheria (F)
(Me-Wuk Tribe)
Established: 1907
640 acres

Cuyapaipe Reservation (F)
(Cuyapaipe Band of Mission
　Indians)
Established: 1893
4,103 acres

Dry Creek Rancheria (F)
(Pomo Tribe)
Established: 1906
75 acres

Enterprise Rancheria (F)
(Maidu Tribe)
Established: 1906
40 acres

Fort Bidwell Reservation (F)
(Paiute Tribe)
Established: 1897
3,335 acres

Fort Independence Reservation (F)
(Paiute Tribe)
Established: 1915
234 acres

Fort Mojave Reservation (F)
(Mojave Tribe)
Established: 1848
32,697 acres

Fort Yuma Reservation (F)
(Quechan Tribe)
Established: 1884
43,561 acres

Grindstone Creek Rancheria (F)
(Wintun Tribe)
Established: 1906
80 acres

Hoopa Extension Reservations (F)
(Yurok Tribe)
Established: 1891
7,015.69 acres

Hoopa Valley Reservation (F)
(Hoopa Tribe)
Established: 1876
85,445 acres

Hopland Rancheria (F)
(Pomo Tribe)
Established: 1907
48 acres

Inaja-Cosmit Reservation (F)
(Inaja-Cosmit Band of Mission
  Indians)
Established: 1875
852 acres

Jackson Rancheria (F)
(Me-Wuk Tribe)
Established: 1893
331 acres

La Jolla Reservation (F)
(La Jolla Band of Mission
  Indians)
Established: 1875
8,541 acres

La Posta Reservation (F)
(La Posta Band of Mission
  Indians)
Established: NA
3,556 acres

Laytonville Reservation (F)
(Cahto Tribe)
Established: 1906
200 acres

Likely Reservation (F)
(Pit River Tribe)
Established: 1922
1.32 acres

Lone Pine Reservation (F)
(Paiute and Shoshone Tribes)
Established: 1939
237 acres

Lookout Rancheria (F)
(Pit River Tribe)
Established: 1913
40 acres

Los Coyotes Reservation (F)
(Los Coyotes Band of Mission
  Indians)
Established: 1889
25,049.63 acres

*Manchester-Point Arena
Rancheria* (F)
(Pomo Tribe)
Established: 1909
363 acres

Manzanita Reservation (F)
(Manzanita Band of Mission
  Indians)
Established: 1893
3,579 acres

Mesa Grande Reservation (F)
(Mesa Grande Band of Mission
  Indians)
Established: 1875
20 acres

Middletown Rancheria (F)
(Pomo Tribe)
Established: 1910
109 acres

Montgomery Creek Rancheria (F)
(Pit River Tribe)
Established: 1915
72 acres

Morongo Reservation (F)
(Morongo Band of Mission
  Indians)
Established: 1908
32,362 acres

Pala Reservation (F)
(Pala Band of Mission Indians)
Established: 1875
11,893 acres

Pauma and Yuima Reservation
(F)
(Pauma Band of Mission
   Indians)
Established: 1872
5,877 acres

Pechanga Reservation (F)
(Pechanga Band of Mission
   Indians)
Established: 1882
4,394 acres

Ramona Reservation (F)
(Cahuilla Band of Mission
   Indians)
Established: 1893
560 acres

Resighini Rancheria (F)
(Coast Indian Community)
Established: 1938
228 acres

Rincon Reservation (F)
(San Luiseno Band of Mission
   Indians)
Established: 1875
4,276 acres

Roaring Creek Rancheria (F)
(Pit River Tribe)
Established: 1915
80 acres

Round Valley Reservation (F)
(Pomo, Nom-Iaka and Wintun
   Tribes)
Established: 1864
30,538 acres

Rumsey Rancheria (F)
(Wintun Tribe)
Established: 1907
185 acres

San Manuel Reservation (F)
(San Manuel Band of Mission
   Indians)
Established: 1893
658 acres

San Pasqual Reservation (F)
(San Pasqual Band of Mission
   Indians)
Established: 1910
1,379.58 acres

Santa Rosa Rancheria (F)
(Tachi Tribe)
Established: 1921
170 acres

Santa Rosa Reservation (F)
(Santa Rosa Band of Mission
   Indians)
Established: 1907
11,092.60 acres

Santa Ynez Reservation (F)
(Santa Ynez Band of Mission
   Indians)
Established: 1901
127 acres

Santa Ysabel Reservation (F)
(Santa Ysabel Band of Mission
   Indians)
Established: 1893
15,527 acres

Sheep Ranch Rancheria (F)
(Me-Wuk Tribe)
Established: 1916
.92 acre

Soboba Reservation (F)
(Soboba Band of Mission
   Indians)
Established: 1883
5,916 acres

Stewarts Point Rancheria (F)
(Kashia Band of Pomo Indians)
Established: NA
40 acres

Sulphur Bank Rancheria (F)
(Pomo Tribe)
Established: 1949
50 acres

Susanville Rancheria (F)
(Paiutek Maidu, Pit River and
   Washoe Tribes)
Established: 1923
150 acres

Sycuan Reservation (F)
(Sycuan Band of Mission
   Indians)
Established: 1875
640 acres

Table Mountain Rancheria (F)
Established: 1916
61 acres

Torres-Martinez Reservation (F)
(Torres-Martinez Band of Mission Indians)
Established: 1876
24,024 acres

Trinidad Rancheria (F)
(Yurok Tribe)
Established: 1917
47 acres

Tule River Reservation (F)
(Tule River Tribe)
Established: 1873
55,356 acres

Tuolumne Rancheria (F)
(Tuolumne Band of Me-Wuk
   Indians)
Established: 1910
336 acres

Twentynine Palms Reservation (F)
(Twentynine Palms Band of
   Mission Indians)
Established: 1895
402 acres

Upper Lake Rancheria (F)
(Pomo Tribe)
Established: 1907
19 acres

Viejas Reservation (F)
(Viejas Group of Capitan
   Grande Band of Mission
   Indians)
Established: 1875
1,609 acres

X L Ranch Reservation (F)
(Pit River and Paiute Tribes)
Established: 1938
9,254.86 acres

COLORADO

Southern Ute Reservation (F)
(Mouache and Capote Ute
   Tribes)
Established: 1873
310,002 acres

Ute Mountain Reservation (F)
(Wiminuche Ute Tribe)
Established: 1873
447,850 acres

CONNECTICUT

Eastern Pequot Reservation (S)
(Pequot and Mohegan Tribes)
Established: 1683
220 acres

*Mashantucket (Western) Pequot
Reservation (F)*
(Pequot and Mohegan Tribes)
Established: 1667
1,201 acres

Golden Hill Reservation (S)
(Pequot and Mohegan Tribes)
Established: 1886
.26 acres

Schaghticoke Reservation (S)
(Schaghticoke Tribe)
Established: 1744
400 acres

FLORIDA

Big Cypress Reservation (F)
(Seminole Indian Tribe)
Established: NA
42,728 acres

Brighton Reservation (F)
(Seminole Indian Tribe)
Established: NA
35,805 acres

Florida State Reservation (S)
(Miccosukee and Seminole Indian Tribes)
Established: NA
104,000 acres

Hollywood Reservation (F)
(Seminole Indian Tribe)
Established: NA
480.87 acres

Miccosukee Reservation (F)
(Miccosukee Indian Tribe)
Established: NA
75,146 acres

IDAHO

Coeur d'Alene Reservation (F)
(Coeur d'Alene Tribe)
Established: 1867
67,981 acres

Fort Hall Reservation (F)
(Shoshone and Bannock Tribes)
Established: 1868
522,510 acres

Kootenai Reservation (F)
(Kootenai Tribe)
Established: 1867
2,072 acres

Nez Percé Reservation (F)
(Nez Percé Tribe)
Established: 1855
85,661 acres

IOWA

Sac and Fox Reservation (F)
(Sac and Fox [Mesquakie]
   Tribes)
Established: 1856
3,540 acres

KANSAS

Iowa Reservation (F)
(Iowa Tribe)
Established: 1836
1,072 acres

Kickapoo Reservation (F)
(Kickapoo Tribe)
Established: 1832
6,660 acres

Potawatomi Reservation (F)
(Potawatomi Tribe)
Established: 1846
21,479 acres

Sac and Fox Reservation (F)
(Sac and Fox Tribes)
Established: 1842
354 acres

LOUISIANA

Chitimacha Reservation (F)
(Chitimacha Indian Tribe)
Established: 1830
283 acres

Coushatta Reservation (F)
(Coushatta Tribe)
Established: NA
154 acres

Tunica-Biloxi Reservation (F)
(Tunica-Biloxi Tribe)
Established: In process of placing their land in reservation status.
134 acres

MAINE

Penobscot Reservation (S)
(Penobscot Tribe)
Established: 1820
127,838 acres

Pleasant Point and Indian Township Reservations (S)
(Passamaquoddy Tribe)
Established: 1820
23,200 acres

MASSACHUSETTS

Hassanamisco Reservation (S)
(Hassanamisco-Nipmuc Tribe)
Established: 1848
11.9 acres

Gay Head Wampanoag (F Trust)
(Gay Head Wampanoag Tribe)
Established: NA
156 acres

MICHIGAN

Bay Mills Reservation (F)
(Chippewa Tribe)
Established: 1850
2,209 acres

Grand Traverse Reservation (U)
(Chippewa Tribe)
Established: NA
acres NA

Hannahville Reservation (F)
(Potawatomi Tribe)
Established: 1913
3,411 acres

Huron Potawatomi Band, Inc. (S)
(Potawatomi Tribe)
Established: 1845
120 acres

Isabella Reservation (F)
(Saginaw Chippewa Tribe)
Established: 1864
138,240 acres

Lac Vieux Desert Reservation (U)
(Lac Vieux Desert Band of Chippewa)
Established: NA
104 acres

L'anse (Keeweenaw Bay) Reservation (F)
(Lake Superior Band, Chippewa Tribe)
Established: 1854
13,750 acres

Sault St. Marie Reservation (U)
(Sault St. Marie Chippewa)
Established: NA
293 acres

MINNESOTA

Fond Du Lac Reservation (F)
(Mississippi Band of Chippewa)
Established: 1854
21,932 acres

Grand Portage Reservation (F)
(Chippewa Tribe)
Established: 1854
44,844 acres

Leech Lake Reservation (F)
(Chippewa Tribe)
Established: 1855
27,853 acres

Lower Sioux Reservation (F)
(Eastern or Mississippi Sioux Tribe)
Established: 1887
1,745 acres

Mille Lacs Reservation (F)
(Chippewa Tribe)
Established: 1855
3,863 acres

Nett Lake Reservation (F)
(Chippewa Tribe)
Established: 1854
41,864 acres

Prairie Island Reservation (F)
(Eastern or Mississippi Sioux
    Tribe)
Established: 1887
571 acres

Shakopee Community (F)
(Shakopee Mdewakanton Sioux
    Tribe)
Established: 1969
293 acres

Red Lake Reservation (F)
(Chippewa Tribe)
Established: 1863
564,452 acres

Upper Sioux Community (F)
(Eastern Mississippi Sioux
    Tribe)
Established: 1938
745 acres

White Earth Reservation (F)
(Chippewa Tribe)
Established: 1867
56,078 acres

MISSISSIPPI

Choctaw Reservation (F)
(Choctaw Tribe)
Established: 1830
17,926 acres

MONTANA

Blackfeet Reservation (F)
(Blackfeet Tribe)
Established: 1855
937,838 acres

Crow Reservation (F)
(Crow Tribe)
Established: 1868
1,517,406 acres

Flathead Reservation (F)
(Salish and Kootenai Tribes)
Established: 1855
627,070 acres

Fort Belknap Reservation (F)
(Gros Ventre and Assiniboine
    Tribes)
Established: 1888
588,756 acres

Fort Peck Reservation (F)
(Assiniboine and Sioux Tribes)
Established: 1873
904,683 acres

Northern Cheyenne Reservation
(F)
(Northern Cheyenne Tribe)
Established: 1884
436,948 acres

Rocky Boy's Reservation (F)
(Chippewa-Cree Tribe)
Established: 1916
108,334 acres

NEBRASKA

Omaha Reservation (F)
(Omaha Tribe)
Established: 1854
26,792 acres

Santee Reservation (F)
(Santee Sioux Tribe)
Established: 1863
9,358 acres

Winnebago Reservation (F)
(Winnebago Tribe)
Established: 1865
27,538 acres

NEVADA

Alpine Colony (F)
(Washoe Tribe)
Established: 1970
80 acres

Battle Mountain Colony (F)
(Shoshone Tribe)
Established: 1917
688 acres

Carson Colony (F)
(Washoe Tribe)
Established: 1917
160 acres

Dresslerville Colony (F)
(Washoe Tribe)
Established: 1917
40 acres

Duck Valley Reservation (F)
(Shoshone and Paiute Tribes)
Established: 1877
289,819 acres

Duckwater Reservation (F)
(Shoshone Tribe)
Established: 1940
3,815 acres

Elko Colony (F)
(Shoshone Tribe)
Established: 1918
193 acres

Ely Colony (F)
(Shoshone Tribe)
Established: 1931
100 acres

Fallon Colony and Reservation (F)
(Paiute and Shoshone Tribes)
Established: 1887
8,180 acres

Fort McDermitt Reservation (F)
(Paiute and Shoshone Tribes)
Established: 1892
16,497 acres

Las Vegas Colony (F)
(Paiute Tribe)
Established: 1911
3,723 acres

Lovelock Colony (F)
(Paiute Tribe)
Established: 1907
20 acres

Moapa River Reservation (F)
(Paiute Tribe)
Established: 1875
71,955 acres

Pyramid Lake Reservation (F)
(Paiute Tribe)
Established: 1874
476,689 acres

Reno-Sparks Colony (F)
(Washoe and Paiute Tribes)
Established: 1917
28.38 acres

Ruby Valley (Te-Moak)
Reservation (F)
(Shoshone Tribe)
Established: 1887
13,050 acres

South Fork and Odgers Ranch
Reservations (F)
(Shoshone Tribe)
Established: 1941
15,036.56 acres

Summit Lake Reservation (F)
(Paiute Tribe)
Established: 1913
10,863 acres

Walker River Reservation (F)
(Paiute Tribe)
Established: 1871
323,406

Winnemucca Colony (F)
(Paiute and Shoshone Tribes)
Established: 1917
340 acres

Woodsford Colony (F)
(Washoe Tribe)
Established: 1887
580 acres

Yerington Colony and Reservation
(F)
(Paiute Tribe)
Established: 1836
1,632 acres

Yomba Reservation (F)
(Shoshone Tribe)
Established: 1937
4,718.46 acres

NEW MEXICO

Acoma Pueblo (F)
(Keresan Tribe)
Established: 1864
263,611 acres

Alamo Reservation (F)
(Navajo Tribe)
Established: 1868
63,109 acres

Canoncito Reservation (F)
(Navajo Tribe)
Established: 1868
76,813 acres

Cochiti Pueblo (F)
(Keresan Tribe)
Established: 1864
50,669 acres

Isleta Pueblo (F)
(Tano-Tiwa Tribe)
Established: 1864
211,034

Jemez Pueblo (F)
(Tano-Jemez Tribe)
Established: 1864
89,619 acres

Jicarilla Reservation (F)
(Jicarilla Apache Tribe)
Established: 1874
823,580 acres

Laguna Pueblo (F)
(Keresan Tribe)
Established: 1864
461,099 acres

Mescalero Reservation (F)
(Mescalero Apache Tribe)
Established: 1873
460,678 acres

Nambe Pueblo (F)
(Tano-Tiwa Tribe)
Established: 1864
19,075 acres

Picuris Pueblo (F)
(Tano-Tiwa Tribe)
Established: 1864
14,947 acres

Pojoaque Pueblo (F)
(Tano-Tewa Tribe)
Established: 1864
11,602 acres

Ramah Reservation (F)
(Navajo Tribe)
Established: 1868
146,953 acres

Sandia Pueblo (F)
(Tano-Tiwa Tribe)
Established: 1864
22,871 acres

San Felipe Pueblo (F)
(Keresan Tribe)
Established: 1864
48,929.90 acres

San Ildefonso Pueblo (F)
(Tano-Tewa Tribe)
Established: 1864
26,198 acres

San Juan Pueblo (F)
(Tano-Tewa Tribe)
Established: 1864
12,237 acres

Santa Ana Pueblo (F)
(Keresan Tribe)
Established: 1883
61,414 acres

Santa Clara Pueblo (F)
(Tano-Tewa Tribe)
Established: 1909
45,748 acres

Santo Domingo Pueblo (F)
(Keresan Tribe)
Established: 1864
69,259.82 acres

Taos Pueblo (F)
(Tano-Tiwa Tribe)
Established: 1864
95,341 acres

Tesuque Pueblo (F)
(Tano-Tewa Tribe)
Established: 1864
16,813 acres

Zia Pueblo (F)
(Keresan Tribe)
Established: 1864
117,680 acres

Zuni Pueblo (F)
(Zuni Tribe)
Established: 1864
409,182 acres

NEW YORK

Allegany Reservation (S)
(Seneca Nation of Indians)
Established: 1794
30,984 acres

Cattaraugus Reservation (S)
(Seneca Nation of Indians)
Established: 1794
22,013 acres

Oil Springs Reservation (S)
(Seneca Tribe)
Established: 1877
640 acres

Oneida Reservation (U)
(Oneida Nation)
Established: 1794
32 acres

Onondaga Reservation (S)
(Onondaga and Oneida Tribes)
Established: 1784
7,300 acres

Poospatuck Reservation (S)
(Poospatuck Tribe)
Established: 1666
60 acres

St. Regis Mohawk Reservation (S)
(St. Regis Mohawk Tribe)
Established: 1796
14,640 acres

Shinnecock Reservation (S)
(Shinnecock Tribe)
Established: NA
400 acres

Tonawanda Reservation (S)
(Tonowanda Band of Seneca
Tribe)
Established: 1863
495 acres

Tuscarora Reservation (S)
(Tuscarora Tribe)
Established: 1784
5,778 acres

NORTH CAROLINA

Cherokee Reservation (F)
(Eastern Band of Cherokee)
Established: 1874
56,573 acres

NORTH DAKOTA

Fort Berthold Reservation (F)
(Mandan, Hidatsa and Arikara
  Tribes)
Established: 1871
419,362 acres

Devils Lake Reservation (F)
(Formerly Fort Totten
  Reservation)
(Devils Lake Sioux Tribe)
Established: 1867
53,239 acres

Standing Rock Reservation (F)
(Sioux Tribe)
Established: 1868
847,254 acres

Turtle Mountain Reservation (F)
(Chippewa Tribe)
Established: 1882
33,319 acres

OKLAHOMA

*Absentee Shawnee Tribe (Historic
Indian Area)*
Established: NA
13,479.90 acres

*Caddo Tribe (Historic Indian
Area)*
Established: 1866
63,608 acres

*Cherokee Tribe (Historic Indian
Area)*
Established: 1833
17,718 acres

*Cheyenne and Arapaho Tribes
(Historic Indian Area)*
Established: 1869
98,020 acres

*Chickasaw Tribe (Historic Indian
Area)*
Established: 1855
96,309 acres

*Choctaw Tribe (Historic Indian
Area)*
Established: 1833
145,069 acres

*Citizen Band of Potawatomi Tribe
(Historic Indian Area)*
Established: 1867
4,371.50 acres

*Comanche Tribe (Historic Indian
Area)*
Established: 1867
234,299.45 acres

*Creek Tribe (Historic Indian
Area)*
Established: 1833
4,061.22 acres

*Delaware Indian Tribe of Western
Oklahoma (Historic Indian Area)*
Established: 1866
63,608 acres

*Eastern Shawnee Tribe (Historic
Indian Area)*
Established: 1936
1,048.35 acres

*Fort Sill Apache Tribe (Historic
Indian Area)*
Established: 1913
3,568.07 acres

*Iowa Tribe of Oklahoma (Historic
Indian Area)*
Established: 1883
1,521.77 acres

Kaw Tribe (Historic Indian Area)
Established: 1872
20 acres

*Kickapoo Tribe of Oklahoma
(Historic Indian Area)*
Established: 1883
6,134.06 acres

*Kiowa Tribe (Historic Indian
Area)*
Established: 1867
234,299.45 acres

*Kiowa-Apache Tribe (Historic
Indian Area)*
Established: 1867
239,299.45 acres

Osage Reservation (F)
(Osage Tribe)
Established: 1870
168,794 acres

*Otoe-Missouria Tribe (Historic
Indian Area)*
Established: 1881
29,343.27 acres

*Pawnee Tribe (Historic Indian
Area)*
Established: 1868
23,221.35 acres

*Ponca Tribe (Historic Indian
Area)*
Established: 1876
17,784.77 acres

*Quapaw Tribe (Historic Indian
Area)*
Established: 1833
12,772 acres

Sac and Fox Tribe (Historic Indian Area)
Established: 1891
18,139.44 acres

Seminole Tribe (Historic Indian Area)
Established: 1866
35,763 acres

Seneca-Cayuga Tribe (Historic Indian Area)
Established: 1831
4,725.83 acres

Tonkawa Tribe of Oklahoma (Historic Indian Area)
Established: 1884
481.24 acres

Wichita Tribe (Historic Indian Area)
Established: 1866
63,608 acres

OREGON

Burns Paiute Reservation (F)
(Paiute Tribe)
Established: 1863
11,466 acres

Celilo Village (F)
Established: 1947
30.39 acres

Coos, Lower Umpqua and Siuslaw Reservation (U)
(Coos, Lower Umpqua and Siuslaw Tribes)
Established: NA
6 acres

Cow Creek Reservation (U)
(Umpqua Tribe)
Established: NA
28 acres

Grand Ronde Reservation (U)
(Umpqua Tribe)
Established: 1855
9,811 acres

Siletz Reservation (U)
(Siletz Tribe)
Established: 1855
3,673 acres

Umatilla Reservation (F)
(Cayuse, Wallawalla, and Umatilla Tribes)
Established: 1855
85,256 acres

Warm Springs Reservation (F)
(Warm Springs, Northern Paiute and Wasco Confederated Tribes)
Established: 1855
643,507 acres

SOUTH DAKOTA

Cheyenne River Reservation (F)
(Sioux Tribe)
Established: 1889
1,395,905 acres

Crow Creek Reservation (F)
(Sioux Tribe)
Established: 1863
125,483 acres

Flandreau Reservation (F)
(Flandreau Santee Sioux Tribe)
Established: 1935
2,183 acres

Lower Brule Reservation (F)
(Sioux Tribe)
Established: 1868
130,239 acres

Pine Ridge Reservation (F)
(Oglala Sioux Tribe)
Established: 1868
1,780,444 acres

Rosebud Reservation (F)
(Sioux Tribe)
Established: 1868
954,572 acres

Sisseton Reservation (F)
(Sisseton-Wahpeton Sioux Tribe)
Established: 1867
105,543 acres

Yankton Reservation (F)
(Yankton Sioux Tribe)
Established: 1853
36,559 acres

TEXAS

Alabama-Coushatta Reservation (S)
(Alabama and Coushatta Tribes)
Established: 1854
4,400 acres

Ysleta Del Sur Pueblo (S)
Formerly Tigua Reservation
(Tigua Tribe)
Established: 1967
(The pueblo was established in 1682 and recognized as Indian land in 1967 by the State of Texas & later by the federal government.)
73 acres

UTAH

Goshute Reservation (F)
(Goshute Tribe)
Established: 1863
7,489 acres

Skull Valley Reservation (F)
(Goshute Tribe)
Established: NA
17,444 acres

Paiute of Utah Reservation (S)
formerly Southern Paiute
Reservation
(Southern Paiute Tribe)
Established: 1972
425 acres

*Uintah and Ouray Reservation
(F)*
(Ute Tribe)
Established: 1863
1,021,558 acres

VIRGINIA

Mattaponi Reservation (S)
(Mattaponi Indians [Pow-
hatan])
Established: 1658
125 acres

Pamunkey Reservation (S)
(Pamunkey Indians [Pow-
hatan])
Established: 1677
800 acres

WASHINGTON

Chehalis Reservation (F)
(Chehalis Tribe)
Established: 1864
2,076 acres

Colville Reservation (F)
(Confederated Tribes)
Established: 1872
1,063,043 acres

Hoh Reservation (F)
(Hoh Tribe)
Established: 1893
443 acres

Jamestown Klallam Reservation (U)
(Klallam Tribe)
Established: NA
11 acres

Kalispel Reservation (F)
(Kalispel Tribe)
Established: 1855
4,557 acres

Lower Elwha Reservation (F)
(Clallam Tribe)
Established: 1968
427 acres

Lummi Reservation (F)
(Lummi and Nooksack Tribes)
Established: 1849
7,678 acres

Makah Reservation (F)
(Makah Tribe)
Established: 1855
27,244 acres

Muckleshoot Reservation (F)
(Muckleshoot Tribe)
Established: 1857
1,275 acres

Nisqually Reservation (F)
(Nisqually Tribe)
Established: 1854
930 acres

Ozette Reservation (F)
(Makah Tribe)
Established: 1893
719 acres

Port Gamble Reservation (F)
(Clallam Tribe)
Established: 1936
1,303 acres

Port Madison Reservation (F)
(Suquamish Tribe)
Established: 1855
2,872 acres

Puyallup Reservation (F)
(Puyallup Tribe)
Established: 1855
103 acres

Quileute Reservation (F)
(Quileute Tribe)
Established: 1889
814 acres

Quinault Reservation (F)
(Quinault Tribe)
Established: 1855
129,221 acres

Sauk-Suiattle Reservation (U)
(Sauk-Suiattle Tribe)
Established: NA
23 acres

Shoalwater Reservation (F)
(Quinault, Chinook, and
Chehalis Tribes)
Established: 1866
335 acres

Skokomish Reservation (F)
(Skokomish Tribe)
Established: 1855
2,987 acres

Spokane Reservation (F)
(Spokane Tribe)
Established: 1881
133,302 acres

Squaxin Island Reservation (F)
(Squaxin Island Tribe)
Established: 1854
971 acres

*Swinomish Indian Tribal
Community* (F)
(Swinomish Tribe)
Established: 1855
3,602 acres

Tulalip Reservation (F)
(Snohomish Tribe)
Established: 1855
10,667 acres

Upper Skagit Reservation (U)
(Skagit Tribe)
Established: NA
74 acres

Yakima Reservation (F)
(Confederated Tribes and Bands
   of the Yakima Indian Nation)
Established: 1859
1,130,286 acres

WISCONSIN

Bad River Reservation (F)
(Bad River Band of Chippewa
   Indians)
Established: 1854
56,558 acres

Lac Courte Oreilles Reservation
(F)
(Lac Courte Oreilles Band of
   Chippewa Indians)
Established: 1854
48,139 acres

Lac Du Flambeau Reservation (F)
(Lac du Flambeau Band of
   Chippewa Indians)
Established: 1854
44,726 acres

Menominee Reservation (F)
(Menominee Tribe)
Established: 1848
222,552 acres

*Sokaogon Chippewa Community
Reservation* (F)
(Mole Lake Band of Chippewa
   Indians)
Established: 1826
1,694 acres

Oneida Reservation (F)
(Oneida Tribe)
Established: 1838
2,751 acres

Potawatomi Reservation (F)
(Potawatomi Tribe)
Established: NA
11,692 acres

Red Cliff Reservation (F)
(Red Cliff Band of Chippewa
   Indians)
Established: 1854
7,495 acres

St. Croix Reservation (F)
(St. Croix Band of Chippewa
   Indians)
Established: 1938
1940 acres

Stockbridge-Munsee Reservation
(F)
(Stockbridge [Mahican] and
   Munsee Tribes)
Established: 1856
15,603 acres

Winnebago Reservation (F)
(Winnebago Tribe)
Established: 1875
4,245 acres

WYOMING

Wind River Reservation (F)
(Shoshone and Arapaho Tribes)
Established: 1863
1,888,588 acres

APPENDIX III

Chronology of Indian Treaties 1778–1868

The list of treaties that follows indicates for a particular tribe the first and last treaties signed and those years when treaty commissioners negotiated one a year, several a month, almost two dozen a year, or none at all. Although hundreds of treaties were negotiated, some tribes like the Chippewa, Potawatomi, and Delaware, treatied repeatedly. Different branches of these three nations alone account for some 100 treaties, while the Navajo signed two, and some groups, like the Wampanoags of Massachusetts and many tribes in California, never signed any.

1778
September 17—Treaty with the Delaware
1784
October 22—Treaty with the Six Nations Iroquois
1785
January 21—Treaty with the Wyandot, Delaware, Chippewa, and Ottawa
November 28—Treaty with the Cherokee
1786
January 3—Treaty with the Choctaw
January 10—Treaty with the Chickasaw
January 31—Treaty with the Shawnee
1789
January 9—Treaty with the Wyandot, Delaware, Ottawa, Chippewa, Potawatomi, and Sac

January 9—Treaty with the Six Nations Iroquois
1790
August 7—Treaty with the Creek
1791
July 2—Treaty with the Cherokee
1794
June 26—Treaty with the Cherokee
November 11—Treaty with the Six Nations Iroquois
December 2—Treaty with the Oneida, Tuscarora, and Stockbridge
1795
August 3—Treaty with the Wyandot, Delaware, Shawnee, Ottawa, Chippewa, Potawatomi, Miami, Eel River, Wea, Kickapoo, Piankashaw, and Kaskaskia
1796
May 31—Treaty with the Seven Nations of Canada
June 29—Treaty with the Creek
1797
March 29—Treaty with the Mohawk
1798
October 2—Treaty with the Cherokee
1801
October 24—Treaty with the Chickasaw
December 17—Treaty with the Choctaw

1802
June 16—Treaty with the Creek
June 30—Treaty with the Seneca
June 30—Treaty with the Seneca
October 17—Treaty with the Choctaw
1803
June 7—Treaty with the Delaware, Shawnee, Potawatomi, Miami, Eel River, Wea, Kickapoo, Piankashaw, and Kaskaskia
August 7—Treaty with the Eel River, Wyandot, Piankashaw, Kaskaskia, and Kickapoo
August 13—Treaty with the Kaskaskia
August 31—Treaty with the Choctaw
1804
August 18—Treaty with the Delaware
August 27—Treaty with the Piankashaw
October 24—Treaty with the Cherokee
November 3—Treaty with the Sac and Fox
1805
July 4—Treaty with the Wyandot, Ottawa, Chippewa, Munsee, Delaware, Shawnee, and Potawatomi
July 23—Treaty with the Chickasaw
August 21—Treaty with the Delaware, Potawatomi, Miami, Eel River, and Wea
October 25—Treaty with the Cherokee
October 27—Treaty with the Cherokee
November 14—Treaty with the Creek
November 16—Treaty with the Choctaw

287

December 30—Treaty with the
    Piankashaw

1806
January 7—Treaty with the Cherokee

1807
November 17—Treaty with the Ottawa,
    Chippewa, Wyandot, and Potawatomi

1808
November 10—Treaty with the Osage
November 25—Treaty with the
    Chippewa, Ottawa, Potawatomi,
    Wyandot, and Shawnee

1809
September 30—Treaty with the Delaware,
    Potawatomi, Miami, and Eel River
September 30—Treaty with the Miami
    and Eel River
September 30—Treaty with the Miami
    and Eel River
October 26—Treaty with the Wea
December 9—Treaty with the Kickapoo

1814
July 22—Treaty with the Wyandot,
    Delaware, Shawnee, Seneca, and
    Miami
August 9—Treaty with the Creek

1815
July 18—Treaty with the Potawatomi
July 18—Treaty with the Piankashaw
July 19—Treaty with the Teton
July 19—Treaty with the Sioux of the
    Lakes
July 19—Treaty with the Sioux of St.
    Peter's River
July 19—Treaty with the Yankton Sioux
July 20—Treaty with the Makah
September 2—Treaty with the Kickapoo
September 8—Treaty with the Wyandot,
    Delaware, Seneca, Shawnee, Miami,
    Chippewa, Ottawa, and Potawatomi
September 12—Treaty with the Osage
September 13—Treaty with the Sac
September 14—Treaty with the Fox
September 16—Treaty with the Iowa
October 28—Treaty with the Kansa

1816
March 22—Treaty with the Cherokee
March 22—Treaty with the Cherokee
May 13—Treaty with the Sac
June 1—Treaty with the Sioux
June 3—Treaty with the Winnebago

June 4—Treaty with the Wea and
    Kickapoo
August 24—Treaty with the Ottawa,
    Chippewa, and Potawatomi
September 14—Treaty with the Cherokee
September 20—Treaty with the
    Chickasaw
October 24—Treaty with the Choctaw

1817
March 30—Treaty with the Menominee
June 24—Treaty with the Oto
June 25—Treaty with the Ponca
July 8—Treaty with the Cherokee
September 29—Treaty with Wyandot,
    Seneca, Delaware, Shawnee,
    Potawatomi, Ottawa, and Chippewa

1818
January 22—Treaty with the Creek
June 18—Treaty with the Grand Pawnee
June 19—Treaty with the Noisy Pawnee
June 20—Treaty with the Pawnee
    Republic
June 22—Treaty with the Pawnee
    Marhar
August 24—Treaty with the Quapaw
September 17—Treaty with the Wyandot,
    Seneca, Shawnee, and Ottawa
September 20—Treaty with the Wyandot
September 25—Treaty with the Peoria,
    Kaskaskia, Mitchigamia, Cahokia,
    and Tamarois
September 25—Treaty with the Osage
October 2—Treaty with the Potawatomi
October 2—Treaty with the Wea
October 3—Treaty with the Delaware
October 6—Treaty with the Miami
October 19—Treaty with the Chickasaw

1819
February 27—Treaty with the Cherokee
July 30—Treaty with the Kickapoo
August 30—Treaty with the Kickapoo
September 24—Treaty with Chippewa

1820
June 16—Treaty with the Chippewa
July 6—Treaty with the Ottawa and
    Chippewa
July 19—Treaty with the Kickapoo
August 11—Treaty with the Wea
September 5—Treaty with the Kickapoo
October 18—Treaty with Choctaw

1821
January 8—Treaty with the Creek
January 8—Treaty with the Creek
August 29—Treaty with the Ottawa,
    Chippewa, and Potawatomi

1822
August 31—Treaty with the Osage
September 3—Treaty with the Sac and
    Fox

1823
September 18—Treaty with the Florida
    Tribes

1824
August 4—Treaty with the Sac and Fox
August 4—Treaty with the Iowa
November 15—Treaty with the Quapaw

1825
January 20—Treaty with the Choctaw
February 12—Treaty with the Creek
June 2—Treaty with the Osage
June 3—Treaty with the Kansa
June 9—Treaty with the Ponca
June 22—Treaty with the Teton,
    Yankton, and Yanktonies Bands of
    Sioux
July 5—Treaty with the Sioux and
    Oglala Bands of Sioux
July 6—Treaty with the Cheyenne
July 16—Treaty with the Hunkpapa
    Band of Sioux
July 18—Treaty with the Arikara
July 30—Treaty with the Minitaree
    Tribe
July 30—Treaty with the Mandan
August 4—Treaty with the Crow
August 10—Treaty with the Great and
    Little Osage
August 16—Treaty with the Kansa
August 19—Treaty with the Sioux,
    Chippewa, Sac and Fox, Menominee,
    Iowa, Winnebago, and a portion of
    the Ottawa, Chippewa, and
    Potawatomi
September 26—Treaty with the Oto and
    Missouri
September 30—Treaty with the Pawnee
October 6—Treaty with the Makah
November 7—Treaty with the Shawnee

1826
January 24—Treaty with the Creek

August 5—Treaty with the Chippewa
October 16—Treaty with the Potawatomi
October 23—Treaty with the Miami

1827
August 11—Treaty with the Chippewa,
Menominee, and Winnebago
September 19—Treaty with the
Potawatomi
November 15—Treaty with the Creek

1828
February 11—Treaty with the Miami
May 6—Treaty with the Western
Cherokee
August 25—Treaty with the
Winnebago, Sac and Fox,
Potawatomi, Ottawa and Chippewa
September 20—Treaty with the
Potawatomi

1829
July 29—Treaty with the Chippewa,
Ottawa and Potawatomi
August 1—Treaty with the Winnebago
August 8—Treaty with the Delaware
September 24—Treaty with the Delaware

1830
July 15—Treaty with the Confederated
Tribes of the Sac and Fox, Medawah-
Kanton, Wahpacoota, Wahpeton, and
Sisseton Bands of Sioux, Omaha,
Iowa, Oto, and Missouri
September 27—Treaty with the Choctaw

1831
February 8—Treaty with the Menominee
February 17—Treaty with the
Menominee
February 28—Treaty with the Seneca
July 20—Treaty with the Seneca and
Shawnee
August 8—Treaty with the Shawnee
August 30—Treaty with the Ottawa

1832
January 19—Treaty with the Wyandot
March 24—Treaty with the Creek
May 9—Treaty with the Seminole
September 15—Treaty with the
Winnebago
September 21—Treaty with the Sac and
Fox

October 11—Treaty with the
Appalachicola Band
October 20—Treaty with the Potawatomi
October 20—Treaty with the Chickasaw
October 22—Treaty with the Chickasaw
October 24—Treaty with the Kickapoo
October 26—Treaty with the Potawatomi
October 26—Treaty with the Shawnee
and Delaware
October 27—Treaty with the Potawatomi
October 27—Treaty with the Kaskaskia
and Peoria of Illinois Tribes
October 27—Treaty with the Menominee
October 29—Treaty with the Piankashaw
and Wea
December 29—Treaty with the Seneca
and Shawnee

1833
February 14—Treaty with the Western
Cherokee
February 14—Treaty with the Creek
February 18—Treaty with the Ottawa
March 28—Treaty with the Seminole
May 13—Treaty with the Quapaw
June 18—Treaty with the Appalachicola
Band
September 21—Treaty with the Oto and
Missouri
September 26—Treaty with the
Chippewa, Ottawa, and Potawatomi
October 9—Treaty with the Pawnee

1834
May 24—Treaty with the Chickasaw
October 23—Treaty with the Miami
December 4—Treaty with the Potawatomi
December 10—Treaty with the
Potawatomi
December 16—Treaty with the
Potawatomi
December 17—Treaty with the
Potawatomi

1835
July 1—Treaty with the Caddo
August 24—Treaty with the Comanche
and Witchita "and their associated
bands" and between "these nations or
tribes, and the Cherokee, Muscogee,
Choctaw, Osage, Seneca, and Quapaw
Nations or Tribes of Indians."
December 29—Treaty with the Cherokee

1836
March 26—Treaty with the Potawatomi
March 28—Treaty with the Ottawa and
Chippewa
March 29—Treaty with the Potawatomi
April 11—Treaty with the Potawatomi
April 22—Treaty with the Potawatomi
April 22—Treaty with the Potawatomi
April 23—Treaty with the Wyandot
May 9—Treaty with the Chippewa
August 5—Treaty with the Potawatomi
September 3—Treaty with the Menominee
September 10—Treaty with the Sioux of
Wahashaw's Tribe of Indians
September 17—Treaty with the Iowa and
Sac and Fox of Missouri
September 20—Treaty with the
Potawatomi
September 22—Treaty with the
Potawatomi
September 23—Treaty with the
Potawatomi
September 27—Treaty with the Sac and
Fox
September 28—Treaty with the Sac and
Fox
September 28—Treaty with the Sac and
Fox
October 15—Treaty with the Oto,
Missouri, Omaha, Yankton, and
Santee Bands of Sioux
November 30—Treaty with the
Wahpaakootah, Sisseton and
Mdewakanton Bands of Sioux

1837
January 14—Treaty with the Chippewa
January 17—Treaty with the Choctaw
and Chickasaw
February 11—Treaty with the
Potawatomi
May 26—Treaty with the Kiowa, Ka-
ta-ka and Ta-wa-ka-ro
July 29—Treaty with the Chippewa
September 29—Treaty with the Sioux
October 21—Treaty with the Sac and Fox
October 21—Treaty with the Yankton
Sioux
October 21—Treaty with the Sac and Fox
November 1—Treaty with the Winnebago
November 23—Treaty with the Iowa
December 20—Treaty with the Chippewa

1838

January 15—Treaty with the New York Indians
January 23—Treaty with the Chippewa
February 3—Treaty with the Oneida
October 19—Treaty with the Iowa
November 6—Treaty with the Miami
November 23—Treaty with the Creek

1839

January 11—Treaty with the Osage
February 7—Treaty with the Chippewa
September 3—Treaty with the Stockbridge and Munsee

1840

November 28—Treaty with the Miami

1842

March 17—Treaty with the Wyandot
May 20—Treaty with the Seneca
October 4—Treaty with the Chippewa
October 11—Treaty with the Sac and Fox

1845

January 4—Treaty with the Creek and Seminole

1846

January 14—Treaty with the Kansa
May 15—Treaty with the Comanche, Aionai, Anadarko, Caddo, Lepan, Long-wha, Keechy, Tah-wa-carro, Wichita, and Waco
June 5 and 17—Treaty with the Potawatomi
August 6—Treaty with the Cherokee
October 13—Treaty with the Winnebago

1847

August 2—Treaty with the Chippewa of the Mississippi and Lake Superior
August 21—Treaty with the Pillager Band of Chippewa

1848

August 6—Treaty with the Pawnee (Grand Pawnee, Pawnee Loupe, Pawnee Republican, Pawnee Tappage)
October 18—Treaty with the Menominee
November 24—Treaty with the Stockbridge

1849

September 9—Treaty with the Navajo
December 30—Treaty with the Utah

1850

April 1—Treaty with the Wyandot

1851

July 23—Treaty with the Sioux-Sisseton and Wahpeton Bands
August 5—Treaty with the Mdewakanton and Wahpakoota Bands of Sioux
September 17—Treaty with the Sioux, Cheyenne, Arapaho, Crow, Assiniboine, Gros Ventre, Mandan, and Arikara

1852

June 22—Treaty with the Chickasaw
July 1—Treaty with the Apache

1853

July 27—Treaty with the Comanche, Kiowa, and Apache
September 10—Treaty with the Rogue River
September 19—Treaty with the Umpqua and Cow Creek Band

1854

March 15—Treaty with the Oto and Missouri
March 16—Treaty with the Omaha
May 6—Treaty with the Delaware
May 10—Treaty with the Shawnee
May 12—Treaty with the Menominee
May 17—Treaty with the Iowa
May 18—Treaty with the Sac and Fox
May 18—Treaty with the Kickapoo
May 30—Treaty with the Kaskaskia, Peoria, Piankashaw, and Wea
June 5—Treaty with the Miami
June 13—Treaty with the Creek
September 30—Treaty with the Chippewa
November 4—Treaty with the Choctaw and Chickasaw
November 15—Treaty with the Rogue River
November 18—Treaty with the Chasta, Scoton, and Umpqua
November 29—Treaty with the Umpqua and Kalapuya
December 9—Treaty with the Confederated Oto and Missouri
December 26—Treaty with the Nisqually, Puyallup, Steilacoom, Squawskin, S'Homamish, Stehchass, T'Peeksin, Squiaitl, and Saheh-wamish

1855

January 22—Treaty with the Kalapuya Confederated Bands of Indians
January 22—Treaty with the Dwamish, Suquamish, and Allied Bands of Indians
January 26—Treaty with the S'Klallam
January 31—Treaty with the Wyandot
January 31—Treaty with the Makah
February 22—Treaty with the Chippewa
February 27—Treaty with the Winnebago
June 9—Treaty with the Wallawalla, Cayuse, and Umatilla
June 9—Treaty with the Yakima
June 11—Treaty with the Nez Percé
June 22—Treaty with the Choctaw and Chickasaw
June 25—Treaty with the Middle Oregon Tribe
July 1—Treaty with the Quinault and Quileute
July 16—Treaty with the Flathead, Kootenai, and Upper Pend d'Oreille
July 31—Treaty with the Ottawa and Chippewa
August 2—Treaty with the Chippewa of Michigan
August 2—Treaty with the Chippewa of Saginaw, Swan Creek, and Black River
October 17—Treaty with the Blackfeet, Gros Ventre, Flathead, and Nez Percé
December 21—Treaty with the Molala

1856

February 5—Treaty with the Stockbridge and Munsee
February 11—Treaty with the Menominee
August 7—Treaty with the Creek and Seminole

1857

September 24—Treaty with the Pawnee
November 5—Treaty with the Tonawanda Band of Seneca

1858

March 12—Treaty with the Ponca
April 19—Treaty with the Yankton Sioux
June 19—Treaty with the Mdewakanton and Wahpahoota Bands of Sioux

June 19—Treaty with the Sisseton and Wahpeton Bands of Sioux

1859

April 15—Treaty with the Winnebago

July 16—Treaty with the Swan Creek and Black River Chippewa and Munsee or "Christian Indians"

October 1—Treaty with the Sac and Fox

October 5—Treaty with the Kansa

1860

May 30—Treaty with the Delaware

1861

February 18—Treaty with the Arapaho and Cheyenne

March 6—Treaty with the Sac and Fox

July 2—Treaty with the Delaware

November 15—Treaty with the Potawatomi

1862

March 13—Treaty with the Kansa

June 24—Treaty with the Ottawa

June 28—Treaty with the Kickapoo

1863

March 11—Treaty with the Mississippi, Pillager, and Lake Winnibigoshish Bands of Chippewa

June 9—Treaty with the Nez Percé

July 2—Treaty with the Eastern Shoshone

July 30—Treaty with the Northwestern Bands of Shoshone

October 1—Treaty with the Western Shoshone

October 2—Treaty with the Red Lake and Pembina Bands of Chippewa

October 7—Treaty with the Tabeguache Band of Utah Indians

October 12—Treaty with the Shoshone-Goshute

1864

April 12—Treaty with the Red Lake and Pembina Bands of Chippewa

May 7—Treaty with the Chippewa, Mississippi, Pillager, and Lake Winnebigoshish Bands of Chippewa City

October 14—Treaty with the Klamath, Modoc, and Snake Indians

October 18—Treaty with the Chippewa of Saginaw, Swan Creek, and Black River

1865

March 6—Treaty with the Omaha

March 8—Treaty with the Winnebago

March 10—Treaty with the Ponca

August 12—Treaty with the Snake

September 29—Treaty with the Osage

October 10—Treaty with the Miniconjou Band of Sioux

October 14—Treaty with the Lower Brulé Sioux

October 14—Treaty with the Cheyenne and Arapaho

October 17—Treaty with the Apache, Cheyenne, and Arapaho

October 18—Treaty with the Comanche and Kiowa

October 19—Treaty with the Two Kettle Band of Sioux

October 19—Treaty with the Blackfeet Sioux

October 20—Treaty with the San Arcs Band of Sioux

October 20—Treaty with the Hunkpapa Band of Sioux

October 20—Treaty with the Yanktonai Band of Sioux

October 28—Treaty with the Upper Yanktonai Band of Sioux

October 20—Treaty with the Oglala Band of Sioux

November 15—Treaty with the Middle Oregon Tribes

1866

March 21—Treaty with the Seminole

March 29—Treaty with the Potawatomi

April 7—Treaty with the Bois Fort Band of Chippewa

April 28—Treaty with the Choctaw and Chickasaw

June 14—Treaty with the Creek

July 4—Treaty with the Delaware

July 19—Treaty with the Cherokee

1867

February 18—Treaty with the Sac and Fox

February 19—Treaty with the Sisseton and Wahpeton Bands of Sioux

February 23—Treaty with the Seneca, Mixed Seneca, Shawnee Quapaw, Confederated Peoria, Kaskaskia, Wea and Piankashaw, Miami Ottawa, and Wyandot

February 27—Treaty with the Potawatomi

March 19—Treaty with the Chippewa of the Mississippi

October 21—Treaty with the Kiowa and Comanche

October 21—Treaty with the Kiowa, Comanche, and Apache

October 28—Treaty with the Cheyenne and Arapaho

1868

March 2—Treaty with the 7 Bands of Ute

April 27—Treaty with the Cherokee

April 29—Treaty with the Brulé, Oglala, Miniconjou, Yanktonai, Hunkpapa, Blackfeet, Cuthead, Two Kettle, San Arcs, and Santee Bands of Sioux and Arapaho

May 7—Treaty with the Crow

May 10—Treaty with the Northern Cheyenne and Northern Arapaho

June 1—Treaty with the Navajo

July 3—Treaty with the Eastern Band of Shoshone and Bannock

August 13—Treaty with the Nez Percé

APPENDIX IV
Native Landmarks

ALABAMA

Museums

Alabama Department of Archives and History Museum, Montgomery

Archaeological and Historical Sites

Ceremonial Indian Mound and Museum, Florence
Mound State Monument, Moundville

ALASKA

Museums

Anchorage Museum of History and Art, Anchorage
Dillingham Heritage Museum, Dillingham
Hoonah Cultural Center and Museum, Hoonah
Inupiat University Museum, Barrow
Nana Museum of the Arctic, Kotzebue
Sealaska Gallery Cultural Museum, Juneau
Yugtaruik Regional Museum, Bethel

ARIZONA

Museums

Ak Chin Him Dak, Maricopa
Arizona State Museum, Tucson
Colorado River Tribal Museum/ Library, Parker
Havasupai Reservation Tribal Museum, Supai
Heard Museum, Phoenix

Hualapai Tribal Museum, Peach Springs
Mohave Museum of History and Arts, Kingman
Museum of Northern Arizona, Flagstaff
Navajo Tribal Museum, Window Rock
Ned A. Hatathli Center Museum, Tsaile
Quechen Museum, Yuma
Salt River Pima-Maricopa Tribal Museum, Scottsdale
Yavapai Museum, Grand Canyon

Archaeological and Historical Sites

Aztec Ruins National Monument, Aztec
Canyon de Chelly National Monument, Chinle
Casa Grande National Monument, Coolidge
Montezuma Castle National Monument, Clarksdale
Navajo National Monument, Tonalea
Old Oraibi Village, Third Mesa
Pueblo Grande Museum and Hohokam Indian Ruins, Phoenix
Tonto National Monument, Roosevelt
Walpi Pueblo, Tuba City
Window Rock Tribal Park, Window Rock

General Interest

Fort Apache Cultural Center, Fort Apache

Gila River Arts and Crafts Center, Sacaton
Hopi Cultural Center, Second Mesa
Navajo Nation Zoological Park, Window Rock
White Mountain Apache Cultural Center, Old Fort Apache

ARKANSAS

Museums

Arkansas State University Museum, Jonesboro

Archaeological and Historical Sites

Nodena Site, Wilson
Toltec Indian Mound State Park, England

CALIFORNIA

Museums

Aqua Caliente Cultural Museum, Palm Springs
American Indian Contemporary Art Gallery, San Francisco
Hearst Museum of Anthropology (formerly the Robert H. Lowie Museum of Anthropology), Berkeley
Hoopa Tribal Museum, Hoopa
Malki Museum, Inc., Banning
Museum of Man, San Diego
Palm Springs Desert Museum, Palm Springs
San Luiseño Band of Mission Indians Museum, Valley Center
Southwest Museum, Los Angeles

Gila River Arts and Crafts Center, Gila River Pima-Maricopa Indian Community, Sacaton, Arizona. This complex, owned and operated by the Gila River Indian Community, includes an Indian culture center and museum and an outdoor heritage park with replicas of the villages of the five Gila River Basin cultures. Photograph by Karen Warth.

Ned A. Hatathli Center, Tsaile, Navajo Nation, Arizona. The center, located on the campus of Navajo Community center, houses the Hatathli Museum which includes exhibits on Navajo history and culture as well as Plains Indian cultures. Photograph by Karen Warth.

Archaeological and Historical Sites

Big and Little Petroglyph Canyons, China Lake

Blythe Intaglios, Blythe

Calico Early Man Archaeological Site, Barstow

Chaw-Se Indian Grinding Rocks State Park, Jackson

General Interest

Cupa Cultural Center, Pala

Elch-Qua-Nun (Land of the People) Community Library, Santa Ysabel

Intertribal Friendship House, Oakland

Lake Mendocino Cultural Center, Ukiah

Owens Valley Paiute-Shoshone Indian Cultural Center, Bishop

Rincon Tribal Education Center, Valley Center

The Sun House, Ukiah

United Native American Education Center, Sacramento

COLORADO

Museums

Denver Art Museum, Denver

Denver Museum of Natural History, Denver

Mesa Verde National Park Museum, Mesa Verde

Ute Indian Museum, Montrose

Archaeological and Historical Park

Chimney Rock, Pagosa Springs

Excalante and Dominguez Ruins, Cortez

Ute Mountain Tribal Park, Towaoc

General Interest

Southern Ute Tourist Center, Ignacio

CONNECTICUT

Museums

Institute for the American Indian, Washington

Peabody Museum of Natural History, Yale University, New Haven

Tantaquidegon Indian Museum, Uncasville

Archaeological and Historical Sites

Mashantucket Pequot Research Library, Ledyard

DELAWARE

Museums

Delaware State Museum, Dover

Island Field Archaeological Museum and Research Center, South Bower

Nanticoke Indian Association Museum, Millsboro

FLORIDA

Museums

Ah-Tha-Thi-Ki Museum, Hollywood

Florida State Museum, University of Florida, Gainsville

Miccosukee Cultural Center, Miami

Seminole Tribal Museum, Tampa

Archaeological and Historical Sites

Crystal River State Archaeological Site, Crystal River

GEORGIA

Museums

Kolomoki Mounds Museum, Blakely

Archaeological and Historical Sites

Cherokee Nation Memorial and Chief Vann House State Historic Site, Chatsworth

Etowah Mounds Archaeological Area, Cantersville

New Echota Historic Site, Calhoun

IDAHO

Museums

Fort Hall Indian Museum, Fort Hall

Nez Percé National Historic Park and Museum, Spalding

ILLINOIS

Museums

Cahokia Mounds State Historic Site and Museum, East St. Louis

Dickson Mounds Museum, Lewiston

Field Museum of Natural History, Chicago

Archaeological and Historical Sites

Kampsville Archaeological, Kampsville

INDIANA

Museums

Eiteljorg Museum of American Indian and Western Art, Indianapolis

Archaeological and Historical Sites

Angel Mounds State Historical Site, Evansville

Mounds State Park, Anderson

IOWA

Museums

Iowa State Historical Museum, Des Moines

Archaeological and Historical Sites

Effigy Mounds National Monument, McGregor

KANSAS

Museums

El Quartelejo Kiva Indian Museum, Scott City

Kansas Museum of History, Topeka

Mid-America All-Indian Center and Museum, Witchita

University of Kansas Museum of Anthropology, Lawrence

KENTUCKY

Museums

Ancient Buried City, Archaeology Museum, Wickliffe

Archaeological and Historical Sites

Adena Park, Lexington

LOUISIANA

Museums

Coushatta Tribe Visitors Center and Museum, Elton
Tunica-Biloxi Regional Indian Center and Museum, Marksville

MAINE

Museums

Maine Tribal Unity Museum, Unity
Old Town Museum, Old Town
Wabanaki Museum and Resource Center, Pleasant Point

MARYLAND

Museums

Archaeological Society of Maryland, Silver Spring
Piscataway Museum Project, Indian Head

MASSACHUSETTS

Museums

Children's Museum, Inc., Boston
Peabody Museum of Archaeology and Ethnology, Harvard University, Cambridge
Wampanoag Indian Program of Plymouth Plantation, Plymouth

Archaeological and Historical Sites

Mashpee Tribal Meeting House, Mashpee

MICHIGAN

Museums

Cranbrook Institute of Science, Bloomfield Hills
Great Lakes Indian Museum, Detroit

Archaeological and Historical Sites

The Anishinabe Aki Village, Flint

MINNESOTA

Museums

Mille Lacs Indian Museum, Onamia
Minneapolis American Indian Center Museum, Minneapolis
The Science Museum of Minnesota, St. Paul

Archaeological and Historical Sites

Indian Mounds Park, St. Paul
Mound Group, International Falls
Pipestone National Monument, Pipestone

MISSISSIPPI

Museums

The Choctaw Museum of the Southern Indian, Philadelphia

Archaeological and Historical Sites

Chickasaw Indian Village Site, Tupelo
The Grand Village of the Natchez Indians, Natchez

MISSOURI

Museums

Line Creek Museum, Kansas City
Museum of Man, Art and Archaeology, University of Missouri, Columbia
William Rockhill Nelson Gallery and Atkins Museum of Fine Arts, Kansas City

MONTANA

Museums

Flat Head Indian Museum, St. Ignatius

Fort Peck Tribal Museum, Poplar
Museum of the Plains Indian, Browning
Northern Cheyenne Tribal Museum, Lame Deer

Archaeological and Historical Sites

Little Big Horn National Monument, Crow Agency
Madison Buffalo Run, Logan

General Interest

Crow Tribe Historical and Cultural Commission, Crow Agency

NEBRASKA

Museums

Fort Robinson Museum, Nebraska State Historical Society, Crawford
University of Nebraska State Museum, Lincoln

NEVADA

Museums

Museum of Natural History, Las Vegas
Northeastern Nevada Museum, Elko

Archaeological and Historical Sites

Lake Mead National Recreation Area, Boulder City

NEW HAMPSHIRE

Museums

Dartmouth College Museum and Galleries, Hanover

NEW JERSEY

Museums

The Montclair Art Museum, Montclair

The Iroquois Indian Museum, Howes Cave, New York. Fashioned after Six Nations (Iroquois) longhouses of the past, the museum features modern arts, archaeological, and historical exhibits. Performances take place in the tent. Photograph by Stephen J. Levine.

NEW MEXICO

Museums

Acoma Museum, Acoma Pueblo

Institute of American Indian Arts Museum, Santa Fe

Jicarilla Arts and Crafts Museum, Dulce

Maxwell Museum of Anthropology, Albuquerque

Mescalero Apache Cultural Center Museum, Mescalero

Millicent Rogers Museum, Taos

Museum of Indian Arts and Culture-Laboratory of Anthropology, Santa Fe

Picuris Pueblo Museum, Penasco

San Ildefonso Pueblo Museum, Santa Fe

The Wheelwright Museum of the American Indian, Santa Fe

Zuni Museum, Zuni

Archaeological and Historical Sites

Aztec Ruins National Monument, Aztec

Bandelier National Monument, Los Alamos

Chaco Culture National Historical Park, Bloomfield

General Interest

Indian Pueblo Cultural Center, Albuquerque

Jemez Visitor's Center, Jemez Pueblo, Jemez

Santo Domingo Cultural Center, Santo Domingo

School of American Research, Santa Fe

Zia Pueblo Cultural Center, San Ysidro

NEW YORK

Museums

Akwesasne Museum, Hogansburg

American Museum of Natural History, New York

The Brooklyn Museum, Brooklyn

Canandaigua Historical Society Museum, Canandaigua

Cayuga Museum of History and Art, Auburn

Iroquois Indian Museum, Howes Cave

Mohawk-Caughnawaga Museum, Fonda

National Museum of the American Indian/Smithsonian Institution, New York

Six Nations Indian Museum, Onchiota

Seneca-Iroquois National Museum, Salamanca

Tonawanda-Seneca Museum, Basom

American Indian Community House Gallery, New York

Native American Centre for the Living Arts, Inc., Niagara Falls

NORTH CAROLINA

Museums

Museum of the Cherokee Indian, Cherokee

Archaeological and Historical Sites

Oconaluftee Indian Village, Cherokee

Town Creek Indian Mound State Historic Site, Mt. Gilead

General Interest

Haliwa-Saponi Library, Hollister

NORTH DAKOTA

Museums

Four Bears Museum, New Town

Standing Rock Reservation Museum, Fort Yates

Three Affiliated Tribes Museum, New Town

General Interest

Anishinaubag Center and St. Paul Indian Ministries, Belcourt

Turtle Mountain Chippewa Heritage Center, Belcourt

OHIO

Museums

Cincinnati Museum of Natural History, Cincinnati

Moundbuilders State Memorial and Museum, Newark

Serpent Mound State Memorial and Museum, Locust Grove

Archaeological and Historical Sites

Campbell Mound, Columbus

Mound City Group National Monument, Chillicothe

OKLAHOMA

Museums

Anadarko Museum, Anadarko

Apache Tribal Museum, Anadarko

Bacone College Museum, Atalon Art Lodge, Muskogee

Cherokee National Museum, Tahlequah

Chickasaw Council House Museum, Tishomingo

Choctaw Council House and Museum, Skullyville

Choctaw Nation Historical Museum, Tuskahoma

Comanche Culture Center Museum, Cache

Creek Council House Museum, Okmulgee

Delaware Tribal Museum, Anadarko

Five Civilized Tribes Museum, Muskogee

Fort Sill Apache Museum, Apache

Muskogee Creek National Museum, Okmulgee

Kiowa Tribal Museum, Carnegie

Osage Tribal Museum, Pawhuska

Philbrook Art Center, Tulsa

Potawatomi Indian Nation Archives and Museum, Shawnee

Sac and Fox Tribal RV Park and Museum/Cultural Center, Stroud

Seminole Nation Museum, Weweoka

Southern Plains Indian Museum, Anadarko

Thomas Gilcrease Institute of American History and Art, Tulsa

Tonkawa Tribal Museum, Tonkawa

General Interest

Jim Thorpe's Home, Yale

Oklahoma City Native American Indian Center, Oklahoma City

Sequoyah Home Site, Sallisaw

Wichita Tribal Cultural Center, Anadarko

OREGON

Museums

Klamath Tribe Museum, Chiloquin

Warm Springs Museum, Shitike Creek

PENNSYLVANIA

Museums

University Museum, University of Pennsylvania, Philadelphia

Archaeological and Historical Sites

Carlisle Indian School, Carlisle

Jim Thorpe Memorial, Jim Thorpe

RHODE ISLAND

Museums

Haffenreffer Museum of Anthropology, Brown University, Bristol

Narragansett Museum, Exeter

Tomaquag Indian Memorial Museum, Exeter

SOUTH CAROLINA

Archaeological and Historical Sites

Santee Indian Mounds, Santee State Park, Santee

SOUTH DAKOTA

Museums

Buechel Memorial Lakota Museum, St. Francis

Harvey Johnson American Indian Cultural Center Museum, Eagle Butte

Red Cloud Indian Museum, Kadoka

Sioux Indian Museum, Rapid City

Yankton Sioux Museum, Marty

Archaeological and Historical Sites

Grave of Chief Sitting Bull, Mobridge

Wounded Knee Monument, Wounded Knee

TENNESSEE

Museums

Chucalissa Indian Town and Museum, Memphis

Archaeological and Historical Sites

Pinson Mounds State Archaeological Area, Pinson

Red Clay State Historical Park, Cleveland

TEXAS

Museums

Alabama-Coushatta Indian Museum, Livingston

Ysleta Del Sur Pueblo Museum, El Paso

Archaeological and Historical Sites

Alibates Flint Quarries National Monument, Fritch

Caddoan Mounds State Historic Park, Alto

General Interest

Native American Cultural Heritage Center, Dallas

UTAH

Museums

Ute Tribal Museum, Fort Duchesne

Archaeological and Historical Sites

Anasazi Indian Village State Historical Monument, Boulder
Canyonlands National Park, Moab

VERMONT

Museums

Robert Hull Fleming Museum, University of Vermont, Burlington

VIRGINIA

Museums

Hampton Institute Museum, Hampton
Mattaponi Indian Museum and Trading Post, West Point
Pamunkey Cultural Center Museum, King William

WASHINGTON

Museums

Colville Confederated Tribes Museum, Coulee Dam
Lelooska Family Museum, Ariel

Puyallup Tribe Museum, Tacoma
Suquamish Museum, Suquamish
Toppenish Museum, Toppenish
Washington State Museum, Thomas Burke Memorial, University of Washington, Seattle
Yakima Nation Museum, Toppenish

Archaeological and Historical Sites

Chief Joseph Memorial, Nespelem

General Interest

Daybreak Star Arts Center, Seattle
Makah Cultural Research Center, Neah Bay
Spokane Tribe Community Center, Wellpinit
Steilacoom Cultural Center, Steilacoom

WASHINGTON D.C.

Museums

National Museum of American History/Smithsonian Institution
National Museum of Natural History/Smithsonian Institution

WEST VIRGINIA

Museums

Archaeology Museum, West Virginia University, Morgantown
Mound Museum, Moundsville

Archaeological and Historical Sites

East Steubenville Site, East Steubenville

Grave Creek Indian Mound, Moundsville

WISCONSIN

Museums

Lac Du Flambeau Indian Museum, Lac Du Flambeau
Milwaukee Public Museum, Milwaukee
Ojibwa Nation Museum, Hayward
Oneida Nation Museum, Oneida
Red Cliff Tribal Museum, Bayfield
Stockbridge-Munsee Historical Library and Museum, Bowler
Winnebago Indian Museum, Wisconsin Dells

Archaeological and Historical Sites

Effigy Mounds in Animal Forms, Devil's Lake State Park, Baraboo
Menasha Mounds, Menasha

General Interest

Bad River Living History, Odanah

WYOMING

Museums

Arapahoe Cultural Museum, Ethete
Plains Indian Museum, Cody

General Interest

Shoshone Tribal Cultural Center, Fort Washakie

APPENDIX V
Chronology

1492, October 12 Christopher Columbus (Colon [Spanish]; Columb [French]; Colom [Portuguese]) landed on the Caribbean island that the people living there called Guanahani, which he named San Salvador. He called the people Indios (Indians). They called themselves Arawaks. Columbus wanted gold, a word appearing 75 times in the first two weeks of his journal entries.

1494 Christopher Columbus initiated the enslavement of Native Americans by Europeans by sending more than 500 of them to Spain to be sold.

1540–1542 From Mexico, the Spanish began their intrusion of Pueblo country in the southwest, conquering the Zuni Pueblo in what is now New Mexico. Finding no gold or silver and encountering native resistance, they temporarily withdrew.

1564 Jacques Le Moyne, part of the French Huguenot colony on St. Johns River in Florida, made the first known European pictures of Indians.

c. 1570 According to written sources, the Five Nations [Iroquois] Confederacy (Cayugas, Mohawks, Oneidas, Onondagas, and Senecas) was founded by Deganawidah, a Huron prophet, and Mohawk statesman Hiawatha. A sixth nation, the Tuscaroras, joined the confederacy in 1722.

1598–1599 Ignoring Pueblo land ownership, the Spanish took possession of "New Mexico." They attacked and virtually destroyed Acoma Pueblo killing, maiming, and enslaving the people.

1605–1619 English ships visited the New England coast trading with Algonquians and kidnapping many. Tisquantum, or Squanto, a Patuxet, was carried off to Spain but managed to get back, only to find his people wiped out by disease.

1607 The English established Jamestown, Virginia, in the territory of the Powhatan Confederacy, led by Wahunsonacock (Powhatan). The Powhatans captured an exploratory party led by English soldier Captain John Smith, who was released at the request of Pocahontas, Wahunsonacock's daughter.

1614 The English negotiated a peace treaty with Wahunsonacock (Powhatan), leader of the Powhatan Confederacy, an alliance of at least thirty tribes. John Rolfe of Jamestown married Pocahontas, a marriage sanctioned by her father. She went to England with him and died there.

1616 The English in Virginia, unable to raise their own food, tried to collect tribute but the Chickahominy refused. The English invaded, captured, and killed several leaders, and forced the payment of tribute.

1621, March 22 Massasoit, Wampanoag chief, and the Pilgrims of Plymouth made a treaty of alliance (recorded in William Bradford's *Of Plymouth Plantation*, 1621). Massasoit faithfully kept the treaty terms until his death over forty years later despite the fact the burden of peace-keeping was placed on the Wampanoags.

1622, March 22 Opechancanough, Powhatan, brother of Wahunsonacock led the Powhatans and other Tidewater tribes in a rebellion against the English colony of Jamestown, killing almost 350, trying to expel them from Jamestown. The English recovered and the war continued for almost ten years. This was the first recorded Indian uprising.

1626, May 6 In the now-famous transaction, Canarsee Indians who occupied the southern end of the island of what is now Manhattan (and who appeared to possess the whole island) sold it to Peter Minuit, Dutch governor of New Amsterdam, now New York, for 60 Dutch guilders, or the equivalent of $24. When settlers moved to the upper end of the island, the long-time resident Weckquaesgeek were unwilling to abandon their homes, planting fields, fishing grounds, and ancestral graves. Conflicts, bloodshed, and property damage resulted from the misunderstood bargain for the purchase of Manhattan.

1636–1637 English aggression in New England resulted in the Pequot War during which the Pequots tried to resist invasion by settlers. The Narragansetts and Mohegans helped the English, led by Captain John Mason, and hundreds of Pequots were killed in their village near Mystic, Connecticut or sold into slavery.

1638, November 14 English colonists in what is now New Haven, Connecticut, negotiated a land sale with Quinnipiac Indians and established what is called the first reservation in the United States.

1644 Opechancanough led the Powhatans in another war for freedom against the English colony of Jamestown, Virginia, but the English captured and murdered him in 1646, ending the revolt.

1649 The English Assembly at Jamestown ordered that Indian town boundaries be clearly marked and defined. This was a device whereby the whites would not have to recognize Indian title to any lands beyond the town boundaries.

1650 About this time, the Cheyennes abandoned their farms on the Minnesota, Mississippi, and Red Rivers and began moving west, becoming buffalo hunters.

1651–1661 With authority from the Massachusetts General Court, John Eliot, a missionary known as the "Apostle to the Indians," began the organization of "praying towns" in New England, designed to bring Christian Indians under colonial rule and to segregate them from unconverted neighbors. He established the first Indian church in New England and began printing religious texts, including the Bible, in the Algonquian language.

1659 The Governor at Santa Fe sent to Mexico City a report of a raid by a band of mounted Navajo Apaches, the first documented evidence of the use of horses by Indians in the American West.

1661 Spanish authorities raided Pueblo kivas (sacred ceremonial chambers) and destroyed hundreds of sacred Kachina masks and other sacred objects in an effort to destroy Indian religion.

1670, August 22 John Eliot and John Cotten ordained Hiacoomes as a Christian missionary. He preached his first service to his own people, the Wampanoags, on Martha's Vineyard.

1675–1676 The Five Nations launched an all out war against the Susquehannas, their old trade rival. Blaming the Susquehannas for raids actually carried out by the Senecas, frontier whites also turned on the Susquehannas, their one-time allies. The Susquehannas, once a powerful barrier to the expansion of the Five Nations, were dispersed.

1675–1676 Southern New England tribes tried to halt English expansion.

Metacomet, called King Philip by the English, began a war against the New England colonists. He gathered some 20,000 Indians who fought for a year but failed to win back their country.

1675, December 19 Captain Benjamin Church of the Plymouth Colony militia led colonial forces against the Narragansetts in Rhode Island who were slaughtered or sold into slavery.

1676, August 12 Metacomet was killed by New England troops. His wife and son were sold into slavery in the West Indies.

1677, May 29 The British government made a peace treaty with the Powhatan nations after realizing that the Indians had been greatly wronged in the Anglo–Susquehanna war. Since many whites had already established themselves in that area, they could easily encroach on Native property.

1680–1683 Aided by some Shawnees, the English in South Carolina destroyed all but fifty of their allies, the Westos, in order to get slaves and better access to the interior. The survivors eventually joined the Creeks.

1680, August 10 The well-planned liberation struggle launched by pueblo religious leaders forced the Spanish invaders to flee New Mexico. Twenty-one Franciscans and about 400 Spanish were killed in the revolt. On August 21, Governor Antonio de Otermin gave orders to exit the Santa Fe area. Although Pueblo people never divulged the names of the leaders of the revolt, some became known. Historical literature generally credits Pope, a San Juan medicine man as leader, however representatives from each village, including Jaca from Taos, Catiti of Santo Domingo, and Tupati of Picuris, helped plan and execute the revolt.

1682 The Delaware Indians made a treaty of good will with William Penn, English Quaker and founder of Pennsylvania, at the village of Shackamaxon on the Delaware River.

1691 English people who married Indians, blacks, or mullatoes were banished from Virginia.

1692, August 16 General Diego de Vargas began a four month campaign to restore twenty-three pueblo villages to the Spanish crown, boasting that he did the feat "without wasting a single ounce of powder, unsheathing a sword, or without costing the Royal Treasury a single maravedi."

1705 The Virginia Assembly restricted the rights of Indians guaranteed by the Treaty of 1677. Indians were not allowed to gather wild foods on English lands, vote, hold public office, testify in court as witnesses, or carry weapons dangerous to the English.

1713, March 25 Colonel James Moore of South Carolina attacked Tuscaroras in North Carolina. Those fortunate to escape death or slavery moved north to New York where they were eventually accepted in 1722 as the sixth nation in the Iroquois Confederacy.

1715, April 15 The great revolt of southern Indians against the English was spearheaded by the Yamassees of South Carolina who resented English slave-catching practices, land encroachment, rum selling, and shady fur trade deals. Many Cherokees did not join and the Chickasaws remained pro-English. It is estimated that Indians killed 90 percent of the Indian traders in South Carolina within the first few months of the war.

1717–1718 The English, French, and Spanish all tried to win over the Creek Confederacy to secure its trade, but the Creek were not dominated by any European group and became a powerful independent force.

1720, August 13 The Pawnees and Otoes wiped out a Spanish army on the Platte River and prevented the Spanish invasion of the Plains.

1723 The first permanent Indian school in the British colonies opened at William and Mary College in Williamsburg, Virginia.

1725, February 19 Captain John Lovewell led an attack against Indians in Wakefield, New Hampshire. His troops took Indian scalps, the first record of scalping by colonists.

1737, August 25 In Philadelphia, the "Walking Purchase Treaty" was signed by Delawares' Lappawinzo, Nutimus, and

Sassoonan with Pennsylvania colonists. According to convention, land was ceded in terms of the distance a man could walk in a day. The English used trained "walkers" who covered sixty-seven miles in a day and a half, a distance far in excess of the Delawares' intent.

1754–1763 During the "French and Indian War," most Algonquian Indians sided with the French but others, especially the Iroquois, helped the English.

1754, June 19–July 10 The Albany Congress was held in New York in which commissioners of the British colonies tried to develop a united colonial Indian policy, conciliate the Iroquois, and insure its support against France. Benjamin Franklin proposed a union among the colonists said to be modeled after the Six Nations Confederacy. The plan was never adopted.

1758, August 29 The first state Indian reservation in North America, called Brotherton, was established by the New Jersey colonial assembly in Burlington County. About 200 Indians, possibly Unamis, settled on the tract until it was sold in 1801.

1763 The British issued a proclamation forbidding settlers to move westward across the Appalachians. The proclamation, unpopular with American colonists, was ignored.

1763, May 7 The Ottawa leader Pontiac, and his pan-Indian confederacy, launched its attack on the English in the Great Lakes region with a surprise assault on Detroit. The alliance captured all British forts west of Niagara except for Fort Detroit and Fort Pitt (Pittsburgh). At General Jeffrey Amherst's suggestion, Henry Bouquet ordered the distribution of smallpox-infected blankets as gifts to Indians near Fort Pitt. The smallpox epidemic contributed to the collapse of Pontiac's alliance. Pontiac signed a peace treaty with the British on August 17, 1765.

1769 Junipero Serra, Franciscan missionary from Spain who was considered the architect of the California mission system, founded San Diego de Alcala, the first in a series of twenty-one missions

built along the coastal trail of California. By 1834, the end of the mission period, thousands of Hoopa, Kumeyaay, Cahuilla, Pauma, Malki, Cupa, and other tribal peoples were forced to convert, labor, and radically change their identity, were confined and punished, and eventually became sapped by disease and died. From the beginning of missionization, uprisings took place frequently.

1775–1783 Tribes were drawn into the American Revolution mainly on the side of the British. The Oneidas and Tuscaroras allied with the Americans against the British in the War for Independence, thus breaking the unity of the Six Nations [Iroquois] Confederacy.

1775, July 21 An Act of Congress divided Indian country into three geographic departments: northern, middle, and southern. Each division had commissioners authorized to make treaties and to arrest British agents.

1775, November 5 The Kamias destroyed the mission at San Diego in the first serious revolt against the missions.

1778, September 17 The first treaty between the Delawares and the newly-organized United States took place at Fort Pitt. The treaty, which guaranteed Delaware territorial rights, asked that peace be established and that U.S. troops be allowed to travel through Delaware land.

1779, August General George Washington sent General John Sullivan to invade the country of the Six Nations [Iroquois] Confederacy who were aiding the English in western Pennsylvania and New York. Sullivan destroyed forty Indian towns, cut down peach trees, and burned 160,000 bushels of corn and other vegetables. The Iroquois were not conquered. As one future president, James Madison, wrote to another, Thomas Jefferson, "The expedition of General Sullivan . . . seems by its effects rather to have exasperated than to have terrified or disabled [the Iroquois]."

1786, June 28 Congress reorganized Indian affairs into the Northern and Southern Departments so that Indian relations might be more effectually controlled.

1787 The Constitution gave the gov-

ernment power to "regulate commerce with foreign nations and among the several states and with the Indian tribes within the limits of any states . . ." This clause, along with the power to make laws and treaties, was the basis for subsequent legislation and decisions regarding Indians.

1787, August 7 The Northwest Ordinance created the basis for the settlement of whites beyond the Alleghenies. It provided that the Indians' land should never be taken from them without their consent.

1788 A smallpox epidemic virtually wiped out Pecos Pueblo leaving about 180 survivors.

1790, July 22 Congress passed a measure that provided for licensing Indian traders. This was the first in a series of acts known as the Indian Trade and Intercourse Acts that regulated trade with Indians and gave the President vast regulatory powers.

1791, November 4 Tribes in Ohio (Shawnees, Delawares, Miamis, Wyandots, Kickapoos, Ottawas, Potawatomis and others) led by Miami Little Turtle annihilated the army of General Arthur Saint Clair, Governor of the Northwest Territory, near present-day Fort Wayne, Indiana. This has been called the worst defeat in U.S. history.

1794, August 20 General Anthony Wayne defeated the Ottawa, Shawnee, and other Ohio Indians led by Shawnees Blue Jacket and Tecumseh at the Battle of Fallen Timbers, near present-day Toledo, Ohio.

1794 The Jay Treaty between Great Britain and the United States guaranteed Indians on both sides the right to pass freely across the U.S.–Canada border.

1795–1822 The U.S. government established twenty-eight factories (federal stores or trading houses) to control trade with Indians and to counteract the Spanish and British influence. Factories were designed to insure a good price for furs and supply the Indians with cheaper and better goods.

1799, June 15 During the Strawberry Festival, while Seneca prophet Handsome Lake was ill, he had his first vision during which messengers told him to preach messages against alcohol, witchcraft, love magic, and abortion. Other visions propelled Handsome Lake into founding a religion, a combination of ancient tradition, Christian elements, and the prophet's innovations, that spiritually renewed his people, who had been devastated by the American Revolution, factionalism, illness, and land cession.

1802–1820s The U.S. government tried to force, bribe, and persuade all Indian tribes to move from east to west of the Mississippi River. Many moved, but others resisted.

1804, May William Clark and Meriwether Lewis, co-leaders of a government-financed expedition into the newly-acquired Louisiana Territory, departed from St. Louis. The expedition eventually encountered around fifty tribes. Back in St. Louis by September 1806, Lewis and Clark reported their findings about topography, Indians, and wildlife to President Thomas Jefferson.

1811, November 7 General William Henry Harrison, along with a force of Indian militia and troops fought the Shawnees and allied tribes near the upper Wabash River in northeast Indiana. This confrontation became known as the Battle of Tippecanoe. Harrison drove off the Indians, led by the Prophet Tenskwatawa, brother of Tecumseh, who was away at the time gathering support among southern tribes. The fighting weakened Tecumseh's confederation.

1813, October 5 Tecumseh, Shawnee warrior and chief, tried to stop the westward flow of American settlers and allied with the British in the War of 1812. He was killed in the Battle of Thames in Ontario, Canada.

1814, March 27 The Creek tribe was defeated in the Battle of Horseshoe Band, Alabama by militia led by Andrew Jackson.

1819, March 3 Congress set up a program for the "civilization" of Indians. The funds were distributed among mission groups, enabling them to widen educational programs among Indians.

1821 Sequoyah, a Cherokee, finished work on an eighty-six symbol syllabary

Sequoyah was honored by the postal service in December of 1980 for his great achievement in creating a syllabary that enabled his people, the Cherokee, to read and write the Cherokee language. Courtesy the U.S. Postal Service.

representing different sounds in the Cherokee language. Based on the Roman alphabet and other symbols, the Cherokee people learned to read within a few months. Sequoyah was honored with a U.S. postage stamp on December 27, 1980.

1822 The factory system was abolished and the remaining goods were to be sold at public auctions. Private traders were to handle trade with the Indians.

1824, March 11 Thomas L. McKenney was appointed "head" of the Indian Office, newly established within the War Department where it remained until 1849.

1827 Stanislaus, an Indian, escaped from San Jose Mission and led the first successful Indian-organized revolt at Santa Clara and San Jose missions.

1828, February 21 The Cherokee Tribal Council in New Echota, Georgia, published the first issue of the weekly *Cherokee Phoenix*, the first Indian-language newspaper in the United States. Edited by Cherokee Elias Boudinot, the paper was printed in English and the Cherokee syllabary developed in 1821 by Sequoyah. The paper continued until

1834, when the state of Georgia suppressed it.

1830–1838 At the request of President Andrew Jackson, Congress passed the Indian Removal Act forcing 92 percent of all Indians living east of the Mississippi River to Indian territory west of the Mississippi. The Cherokees, Chickasaws, Yuchis, Creeks, Choctaws, and Alabamas were forced to give up their lands in the southeast. Many died from disease and exposure in forced migrations at gun point.

1832, August 1–2 At the Bad Axe River in Wisconsin, U.S. volunteer troops led by Henry Atkinson massacred hundreds of unarmed women, children, and elders led by Black Hawk, Sac leader. Black Hawk was leading them across the Mississippi River in hopes of restoring their villages and planting crops on lands from which they had been removed by treaty. Black Hawk was captured and the remainder of the band forced to give up the eastern part of Iowa as punishment for the war. In 1989, the Wisconsin Assembly presented an apology to the Sac and Fox Nation expressing regret for the Black Hawk War and Bad Axe Massacre, admitting "the campaign was marked by faulty intelligence, blunders, violence against non-combatants, and other improper conduct by troops and territorial militia."

1834, October The Tongva and Iviatim of the San Bernardino region rebelled and were punished. In December, they rebelled again and sacked and burned the buildings of the mission.

1835, December 28 Major Francis L. Dade and his column were ambushed near Wahoo Swamp by Seminoles and blacks under Alligator, Jumper, and Micanopy during the second Seminole War. Dade and about half of his men died. Seminoles were angry about being forced to move from Florida to Indian Territory.

1847, November 29 A group of Cayuse attacked the Presbyterian mission in Oregon Territory killing the missionaries. They retaliated against the increasing number of whites in the area and for the devastating measles epidemic killing Indians who had no immunity to the disease.

1848, February 2 The Treaty of Guadalupe Hildago with Mexico brought many new tribes under U.S. jurisdiction.

1849 A congressional act transferred the Indian Office from the War Department to the newly created Interior Department.

1849–1885 There were fifteen million buffalo on the Plains in two great herds. By 1880, the southern herd was wiped out and by 1885 the northern herd was almost exterminated. The slaughter of buffalo by white hunters destroyed the Indians' basis of subsistence.

1851, September 17 The Treaty of Fort Laramie with the Plains Indians defined their territories. In return for ending hostilities, Indians were promised annuities, later cut down by the U.S. Senate.

1851, May 13–July 8, 1852 Because of the intervention of California politicians and entrepreneurs, the California legislature opposed eighteen treaties negotiated between federal commissioners and representatives of California Indian groups and instructed its congressional representatives to do likewise. On July 8, 1852, the Senate rejected each of the treaties. The U.S. did not inform the Indians that the treaties were rejected and drove them off the land.

1861–1865 Many Indian tribes were caught in the middle during the U.S. Civil War, especially tribes in Indian Territory (Oklahoma). Chickasaws and Choctaws were mostly pro-Confederate, Cherokees and Creeks evenly divided, and the Kickapoos anti-Confederate. Indian units fought on both sides during the war.

1862 Secretary of the Interior Caleb Smith advocated a sharp change in Indian policy stating that tribes should no longer be regarded as independent (self-governing) nations but rather as "wards of the government." The policy, gradually put into effect, was in full operation by the 1880s.

1862 The Homestead Act brought vast numbers of settlers on to public domain lands in Kansas and Nebraska to claim 160 acres of land for each head of the family. Many settled on land belonging to Indian tribes and were certified as owners of the illegally taken land.

1862, December 26 The easternmost Dakotas (Sioux) who suffered broken promises, loss of their hunting grounds, and the invasion of their territories by whites who drove away the game on which they depended, resisted white aggression in the so-called "Minnesota Sioux War" under the leadership of Little Crow. After much fighting, 300 Dakotas were captured and thirty-eight of them publicly hanged in Mankato, Minnesota in the largest mass execution in U.S. history.

1864 Reversing previous policies, a federal law was passed that regarded Indians as competent witnesses and allowed them to testify in trials involving white people.

1864, March 6 The Navajo Long Walk began. Altogether, some 8,000 Navajos were force marched from their homeland in northeastern Arizona to Fort Sumner, New Mexico facing freezing weather, kidnapping, hunger, dysentery, and death along the 350-mile route. They surrendered to the U.S. Army after a scorched-earth policy destroyed their livestock and grain fields. They were imprisoned at Bosque Redondo, along with Apaches, under wretched conditions until 1868, when they were allowed to return to their homeland, reduced to one-fifth the size of the original territory.

1864, November 29 Colonel John Chivington, commander of the Colorado military district in 1863, led Colorado volunteers in a surprise attack, authorized by Governor John Evans of Colorado Territory, against Black Kettle's peaceful Cheyenne camp at Sand Creek in southeastern Colorado. Estimates of those killed and mutilated range from 200 to 500 men, women, and children. In March 1865, the Sand Creek Massacre (also known as the Chivington Massacre) was investigated by a joint military-Congressional group. Chivington was censured for his conduct at Sand Creek but never court-martialed.

1866, August 1 The War Department ordered the U.S. Indian Scouts established within the Army to provide in Indian country "a force of Indians not to exceed one thousand, to act as scouts." They were required to supply Army posts with fresh meat as well. The number of scouts declined from 474 in 1867 to 24 in 1915. The scout program was discontinued in 1947 as a distinct element of U.S. military forces.

1866, December 21 A force of about 2,000 Sioux, Cheyennes, and Arapahos ambushed a detachment of eighty troops led by Captain William J. Fetterman on the Bozeman Trail. Captain Fetterman and his troopers chased a small number of warriors who had lured them into a trap where concealed warriors killed them all.

1867 The U.S. bought Alaska from Russia and added Inuit, Aleut, and Indian populations to its own. Many Christian missions established themselves in Native communities over the next twenty years.

1867–1868 The Surgeon General's office sent a series of memoranda to army medical officers instructing them to collect Indian crania from graves and battlefields for the Army Medical Museum.

1867, October 21–28 The largest gathering of Indians and whites in the history of the United States took place at Medicine Lodge Creek in Kansas Territory during which several treaties were negotiated.

1868, November 27 Lt. Colonel George A. Custer and the 7th Cavalry attacked the Cheyenne camp of Chief Black Kettle on the Washita River in Oklahoma, killing Black Kettle and over 100 others.

1869, January 29 Near Mulberry Creek in Kansas, the Tenth Cavalry detachment and five settlers massacred at least eight Pawnees recently discharged from a special Army unit known as the Pawnee Scouts. B.E. Fryer, Post Surgeon at Fort Harker, Kansas, shipped six skulls from these dead Indians to the Army Medical Museum in Washington, D.C.

1869, April 10 Congress established the Board of Indian Commissioners responding to a demand for a non-partisan group to oversee the administration of Indian affairs. Staffed by reformers, it frequently disagreed with the Interior Department in its sixty-five year history.

1869, April 21 President Grant appointed Brigadier General Ely Samuel Parker, Tonawanda Seneca chief, to become Commissioner of Indian Affairs. The first Indian to fill the position, he served until December 1871.

1870 The prophet Wodziwob (Wovoka) founded the Ghost Dance of 1870, a religious movement on the Northern Paiutes' Walker River Reservation in Nevada. Promising a restoration to traditional days during a time of suffering and despair, the movement spread to California tribes and the Great Basin.

1870, January 23 Colonel E. M. Baker attacked an encampment of Blackfeet in Montana, killing 173 men, women, and children. Commonly known as Baker's Massacre, this was the only armed conflict between the Blackfeet and U.S. troops.

1871, March 3 Congress ended treaty making with Native Americans but also declared existing treaties would remain in effect. Thereafter, agreements were made by Congressional act, executive orders, and executive agreements.

1871, April 30 At least 150 of Apache chief Eskiminzin's people were killed by a citizen army at Camp Grant near Tucson who blamed his band for Apache raids in the region. The citizens were acquitted at trial in December of 1871.

1873, June 1 Kintpuash (nicknamed Captain Jack by whites), leader of the Modoc War of 1872–73 surrendered along with some eighty Modoc warriors who refused to return to a joint reservation with Klamath Indians in Oregon. Kintpuash had defended their lava bed stronghold near Tule Lake in northern California for several months against U.S. troops. Betrayed by other Modoc warriors who helped track Kintpuash down for the army, Captain Jack and three other warriors were hanged on October 3, 1873. Their heads were removed and shipped to the Army Medical Museum in Washington D.C. Captain Jack's skull later went to the Smithsonian Institution and was eventually returned to members of the Indian community.

1874, July 30 Gold was discovered on French Creek in the Black Hills of South Dakota. Eager miners rushed into Indian territory ignoring treaties that protected Indian lands.

1876, June 25 Sioux and Cheyenne warriors annihilated Lieutenant Colonel · George Armstrong Custer and his 7th Cavalry regiment at the Little Big Horn in present-day southeastern Montana in a battle that continues to fascinate people around the world. Custer's precise movements have never been determined, but accounts of the battle by Indians who participated in it tell how his command was destroyed in fierce fighting.

1876, November 25 The 4th Cavalry under the command of General George Crook attacked Dull Knife's Band on the Powder River in Wyoming, destroying food and clothing supplies of the Northern Cheyenne leader and his followers. In May 1877, Dull Knife, Little Wolf, and their followers surrendered at Fort Robinson in Nebraska.

1877, May 6 Chief Crazy Horse and 900 Sioux Indians surrendered to the U.S. government at Fort Robinson, Nebraska, where he was murdered in a guard house. Crazy Horse never signed a treaty with the government.

1877, October 5 Chief Joseph and his Nez Percé followers made a heroic 1,700 mile run to seek refuge in Canada with Sitting Bull's people. U.S. troops blocked the escape route of the weary and starving Indians only thirty miles from the Canadian border. Chief Joseph, whose strategic and technical methods are cited by military historians, delivered an often-quoted surrender speech that began: "I will fight no more forever." A commemorative stamp was issued November 4, 1968.

1878 The U.S. government established Indian police forces for reservation supervision.

1878, April 13 Fifteen hostages from Fort Marion in St. Augustine, Florida, arrived at Hampton Normal and Agricultural Institute in Virginia, a ten-year old school for African Americans. Beginning an unprecedented experiment in Indian education, more than 1,300 students from sixty-five tribes eventually

Postal service honored Chief Joseph, the heroic Nez Percé leader, with a commemorative stamp in 1968. Beginning in the summer of 1877, Chief Joseph led 750 men, women, and children from Oregon toward Canada where they hoped to find freedom. Pursued the entire way by 2,000 veteran Army troops, Chief Joseph succeeded in eluding the soldiers until October 5 when exhaustion, freezing weather, and the end of supplies forced him to surrender. Courtesy the U.S. Postal Service.

studied at Hampton over a forty-five-year period. The Indian education program, fashioned after the program developed for African-American students, provided students with academic courses, manual training, and Christian education.

1878, September 9 Nearly 300 Northern Cheyenne men, women, and children, led by Dull Knife and Little Wolf, fled the Cheyenne-Arapaho Reservation in Indian territory to return to their Tongue River homeland in northern Wyoming and southern Montana. Dull Knife and Little Wolf were eventually captured. The Northern Cheyenne were officially granted the Tongue River Reservation in Montana in 1884, but Dull Knife had died the year before. Little

Wolf went into voluntary exile because he had killed a fellow Cheyenne during a dispute.

1879 Captain Richard Henry Pratt founded Carlisle Indian School in Pennsylvania in an abandoned military barracks. The school, the first federally funded, nonreservation boarding school for Indians, isolated Indians from reservation life. During vacations, Pratt sent students to live and work with white families (the "outing" system) so they could be assimilated into non-Indian society. Pratt said, "to civilize the Indian, put him in the midst of civilization. To keep him civilized, keep him there."

1879, September 29 The Ute Colorow and his followers killed Major Thomas T. Thornburgh and Nathan C. Meeker, agent at White River Agency at the Battle of Milk Creek. Colorow was pardoned for his role because he was engaged in what was deemed a fair fight.

1881, August 5 Crow Dog, leader of one faction of Brulé Sioux, killed Brulé Chief Spotted Tail, suspecting his honesty and integrity. According to tribal custom, Crow Dog paid money for murdering Spotted Tail but Washington officials made him stand trial. Although a jury convicted him of murder and sentenced him to die, the U.S. Supreme Court ruled that the federal court had no jurisdiction over a case of one Indian killing another. Crow Dog was freed.

1881, July 19 Sitting Bull led his starving followers from Canada across the border to the United States, surrendering at Fort Buford, North Dakota. Despite the Army's promise of amnesty, Sitting Bull was held as a military prisoner for two years.

1882, October 26 When a Tlingit shaman was accidentally killed by a whaler, the Northwest Trading Company, responsible for the killing, refused payment in accordance with the Tlingit custom that required compensation for death of a tribesman, and reported the Indians were uprising. The U.S. Navy shelled the Tlingits on October 26 killing six children and destroying the village. Angoon sued the federal government for the bombardment and the villages agreed to an

out-of-court settlement in 1973 for $90,000. In 1982, totem poles were raised in the center of Angoon to the memory of the children during the 100th anniversary of the bombing.

1882, December 16 By executive order, the Hopi Reservation, 3,863 square miles, was set apart for the Hopi Tribe in the Navajo Agency in Arizona.

1883 William Frederick Cody staged his first Wild West show in Omaha, Nebraska. It is believed that Cody's shows, which included reenactments of Indian battles, influenced Hollywood westerns.

1883, October 10 The first Lake Mohonk Conference of Friends of the Indian was held in New Paltz, New York. Growing numbers of reformers met until 1916 exerting a powerful influence on both government policy and private attitudes of many Americans. The conference supported a "reform" plan for allotment, the abolition of the reservations and distribution of tribal lands to individual Indians. Senator Dawes credited the conference for the passage of the Dawes Act in 1887.

1884 Congress acknowledged the rights of Inuits to Alaskan territorial lands.

1885 In the Major Crimes Act, Congress gave federal courts jurisdiction over major criminal offenses in Indian Territory and on reservations.

1886, September 4 Geronimo, Chiricahua Apache leader, and a few of his followers, surrendered to General Nelson A. Miles at Skeleton Canyon, Arizona.

1886, December 14 A federal policy stated "no books in any Indian language must be used or instruction given in that language . . . the rule will be strictly enforced."

1887, February 7 The General Allotment Act or Dawes Severalty Act (named after Senator Henry L. Dawes of Massachusetts) tried to break up tribally-owned lands and divide them among individuals, with the "surplus" (unappropriated lands on reservations) sold to whites, sometimes at very low prices, by unscrupulous public officials. This act de-

stroyed tribal existence and gave Indian agents tremendous power over individual Indians. The law resulted in the transfer of some 90 million acres from Indian to non-Indian owners in the next forty-five years.

1889, April 22 Part of Indian territory was thrown open to white settlers. Some 50,000 people crossed the boundary line to stake their claims on choice acres, formerly Indian lands, and created the new territory of Oklahoma.

1890 The Ghost Dance, a religious movement which originated with the Paiute prophet Wovoka (Jack Wilson), spread among the Sioux and other western Indians.

1890, February 10 In a government-organized "land grab" of former Sioux lands in South Dakota, settlers claimed lots on 11 million acres.

1890, December 15 Sitting Bull, Hunkpapa Lakota leader and medicine man, was killed by Lieutenant Bullhead of the Standing Rock Sioux Indian Police.

1890, December 29 Chief Big Foot and his Minnconjou and Hunkpapa Sioux bands encamped at Wounded Knee, in present-day South Dakota, were surrounded by U.S. 7th Cavalry commanded by Colonel James William Forsyth. In the midst of negotiations between the cavalry and the Lakotas, an unknown person fired a shot. The army opened fire with Hotchkiss guns and some 300 people—almost all women, children, and elderly, were killed, including Big Foot. A court of inquiry absolved Forsyth of wrongdoing. Restored to his command, he was promoted to brigadier general in 1894.

1893–1905 The Dawes Commission appointed by President Grover Cleveland dissolved the governments of the Creek, Chickasaw, Cherokee, Choctaw, and Seminole in Oklahoma and allotted 20 million acres of land to 90,000 individual owners.

1902, January 13 The U.S. Commissioner of Indian Affairs prohibited "wearing of long hair by the male Indian population." A poem, "To wear or not to wear hair," was sent to Indian school superintendents: "Not to be shorn; perchance then not to draw annuities."

1903 "Chief" Charles Bender, Chippewa, started his major league baseball career with the Philadelphia Athletics of the American League. He is considered one of the greatest pitchers of all time.

1908 In the *Winters* doctrine, the Supreme Court laid down the basic tenet of Indian law that the establishment of an Indian reservation implied reservation of sufficient water to enable Indians to live on the lands.

1911, August 29 Ishi ("man" in Yahi), the only survivor of the Yahi tribe walked into Oroville, California. Found by townspeople and put into a prison cell, anthropologists Alfred Kroeber and Thomas Waterman took full responsibility for Ishi. He was a valuable informant of Yahi lifeways for many anthropologists and museum visitors until his death five years later.

1912 Jim Thorpe, Sac, captured the gold medal in both the Pentathlon and the Decathlon at the 1912 Olympics in Stockholm, Sweden.

1912 Dr. Carlos Montezuma, Yavapai-Apache, and one of the original members of the "Society of American Indians" broke away to found *Wassaja*, his own publication, considered the first militant Indian journal of this century. Montezuma desired the immediate abolition of the Bureau of Indian Affairs.

1918, October 10 The Native American Church was incorporated in Oklahoma by members of Ponca, Cheyenne, Comanche, Oto, Kiowa, and Apache tribes.

1922–1924 The All-Pueblo Council and other groups fought and defeated the Bursum Bill in Congress which would have recognized the rights of white squatters to Pueblo lands.

1924, June 2 By congressional act, and in part in gratitude for the Indians' contribution in World War I when they were not subject to the draft, citizenship was granted to all Indians who were not yet citizens. The act gave Indians dual citizenship, as members of tribes and as citizens of the United States.

1925 Clinton Rickard, Tuscarora,

helped to organize the Indian Defense League. The League succeeded in re-establishing the Jay Treaty (1794) right to pass freely back and forth between Canada and the United States.

1928 The *Meriam Report*, prepared by the Institute for Government Research, revealed the gross abuses within the Bureau of Indian Affairs and cited the General Allotment Act as reason for impoverished conditions.

1928 Charles Curtis, of Kaw and Osage descent, was a Kansas congressmen for fourteen years and Senator for twenty years before he became Vice President of the United States serving Herbert Hoover.

1934, June 18 The Indian Reorganization Act (IRA) or Wheeler-Howard Act was signed into law, reversing the allotment policy. The IRA provided for tribal ownership of land and ostensibly gave elected tribal councils the power to control their own budgets, hire attorneys, and incorporate. In reality, the Interior Secretary retained final authority and the Bureau of Indian Affairs retained most of its old power.

1936 The Oklahoma Indian Welfare Act provided for the reorganization of tribeless Indians within the state and restored tribal legal identity to the "Five Civilized Tribes" whose governments were dissolved earlier in the century.

1942, June 16 The Aleuts, required to evacuate the Pribilof Islands for military reasons after the Japanese landed on Kiska and Attu on June 7 had, in many cases, two hours to gather up belongings and were limited to one suitcase each. Boarded on ships for unknown destinations, their villages were subsequently vandalized by occupying American forces.

1942, July 18 The Six Nations (Cayuga, Mohawk, Oneida, Onondaga, Seneca, and Tuscarora) declared war on the Axis powers (Germany, Italy, and Japan) after objecting to U.S. military conscription laws which they believed violated their autonomy.

1944, November 15 Delegates representing more than fifty tribes met in Denver and formed the National Congress of the American Indians (NCAI).

1945, February 23 Marine private Ira

This postage stamp, issued July 11, 1945, honored the marines, including Pima Indian Ira Hayes, who raised the American flag on Mount Suribachi, Iwo Jima. Courtesy the U.S. Postal Service.

Hayes, from the Pima Reservation in Arizona, and five others reenacted the second flag raising on Mount Suribachi, Iwo Jima, for photographer, Joe Rosenthal. A commemorative postage stamp was issued on July 11, 1945, based on Rosenthal's Pulitzer prize winning photograph.

1946 The U.S. Congress established the Indian Claims Commission in order to settle land claims against the United States, provide financial compensation, and acquire title to millions of acres of illegally seized Indian land.

1948, July 15 The Arizona Supreme Court held that Indians had the right to vote in Arizona.

1948, August The Corps of Engineers began construction of the 245-foot-high Oahe Dam near Pierre, South Dakota. The Standing Rock and Cheyenne Sioux Reservations lost a total of 160,889 acres.

1948, August 3 Federal court in New Mexico declared that a New Mexico constitutional provision denying Indians the right to vote was contrary to the Fifteenth Amendment of the U.S. Constitution.

1951 Annie Dodge Wauneka was elected the first Navajo woman to the Navajo Tribal Council composed of seventy-four members.

1952 Allie P. Reynolds, Creek, a pitcher for the Yankees, pitched the most shutouts in 1945 and 1952 and led the American League in strikeouts in 1943 and 1952.

1952–1957 The Bureau of Indian Affairs' "relocation program" moved 17,000 Indians to such cities as Los Angeles, Chicago, Denver, San Francisco, and Oakland.

1953, August 1 The U.S. Congress resolved to terminate the special relationship with tribes in the United States.

1954, August 15 The U.S. Congress passed Public Law 280, empowering any state legislature to take over civil and criminal jurisdiction on Indian reservations without tribal consent. This put an end to Indians' authority to police themselves.

1957, March 10 The Dalles Dam choked back and closed the downstream surge of the Columbia River and Celilo Falls. The ancient, sacred Indian salmon fishing grounds were underwater.

1958, January 18 Armed Lumbee Indians broke up a Ku Klux Klan meeting in Robeson County, North Carolina and received international attention for their victory.

1961, February Basil Williams, President of the Allegany Seneca, appealed to President John F. Kennedy to stop the Kinzua Dam. The plea was ignored and the dam flooded about 10,000 acres of habitable Seneca lands along the Allegheny River in New York and forced one-third of the population to relocate, violating a 1794 treaty, the government's oldest active treaty made with the Six Nations. The dam inundated the Cornplanter Grant, a holy shrine.

1961, June 13 Nearly 800 Indian people from ninety tribes who gathered at the American Indian Chicago Conference prepared the *Declaration of Indian Purpose* which addressed the inherent right of all people to retain spiritual and cultural

values, and called for action toward formulating and adopting policies and programs empowering Indian people.

1961, August A group of Indian youth, mostly college students, met to organize the National Indian Youth Council which began publishing the newspaper *Americans Before Columbus*.

1962, October 1 The Institute of American Indian Arts opened, offering high school diplomas and a two-year postsecondary program for Native students. In 1984, it received accreditation as a junior college.

1962, October 1 The first edition of the *Tundra Times*, published in Fairbanks, Alaska, came off the press. Founded and edited until 1976 by Howard Rock, an Inupiat from Point Hope, the paper kept Natives in 203 villages, as well as subscribers in the "lower 48," informed about their problems. The paper temporarily suspended operations from December 1991 to October 1992 because of financial difficulties.

1963, December 2 President Lyndon B. Johnson presented Annie Dodge Wauneka with the Medal of Freedom, the nation's highest civilian award, for her accomplishments in eradicating tuberculosis among Native people. To date, she is the first and only Native American so honored.

1964 Jeannette Henry and Rupert Costo organized the American Indian Historical Society in San Francisco and began publishing *The Indian Historian*. The organization fought to improve textbook materials about Indians and to publish materials about Indian history.

1965, October 16 The All-Indian Pueblo Council, considered the oldest mutual defense league in the western hemisphere, adopted a constitution and bylaws that combined ancient custom and laws with modern governmental forms.

1966 The Alaska Federation of Natives (AFN) was founded representing Inuits (Eskimos), Aleuts, and Indians.

1968, March 6 In his special message to Congress on Indian Affairs, President Lyndon B. Johnson proposed: "A goal that ends . . . 'termination' of Indian programs and stresses self-determination."

1968, July 29 The American Indian Movement was founded in Minneapolis, Minnesota, to deal with problems faced by urban Indians in the United States.

1969 The first National Indian Education Association conference was held in Minneapolis, Minnesota.

1969, January The Navajo Community College on the Navajo Reservation in Arizona, the first four-year college established and controlled by an Indian tribe, opened its doors to students.

1969, May 5 N. Scott Momaday, a thirty-four-year-old Kiowa, was the first Indian to win a Pulitzer prize for literature for his novel *House Made of Dawn*.

1969, November 20 Members of Indians of All Tribes who occupied Alcatraz Island located in San Francisco Bay claimed the right of possession under an 1868 Sioux Treaty which said unused federal land would revert to Indians. The Indians stayed on the island until June 11, 1971.

1970, December 15 President Richard M. Nixon signed the law restoring the sacred Blue Lake to the people of Taos Pueblo sixty-four years after it was taken from them and made part of Carson National Forest. The Blue Lake area has been used by the Taos people for religious and tribal purposes.

1971 The Native American Rights' Fund (NARF) was organized to preserve tribal existence, protect tribal natural resources, promote human rights, and develop Indian law. Since its founding, NARF has won many battles in court and in Congress by providing expert legal representation.

1971, December 18 President Richard M. Nixon signed into law the Alaska Native Claims Settlement Act (ANCSA) granting Alaska's 60,000 Indians, Inuits, and Aleuts title to 44 million acres of their ancient homeland and $962.5 million in settlement of the century-old question of Native land rights. The money was paid into thirteen regional Native corporations that ANCSA created to invest the money. Individual Natives were enrolled in the corporations and received shares of stock restricted to Natives and heirs until

1991. The land was divided among some 200 villages and the regional corporations which held subsurface rights to village lands.

1972, May 20   Mount Adams, a sacred mountain of the Yakimas in Washington, was restored to the tribe.

1972, November 2–8   Dennis J. Banks and Russell C. Means of the American Indian Movement (AIM) and about 500 Indians occupied the Bureau of Indian Affairs (BIA) in Washington, D.C. The protest, called the "Trail of Broken Treaties," demanded BIA reform, treaty reform, new land policies, and social and economic programs. The demonstrators agreed to leave the BIA building after a series of court actions, White House maneuvers, and strong public reaction.

1973, February 27   Over 200 Lakotas led by Banks and Means seized and occupied the hamlet of Wounded Knee, South Dakota, on the Pine Ridge (Oglala Sioux) Reservation until May 8th. Their goals were to dramatize poverty, corruption, and oppression on the reservation. They called for federal review of treaties and the removal of Chairman Richard Wilson from Oglala Sioux tribal government. Two Indians were killed, two federal marshalls wounded, and 300 Indians arrested during the occupation.

1973, December 22   President Richard M. Nixon signed into law the Menominee Restoration Act which reestablished relations of the tribe with the federal government. Terminated as a tribe in 1961, members of the tribe devoted ten years of time and energy to restoration of federal trust status.

1974   The American Indian Higher Education Consortium was established to provide technical assistance to developing Indian colleges.

1974, February 12   U.S. District Court Judge George W. Boldt of Tacoma, Washington made a landmark decision affirming the fishing rights of fourteen Indian tribes in Washington. Boldt ruled Indian people were entitled to half of the harvestable salmon and steelhead in the treaty area waters in Washington and had the right to fish in their traditional off-reservation sites.

1974, May 19   Rod Curl, Wintu, beat Jack Nicklaus by one stroke to win the Colonial National golf open at Fort Worth, Texas with a four-under par, 276 for 72 holes.

1974, December 22   Congress passed the Navajo-Hopi Land Settlement Act providing for an equal partition of the Joint Use Area (1.8 million acres of the 1882 executive order reservation [2.5 million acres] owned jointly by the two tribes) and the relocation of members of one tribe living on land partitioned to the other. Thousands of Navajos and 100 Hopi families were forced to relocate. Since 1974, Congress passed additional legislation extending relocation deadlines, authorizing acquisition of additional lands for Navajos, allotting more funds for relocation, and granting life estates to some elderly Navajos.

1975, September   The Council of Energy Resource Tribes was formed to protect and manage energy resources on reservations.

1975, January 3   The Havasupai Tribe of Arizona won its sixty-six-year-old struggle for title to a portion of its ancient homeland along the Grand Canyon's south rim when President Gerald Ford signed the Grand Canyon National Park Enlargement Act into law.

1975, January 4   President Gerald Ford signed the Indian Self-Determination and Education Assistance Act by which Congress mandated that the federal government permit Indian tribes to administer their own federal programs if they desired to do so.

1975, June 26   A bloody shoot-out occurred between two FBI agents and several American Indians on South Dakota's Pine Ridge Reservation. Both FBI agents and one Indian were killed. Leonard Peltier, a member of the American Indian Movement, indicted and convicted in 1977 in a Fargo, North Dakota federal court, is serving two life sentences for a crime he claims he did not commit. Two other Indians tried on the same charges brought against Peltier were acquitted.

1975, September 25   Chief Frank Fools Crow, an Oglala Lakota of Kyle, South Dakota, offered the prayer at the convening of the U.S. Senate, the first time in history an American Indian holy man offered such a prayer. Chief Fools Crow spoke in Lakota and the prayer was translated into English.

1978   The American Indian Religious Freedom Act (AIRFA) became law and officially guaranteed constitutional First Amendment religious freedom protection for Native Americans. Considered a policy statement, the act did not give Indians legally enforceable rights.

1978, February 11   The Longest Walk began when some 180 Native Americans set out from San Francisco to walk to Washington, D.C. to commemorate all the forced walks Indians had made in the past.

1978, March 24   In *Mashpee Tribe v. Town of Mashpee*, a federal district court dismissed the Mashpee Wampanoags' land claim suit on grounds that they were not a tribe in 1976 when they filed the suit. This was the first defeat for any eastern tribe under the 1790 Nonintercourse Act.

1978, November 8   The Indian Child Welfare Act was signed into law by President Jimmy Carter. The law protects the integrity of Indian families by eliminating abusive child welfare practices that result in unwarranted Indian parent–child separations.

1980, October 10   President Jimmy Carter signed the Maine Indian Claims Settlement Act authorizing $81.5 million to secure a land and financial base for the Passamaquoddy, Penobscot, and Houlton Band of Maliseet who had maintained that their land was taken illegally in 1794, 1796, and 1818. In return, the tribes relinquished their long-standing legal claim to 12.5 million acres of their traditional lands. The bill also confirmed federal recognition for all three groups, a status they obtained in 1976.

1980, December 2   President Carter signed the Alaska National Interest Lands Conservation Act setting aside just over 100 million acres of public lands in Alaska for national parks, wildlife refuges, and forests while guaranteeing food gathering rights for Alaska Natives.

1981, February 22   The Vietnam Era

Veterans Inter-Tribal Association was inaugurated in Oklahoma to help promote a positive image of Indian Vietnam veterans and to give Indian veterans a united voice in veteran affairs.

1981, July Tim Giago, Lakota, founded the *Lakota Times*, now called *Indian Country Today*.

1982, February 10 Dr. Everett Rhoades, Kiowa, was sworn in as Director of the U.S. Indian Health Service in Washington, D.C. becoming its first American Indian director.

1982, December The Indian Tribal Governmental Tax Status Act was enacted as a means to end discriminatory treatment of tribal governments under the Internal Revenue Code. Under the act, tribal governments may issue bonds in limited circumstances.

1983 Sinte Gleska College on the Rosebud Sioux Reservation in South Dakota was awarded full accreditation by the North Central Association of Colleges and Schools, the first tribally-controlled college on an Indian reservation to receive it at the Baccalaureate level. The name of Sinte Gleska College changed to Sinte Gleska University during a 1992 Founder's Day Celebration.

1983, January 25 The U.S. 7th Circuit Court of Appeals found that the Lac Courte Oreilles Band of Chippewas of Wisconsin retained their hunting, fishing, trapping, and gathering rights when they signed the Treaties of 1837, 1842, and 1854. The U.S. Supreme Court refused to hear an appeal of what became known as the Voight decision.

1983, February 7 The Inuit Circumpolar Conference, an organization of the Inuit people of Alaska, Canada, and Greenland founded in 1977, was granted non-governmental organization status at the United Nations.

1983, November 14 Mary and Carrie Dann, traditional Western Shoshone sisters, were among the seventeen women presented awards by the Wonder Women Foundation in New York City. The women, honored for their defense of Western Shoshone rights to their homeland, have waged a battle since 1972 against the federal government through litigation and civil disobedience.

1984, April 7 The elected leaders of the Eastern Band of Cherokees of North Carolina and the Western Cherokees of Oklahoma met in joint council for the first time since the Cherokee Nation was split by forced removal. The historic reunion was held at Red Clay in southeastern Tennessee, the scene of the last eleven Cherokee Council meetings before the Cherokees were forced to march to Oklahoma.

1984, June 6 The Senate resolved to make the Senate Select Committee on Indian Affairs a permanent committee. It is the only congressional committee that focuses exclusively on Indian issues.

1985 The Jicarilla Apache Tribe of New Mexico was the first tribal government to sell tax-exempt municipal bonds, rated "A" by Standard and Poor's Corporation, to institutional investors.

1985, July 31 The Navajo Tribal Council passed the Navajo Business Preference Law to improve economic opportunities for Navajo business people. The law requires first preference to Navajo-owned businesses on all contract-letting jobs.

1986, November Northern Cheyenne Benjamin Nighthorse Campbell won in Colorado's Third Congressional district, the eighth largest district in the country. A member of the 1964 Olympic Judo team and an expert jeweler, Campbell won a Senate seat in 1992.

1987, January 5 National Native News (produced by Alaska Public Radio), the country's first and only daily radio news service covering Native issues, first aired.

1987, February 25 In *California et al. v. Cabazon Band of Mission Indians et al.*, the U.S. Supreme Court upheld the right of the Cabazon Reservation in Riverside County to hold high-stakes bingo games despite the state's contention that California gambling laws apply on Indian reservations.

1987, July Wilma Mankiller became the first woman elected Principal Chief of the Cherokee Nation of Oklahoma. She has attracted national and worldwide interest for her leadership and accomplishments in economic development, health

This stamp honoring the Lakota leader Red Cloud was issued in August 1987. Courtesy the U.S. Postal Service.

care, and tribal self-governance.

1987, August 15 Representatives of the Oglala Sioux Tribe and U.S. Postal Service commemorated the issue of a new 10-cent stamp honoring Chief Red Cloud, the Sioux leader who negotiated a 1868 treaty between the United States and the Sioux Nation. The Postmaster said the stamp would be printed continuously as the nation's only 10-cent stamp.

1987, December 16 President Ronald Reagan signed a bill establishing the Trail of Tears as a National Historic Trail, commemorating the nine-state march of the Cherokee Indians during their forced removal from their homelands in the southeast to Oklahoma.

1988, February 3 President Reagan signed into law the "1991 Amendments" to the Alaska Native Claims Settlement Act. The passage culminated the work of fifteen congressional hearings, seven Alaska Federation of Natives conventions, and five Native leadership retreats to correct problems that emerged from implementing the Alaska Native Claims Settlement Act of 1971 to settle aboriginal land claims of the Alaska Native peoples. The "1991" law provided automatic protections for land and Native corporate stock.

1988, April 20   Congress repealed the termination resolution of 1953, an action awaited by tribal governments for over thirty years.

1988, August 11   President Reagan signed a law making restitution to Aleut residents of the Pribilof and Aleutian islands for loss of personal and community property and village lands during U.S. military occupation of the islands during World War II.

1989, March 2   The first permanent tribute honoring the Navajo Code Talkers was dedicated in Phoenix, Arizona.

1989, March 24   Exxon's 987-foot oil tanker *Valdez* ran aground on Bligh Reef, Alaska spilling 11 million gallons of North Slope crude oil into Prince William Sound in the nation's worst oil spill. One thousand square miles were affected and will have a lasting, negative impact on Native lands and lifestyle including hunting and fishing, gathering, and commercial fishing.

1989, September 14   Sitting Bull, Hunkpapa Lakota spiritual and political leader, was honored by the U.S. Postal Service with a 28-cent stamp issued in Rapid City, South Dakota.

The postal service honored the legendary Sitting Bull, Lakota spiritual leader and warrior, with a stamp in September 1989. Courtesy the U.S. Postal Service.

1989, November 28   President George Bush signed the National American Indian Museum Act which established the National Museum of the American Indian as part of the Smithsonian Institution in Washington, D.C. and requires the Smithsonian Institution to return Native human remains to requesting tribes.

1990, April 17   The U.S. Supreme Court ruled in *Employment Division, Department of Human Resources of Oregon et al. v. Smith et al.* that the state could deny unemployment benefits to drug rehabilitation counselors terminated for sacramental use of peyote in Native American religious ceremonies. This devastating decision sharply curtails the free exercise provisions of the First Amendment. An extraordinary coalition of forty groups formed to seek a legislative reversal.

1990, October 30   President Bush signed the Native American Language Act into law. It reversed past policy that suppressed and exterminated Native American languages and cultures.

1990, November 16   President Bush signed the Native American Graves Protection and Repatriation Act which requires federal agencies and private museums receiving federal funding to inventory their collections of Native American human remains, funerary objects, sacred objects, and objects of cultural patrimony. Ancestral remains and objects must be returned to requesting tribes proving ownership. The law represents a major shift away from viewing Native American human remains as "archaeological resources" or "federal property."

1990, December 29   People gathered in sub-zero temperature to commemorate the Lakota people murdered at Wounded Knee, South Dakota, by the 7th Cavalry on that date 100 years before. Many of the descendants of the massacre victims attended the ceremony.

1991, February 19   The 99-year Salamanca, New York leases of Seneca lands expired. (Ninety percent of Salamanca sits on the Seneca Allegany Indian Reservation, sixty-five miles south of Buffalo, New York). Many Salamancan residents bitterly opposed the new agreement be-

cause it raised the town's annual lease payments, some as little as $1.00 per year.

1991, April 19   Mississippi Choctaw voters rejected a proposal to allow disposal of manufacturing waste products on land near the reservation that the tribe proposed to purchase and lease for the landfill. Choctaws were the first tribe to put the matter to a referendum vote.

1991, May 6   David Sohappy, Yakima Indian, traditional salmon fisherman, and practitioner of the Seven Drums Religion, died at a nursing home in Oregon. A national symbol of the struggle for Indian treaty rights in the Pacific Northwest, Sohappy, his son, and others were entrapped by Washington State and the federal government in a fish-buying operation called "salmonscam." Family and friends believe prison life ruined Sohappy's health, who was paroled in 1988.

1991, June 12   San Carlos Apache Tribal Council members launched an international campaign to voice their opposition to the telescope project on their sacred Mount Graham, located in Coronado National Forest near the reservation in Arizona.

1991, June 12   The Oregon Legislature approved a bill intended to allow use of peyote in Native American religious ceremonies.

1991, August 4   Sacred objects stolen from the Omaha Tribe in 1898 were returned during the tribe's annual harvest festival by the Smithsonian Institution's National Museum of the American Indian. The year before, the tribe also got back its sacred pole and over 200 objects from Harvard's Peabody Museum in Cambridge, Massachusetts.

1991, September   Skeletal remains of nearly 756 Kodiak Island natives were reburied in a Russian Orthodox ceremony nearly sixty years after the Smithsonian Institution took them for research purposes without the islanders' permission.

1991, December 10   President George Bush signed legislation approving the name change from Custer Battlefield National Monument to Little Bighorn

Battlefield National Monument and authorized the construction of a memorial to honor Indians who fought there. The Custer Battlefield was the only National Park Service battlefield named after a person.

1992, February 12 The Mashantucket Pequot Tribe dedicated the Foxwoods High Stakes Bingo and Casino in Ledyard which Connecticut tried to block for two years. More than thirty U.S. and international banks rejected the tribe's request for a construction loan. The Casino became the largest Indian-run gaming operation in the country.

1992, March 27 New York state cancelled a twenty-year contract to buy power from the proposed Hydro-Quebec Great Whale project near James Bay. Quebec wants to build the James Bay hydroelectric complex in the Canadian subarctic, while the Cree and Inuit peoples have long opposed the project, which would have destroyed their way of life and a large area of the Cree homeland that serves as habitat to caribou and migratory birds.

1992, April 3 After nearly two years of protests by Native American groups, the Dickson Mounds Museum of Illinois, the country's last public museum displaying the remains of ancient Indians, closed on the orders of Governor Jim Edgar.

Bibliography

HISTORICAL OVERVIEW OF RELATIONS BETWEEN NATIVE AMERICANS AND WHITES IN THE UNITED STATES

General Resources

Biographical Dictionary of Indians of the Americas. 2 volumes. Newport Beach, CA: American Indian Publishers, 1983.

Hirschfelder, Arlene; Byler, Mary Gloyne; and Dorris, Michael. *Guide to Research on North American Indians.* Chicago: American Library Association, 1983.

Hodge, Frederick Webb, ed. *Handbook of American Indians North of Mexico.* 2 volumes. Bureau of American Ethnology Bulletin 30, Washington, D.C., 1907–1910.

Hoxie, Frederick E. and Markowitz, Harvey. *Native Americans: An Annotated Bibliography.* Englewood Cliffs, NJ: Salem Press, 1991.

Klein, Barry T. *Reference Encyclopedia of the American Indian.* 6th ed. West Nyack, NY: Todd Publications, 1992.

Newberry Library Center for the History of the American Indian Bibliography Series. Bloomington, IN: Indiana University Press, 1976–1983. 30 volumes.

Prucha, Francis Paul. *Atlas of American Indian Affairs.* Lincoln, NE: University of Nebraska Press, 1990.

———. *A Bibliographical Guide to the History of Indian-White Relations in the United States.* Chicago: University of Chicago Press, 1977.

———. *Indian-White Relations in the United States: A Bibliography of Works Published 1975–1980.* Lincoln, NE: University of Nebraska Press, 1982.

Scarecrow Press Native American Bibliography Series. Metuchen, NJ, 1980. (Series projected at more than forty volumes.)

Sturtevant, William C., gen. ed. *Handbook of North American Indians,* 20 volumes. Washington, D.C.: Smithsonian Institution.
  vol. 4: History of Indian-White Relations, 1988
  vol. 5: Arctic, 1984
  vol. 6: Subarctic, 1981
  vol. 7: Northwest Coast, 1990
  vol. 8: California, 1978
  vol. 9: Southwest (Pueblos), 1979
  vol. 10: Southwest (non-Pueblo), 1983
  vol. 11: Great Basin, 1987
  vol. 15: Northeast, 1978

Vaugh, Alden T. *New England Frontier: Puritans and Indians, 1620–1675,* rev. ed. New York: Norton, 1979.

Waldman, Carl. *Atlas of the North American Indian.* New York: Facts on File, 1985.

———. *Who Was Who in Native American History: Indians and Non-Indians from Early Contacts through 1990.* New York: Facts on File, 1990.

Weatherford, Jack. *Native Givers: How the Indians of the Americas Transformed the World.* New York: Crown Publishers, 1989.

———. *Native Roots: How the Indians Enriched America.* New York: Crown Publishers, 1991.

Books

Axelrod, Alan. *Chronicle of the Indian Wars: From Colonial Times to Wounded Knee.* New York: Prentice Hall, 1993.

Axtell, James, ed. *The Indian Peoples of Eastern Amer-*

ica: A Documentary History of the Sexes. New York: Oxford University Press, 1981.

———. *The Invasion Within: The Contest of Cultures in Colonial North America*. New York: Oxford University Press, 1985.

Beider, Robert E. *Science Encounters the Indian, 1820–1880*. Norman, OK: University of Oklahoma Press, 1986.

Berkhofer, Robert E. *White Man's Indian: Images of the American Indian from Columbus to the Present*. New York: Random House, 1979.

Bernstein, Alison R. *American Indians and World War II: Toward a New Era in Indian Affairs*. Norman, OK: University of Oklahoma Press, 1991.

Bourne, Russell. *The Red King's Rebellion: Racial Politics in New England, 1675–1677*. New York: Atheneum, 1990.

Brodeur, Paul. *Restitution: The Land Claims of the Mashpee, Passamaquoddy, and Penobscot Indians of New England*. Boston: Northeastern University Press, 1985.

Brown, Dee. *Bury My Heart at Wounded Knee*. New York: Holt, Rinehart and Winston, 1970.

Burt, Larry W. *Tribalism in Crisis: Federal Indian Policy, 1953–1961*. Albuquerque, NM: University of New Mexico Press, 1982.

Calloway, Colin G. *New Directions in American Indian History*. Norman, OK: University of Oklahoma Press, 1988.

Carlson, Richard G., ed. *Rooted Like the Ash: New England Indians and the Land*. Naugatuck, CT: Eagle Wing Press, 1987.

Churchill, Ward, and Jaimes, M. Annette. *Fantasies of the Master Race: Literature, Cinema, and the Colonization of American Indians*. Monroe, ME: Common Courage Press, 1992.

Cook, Sherburne F. *The Indian Population of New England in the Seventeenth Century*. Berkeley, CA: University of California Press, 1976.

Cornell, Stephen. *Return of the Native American: Indian Political Resurgence*. New York: Oxford University Press, 1988.

Costo, Rupert, and Costo, Jeannette Henry, eds. *The Missions of California: A Legacy of Genocide*. San Francisco: Indian Historian Press, 1987.

Crosby, Alfred W. *The Columbian Exchange: Biological and Cultural Consequences of 1492*. Westport, CT: Greenwood Press, 1972.

Debo, Angie. *A History of the Indians of the United States*. Norman, OK: University of Oklahoma Press, 1970.

Deloria, Vine, Jr. *American Indian Policy in the Twentieth Century*. Norman, OK: University of Oklahoma Press, 1985.

———. *Custer Died for Your Sins: An Indian Manifesto*. 1969, Reprint. Norman, OK: University of Oklahoma Press, 1988.

———. *We Talk, You Listen: New Tribes, New Turf*. New York: Macmillan, 1970.

Deloria, Vine, Jr. and Lytle, Clifford. *American Indians, American Justice*. Austin, TX: University of Texas Press, 1983.

———. *The Nations Within: The Past and Future of American Indian Sovereignty*. New York: Pantheon, 1984.

Denevan, William M., ed. *The Native Population of the Americas in 1492*. 2d ed. Madison, WI: University of Wisconsin Press, 1992.

Dippie, Brian W. *The Vanishing American: White Attitudes and U.S. Indian Policy*. Lawrence, KS: University Press of Kansas, 1982.

Dockstader, Frederick J. *Great North American Indians: Profiles in Life and Leadership*. New York: Van Nostrand Reinhold, 1977.

Dowd, Gregory Evans. *A Spirited Resistance: The North American Indian Struggle for Unity, 1745–1815*. Baltimore, MD: Johns Hopkins University Press, 1991.

Driver, Harold E. *Indians of North America*. Chicago: University of Chicago Press, 1961.

Dunlay, Thomas W. *Wolves for the Blue Soldiers: Indian Scouts and Auxiliaries with the United States Army, 1860–1890*. Lincoln, NE: University of Nebraska Press, 1982.

Edmunds, R. David, ed. *American Indian Leaders: Studies in Diversity*. Lincoln, NE: University of Nebraska Press, 1980.

———. *Tecumseh and the Quest for Indian Leadership*. New York: Little, Brown and Co., 1987.

Fixico, Donald L., ed. *An Anthology of Western Great*

Lakes Indian History. Milwaukee, WI: University of Wisconsin, 1988.

————. *Termination and Relocation, Federal Indian Policy, 1945–1960*. Albuquerque, NM: University of New Mexico Press, 1986.

Fleming, Paula, and Luskey, Judith. *The North American Indians in Early Photographs*. New York: Harper and Row, 1986.

Forbes, Jack. *Native Americans of California and Nevada*. Rev. ed. Happy Camp, CA: Naturegraph Publishers, 1982.

Gibson, Arrell Morgan. *The Chickasaws*. Norman, OK: University of Oklahoma Press, 1963.

Gilbert, Gil. *God Gave Us This Country: Tekamthi and the First American Civil War*. New York: Atheneum, 1989.

Gonzalez, Ray. *Without Discovery: A Native Response to Columbus*. Seattle, WA: Broken Moon Press, 1992.

Goodman, Jeffrey. *American Genesis: The American Indian and the Origins of Modern Man*. New York: Summit Books, 1981.

Graymont, Barbara. *The Iroquois in the American Revolution*. Syracuse, NY: Syracuse University Press, 1972.

Green, Michael. *The Politics of Indian Removal: Creek Government and Society in Crisis*. Lincoln, NE: University of Nebraska Press, 1982.

Hagan, William T. *American Indians*. Rev. ed. Chicago: University of Chicago Press, 1979.

————. *United States-Comanche Relations: The Reservation Years*. Norman, OK: University of Oklahoma Press, 1990.

Hauptman, Laurence M. *The Iroquois and the New Deal*. Syracuse, NY: Syracuse University Press, 1981.

————. *The Iroquois Struggle for Survival: World War II to Red Power*. Syracuse, NY: Syracuse University Press, 1986.

Hauptman, Laurence M., and Wherry, James D., eds. *The Pequots in Southern New England: The Rise and Fall of an American Indian Nation*. Norman, OK: University of Oklahoma Press, 1990.

Heizer, Robert F., ed. *The Destruction of California Indians*. Santa Barbara, CA and Salt Lake City, UT: Peregrine Smith, 1974.

Heizer, R. F., and Whipple, M. A., eds. *The California Indians: A Source Book*. 2d ed. Berkeley, CA: University of California Press, 1971.

Hertzberg, Hazel W. *The Search for An American Indian Identity: Modern Pan-Indian Movements*. Syracuse, NY: Syracuse University Press, 1971.

Hill, Richard. *Skywalkers: A History of Indian Ironworkers*. Brantford, Ontario: Woodland Indian Cultural Educational Centre, 1987.

Horsman, Reginald. *Expansion and American Indian Policy, 1783–1812*. East Lansing, MI: Michigan State University Press, 1967.

Hoxie, Frederick E., *A Final Promise: The Campaign to Assimilate the Indians, 1880–1920*. Lincoln, NE: University of Nebraska Press, 1984.

————. *Indians in American History: An Introduction*. Arlington Heights, IL: Harlan Davidson/Forum Press, 1988.

Hudson, Charles. *Catawba Nation*. Athens, GA: University of Georgia Press, 1970.

————. *Four Centuries of Southern Indians*. Athens, GA: University of Georgia Press, 1975.

————. *The Southeastern Indians*. Knoxville, TN: University of Tennessee Press, 1976.

Iverson, Peter. *The Plains Indians of the Twentieth Century*. Norman, OK: University of Oklahoma Press, 1985.

Jaimes, M. Annette, ed. *The State of Native America: Genocide, Colonization, and Resistance*. Boston: South End Press, 1992.

Jennings, Francis. *The Ambiguous Iroquois Empire: The Covenant Chain Confederation of Indian Tribes with English Colonies from Its Beginnings to the Lancaster Treaty of 1744*. New York: W.W. Norton, 1984.

————. *The Invasion of America: Indians, Colonialism, and the Cant of Conquest*. Chapel Hill, NC: University of North Carolina Press, 1975.

Josephy, Alvin M. *America in 1492*. New York: Knopf, 1991.

Josephy, Alvin M., Jr. *Now That the Buffalo's Gone: A Study of Today's American Indians*. New York: Knopf, 1982.

————. *The Patriot Chiefs: A Chronicle of American Indian Resistance*. New York: Viking Press, 1958.

————. *Red Power: The American Indians' Fight for*

Freedom. New York: American Heritage Press, 1971.

Kammer, Jerry. *The Second Long Walk: The Navajo-Hopi Land Dispute*. Albuquerque, NM: University of New Mexico Press, 1986.

Katz, William Loren. *Black Indians: A Hidden Heritage*. New York: Atheneum, 1986.

Kawano, Kenji, photographer. *Warriors: Navajo Code Talkers*. Flagstaff, AZ: Northland Publishing, 1990.

Kelly, Lawrence C., *The Assault on Assimilation: John Collier and the Origins of Indian Policy Reform*. Albuquerque, NM: University of New Mexico Press, 1983.

————. *Federal Indian Policy*. New York: Chelsea House Publishers, 1990.

Kelsay, Isabel Thompson. *Joseph Brant, 1743–1807, Man of Two Worlds*. Syracuse, NY: Syracuse University Press, 1984.

Kickingbird, Kirke, and Ducheneaux, Karen. *One Hundred Million Acres*. New York: Macmillan, 1973.

Kniffen, Fred B., Gregory, Hiram F., and Stokes, George A. *The Historic Indian Tribes of Louisiana: From 1542 to the Present*. Baton Rouge: Louisiana State University Press, 1987.

Koning, Hans. *Columbus: His Enterprise, Exploding the Myth* (Including *Columbus in the Classroom* by Bill Bigelow). 1972. Reprint. New York: Monthly Review Press, 1991.

Lawson, Michael L. *Damned Indians: The Pick-Sloan Plan and the Missouri River Sioux, 1944–1980*. Norman, OK: University of Oklahoma Press, 1982.

Lazarus, Edward. *Black Hills/White Justice: The Sioux Nation Versus the United States 1775 to the Present*. New York: Harper/Collins, 1991.

Leacock, Eleanor Burke, and Lurie, Nancy Oestreich. *North American Indians in Historical Perspective*. New York: Random House, 1971.

McDonnell, Janet A. *The Dispossession of the American Indian, 1887–1934*. Bloomington, IN: University of Indiana Press, 1991.

McNickle, D'Arcy. *Native American Tribalism: Indian Survivals and Renewals*. New York: Oxford University Press, 1973.

————. *They Came Here First: The Epic of the American Indian*. New York: Octagan Books, 1975.

Mallery, Garrick. *Picture-Writing of the American Indians*. Washington, D.C.: U.S. Government Printing Office, 1893.

Martin, Joel W. *Sacred Revolt: The Muskogees' Struggle for a New World*. Boston: Beacon Press, 1991.

Matthiessen, Peter. *In the Spirit of Crazy Horse*. New York: Viking Press, 1980.

————. *Indian Country*. New York: Viking Press, 1984.

Miner, H. Craig. *The Corporation and the Indian: Tribal Sovereignty and Industrial Civilization in Indian Territory, 1865–1907*. Norman, OK: University of Oklahoma Press, 1988.

Moses, L.G., and Wilson, Raymond, eds. *Indian Lives: Essays on Nineteenth and Twentieth Century Native American Leaders*. Albuquerque, NM: University of New Mexico Press, 1985.

Nabokov, Peter. *Native American Testimony: A Chronicle of Indian-White Relations from Prophecy to the Present, 1492–1992*. New York: Viking Press, 1992.

Nash, Gary B. *Red, White, and Black: The Peoples of Early America*. Englewood Cliffs, NJ: Prentice Hall, 1982.

Olson, James S., and Wilson, Raymond. *Native Americans in the Twentieth Century*. Urbana, IL: University of Illinois Press, 1984.

Ortiz, Alfonso. *New Perspectives on the Pueblos*. Albuquerque, NM: University of New Mexico Press, 1972.

Paul, Doris A. *The Navajo Code Talkers*. Bryn Mawr, PA: Dorrance and Co., 1973.

Pearce, Roy Harvey. *Savagism and Civilization: A Study of the Indian and the American Mind*. Baltimore: Johns Hopkins University Press, 1967.

Philp, Kenneth R. *Indian Self-Rule: First-Hand Accounts of Indian-White Relations from Roosevelt to Reagan*. Salt Lake City, UT: Howe Brothers, 1986.

Porter, Frank W., III. *Strategies for Survival: American Indians in the Eastern United States*. Westport, CT: Greenwood Press, 1986.

Prucha, Francis Paul. *The Great Father: The United*

States Government and the American Indians. 2 volumes. Lincoln, NE: University of Nebraska Press, 1984.

Reber, Bruce. *The United States Army and the Indian Wars in the Trans-Mississippi West, 1860–1898.* Carlisle Barracks, PA: U.S. Army Military History Institute, 1978.

Richter, Daniel K., and Merrell, James. *Beyond the Covenant Chain: The Iroquois and Their Neighbors in Indian North America: 1600–1800.* Syracuse, NY: Syracuse University Press, 1987.

Rountree, Helen C. *The Powhatan Indians of Virginia: Their Traditional Culture.* Norman, OK: University of Oklahoma Press, 1989.

Ruby, Robert H., and Brown, John A. *A Guide to the Indian Tribes of the Pacific Northwest.* Norman, OK: University of Oklahoma Press, 1986.

Salisbury, Neal. *Manitou and Providence: Indians, Europeans, and the Making of New England, 1500–1643.* New York: Oxford University Press, 1982.

Sando, Joe S. *Pueblo Nations: Eight Centuries of Pueblo Indian History.* Santa Fe, NM: Clear Light Publishers, 1992.

Simmons, William S. *Spirit of New England Tribes: Indian History and Folklore, 1620–1984.* Hanover, NH: University Press of New England, 1986.

Smith, Jane F., and Kvasnicka, Robert M. *Indian-White Relations: A Persistent Paradox.* Washington, D.C.: Howard University Press, 1976.

Smith, Sherry L. *The View from Officers' Row: Army Perceptions of Western Indians.* Tucson, AZ: University of Arizona Press, 1990.

Spicer, Edward H. *A Short History of the Indians of the United States.* 1969. Reprint. Malabar, FL: Krieger, 1983.

Stedman, Raymond William. *Shadows of the Indian: Stereotypes in American Culture.* Norman, OK: University of Oklahoma Press, 1982.

Stuart, Paul. *Nations within a Nation: Historical Statistics of American Indians.* Westport, CT: Greenwood Press, 1987.

Sutton, Imre. *Irredeemable America: The Indians' Estate and Land Claims.* Albuquerque, NM: University of New Mexico Press, 1985.

Tanner, Helen Hornbeck. *Atlas of Great Lakes Indian History.* Norman, OK: University of Oklahoma Press, 1987.

Taylor, Theodore W. *The States and Their Indian Citizens.* Washington, D.C.: Bureau of Indian Affairs, 1972. P. 180.

Trafzer, Clifford E. *American Indian Identity: Today's Changing Perspectives.* Sacramento, CA: Sierra Oaks Publishing Co., 1986.

Underhill, Ruth M. *Red Man's America: A History of Indians in the United States.* Chicago: University of Chicago Press, 1953.

Utley, Robert M. *The Indian Frontier of the American West, 1846–1890.* Albuquerque, NM: University of New Mexico Press, 1983.

Vecsey, Christopher, and Starna, William A. *Iroquois Land Claims.* Syracuse, NY: Syracuse University Press, 1988.

Vecsey, Christopher, and Venables, Robert W. *American Indian Environments: Ecological Issues in Native American History.* Syracuse, NY: Syracuse University Press, 1980.

Viola, Herman J. *After Columbus: The Smithsonian Chronicle of the North American Indians.* Washington, D.C.: Smithsonian Books/New York: Orion Books, 1990.

Washburn, Wilcomb, comp. *The American Indian and the United States: A Documentary History.* 4 volumes. New York: Random House, 1973.

———. *The Indian in America.* New York: Harper and Row, 1974.

Weeks, Philip, ed. *The American Indian Experience—A Profile: 1524 to the Present.* Arlington Heights, IL: Forum Press, 1988.

Weibel-Orlando, Joan. *Indian Country, L.A.: Maintaining Ethnic Community in Complex Society.* Urbana: University of Illinois Press, 1991.

Welch, James. *Fools Crow.* New York: Viking Penguin, 1986. P. 80.

Weltfish, Gene. *The Lost Universe: Pawnee Life and Culture.* Lincoln, NE: University of Nebraska Press, 1965.

Weyler, Rex. *Blood of the Land: The Government and Corporate War Against the American Indian Move-*

ment. New York: Everest House Publishers, 1982.

White, Richard. *The Middle Ground: Indians, Empires, and Republics in the Great Lakes Region, 1650–1815*. Cambridge: Cambridge University Press, 1991.

––––––. *The Roots of Dependency: Subsistence, Environment, and Social Change Among the Choctaws, Pawnees, and Navajos*. Lincoln, NE: University of Nebraska Press, 1983.

Wooster, Robert. *The Military and United States Indian Policy, 1865–1903*. New Haven, CT: Yale University Press, 1988.

Worcester, Donald E. *The Apaches: Eagles of the Southwest*. Norman, OK: University of Oklahoma Press, 1979.

Young, Mary Elizabeth. *Redskins, Ruffleshirts, and Rednecks: Indian Allotments in Alabama and Mississippi, 1830–1860*. Norman, OK: University of Oklahoma Press, 1961.

NATIVE AMERICANS TODAY

American Indian Lawyer Training Program, Inc. *Indian Tribes as Sovereign Governments: A Sourcebook on Federal-Tribal History, Law, and Policy*. Oakland, CA: AIRI Press, 1988.

Cook, Sherburne F. *The Indian Population of New England in the Seventeenth Century*. Berkeley, CA: University of California Press, 1976.

Dobyns, Henry F. *Their Numbers Become Thinned: Native American Population Dynamics in Eastern North America*. Knoxville, TN: University of Tennessee Press, 1983.

Hale, Duane Kendall. *Researching and Writing Tribal Histories*. Grand Rapids, Michigan: Michigan Indian Press/Grand Rapids Inter-Tribal Council, 1991.

O'Brien, Sharon. *American Indian Tribal Governments*. Norman, OK: University of Oklahoma, 1989.

Snipp, Matthew. *American Indians: The First of This Land*. [The Population of the United States in the 1980s, Census Monograph Series] New York: Russell Sage Foundation, 1989.

Swanton, John R. *The North American Tribes of North America*. Bureau of American Ethnology Bulletin 145. Washington, D.C.: Smithsonian Institution Press, 1952.

Thornton, Russell. *American Indian Holocaust and Survival: A Population History Since 1492*. Norman, OK: University of Oklahoma Press, 1987.

––––––. *The Cherokees: A Population History*. Lincoln, NE: University of Nebraska Press, 1990.

U.S. Department of Commerce. *Federal and State Indian Reservations and Indian Trust Areas*. Washington, D.C.: U.S. Government Printing Office, 1974.

TREATIES/SUPREME COURT DECISIONS

American Friends Service Committee. *Uncommon Controversy: Fishing Rights of the Muckleshoot, Puyallup, and Nisqually Indians*. Seattle, WA: University of Washington Press, 1970.

Cohen, Fay G. *Treaties on Trial: The Continuing Controversy over Northwest Indian Fishing Rights*. Seattle, WA: University of Washington Press, 1986.

Cohen, Felix S. *Handbook of Federal Indian Law*. Washington, D.C.: Department of the Interior, 1942. Numerous revisions.

Costo, Rupert, and Henry, Jeannette. *Indian Treaties: Two Centuries of Dishonor*. San Francisco: Indian Historian Press, 1977.

Doherty, Robert. *Disputed Waters: Native Americans and the Great Lakes Fishery*. Louisville, KY: University Press of Kentucky, 1991.

Kappler, Charles J., comp. *Indian Affairs: Laws and Treaties*. 5 volumes. Washington, D.C.: U.S. Government Printing Office, 1904–1941; New York: AMS Press, 1971.

Kickingbird, Kirke; Kickingbird, Lynn; Chibitty, Charles J.; and Berkey, Curtis. *Indian Sovereignty*. Washington, D.C.: Institute for the Development of Indian Law, 1977.

Kickingbird, Kirke; Kickingbird, Lynn; Skibine, Alexander Tallchief; and Chibitty, Charles. *Indian Treaties*. Washington, D.C.: Institute for the Development of Indian Law, 1980.

Native American Rights Fund. *The NARF Legal Review*. Quarterly publication. Boulder, Colorado.

Peavar, Stephen L. *The Rights of Indians and Tribes: The Basic ACLU Guide to Indian and Tribal Rights*. 2d ed. Carbondale, IL: Southern Illinois University Press, 1992.

Prucha, Francis Paul, ed. *Documents of United States Indian Policy*. 2d ed. Lincoln, NE: University of Nebraska Press, 1990.

Tribal Constitutions: A Handbook for BIA Personnel. Washington, D.C.: U.S. Department of the Interior, Bureau of Indian Affairs, Tribal Relations Branch, June 1987.

Wilkinson, Charles F. *American Indians, Time, and the Law: Native Societies in a Modern Constitutional Democracy*. New Haven, CT: Yale University Press, 1987.

Kvasnicka, Robert M., and Viola, Herman J., eds. *The Commissioners of Indian Affairs, 1824–1977*. Lincoln, NE: University of Nebraska Press, 1979.

Porter, Frank W. III. *The Bureau of Indian Affairs*. New York: Chelsea House Publishers, 1988.

Schmeckebier, Laurence. *The Office of Indian Affairs: Its History, Activities and Organization*. Institute For Government Research Service Monographs of the United States Government No. 48. Baltimore: The Johns Hopkins Press, 1927.

Stone, Eric. *Medicine Among the American Indians*. New York: Paul B. Hoeber, Inc., 1932. P. 22.

Taylor, Theodore W. *The Bureau of Indian Affairs*. Boulder, CO: Westview Press, 1984.

Vogel, Virgil J. *American Indian Medicine*. Norman, OK: University of Oklahoma Press, 1970.

THE BUREAU OF INDIAN AFFAIRS AND THE INDIAN HEALTH SERVICE

Barrow, Mark V.; Niswander, Jerry D.; and Fortuine, Robert. *Health and Disease of American Indians North of Mexico: A Bibliography*. Gainesville, FL: University of Florida Press, 1972.

Bureau of Indian Affairs. *Department of the Interior Departmental Manual*, part 130, 1986.

Commissioners of Indian Affairs, 1849–1967. *Annual Reports to the Secretary of the Interior*. Washington, D.C.: U.S. Government Printing Office; New York: AMS Press, 1976–1977.

Dorris, Michael. *The Broken Cord*. New York: Harper and Row, 1989.

Gorman, Carl N. *Navajo Theory of Disease and Healing Practices*. Window Rock, AZ: Navajo Health Authority, 1973.

Indian Health Service. *Trends in Indian Health— 1992* (Charts and Tables). Rockville, MD: Department of Health and Human Services, 1992.

Jackson, Curtis and Marcia Galli. *A History of the Bureau of Indian Affairs and its Activities Among Indians*. San Francisco: R & E Research Associates, Inc. 1977.

LANGUAGES

Booker, Karen M. *Languages of the Aboriginal Southeast: An Annotated Bibliography*. Metuchen, NJ: Scarecrow Press, 1991.

Bright, William. *Bibliography of the Languages of Native California: Including Closely Related Languages of Adjacent Areas*. Metuchen, NJ: Scarecrow Press, 1982.

Campbell, Lyle, and Methun, Marianne, eds. *The Languages of Native America: Historical and Comparative Assessment*. Austin, TX: University of Texas, 1979.

Dictionary of American Naval Fighting Ships. 8 volumes. Washington, D.C.: Department of the Navy, Naval History Division, 1959–1981.

Garland Studies in American Indian Linguistics. Series of Monographs containing research in Linguistics field. New York: Garland Publishing Inc., 1976.

Holmes, Ruth Bradley, and Smith, Betty Sharp. *Beginning Cherokee*. Norman, OK: University of Oklahoma Press, 1976.

Pilling, James Constantine. *Bibliographies of the Languages of the North American Indian*. 1887–1894. Reprint. New York: AMS Press, 1973. Reprint of volumes published from 1887 to 1894.

Young, Robert W. and Morgan, William, Sr. *The Navajo Language: A Grammar and Colloquial Dictionary.* Albuquerque, NM: University of New Mexico Press, 1987.

EDUCATION

Boyer, Paul. *Tribal Colleges: Shaping the Future of Native America.* Princeton, NJ: Carnegie Foundation for the Advancement of Teaching, 1989.

Cahape, Patricia, and Howley, Craig B., eds. *Indian Nations at Risk: Listening to the People. Summaries of Papers Commissioned by the Indian Nations At Risk Task Force of the U.S. Department of Education.* Washington, D.C.: U.S. Department of Education, 1991.

Fuchs, Estelle, and Havighurst, Robert J. *To Live on This Earth: American Indian Education.* Garden City, NY: Doubleday, 1972.

Hyer, Sally. *One House, One Voice, One Heart: Native American Education at the Santa Fe Indian School.* Santa Fe, NM: Museum of New Mexico Press, 1990.

Indian Education: A National Tragedy—A National Challenge. Senate Report No. 501, 12836-1.

Lame Deer, John (Fire) and Richard Erdoes. *Lame Deer, Seeker of Visions.* New York: Simon & Schuster, 1972.

More, Arthur. "Native Indian Learning Styles: A Review for Researchers and Teachers." *Journal of American Indian Education.* August, 1989, pp. 15–28.

National Advisory Council on Indian Education, U.S. Department of Education, Annual Reports, 1973. Washington, D.C.: U.S. Government Printing Office.

Oppelt, Norman T. *The Tribally Controlled Indian Colleges: The Beginnings of Self-Determination in American Indian Education.* Tsaile, AZ: Navajo Community College Press, 1990.

Prucha, Francis Paul. *The Churches and the Schools.* Lincoln, NE: University of Nebraska Press, 1979.

Reyhner, Jon, and Eder, Jeanne. *A History of Indian Education.* Billings, MT: Native American Studies, Eastern Montana College, 1989.

Roessel, Robert A., Jr. *Navajo Education in Action: The Rough Rock Demonstration School.* Chinle, AZ: Navajo Curriculum Center, 1977.

Szasz, Margaret Connell. *Education and the American Indian: The Road to Self-Determination, 1928–1973.* Albuquerque, NM: University of New Mexico Press, 1975.

———. *Indian Education in the American Colonies, 1607–1783.* Albuquerque, NM: University of New Mexico, 1988.

Trennert, Robert A. *The Phoenix Indian School: Forced Assimilation in Arizona, 1891–1935.* Norman, OK: University of Oklahoma Press, 1988.

RELIGION

Barrett, H. G.: *Indian Shakers: A Messianic Cult of the Pacific Northwest.* Carbondale: Southern Illinois University Press, 1957.

Beck, Peggy V., Walters, Anna Lee, and Francisco, Nia. *The Sacred: Ways of Knowledge, Sources of Life.* Tsaile, AZ: Navajo Community College Press, 1992.

Benedict, Ruth. *The Concept of the Guardian Spirit in North America.* 1923. New York: Kraus Reprint Corp., 1964.

Berkhofer, Robert F. *Salvation and the Savage: An Analysis of Protestant Missions and American Indian Response, 1787–1862.* Lexington, KY: University of Kentucky Press, 1965.

Bowden, Henry Warner. *American Indians and Christian Missions: Studies in Cultural Conflict.* Chicago: University of Chicago Press, 1981.

Coleman, Michael C. *Presbyterian Missionary Attitudes toward American Indians, 1837–1893.* Jackson: University Press of Mississippi, 1985.

Deloria, Vine, Jr. *God Is Red.* New York: Dell, 1973.

Eastman, Charles A. *The Soul of an Indian.* Reprint.

1980. Boston: Houghton Mifflin, 1911.

Gill, Sam D. *Native American Religions: An Introduction*. Belmont, CA: Wadsworth, 1982.

———. *Native American Religious Action: A Performance Approach to Religion*. Columbia, SC: University of South Carolina Press, 1987.

Green, Rayna, and Mitchell, Nancy Marie, comps. *American Indian Sacred Objects, Skeletal Remains, Repatriation, and Reburial: A Resource Guide*. Washington, D.C.: American Indian Program, National Museum of American History, Smithsonian Institution, 1990.

Harrod, Howard L. *Renewing the World: Plains Indian Religion and Morality*. Tucson, AZ: University of Arizona Press, 1987.

Heth, Charlotte. *Native American Dance: Ceremonies and Social Traditions*. Washington, D.C.: National Museum of the American Indian, Smithsonian Institution, 1992.

Hirschfelder, Arlene, and Molin, Paulette. *Encyclopedia of Native American Religions*. New York: Facts on File, 1992.

Horse Capture, George P., ed. *The Concept of Sacred Materials and Their Place in the World*. Cody, WY: Buffalo Bill Historical Center, 1989.

Hultkrantz, Ake. *The Religions of the American Indian*. Berkeley, CA: University of California Press, 1967.

———. *Belief and Worship in Native North America*. Edited by Christopher Vecsey. Syracuse, NY: Syracuse University Press, 1981.

———. *The Study of American Indian Religions*. Edited by Christopher Vecsey. New York: Crossroad, 1983.

———. *Native Religions of North America: The Power of Visions and Fertility*. New York: Harper and Row, 1987.

Jorgenson, Joseph G. *The Sun Dance Religion*. Chicago: University of Chicago Press, 1972.

Kehoe, Alice Beck. *The Ghost Dance: Ethnohistory and Revitalization*. New York: Holt, Rinehart and Winston, 1989.

LaBarre, Weston. *The Ghost Dance: Origins of Religion*. Garden City, NY: Doubleday, 1970.

———. *The Peyote Cult*. Norman, OK: University of Oklahoma Press, 1989.

Milner, Clyde A., and O'Neil, Floyd A. *Churchmen and the Western Indians, 1820–1920*. Norman, OK: University of Oklahoma Press, 1989.

Moore, James T. *Indian and Jesuit: A Seventeenth Century Encounter*. Chicago: University of Chicago Press, 1982.

Paper, Jordan. *Offering Smoke: The Sacred Pipe and Native American Religion*. Moscow, ID: University of Idaho Press, 1988.

Rahill, Peter J. *The Catholic Indian Missions and Grant's Peace Policy, 1870–1884*. Washington, D.C.: Catholic University of America Press, 1953.

Ruby, Robert H., and Brown, John A. *Dreamer-Prophets of the Columbia Plateau*. Norman, OK: University of Oklahoma Press, 1989.

Seattle. Speech published in *Seattle Sunday Star*, October 29, 1887. Translated by Henry Smith.

Stewart, Omer C. *Peyote Religion: A History*. Norman, OK: University of Oklahoma Press, 1987.

Trafzer, Clifford. *American Indian Prophets*. Sacramento, CA: Sierra Oaks, 1986.

Underhill, Ruth M. *Red Men's Religion: Beliefs and Practices of the Indians North of Mexico*. Chicago: University of Chicago, 1965.

United States Commission on Civil Rights. *Religion in the Constitution: A Delicate Balance*. Clearinghouse publication No. 80. Washington, D.C.: U.S. Commission on Civil Rights, 1983.

Vecsey, Christopher. *Handbook of American Indian Religious Freedom*. New York: Crossroad, 1991.

———, ed. *Religion in Native North America*. Moscow, ID: University of Idaho Press, 1990.

Walker, Deward E., Jr., ed. *Systems of North American Witchcraft and Sorcery*. Moscow: University of Idaho Press, 1970.

Wall, Steve, and Arden, Harvey. *Wisdomkeepers: Meetings with Native American Spiritual Elders*. Hillsboro, OR: Beyond Words Publishing, 1990.

Wallace, Anthony F. C. *The Death and Rebirth of the Seneca*. New York: Knopf, 1970.

GAMES AND SPORTS

Blanchard, K. *The Mississippi Choctaws at Play: The Serious Side of Leisure*. Urbana, IL: University of Illinois Press, 1981.

Culin, Stewart. *Games of the North American Indians*. The Twenty-Fourth Annual Report of the Bureau of American Ethnology. 1907. Reprint. New York: Dover Press, 1975.

Nabokov, Peter. *Indian Running*. Santa Barbara, California: Capra Press, 1981.

Oxendine, Joseph B. *American Indian Sports Heritage*. Champaign, IL: Human Kinetics Books, 1988.

Wheeler, R. W. *Jim Thorpe: World's Greatest Athlete*. Norman, OK: University of Oklahoma Press, 1979.

ARTISTS

Adair, John. *Navajo and Pueblo Silversmiths*. Norman, OK: University of Oklahoma Press, 1944.

Bataille, Gretchen M., and Silet, Charles L. P., eds. *The Pretend Indians: Images of Native Americans in the Movies*. Ames, IA: Iowa State University Press, 1980.

Berlant, Anthony, and Ralenberg, Mary Hunt. *Walk in Beauty*. Boston: Little, Brown and Co., 1977.

Coe, Ralph T. *Lost and Found Traditions: Native American Art 1965–1985*. New York: American Federation of the Arts, 1986.

———. *Sacred Circles: Two Thousand Years of North American Indian Art*. Kansas City, MO: Nelson Gallery of Art-Atkins Museum of Fine Art, 1977.

Dunn, Dorothy. *American Indian Painting of the Southwest and Plains Areas*. Albuquerque, NM: University of New Mexico Press, 1968.

Faucett, David M., and Callander, Lee A. *Native American Painting*. New York: Museum of the American Indian/Heye Foundation, 1982.

Friar, Ralph E., and Natasha A. *The Only Good Indian: The Hollywood Gospel*. New York: Drama Book Specialists, 1972.

Heth, Charlotte, ed. *Native American Dance: Ceremonies and Social Traditions*. Washington, D. C.: National Museum of the American Indian with Starwood Publishing, Inc., 1992.

Hilger, Michael. *The American Indian in Film*. Metuchen, NJ: Scarecrow Press, 1986.

Hill, Rick. *Creativity Is Our Tradition: Three Decades of Contemporary Indian Art*. Santa Fe, NM: Institute of American Indian Arts, 1992.

Jones, Eugene H. *Native Americans as Shown on the Stage, 1753–1916*. Metuchen, NJ: Scarecrow Press, 1988.

Koch, Ronald P. *Dress Clothing of the Plains Indians*. Norman, OK: University of Oklahoma Press, 1976.

Lyford, Carrie. *Quill and Beadwork of the Western Sioux*. Washington, D.C.: Bureau of Indian Affairs, 1940.

Miles, Charles. *Indian and Eskimo Artifacts of North America*. New York: Bonanza Books, 1963.

O'Connor, John E. *The Hollywood Indian: Stereotypes of Native Americans in Films*. Trenton, NJ: New Jersey State Museum, 1976.

Orchard, William C. *Beads and Beadwork of the American Indians: A Study Based on Specimens in the Museum of the American Indian, Heye Foundation*. New York: Museum of the American Indian/Heye Foundation, 1975.

———. *The Technique of Porcupine Quill Decoration Among the North American Indians*. New York: Museum of the American Indian/Heye Foundation, 1971.

Petersen, Karen Daniels. *Plains Indian Art from Fort Marion*. Norman, OK: University of Oklahoma Press, 1971.

Powers, William K. *War Dance: Plains Indian Musical Performance*. Tucson, AZ: University of Arizona Press, 1990.

Strickland, Rennard. "Coyote Goes Hollywood, Part 1." *Native Peoples*, vol. 2, no. 3 (Spring 1989): 46-52.

———. "Coyote Goes Hollywood, Part 2." *Native Peoples*, vol. 2, no. 3 (Fall 1989): 38-46.

Tillett, Leslie, ed. *Wind on the Buffalo Grass*. New York: Thomas T. Crowell, 1976.

Wade, Richard, ed. *The Arts of the North American Indian: Native Traditions in Evolution.* New York: Hudson Hills Press, 1986.

Weatherford, Elizabeth, with Seubert, Emelia. *Native Americans on Film and Video.* New York: Museum of the American Indian/Heye Foundation, 1981.

———. *Native Americans on Film and Video.* Volume II. New York: Museum of the American Indian/Heye Foundation, 1988.

Whiteford, Andrew H. *North American Indian Arts.* Racine, WI: Western Publishing Co., 1970.

VOICES OF COMMUNICATION

Allen, Paula Gunn. *Studies in American Literature: Critical Essays and Course Designs.* New York: Modern Language Association of America, 1983.

American Indian Media Image Task Force. *The American Indian and the Media.* Minneapolis, MN: National Conference of Christians and Jews, 1991.

Bataille, Gretchen M., and Sands, Kathleen Mullen. *American Indian Women Telling Their Lives.* Lincoln, NE: University of Nebraska Press, 1984.

Bruchac, Joseph. *Survival This Way: Interviews with American Indian Poets.* Tucson, AZ: University of Arizona Press, 1987.

Brumble, H. David, III. *American Indian Autobiography.* Berkeley, CA: University of California Press, 1988.

———. *An Annotated Bibliography of American Indian and Eskimo Autobiographies.* Lincoln: University of Nebraska Press, 1981.

Colonnese, Tom, and Owens, Louis. *American Indian Novelists: An Annotated Critical Bibliography.* New York: Garland Publishing, 1985.

Coltelli, Laura. *Winged Words: American Indian Writers Speak.* Lincoln: University of Nebraska Press, 1990.

Danky, James P., and Hady, Maureen E. *Native American Periodicals and Newspapers, 1828–1982.* Westport, CT: Greenwood Press, 1984.

Hirschfelder, Arlene B. *American Indian and Eskimo Authors: A Comprehensive Bibliography.* New York: Association on American Indian Affairs, 1973.

Jacobson, Angeline. *Contemporary Native American Literature: A Selected and Partially Annotated Bibliography.* Metuchen, NJ: Scarecrow Press, 1977.

Krupat, Arnold. *The Voice in the Margin: Native American Literature and the Canon.* Berkeley, CA: University of California Press, 1989.

———. *For Those Who Came After: A Study of Native American Autobiography.* Berkeley, CA: University of California Press, 1985.

Larson, Charles R. *American Indian Fiction.* Albuquerque, NM: University of New Mexico, 1978.

Littlefield, Daniel F., Jr., and Parins, James W., eds. *American Indian and Alaska Native Newspapers and Periodicals, 1826–1924* (1984); *American Indian and Alaska Native Newspapers and Periodicals, 1925–1970* (1986); and *American Indian and Alaska Native Newspapers and Periodicals, 1971–1985* (1986). Westport, CT: Greenwood Press.

Littlefield, Daniel F., Jr., and Parins, James W. *A Biobibliography of Native American Writers, 1772–1924.* Metuchen, NJ: Scarecrow Press, 1981.

———. *A Biobibliography of Native American Writers, 1772–1924: A Supplement.* Metuchen, NJ: Scarecrow Press, 1985.

Murphy, James E., and Murphy, Sharon M. *Let My People Know: American Indian Journalism, 1828–1978.* Norman, OK: University of Oklahoma Press, 1981.

Owens, Louis. *Other Destinies: Understanding the American Indian Novel.* Norman, OK: University of Oklahoma Press, 1992.

Rock, Roger O., comp. *The Native American in American Literature: A Selectively Annotated Bibliography.* Westport, CT: Greenwood Press, 1985.

Ruoff, A. LaVonne Brown. *American Indian Literatures: An Introduction, Bibliographic Review, and Selected Bibliography.* New York: Modern Language Association of America, 1990.

Stensland, Anna Lee. *Literature by and about the American Indian: An Annotated Bibliography.* 2d ed. Urbana, IL: National Council of Teachers of English, 1979.

Swann, Brian, and Krupat, Arnold, eds. *I Tell You Now: Autobiographical Essays by Native American Writers.* Lincoln, NE: University of Nebraska Press, 1987.

Vecsey, Christopher. *Imagine Ourselves Richly: Mythic Narratives of North American Indians.* San Francisco: Harper and Row, 1991.

Wiget, Andrew. *Critical Essays on Native American Literature.* Boston: G.K. Hall, 1985.

————. *Native American Literatures.* Boston: Twayne Publishers, 1985.

Wong, Hertha Dawn. *Sending My Heart Back Across the Years: Tradition and Innovation in Native American Autobiography.* New York: Oxford University Press, 1992.

EMPLOYMENT, INCOME, AND ECONOMIC DEVELOPMENT

Ainsworth, Robert G. *An Overview of the Labor Market Problems of Indians and Native Americans.* Washington, D.C.: National Commission for Employment Policy, 1989.

Burton, Lloyd. *American Indian Water Rights and the Limits of Law.* Lawrence, KS: University Press of Kansas, 1991.

DuMars, Charles T.; O'Leary, Marilyn; and Utton, Albert E. *Pueblo Indian Water Rights: Struggle for a Precious Resource.* Tucson, AZ: University of Arizona Press, 1984.

Fixico, Donald L. *Termination and Relocation: Federal Indian Policy, 1945–1960.* Albuquerque, NM: University of New Mexico, 1986.

Glazer, Suzy. "Native American Unemployment," *Indian Truth.* No. 266, January 1986, pp. 6–16.

Hill, Richard, *Skywalkers: A History of Indian Ironworkers.* Brantford, Ontario: Woodland Indian Cultural Educational Center, 1987.

Institute for Government Research Studies in Administration. *The Problem of Indian Administration.* Baltimore: The Johns Hopkins Press, 1928.

Jorgensen, Joseph G., ed. *Native Americans and Energy Development II.* Boston: Anthropology Resource Center and Seventh Generation Fund, 1984.

Nabhan, Gary Paul. *Enduring Seeds: Native American Agriculture and Wild Plant Conservation.* Flagstaff, AZ: North Point, 1991.

Native American Studies. *Economic Development in American Indian Reservations.* Albuquerque, NM: University of New Mexico Press, 1979.

Reno, Philip. *Mother Earth, Father Sky, and Economic Development: Navajo Resources and Their Use.* Albuquerque, NM: University of New Mexico Press, 1981.

Snipp, C. Matthew. *American Indians: The First of This Land.* New York: Russell Sage Foundation, 1989.

Stuart, Paul. *Nations Within a Nation: Historical Statistics of American Indians.* New York: Greenwood Press, 1987.

United States Department of the Interior, Bureau of Indian Affairs. *Indian Service Population and Labor Force Estimates.* Washington, D.C.: 1991.

Viola, Herman J., and Margolis, Carolyn, eds. *Seeds of Change: A Quincentennial Commemoration.* Washington, D.C.: Smithsonian Institution Press, 1991.

White, Robert. *Tribal Assets: The Rebirth of Native America.* New York: Henry Holt, 1990.

Zell, Patricia, ed. *Indian Water Policy in a Changing Environment.* Oakland, CA: American Indian Lawyer Training Program, Inc. 1982.

APPENDIX I/II

Armstrong, Virginia. *I Have Spoken.* Chicago: Swallow Press, 1971.

"Indian Entities Recognized and Eligible to Receive Services from the United States Bureau of Indian Affairs." *Federal Register* Vol. 53 no. 250. Washington, D.C.: 1988, updated 1991.

Klein, Barry T. *Reference Encyclopedia of the American Indian.* 6th ed. West Nyack, NY: Todd Publications, 1992.

Russell, George. *The American Indian Digest: An Insight to American Indian History.* Phoenix: Thunderbird Enterprises, 1992.

Sturtevant, William. *Handbook of North American Indians*. (*See* GENERAL RESOURCES.)

Swanton, John. *The Indian Tribes of North America*. Washington, D.C.: U.S. Government Printing Office, 1952.

United States Bureau of the Census #2, Economics and Statistics Administration. "American Indian Tribes with 1,000 or More American Indians for the United States 1990." *United States Department of Commerce News*. Washington, D.C. CB92-244.

———, Economics and Statistics Administration. *1990 Census Profile: Race and Hispanic Origin*. Washington, D.C.: June 1991.

———, Racial Statistics Branch, Population Division. *American Indian and Alaska Native Areas: 1990*. Washington, D.C. CPH-L-73.

United States Department of the Interior, Bureau of Indian Affairs, Branch of Acknowledgement and Research. *List of Petitioners by Date of Initial Petition*. Washington, D.C.: 1992.

———, Division of Tribal Government Services. *Tribal Leaders Directory*. Washington, D.C.: 1992.

———, Office of Trust Responsibilities. *Annual Report of Indian Lands*. Washington, D.C.: 1985.

Waldman, Carl. *Atlas of North American Indian Tribes*. New York: Facts on File, 1985.

APPENDIX III

Folsom, Franklin, and Folsom, Mary Elting. *America's Ancient Treasures*. Albuquerque, NM: University of New Mexico Press, 1983.

Gattuso, John, ed. *Insight Guide: Native America*. New York: Prentice Hall Travel, 1991.

Gridley, Marion E., comp. *America's Indian Statues*. Chicago, IL: The Amerindian, 1966.

Marquis, Arnold. *A Guide to America's Indians: Ceremonials, Reservations, and Museums*. Norman, OK: University of Oklahoma Press, 1974.

National Native American Cooperative. *Native American Directory: Alaska, Canada, United States*. San Carlos, AZ: National Native American Cooperative, 1982.

Shanks, Ralph, and Shanks, Lisa Woo. *The North American Indian Travel Guide*. Petaluma, CA: Costano Books, 1986.

Tiller, Veronica E., ed. *Discover Indian Reservations USA: A Visitors' Welcome Guide*. Denver, CO: Council Publications, 1992.

Index

DATE DUE